YO-CVP-623

A Short History of Legal Thinking in the West

Stig Strömholm

A Short History of Legal Thinking in the West

NORSTEDTS

To the Master and Fellows
of Magdalene College, Cambridge,
in deep gratitude.

S.S.

All rights reserved. No part of this book may be reproduced, stored in a
retrieval system or transmitted in any form by any means, electronic,
mechanical photocopying, recording of otherwise, without the written
permission of the publisher, Norstedts Förlag AB.

Distribution in the United States and Canada:
Fred B Rothman & Co

ISBN 91-1-857142-5
© Stig Strömholm and Norstedts Förlag AB, Stockholm, Sweden
Cover design: Rolf Hernegran
Studentlitteratur AB
Lund 1985

Preface

The present book purports to be a textbook for law students in that part of "jurisprudence", as commonly taught in European and American law schools, which deals with the growth and development of general ideas and principles in the field of law.

The somewhat pedantic title of the book has been chosen with care, not to induce any reader into error about its contents and scope. "Thinking" is obviously an activity which takes place in all branches of legal science; what is referred to here, however, is something more specific. By "legal thinking" – as opposed to both "the philosophy of law", on one hand and "legal scholarship in general", on the other hand – we have tried to cover, essentially, two elements: not only theory-building about what the law is, as a body of rules, a logical structure, and an element of social organization and social realities, but also thinking about the principal problems raised by the exercise of the lawyer's craft, in particular those related to interpretation of statutes or precedents.

For some fifteen years, the present writer has taught jurisprudence, principally at the University of Uppsala but also in some other European institutions, and for one term, in 1982, in the New World, at the University of Minnesota Law School. The book is based upon the experience gathered in these years. I should like to make three points which are related to that experience and which I have tried to bear in mind throughout the work.

There are – in this field as elsewhere – fundamental differences between Continental and Anglo-American reading and teaching habits, and since this is a book written in English by a Continental author, I feel some comments are called for on this topic. Both methods have obvious advantages and equally obvious drawbacks. The typical Continental textbook expresses the ambition to cover, be it only in one sentence or in a footnote, everything and everybody that "matters" (or has mattered) in the field concerned and to give at least some survey of all those ideas (and persons) that are considered to be of particular importance. The successful student, upon completion of a course of study comprising textbooks of this kind, is expected to possess a kind of knowledge which could be described as encyclopaedic but also, less politely, as systematically shallow: he should have heard all the great names; any reasonably clear reference to the great ideas should call forth a smile of recognition on his lips; he should know who wrote what, who wrote before or after whom, who belonged to this or that school and, in the barest outline, what the school stood for; he should possess, in his head, a clear, but possibly quite pale, and quite small-scale, all-world and all-time map of the whole field of study. The typical Anglo-American textbook contains "cases and materials", or "texts and materials." It presents a small selection of texts which are considered to be particularly important, or to have a particular exemplary value, and which are frequently reprinted at considerable length, with sometimes quite deep-going introductions and commentaries. The idea is, obviously, that upon successful completion of the course of study, the student should have tilled and, by his labour, made his own, at least a few acres of particularly fertile land; he may ignore, on the other hand, what crops are growing on the opposite slope of the hill he has been working on.

In the present book, an attempt has been made, in order to avoid some of the most obvious drawbacks of the Continental tradition, to concentrate upon essential ideas and important writers. At the same time, the ambition of achieving a reasonable coverage of the whole map has been maintained. Whether or not this compromise has been successful, it is not for the author to decide. He is well aware of the fact that intermediary solutions of this kind frequently combine the weaknesses of all the patterns they try to reconcile, without presenting the advantages of any single solution. It is obvious that no secondary reading can ever replace the original texts; no *reading about* a thinker can ever replace *reading him*. The present book should be read together with a reasonably broad selection of important texts. Without some contact with the authentic sources there can be no true living knowledge in this field. "Important" may not necessarily coincide with "typical": according to my experience, few things are more thought-provoking, and more rewarding, in the teaching of historical jurisprudence, than confronting students with a text which shows what gross and sometimes misleading simplifications normal textbooks

Preface

contain (and to some extent must contain) about the great thinkers of the past. More than once, I have used texts by Aristotle, or even St. Thomas of Aquino, which have made intelligent and well-informed students discuss seriously whether they were reading a late 19th century or an early 20th century writer.

My second point can be made more briefly. Whether it is recognized or not – and it usually is not – there is still an English, a French, a German, an Italian, and an American view of the international history of legal thinking; there is certainly also a Spanish and of course, a Russian one, although I am not familiar with either. Nationalism is much more deeply rooted than generally admitted even in a field like this. Insofar as the study of historical jurisprudence tends to analyse the roots of *one's own* present habits of thought in the legal sphere, there is of course nothing wrong with this. If the intellectual quality of jurisprudential thinking *per se* is intended to be the criterion for including and excluding writers and ideas, on the other hand, national bias becomes more perilous. Originating as it does in a small but open intellectual landscape, in a province with no claim to leadership in the history of legal thinking (or indeed of anything) – a judgment which the late, short and now fading glories of "Scandinavian Realism" can hardly invalidate – the present book purports to be, in this respect, reasonably fair and impartial. This humbly selective attitude to the monologues of the mighty is reflected in the bibliographical notices under the headings of chapters: English, French, German, Italian – and some Scandinavian – references are listed indiscriminately, in an attempt to give only the best, irrespective of origin.

Having corrected – I now come to my third point – between 2.500 and 3.000 examination papers by European and American law students from the last fifteen years, I have come to the grim but firm conclusion that discussing – superficially or at depth – the contents of jurisprudential thinking without numerous, elementary, but often lengthy references to the intertwined growth of political, religious, social, economic and intellectual history, is like distributing caviar to the starving masses. Today, no or almost no, knowledge of such factors, of their chronology, or of their impact upon legal thinking can be expected from the average, or even clearly above average, law student. What real understanding of, say, Aristotle's political and ethical thinking is possible without a minimum of knowledge about the Greek city state or the transition into the Hellenistic world? What boots it to study Thomas of Aquino's views upon private property if you believe the great theologian to be vaguely contemporary with King Alfred or Henry VIII, or Frederick the Great (to take three answers I have seen, and not from utter fools or ignoramuses)? The objection which a colleague of thirty years ago would be most likely to have voiced against this book is that general history, and intellectual history in other fields than the law, are given almost as much space as the discussion of jurisprudential topics. This is, on the other hand, the criticism I take most light-heartedly. Today, a full supply of historical information is absolutely necessary. Nothing can be taken for granted. And it seems to me better that the historian of jurisprudence takes it upon him to make his own selection of relevant historical materials than to refer the student to completing or refreshing his knowledge in general works which may not always meet his precise needs.

Where does "history" come to an end and the stream of time become "contemporary"? There is no chance of ever achieving unanimity in answering that question. Good reasons can be given for a number of theoretical standpoints. A practical solution frequently, and unconsciously, adopted even by scholars is that history comes to an end some ten or twenty years before the schooldays of the person concerned: school textbooks of history tend (or at least tended) to be lagging behind by approximately that number of years. The dilemma confronting any historian attempting to find a rational solution is obvious: putting an end too early may cause a lasting lacuna in the student's education; it is a euphemism to say that not all lawyers turn back to fill out what was left in their youth. Carrying "history" too far, on the other hand, and covering what is really "contemporary", may imply a particularly treacherous kind of intellectual dishonesty: ideas and theories which still stir up academic or even political dust are described and judged with the historian's pretention to objectivity, fairness, distance and overview.

All taken together, the latter danger seems to the present writer more serious than the former. Tolerating ignorance is preferable to indulging in intellectual dishonesty. "History", in the present book, comes to an early end: about 1900. What has happened afterwards is, in the slow-moving world of legal ideas, "contemporary" and should be studied as such.

A book covering a field as wide as Occidental jurisprudential thinking from the Greeks to the beginning of the present century cannot, for reasons which hardly call for lengthy explanations, be based upon first-hand research work with all the thinkers covered or referred to. Such a book inevitably has to be a "compilation" – the learned name for a selective and, it is hoped, critical and rational, plundering of other men's work – to a greater extent than the present writer fully realized when starting this work some four or five years ago. Initially, this was something of a shock to an author more familiar with writing monographs, where every idea, and every judgment, is his own. Using other men's flowers also calls for decisions in matters of style which a scholar may sometimes find doubtful from the point of view of intellectual honesty: a journalistic approach is sometimes inevitable. One has to make up one's mind on difficult issues and present sweepingly one or two views, as if they were not only one's own but also based upon lengthy and mature individual reflection and, worst of all, "true", and the only ones with a claim to truth, without explaining why, in detail or at all, precisely these views are picked out among many, which would all deserve in-depth consideration and discussion. Such discussion would obviously make a one-volume history of legal thinking utterly impossible. Furthermore, there is an unpleasant flavour of dishonesty – or at least of claims to knowing, and knowing better – when you present as your own independently found and formulated conclusion what is really a choice between other people's alternatives: you cannot fill your text with all the "would seem", or "may well", or "according to some" which strict truthfulness would call for too often, you have to say "is" or "must", and delete the reference to the anonymous holders of the view you finally accept. Among the many writers to whom I am particularly indebted, mention should be made of three: the late Austrian professor Alfred Verdross, whose *Abendländische Rechtsphilosophie* (Vienna 1958) is a fine example of the Continental textbook at its best; the late Italian professor Guido Fassò, whose three-volume *Storia della filosofia del diritto* (Bologna 1966–1970) is the greatest modern work of its kind; finally my old teacher, Professor Ivar Strahl, of Uppsala University, whose short little survey *Makt och rätt* (7th ed 1981) is a remarkable performance in its kind. For oral inspiration the author wishes to thank, in particular, his younger colleagues, Dr. Åke Frändberg and Dr. Anders Fogelklou, of the Uppsala Faculty of Law. Neil Lowell Kent has kindly read the manuscript with a view to correcting the author's English. I am stubborn, however. My English has served me in writing for some

Preface

thirty years, and I have the same feelings for it as for an old servant. All responsibility falls on my shoulders.

The author is deeply indebted to Mrs. B. Kinnwall, Uppsala, who has for twenty years helped him to transform handwritten hieroglyphs in various languages into readable manuscripts, and also to Mrs. Rut Tärnström, Mrs. Ulla Svedestig, and Miss Maud Rosendal, of the Secretariat of the Uppsala Faculty of Law, for efficient cooperation in producing the present book.

The Royal Swedish Academy of Letters, History and Antiquities and the Swedish Council for Research in the Humanities and Social Sciences have granted substantial contributions towards the printing costs. The author is deeply indebted to these institutions.

Uppsala, May 1985
Stig Strömholm

Contents

Preface 5

Ch. 1 Ancient Greece 13

1. Introduction 13
2. Political, Economic and Social Background 14
3. The Greek Forms of State and Government 18
4. Sources for the Study of Greek Legal Thinking 21
5. A Law without a Legal Technique 23
6. The Earliest Period. The Natural Philosophers 25
7. The Sophists 27
8. Socrates and Plato 29
9. Aristotle 35
10. Cynics and Epicureans 41
11. The Stoics 43

Ch. 2 The Romans 46

1. Introduction 46
2. The Historical and Social Framework 49
3. Sources for the Study of Roman Law and Legal Thinking 53
4. The Contributions of the Philosophers 61
5. A Legal Profession without a Philosophy 64
6. Legal Reasoning 67

Ch. 3 The Emergence of Christian Thinking 71

1. Introduction 71
2. The Jewish Heritage 73
3. The Specific Christian Message 75
4. The propagation of Christianity. Historical Background Facts 77
5. St. Paul and the Early Fathers of the Church 81
6. St. Augustine 89
7. The Centuries of Transition 93
8. The Germanic Element 95

Ch. 4 The High and Late Middle Ages 97

1. Introduction 97
2. Some Historical Background Facts 100
3. The Contributions of Early Scholastic Philosophy 106

4. St. Thomas of Aquino 109
5. Later Scholasticism 112
6. The Glossators 117
7. The Commentators 124
8. The Canonists 129

Ch. 5 The Transition to the Modern Era (1500–1650) 132

1. Introduction 132
2. Some Historical Background Facts 135
3. Major Trends in Religious, Philosophical and Political Thinking 141
4. The Rise of Secularized Natural Law: Grotius and Hobbes 153
5. Legal Reasoning in the Renascence Period 160

Ch. 6 The Era of the Rationalistic Law of Nature (1650–1789) 165

1. Introduction 165
2. Some Historical Background Facts 170
3. Major Trends in Religious, Philosophical and Political Thinking 175
4. The Heyday of Rationalistic Natural Law Theory 187
5. John Locke 191
7. Rousseau 201
8. Legal Reasoning in the Era of Rationalism 205

Ch. 7 Towards a New World: the 19th Century 212

1. Introduction 212
2. Some Historical Background Facts 221
3. Major Trends in Religious, Philosophical and Political Thinking 232
4. Enlightenment Thinking Continued: Jeremy Bentham 249
5. Kant 254
6. The Later German Idealists 259
7. Hegel 260
8. Historicism and Positivism 264
9. Reactions against Positivism 275
10. Marx and Early Marxism 282
11. The Turn of the Century 289
12. Legal Reasoning in the 19th Century 293

Concluding Remarks 301

Alphabetical Index 303

Chapter 1

Ancient Greece

Selected Bibliography: A. Brimo, *Les grands courants de la philosophie du droit et de l'état*, 3ème éd., Paris 1978, pp. 27–42; H.J. van Eikema Hommes, *Major Trends in the History of Legal Philosophy*, Amsterdam 1979, pp. 3–41; G. Fassò, *Storia della filosofia del diritto*, vol. I, Bologna 1966, pp. 15–123; Lord Lloyd of Hampstead, *Introduction to Jurisprudence*, 3rd ed., London 1972, pp.74–78, 89–92; K. Rode, *Geschichte der europäischen Rechtsphilosophie*, Düsseldorf 1974, pp. 4–51; I. Strahl, *Makt och rätt*, 7 uppl., Stockholm 1981, pp. 14–22; A. Verdross, *Abendländische Rechtsphilosophie*, Wien 1958, pp. 1–49; M. Villey, *La formation de la penseé juridique moderne*, Paris 1968, pp. 14–61; E. Wolf, *Griechische Rechtsdenker*, Frankfurt am Main 1950–1957.

1. Introduction

As long as there have been organized societies, "the law" – or laws – in one or more of the numerous acceptions of the word – has been an ever-recurring object of human reflection. Most highly developed early civilizations have left at least some evidence, frequently of great interest, about their preoccupation with legal problems in a wide sense. The *scientific* study of such problems in the Occidental world, however, has its cradle in ancient Greece, at least in the sense that most of the fundamental questions which have kept legal philosophers and lawyers busy ever since were formulated in that civilization. Similarly it is among the Hellenes that we find the first outlines of answers, and the first attempts to draw up a coherent, in principle "scientific", theory about the essence and nature of law.

Greek sources are much less rewarding with regard to such more "technical" matters as the systematical structure of laws and the technique of interpreting and implementing legal rules. In respect of these questions, the intellectual pupils, and military and political masters, of the Greeks – the Romans – have handed over far more important contributions to the development of Western Europe.

One single example to show *how important* the work of Greek thinkers with the fundamental questions of legal philosophy was for future developments: as early as the 5th century B.C. we can distinguish, in Greek philosophical debate, between three – as yet embryonic – concepts of a "law of nature" (*vide* secs. 9 and 11 below). These three are precisely those which, ever after, have been dominating in Occidental discussion: (1) the "theological", or "voluntaristic" one,[1] which is based on the idea of an eternal, unchanging body of "natural laws", the validity of which is due to the fact that it expresses Divine will; (2) the view according to which certain general and immutable rules are founded in the "natural" instincts of all living creatures ("naturalistic" natural law) and (3) the idea of a legal system determined by, and fully accessible to, human reason ("rationalistic" natural law theories). It is characteristic for the wealth of Greek culture, and for the continuous debate which expresses a corresponding intellectual development, that not only these "theories" or attempted explanations were put forward. We also find, in the Greek discussion, most of the principal objections and counter-arguments which will play a decisive role in future European debate.

Another example of to what extent the Greeks determined the scope and direction of future discussion can be taken from political and constitutional discussion. The well-known concepts monarchy – aristocracy – democracy go back to the attemps of ancient theoricians to find a complete and coherent systematical framework which could be used for classifying various political systems.

2. Political, Economic and Social Background

Like all civilizations, the culture of ancient Greece stands in a relation of cross-fertilizing with the given framework within which it developed. That frame is, of course, in the first place determined by geography: although Greek colonies were founded from Western North Africa to the plains north of the Black Sea, and although the Greeks (under Macedonian leadership) founded cities and exercised a considerable influence as far east as Mesopotamia, Greek civilization is nevertheless essentially a product of the eastern Mediterranean. In the mostly narrow valleys, with predominantly light agriculture, such as growing

---

[1] From Latin *voluntas* - will (here God's will).

wine and olives and raising small cattle, the *city* (Greek: pólis) with its surrounding country district was the usual political unity. Communications were easier by sea than by land; numerous harbours traded with the whole Mediterranean basin, and the crafts produced, from an early date, articles of export. In agriculture but particularly in the larger manufacturing enterprises and in the public services, including building and mining, slave manpower played an important part througout antiquity.

This is not the place for a description of the earliest history of Greece. Let us only remind the reader of the fact that the Greeks, or Hellenes, are believed to have immigrated to present Greece in successive waves from the middle of the second pre-Christian millenium onwards. There were fairly important differences not only in dialect but also in customs and political traditions between different tribes, among which mention should be made of the Dorians in the Peloponnese – with Sparta, or Lacedæmon, as the leading state – and the Ionians on the Aegean islands and on the western coast of Asia Minor.

The oldest political constitution in ancient Greece about which we have at least some information is that which is found described in the Homeric poems, the Iliad and the Odyssey. These epic songs were, in all likelihood, put into their present shape some time about 700 B.C., but they reflect societal conditions which had been prevailing at least a couple of centuries earlier. The dominant form of government in Homer's poems is tribal monarchy: the small states were governed by hereditary kings who, in matters of importance, took the advice of an aristocratic assembly. In the Odyssey, which came into being somewhat later than the Iliad, scholars think there are intimations of the ensuing political development: the nobility successively deprived monarchy of political power; in most Greek states, an aristocratic form of republicanism, granting power to landowners of noble and gentle stock, was introduced. In some states, in particular in Sparta, however, monarchy was retained in form.

In the course of the long period of crisis that began in the 8th century B.C., the aristocratic constitution and the corresponding social and economic structures broke down in most Greek cities. A great number of important social and economic problems became evident, and changes took place, roughly at the same time in the leading states, in particular those engaged in trade and shipping. A monetary economy came into being; cities grew, and both a quest for prestige and a feeling of equality in relation to the nobility rose among wealthy plebeians. Overpopulation and insufficient supply of arable land led not only to emigration and colonization, but also to violent conflicts of interest between the landowners and their tenants. For the latter, the introduction of a monetary economy caused great difficulties; they were not seldom ruined and, in the worst case, sold as slaves with their families. The legal machinery was entirely in the hands of the landowning nobility; the laws were considered as exalted secrets, handed over from father to son in the aristocratic families that administered the law.

In the period of strife which has thus been characterized, claims were raised and solutions were proposed which are still recognizable and which have in fact been reiterated, in similar crises, throughout the development of western Europe. In some Greek states, the political supremacy of the aristocracy was replaced by that of the new *bourgeoisie*. Elsewhere, particularly in Sparta and the Dorian states in the Peloponnese, the nobility managed to retain its position. In some states a tyrant (a Greek word which had then no pejorative connotation; it simply meant an absolute ruler of a kind distinct from the old tribal kings) became head of the state. Such rulers were often supported by the lower classes. Finally – the foremost example is Athens – the political development led to longer or shorter periods of more or less radical democracy.

One of the claims that were raised in the violent and frequently ferocious struggles that marked the transition from the rule of traditional aristocracy to other forms of government was that *laws should be made public by promulgation*. It had been a prominent feature of the oligarchic communities that the rules of the law were a kind of professional secret within the ruling class. Clear rules, easily accessible to everybody, were held up as indispensable conditions for equality before the law *(isonomy)*. This claim was often combined with endeavours to modify the substantive contents of the laws, e.g. by introducing rules that cancelled all debts incurred before the passing of the law, or at least mitigated the treatment of insolvent debtors; in some states, land reforms by means of redistribution of real property were attempted. In this period, it occurred with some frequency that states called in particularly wellknown and respected statesmen or scholars from abroad to reform their legislation with that impartiality which, it was held, only a foreigner could achieve.

The classical period of the Greek world is the 5th century B.C. The fight against the expansion of the immense Persian Empire, which had conquered the Greek cities on the western coast of Asia Minor and the neighbouring isles, was a sufficiently strong incentive for the Greek states to forget their quarrels and act in common. Heroic resistance, under Spartan leadership, in the vital mountain pass of Thermopylae in northern Greece, the victory of Marathon and the decisive naval battle of Salamis (490–480 B.C.) eliminated for a long time the threat from the east. The "all-Greek" *(pan-hellenic)* unity again gave way to internal fighting. Athens, which had gone through an initially slow but soon more and more rapid evolution towards democracy, used its naval superiority to build up an "Empire" which comprised in particular, cities in the Aegean archipelago and which was, by Greek standards, very large and strong; a great number of small states were forced, bullied or frightened into joining the Athenian league as "allies". The grandeur and glory of Athens found expressions in magnificent public buildings, in vast fortifications, and in the construction and extension of the harbour and naval yard of Piraeus. Against Athenian naval power and Athenian democracy the Peloponnesian states rallied round Sparta. In 431 B.C., a war broke out between the two blocks ("the Peloponnesian War"). It was to last for almost 30 years and, by loss of men and destruction of property as well as by the increasing ruthlessness of both politics and warfare, wrought havoc to Greece, in the first place to Athens, to an extent which no future work could undo.

The following century, the fourth B.C., is characterized by political decline, usually unsuccessful attempts to create greater political units, or federations, interferences both by Persia and by the growing northern neighbour, the Kingdom of Macedonia. About 340 B.C., King Phillip of Macedonia conquered Greece; soon after, he was succeeded by his son, Alexander the Great, who dragged the halfwilling Greeks with him on his heroic crusade into Asia, where he crushed the Persian Empire. When Alexander died, after a short reign, and his dominions were divided upon his principal followers, Greece became part of the Kingdom of Macedonia. When, about 175 B.C., that state was defeated by the new masters of the Mediterranean world, the Romans, the Greek states became part of the Roman Empire.

Under the sceptre of Rome, Greece enjoyed, in the first place, external peace and internal order. It was part of the policy of Roman imperialism to grant the subdued peoples a fairly high degree of autonomy. The deep admiration of educated Romans for Greek culture, which they had tried to acquire since the 3rd century B.C., contributed to make Greece a relatively favoured province in the great Empire; the Greek peninsula became a goal for the tourism of the wealthy, and it was held an indispensable or at least highly desirable part of the education of a Roman gentleman to have spent at least some time at the schools of Athens, which became and remained for a long time the most famous, albeit somewhat decadent and provincial, university and school centre.

This special position, as the learned, antiquarian, tourist and museum province of the Empire was retained as long as the ancient civilization survived, When, about 400 A.D., Rome was divided into an Eastern and a Western Empire, of which the latter was soon to fall into pieces under the onslaught of Germanic tribes and Huns, Greece fell to the Eastern Empire, with Byzantium as its capital, and thus could give important contributions to the Byzantine culture of the Middle Ages. At that time, however, the Athenian Schools of philosophy which had exercised an enormous influence upon intellectual development, were closed at the order of the Christian Emperor.

3. The Greek Forms of State and Government

Before giving a brief description of the main features of ancient Greek discussion concerning legal and political philosophy – inseparable in the Greek world – we shall try to convey at least some picture of that "state" to which the discussion refers and of the role played by the state in the life of the citizens.

A modern observer has to exert his imaginative powers very considerably to obtain an idea of how the Greek *pólis*, or city- state, was seen and understood by its citizens in the period 700–400 B.C. It is characteristic for modern thinking that individual and community are considered as distinct from each other, and to some extent as opposed to each other. In the Greek city states, it would have been difficult to make such opposition real and credible. Even if there were in fact dissenters, who "dropped out" and opposed the individual against collective interests, it is not an exaggeration to pretend about most Greek thinkers that the City was the very centre of their existence. Citizenship meant membership, part-ownership. At least in so far as the reasonably well-to-do inhabitants were concerned, active and direct participation in public activities of all kinds was not only considered a natural right and duty, but also a pursuit to which the greatest and most important part of a man's life should be devoted. While modern communities frequently discuss how to strike the proper balance between the community and its claims on the one hand, the individual on the other hand, the main problem in Greek public debate was how to determine each group's and each citizen's proper place in the state, how *the degree of participation* should be fixed. Religion, which modern societies consider as something highly personal, intimate and private, was closely connected with the life of the community. The cult of the local god or gods was a matter of state, like the plays and theatrical performances which were frequently part of that cult had the character of official acts. The "good life", in the eyes of the Greek city inhabitant, was *not* a pleasant private or family life (woman and family generally held a position in the shade in ancient Greece) but continuous active participation in public business. In many states more important decisions were passed by open and direct voting.

It is of some importance to stress that this view of the state, and this ideal for the community and the good life are prevailing in the writings of those two Greek writers who came to mean most to posterity, *viz.* *Plato* (d. 347 B.C.), and his pupil *Aristotle* (d. 322 B.C.). Although the latter was attached for long periods to the Macedonian court and had time, before he died, to see Alexander the Great conquer and at least begin to organize the whole Near East, the new kind of large territorial state which came into existence at that time is not only unknown but obviously unacceptable to him. In his very extensive writings Aristotle is firmly and strictly confined to the world of the *pólis*. When the analyses and proposals of these two – and also other – Greek writers were later read and used, it was frequently forgotten that their ideas are adapted to states of the classical Greek type, and this has given rise to many errors and misunderstandings. Neither Plato nor Aristotle had any experience of, or spoke about, states with a vast territory, numerous cities and a population of millions or tens of millions. The leading "great power", Athens, is likely to have had, in Plato's days, a population numbering considerably less than 200.000 citizens (to whom should be added rather more than 100.000 slaves, and at least some tens of thousands of free immigrants without citizenship).

The difference between the city states and the large empires which were founded by Alexander and his successors is of great importance. An eminent modern American historian of political ideas (Professor

G.H. Sabine) has gone so far as to describe Aristotle's death as the greatest break in Occidental political philosophy: after that event, the debate could go on without any real interruption. This seems to imply an obvious exaggeration. Even leaving aside the impact which the Industrial Revolution has had upon life in the Occidental societies of the last 100–150 years, the creation and fall of the Roman Empire, the medieval period, and the emergence of a new kind of territorial, national state from the late Middle Ages onwards brought so much new experience, to be processed by political thinkers, that Professor Sabine's contention, although, of course, impossible to disprove, seems untenable. There is no doubt, on the other hand, that the political development which transformed the free city states into more or less independant "municipalities" – atoms, as it were, of large monarchies – must have been a revolution with deep-going and far-reaching effects on human attitudes and on human thinking in matters of state, law and politics.[2] Although the political failures and corruption of the 4th century B.C. had given rise to criticism of the city state, and also had seen the emergence of "drop-out" philosophies, which glorified the unpolitical private life, nevertheless the vast majority of citizens of the small states must have found themselves in an entirely new situation when the centre of their public life, and the depository of the essential values in their lives, was degraded from an autonomous state into a local government district. It must be remembered that unlike most modern territorial states, the ancient monarchies were not based upon *nationality;* nor could they profit from any common historical or national ideology, which could compensate for anonymity (The Roman state ideology was originally available only to the native citizens of Rome; later on, in the Imperial era, some common objects of cult did in fact develop and undoubtedly contributed to creating a sort of Roman "national feeling" in the educated classes). The Hellenistic[3] monarchies were nothing but territories brought together

---

[2] It should be stressed, on the other hand, that throughout Antiquity, the *city* remained, wherever cities existed, the administrative unit both of Macedonians and Romans, that cities enjoyed a very considerable autonomy, and that the sometimes disastrous financial results of local patriotism and fierce competition between cities represented a problem for Roman governors even in late Roman times. See A.H.M. Jones, *The Greek City from Alexander to Justinian,* Oxford 1979.

[3] The term "Hellenistic" is used to denote Greek civilisation – in and outside Greece – from the 4th century B.C. onwards.

with the right of conquest. The absolute monarch, an army and a growing bureaucracy were the only factors that kept them together.

Thus, about 300 B.C., the citizens of the Greek city states, including their philosophers and lawyers, were confronted with the task of adapting their lives and their ideas to a world which was infinitely larger and, consequently, much less intimate and secure than that local community where the temple of their home town had been the obvious centre. There are features in the Hellenistic philosophies of law and state which can be understood only against that background.

It is at this time that the modern debate concerning the relationship between *individual and community,* and ideas about *individual rights* come into existence – initially on a very modest scale. It is also in the Hellenistic period that the idea of a *universal legal system,* not attached to any *pólis* but immutable and valid throughout the world, is gradually gaining ground. Furthermore, however, Oriental political ideas such as the *divinity of the reigning monarch,* penetrate also into the Greek world. At the same time, however, royal legislation and bureaucratic administration are sometimes praised as enlightened and rational when compared with the public life of the city state, which had been increasingly discredited as marked by political strife and narrow group and class interests.

Finally, it should be pointed out that the breakdown of the city states and the emergence of large monarchies – an event that was frequently brought about by protracted and bloody wars – as well as the merging of Greek and Oriental religious ideas and ideals contributed to preparing the ground for a new type of religions: creeds, frequently of Oriental origin, which were characterized by personal and intimate feeling, often by mystic elements, and by an intense longing for some kind of individual "salvation". In this sense, the road was prepared for the rapid dissemination of Christianity in the first centuries of our era.

4. *Sources for the Study of Greek Legal Thinking*

Ancient Greek law is far less known and has been far less explored than Roman law. This is, of course, to some extent due to the fact that the study of Greek law raises more practical obstacles, both because it requires a philological and historical scholarship which few lawyers and historians of law command, and also because the source material is far less abundant.

As for Greek *legal philosophy,* the situation is more favourable.

The sources for the study of ancient Greek law and of ideas and theories connected with law and legal science can be divided into five groups.

No *legal writing* in the modern sense has been preserved, and there does not seem to have existed any literature of that kind. Some fragments of a textbook "on the laws" from the 4th century B.C. are still extant; characteristically, it is the work of a philosopher, *Theophrastos* (Aristotle's principal pupil, and after the master's death head of the Aristotelian, or "Peripathetic", school of philosophy).

Much can be learnt from the works of the great orators, in particular those of Athens. Among them should be mentioned *Lysias, Isocrates,* and *Demosthenes,* all active in the 4th century B.C., and authors of famous political and forensic speeches which have been preserved. These pleadings cannot, of course, convey a complete or a systematic picture of Greek law and its administration, but they provide a number of case studies which illustrate in a concrete way both institutions, single rules of law, and – above all – legal reasoning and legal habits of thought. The courts in which these speeches were held were almost invariably composed of laymen who had been elected or even picked out by casting lots. Moreover, they were very large; a court could consist of hundreds or even thousands of members, and the art of persuasion developed by counsel therefore frequently came closer to the technique of a political orator rather than the close reasoning of a lawyer before an ordinary court.

A third but meagre and uneven source of information are the various *inscriptions* which have been preserved. They mostly deal with public law and or with religious rules and rituals.

Private law rules and commercial contracts can be studied in the still growing body of *papyrus* documents which are found especially in Egypt.

In so far as legal thinking and legal philosophy are concerned, the most important sources are, by far, the writings of philosophers; a vast mass has been preserved. It is of course impossible to draw any safe conclusions about the role, if any, which these theoretical treatises played for "the living law". What is certain, however, is that Greek legal philosophy was to exercise a decisive influence on the development both of general ideas in the realm of law in Western Europe, and of the principles of substantive law.

5. A Law without a Legal Technique

It is characteristic for modern legal thinking that, fully conscious about the difficulty of transforming the principle into concrete and practical action, it draws a dividing line between "legal", "political" and "moral" questions. What is most typical for the "law" in this context would seem to be that it is implemented by use of a method of decision and of reasoning which has for its object a body of norms considered to be, and treated as, binding and which implies a specific technique, also of a normative character. The delimitation of a specialised "legal" field of problems and of decisions has often been criticized, from various quarters, as artificial and apt to conceal the true underlying interests and the fundamentally political character of most controversies in a developed society. However, the delimitation has mostly been greeted as a decisive progress. It is, in the main, the work of the Roman lawyers. The Greeks do not seem to have known it. This is in all likelihood due to, or at least connected with, the absence of a real "legal profession" in ancient Greece and with the composition and methods of her courts. The Greeks hardly ever distinguished between such arguments as were related to legal, political and moral problems. This fact is illustrated both by the works of the Attic orators and by the poverty, in classical Greek, of such terms as serve to denote differences of the kind referred to. This does not mean, of course, that the Greeks should not have invented and used, with great satisfaction, highly sophisticated *procedural* rules and arguments.

Nor does the statement that the Greeks had no "legal technique" imply that they would have lived without *laws*. On the contrary, the concept of "the law" – the clear, written law, adopted according to an established procedure and duly published – was highly important in Greece; more so, in fact, than in Rome, where the inhabitants were far more prepared to accept a legal development by court precedents. Greek literature contains a wealth of pointed slogans and *bons mots* where the rule of the law is defined and glorified. One such *bon mot* was νόμος βασιλεύς "the Law as King", and Aristotle has described eloquently a society where everybody is living under the law, a "master without passions".

It is generally held by modern scholars that the supremacy of the law in the Greek society was in fact so strong that there was no room for the creation of a customary law, or for "equity" in the sense of derogations from the letter of the law. As will be developed below, however, Aristotle formulates the problem of equity in a way that was to determine all further Occidental discussion of this question. Legal rules, it was generally held, could not under any circumstances be set aside. In all likelihood, there were, in actual practice, areas in which local religious and similar traditions must have possessed considerable importance, but what seems clear is that custom and usage were hardly ever *invoked* as authorities. It was preferred, in such cases, to refer to mythical lawgivers or divine commands to justify legal solutions.

We are not informed about any specific *doctrine of the sources of law* and their use in ancient Greece. Again, there are good reasons to believe that the prevailing court organization was an obstacle against a more advanced development. There does not seem to have been any consciousness about the problems of interpretation. Principles and methods for the construction of literary texts, and a specialized terminology covering the various elements of that activity, were developed in the Hellenistic era by grammarians and scholars in the field of literary history, but there is no evidence about any influence from these quarters upon the interpretation of legal texts. An Athenian writer recommends, about 380 B.C., that the courts judge according to the law, and if there are no specific statutory provisions in point, according to the best justice they can find. It should be added that not even Aristotle, who is the theorician otherwise most open to practical problems of this kind, gives any attention to questions concerning the construction of statutes.

Little is known about early Greek influence upon *Roman* law (in the period 5th–3rd centuries B.C.), although the drafters of the Roman Code of the Twelve Tables visited Greece, according to Roman tradition, to study, i.a., Solon's reform work at Athens. In *late* Roman law, some special institutions of Greek origin were introduced. In spite of the political supremacy of Rome in the Mediterranean world from the 3rd century B.C., Roman law seems to have had a very small impact upon local Greek law. One explanation may be that Roman private law was to such a great extent a customary law, which already for that reason had difficulty in penetrating into the codified Greek systems.

The great gift of Greek legal science to Rome, and to later Occidental civilization, was thus not to be found in rules or institutions. It was the philosophical analyses of the theoretical foundations of law and justice. From at least the 2nd century B.C., Greek legal philosophy exercised a strong influence among Roman lawyers, and among the Roman upper classes in general. The leading lawyers invariably belonged to that stratum of the Roman society.

The first evidence of theoretical analyses and attempts at explanations in the Greek world are to be found in the field of the natural sciences. In the 5th century, a decisive change took place: the critical and analytical methods and techniques of reasoning which had been developed in the course of these early studies of nature were now put to use in the discussion of human and societal questions. Those who devoted themselves to such discussion, and who taught their methods to others were called *Sophists* – a word which has got a pejorative ring, principally as a result of Plato's descriptions of Socrates' disputations with pettyfogging Sophists, but which simply meant "teachers of wisdom", or "specialists in wisdom" (Greek "sophia" means "wisdom").

From the 5th century B.C. until the end of Antiquity, a wealth of schools, theories and movements came into existence. One decisive turn of the tide has already been mentioned: the transition from the world of the "pólis", or City state, to the large Hellenistic monarchies deeply marked theoretical discussion. That discussion was largely connected with the more or less firmly organized schools, of which the most famous ones were the Academy (founded by Plato and extant until the 5th century A.D.), the Lyceum (also called the Peripathetic school, which was the work of Aristotle), the Stoa or Stoic school (founded by Zeno about 300 B.C.), the Epicurean school (also from about 300 B.C.). More temporary and less firmly organized schools of thought and groups of philosophers are represented by the Sophists and by Cynics and Sceptics in Hellenistic days.

6. *The Earliest Period. The Natural Philosophers*

It was to take a long time before the Greek language developed general terms with a sense approximately corresponding to the word "law" (Swedish "rätt", German "Recht", French "droit"), and when that linguistic innovation came to pass, these words bore the character of artificial specialized terms. In the earliest language, that of the Homeric poems, two key words appear in contexts where the "law" in the sense of a system of rules, or that which is legally acceptable, is being referred to. One of these words is *themis,* the other is *dike.* In Greek mythology, both words are used to denote goddesses of justice, and both words can be translated into "law", but in a highly specialized sense.

Themis appears frequently in the Homeric poems. A more precise definition of the sense of the word would seem to be "that which is proper", or "appropriate", the "reasonable and proper order of things". The term refers to a settled and functioning social system and what pertains to it, i.e. courts of justice and a settled legal procedure. Thus in the Odyssey, it is said about the wild and one-eyed Cyclops – in order to show what inhuman barbarians they were – that this people knows not of court meetings and *themistes,* i.e. judges. *Themis* is not a legal system in the technical sense of the word; it is a network of norms, an impersonal and flexible "order", the principal function of which is to draw up the lines of demarcation delimiting each man's "proper" sphere of action. To commit wrong is to exceed that area; worst of all is to enter another man's sphere with violence.

Dike can be paraphrased with "that which is right in the individual case". The term is frequently used to denote a (correct) *decision* in an individual case before a court. In other words, *dike* means the determination of the concrete content of a norm which is part of *themis:* the proper and authoritative expression, *in casu,* of the social order.

From the troubled period 750–500 B.C., there is a fair amount of evidence both about growing (and frequently negative) experience of legal solutions and legal procedures, and about deepened and more systematic reflection concerning law and the philosophy of law. The poet Hesiod complains, towards the end of the aristocratic era, in the 8th century, of "gift-devouring judges"; the claims for unambiguous laws easily accessible to everybody and enacted with the consent of the people is evidence of growing insight into the functions and role of courts and legal rules. Corrupt judges and obscure laws were certainly not the only mischiefs calling for remedies. Another frequently raised problem was the inefficiency of the law in a society with small resources and undeveloped public services. In the Athenian reform legislation of Solon (6th century B.C.), an attempt was made to solve the problem of inefficiency i.a. by introducing a general right to prosecute certain crimes *(actio popularis).* In the course of time, this was to prove a dangerous device.

In early Greek philosophy, before the Sophists, we find scattered evidence about reflections concerning state and law. Many of those thinkers who are usually described as representatives of "natural philosophy" took an active part in public life, and they frequently use images and terms from that field of activity to describe and illustrate theories about natural phenomena. In the writings of *Heraclitos* (7th–6th century B.C.) we find, for the first time, expressions of an idea which was to be developed in various theories of natural law: "all human laws", he says, "are nourished by one single divine law"; and *Pythagoras* (580–500 B.C.) discusses questions of justice in the context of his description of the world order and harmony of the world, which he considered to be a perfect mathematical equilibrium in all relations. *Democritos* (b. about 460 B.C.), the author of the first "theory of atoms," goes deeper into ethical questions. He lays down moral precepts of a purely individual character, distinct from those norms which are maintained only by fear of punishment.

A famous and widely celebrated expression of early reflection concerning the dichotomy positive law v. ethics is found in *Sophocles'* tragedy "Antigone" from the middle of the 5th century B.C. The heroine of the tragedy, Antigone, gives her brother, fallen in battle as an outlaw and a rebel, a ritual funeral although the King of the state has severely prohibited all subjects to give any attention to the dead man's corpse. Antigone is arrested. Against the laws of worldly power, she invokes the duties of a higher moral order; the obligation to bury one's kinsmen according to the rites is one of these duties. It is not advisable to insist too heavily on Antigone's famous speech as an expression of legal philosophy, but it deserves attention and admiration as a classical illustration of an eternal ethical problem.

7. *The Sophists*

The contributions of the Sophists to the critical analysis of inherited conventional ideas about law and justice covered a wide area; they represented all nuances and shadows of scepticism and relativism, but also other fundamental attitudes and other ideas are represented among them. One of the most famous expressions of relativism is the so-called *homo mensura* maxim of *Protagoras* (d. about 410 B.C.): "man is the measure of all things". Historians have sometimes described the age of the Sophists as "the Greek Enlightenment"; there are in fact many similarities between this early rationalistic movement and some of the most salient trends in European 18th century philosophy.

Thus the Sophists questioned, and many among then flatly rejected, the idea that law and justice have a religious foundation. They made law and legal institutions the object of empirical studies in the same way as they examined other social and psychological phenomena.

The Sophists were the first to formulate, albeit in a preliminary way, without the terminology later to be adopted and without pursuing this line of investigation systematically, the fundamental problem of all natural law thinking: is there such a thing as a legal system above or alongside that created by men in human societies? Many of the Sophists pushed their enquiry further, however, and tried to ascertain, by empirical observations, what would be the nature and the contents of a "natural" system of this kind. Some of them tried to demonstrate, in this context, that in the state of nature, the stronger usually hold sway over the weaker; this, some Sophists openly proclaimed, is the only reasonable state of affairs. Others insist on the observation that those differences in rank, position and conditions of life which are characteristic for human societies cannot be found in nature. Consequently, the "natural" legal system can be described as a state of liberty and equality. Moreover, we find, among the Sophists, representatives, or at least forerunners, of "theological", as well as of "naturalistic" and "rationalistic" natural law thinking. Finally, a few writers belonging to the Sophist movement express, in an embryonic state, the idea that law and society are based upon a contract between those concerned ("the social contract") and that this fact has an impact upon the contents of legal systems and also upon the limits which such systems have to observe.

Many Sophists undoubtedly expressed a naive and exaggerated belief both in rational analysis and in the possibility for sufficiently acute reasoning to arrive at the truth. Among them there were also many who devoted themselves to hairsplitting and who boasted with their refined technique of argumentation. However, the mostly negative impression left to posterity by these early representatives of social and legal thinking is to a great extent unjust. The Sophists were unfortunate enough to displease, and come into conflict with, one of the noblest characters in the history of philosophy, Socrates. They were therefore attacked, and caricatured, by one of the greatest philosophers and literary artists of all times: Plato. Their reputation has suffered incurable prejudice from this conflict.

8. Socrates and Plato

Socrates, the Athenian "street philosopher", put to death under a sentence by a people's court in 399 B.C., has not left any written works; his teaching was oral, and what we know about it is what we find in the works of his pupils, in the first place Plato.

Socrates lived and worked in a social and intellectual *milieu* which was at the same time characterized by old-fashioned religious convictions and conventions, by a strong belief in the City of Athens and in her strength and divine protection, and by the wave of relativism and scepticism that followed in the wake of the Sophist movement. Socrates served with great gallantry as an infantry man in the Athenian citizen army in the Peloponnesian war. Towards the end of his life, the political and ideological controversy which was always at least latent in the Athenian Republic became acute under the pressure of the war effort, the defeats suffered by Athens and the approach of the final catastrophe. The death sentence passed upon Socrates would seem to reflect the distrust and dislike which the common burghers of Athens harboured against "intellectuals" in general. Socrates was accused of being and sentenced as an enemy of religion and a seducer of the young. This was, as far as we can see, not only an injustice but also a misunderstanding. Socrates' teaching is, in several respects, a *reaction* against the theories and maxims of the Sophists. It reflects a search for a system of ethics on religious foundations, but few links obviously connected it with the narrow and in many respects still primitive and formalistic official State religion. Like the Sophists, and like most Greek thinkers – the essentially empirical Aristotle being the principal exception – Socrates is a *rationalist*. Virtue, which Socrates' teaching purports to achieve, is found and practised by theoretical understanding: to be virtuous is a matter of knowledge; to understand the true interplay of causes and effects also implies an understanding of, and a sufficiently strong wish to achieve, moral perfection. In this respect, Socrates is, as compared with the sceptical Sophists, an optimist.

Strong personal and internalized ethical convictions, combined with great respect both for traditional religion and for the laws and institutions of the state are the most salient feature of Socrates' philosophy. Another characteristic element is his technique of reasoning, which starts from everyday language, and familiar ideas. On this basis, he goes on to formulate definitions of concepts which contribute to create clarity in the questions taken up for discussion. To a great extent, Socrates worked with carefully chosen questions, which made his dialogue partners reflect and reconsider their opinions. In this way, it is the partner himself who arrives at the conclusions which the philosopher wanted to see drawn. Socrates himself describes his method at "majeutic," from the Greek word for the (medical) art of delivery.

Socrates' most eminent pupil was *Plato* (427–347 B.C.), one of the greatest and most influential thinkers of all times. Although state and laws were at the centre of Plato's interests, his works in these fields are only part of his extensive still preserved productions. Plato's best-known, and perhaps most lasting, contribution in the area of general philosophy is his "doctrine of ideas," *i.e.* the theory that those things which we perceive in the world of observable realities are only reflections of the "ideas" of these things – their everlasting and unchangeable originals, or "archetypes". For Occidental philosophy and religion, as well as for art and literature, Platonism has been an immeasurable, ever recurring source of inspiration. It is enough to remind the reader of the development undergone by the term and notion, "idea" in the Occidental languages: "idealism" has remained one of the great main currents in the history of ideas in the West. The lasting success of Plato's teaching is undoubtedly due also to the artistic qualities of the works where it is presented.

Plato was an Athenian of aristocratic origin. Family tradition would have made statecraft his natural field of activity, but both the excesses of the democratic *régime* of Athens towards the end of the Peloponnesian war and the brutal reactionary government which came into power after the defeat of Athens (and which was responsible for the execution of Plato's deeply respected and loved teacher, Socrates) disgusted him, and he chose to lead the life of a private scholar, writing and teaching in his home. In his later years, he taught in a garden called Academia, near Athens, which was to remain an influential school of philosophy until the end of the ancient world. On a couple of occasions, Plato tried to realize his ideas about the ideal state, acting on the invitation of a "tyrant," i.e. an absolute monarch, in one of the Greek colonies in Sicily. These attempts resulted in failure, however, and Plato's development as a thinker is marked by disappointment and dwindling belief in the possibility to create ideal societies.

Among Plato's many writings, three are of particular interest from the point of view of legal philosophy: *The Republic*, *The Statesman*, and *The Laws*. The dating of Plato's work is an old and complicated controversial question, which cannot be discussed here. What seems certain is that *The Republic* is the earliest of these three books, and that the later two reflect Plato's negative experience in Sicily. *The Republic* is the picture of an ideal society, a *utopia* (a Greek word which can be translated by "Nowhere"), and it seems obvious that Plato was forced to doubt its possibility. *The Statesman* and *The Laws* express attempts to find the second best, i.e. forms of states which do not raise the same exclusive claims but which are nevertheless superior to what Plato found in contemporary Greece.

We do not intend to give a description of the contents of Plato's works in the field of legal and political philosophy. It should only be kept in mind that none of them contains analyses of existing states or societies; even in the latter works, Plato is drawing up a programme for future, reformed states. In *The Republic,* he presents, in fairly great detail, the outline of a society which has been described with such various names as "élite society" and "extreme state socialism." Plato proposes a rigorous division of the population into three classes, or "castes", each with a specific function: at the top we find those who govern the republic, the wise and knowledgeable, picked out through a severe procedure of selection and education; below them come the warriors, or guardians, also carefully selected and subject to rigorous demands with regard to courage, ability, and – to use a modern term – "professional ethics." At the bottom, there is the mass of the population, engaged in agriculture and other economic activities. Only this lowest class is allowed to live in families and to possess private property. In the eyes of a modern observer, Plato's "Republic" has the features of an inhuman and meticulously regulated social machine. It should be remembered that the proper term of comparison is not a modern society but the Greek *pólis:* the system proposed by Plato certainly appeared less frightening and less foreign to his contemporaries; the extant city states constituted far-reaching and deep-going communities of life, and the modern "problematization" of the relationship between the community and the individual was unknown.

In *The Laws,* which seem to express the final stage in Plato's development, the philosopher describes a society of a corporate character, also divided into classes, but less rigorously. Its salient feature is the complete predominance of the *laws,* expressions of accumulated collective experience and respected as a kind of impersonal rulers of the city.

When trying to single out and emphasize the principal elements of Plato's philosophy of law and of the state, it should first be noted that Plato is a *rationalist* in the same way as Socrates: virtue means knowledge and knowledge leads to virtue. There is, objectively, such a thing as a "good life" which can be taught and learnt. In order to improve people morally or, more generally, train them for civic purposes, you have to teach them to see and understand. On this score, Plato is in conscious and explicit opposition to many Sophists, who considered both knowledge and virtue to be inaccessible, or even simply nonexistant. But these ideas are also in opposition to such modern views as presuppose, as a general principle, a clear dividing line between that which can be objectively ascertained and subjective evaluations. Plato – like most early thinkers – represents an *objective theory of values:* what is "good" or "valuable" can be determined in the same way and with the same degree of certainty as the colour or the weight of an object can be ascertained. This part of Plato's thinking has a religious character; it is obviously connected with the supposed objective existence of ideas (including the ideas of moral qualities, such as "good," "virtuous", "just") and, by implication, their accessibility to objective knowledge. The view – or the illusion – that knowledge necessarily leads to virtue is one of those ideas that recur, time and again, in the development of Western thought, e.g. in the era of Enlightenment in the 18th century and in some schools of thought in modern pedagogics. The fruits which these ideas have carried have not always been convincing.

Plato, now, does not push the contention that what is good can be found out objectively to the point of pretending that such knowledge is easily accessible to all. He had obviously been impressed with the requirements of precision and exactitude formulated in particular by mathematics and geometry. He insisted on the same intellectual prerequisites for knowledge about moral values. The result is that such knowledge is accessible only to the wise, the philosophers. Plato's theories are far from "democratic." On the contrary, they are early expressions of that *élite* thinking, or rather that belief in *specialization* and *expert knowledge*, which is a frequently recurring element in Occidental political and social thinking. Since "virtue" – the goal of life in society – may be taught and learnt, it is a natural field of activity for "him who knows," the expert. The good politician appears, in Plato's works, as a kind of medical man. In "The Statesman," the idea of the knowledgable leader is of great importance.

It is particularly in the earliest of the three great works on political and legal philosophy that Plato's rationalism seems rigid and not without naiveté. He establishes (in this, however, he is not alone) a hierarchy of virtues: first comes wisdom, then courage, and finally moderation. The three classes of the ideal republic correspond to this order: the rulers, the guardians, and those engaged in gainful occupations. In other contexts, it should be added, Plato like Aristotle describes *justice* as the principal among virtues, the essence of them all.

However, along with this highly schematized thinking, Plato's work expresses insight of a different and far more deep-going kind. He does not consider society to be the product of any "social contract" or similar agreement, but as a necessary organization for the satisfaction of basic human needs. He holds – in opposition to the views of contemporary democratic politicians – that a highly developed distribution of tasks, under which each citizen can concentrate upon what he knows best, secures the most efficient satisfaction of needs.

Within the Platonic system, the question of *justice* between the different classes of the community (and between individuals, although Plato hardly discusses them) becomes, for all practical purposes, a question of finding a harmonious, rational, and practically justifiable equilibrium between the rôles and the degrees of participation granted to each group in the common work for the state. Plato is far from any abstract principle of equal shares or of complete equality. It is not probable that he would have understood that kind of reasoning, given his basic assumptions. Again, it should be remembered that Plato's frame of reference was the Greek city state. It was an axiom for him that what was useful for the public was also useful for each individual who is a member of that public. The state, to Plato as to most other Greek thinkers, was an all-embracing community of life, not a "public sector" as distinct from a private sphere of life.

The notion of justice in the sense of "equilibrium between groups" – not in the sense of a mechanical distribution of power, or of wealth, according to the number of heads – is elaborated with particular care in *The Laws*. The society outlined in this work is characterized by aristocratic corporativism, with elements of monarchic rule. There is no "ruling class" corresponding to the philosophers in *The Republic;* the different classes of the population have a right of vote proportional to their property. Private wealth, family life, and monogamous marriage are accepted for all classes. The system is based upon slavery in agriculture, and – what may seem more astonishing – on the principle that industry and trade are entirely in the hands of foreigners, non-citizens. Plato had a strong preference for agrarian societies and harboured a corresponding distrust of urban occupations and of large cities (in particular sea ports) – a feature he shares with many conservative thinkers throughout history. Impressions and memories from the life of Athenian democracy, with its turbulent mobs, frequently enforced by sailors and aliens, certainly played an important part in determining Plato's negative view of the city as a centre of political life.

In *The Laws*, a dilemma, an internal contradiction in Plato's thinking, appears. In the ideal republic, laws were superfluous, since the wisest were in power, and they should not be bound by any laws. We recognize this attitude from some brands of modern socialism and from fascism: laws are mere obstacles, tools of individualistic or reactionary resistance; when those who know best are in power, no legal rules are necessary. In *The Laws*, Plato stresses the idea that the laws of a society represent *empirical wisdom* – experience and common sense are, as it were, frozen into the laws. Thus Plato seems prepared to accept experience, and also convention, as grounds for legislation. However, this recognition of the value of experience, and even more convention, is frequently difficult to reconcile with the radical rationalism which Plato usually expresses and does not seem to have abandoned in other respects. The tension between empiricism and rationalism, particularly obvious in Plato's thinking, is one of the elements that live on through the whole Occidental development.

There are, in Plato's works, a great number of ideas, or of fragments of ideas, which were to exercise a decisive influence upon all future debate in the fields of legal and political science. We have already made reference to ideas concerning a *division of powers* upon different organs, and to the *"socialism"* and *utopism* of *The Republic*. Other ideas can be mentioned: the outlines of *a typology of forms of government* (monarchy

– tyranny, aristocracy – oligarchy, democracy – ochlocracy), which were to be elaborated by Aristotle; finally elements of a philosophy of history (which goes back upon myths and religious ideas) according to which human societies develop from a happy state of nature, through tyranny and democracy, towards ever greater decay, and catastrophe, whereupon a new cycle commences.

Plato's thinking was to mean more to analytical and critical thinkers – not to speek of dreamers and poets – than to political leaders and legislators. But the ideas of the Athenian have always come back, in one way or another, as immortal, suggestive, severe and challenging elements in the complicated pattern of Occidental thought.

9. Aristotle

When medieval European philosophers and theologians invoked, as an authority, "the Philosopher," they incurred no risk of misunderstanding. The term was reserved for one thinker: Aristotle from Stagira (384–322 B.C.). The high Middle Ages may have been the epoch when his influence was strongest, but there has hardly been any period in European history – including our own times – where his teaching has been completely forgotten. No other individual thinker can claim such a strong, lasting and many-sided importance. Aristotle came from the small town of Stagira in Thrace, but his father, a medical man, was for a long time attached to the court of the Kings of Macedonia. In his youth and early manhood Aristotle was Plato's pupil in the Athenian academy where he stayed till the master's death. In 343 Aristotle became the teacher of Alexander the Great. When that task had been fulfilled, he returned to Athens (335 B.C.) and founded his own school of philosophy, Lyceum (the so-called Peripathetic school). When Alexander died in 323, there was a short outburst of anti-Macedonian feeling in Athens, and Aristotle had to leave the city. He died in exile the following year.

In many important respects Aristotle is the opposite of Plato. Whereas the latter is, among other things, an inspired religious seer and prophet, Aristotle is essentially a pure scholar. Empiricism – both as an attitude of attachment to the world of ascertainable facts and as a method, implying careful observation of those facts – is one of his predominant features. With regard to politics, where the disillusioned aristocrat Plato adopted, from the beginning, an extreme standpoint,

Aristotle is a man of middle ways and of compromises. To borrow a character from the modern European scene, Aristotle is a sober upper middle class scholar, a *bourgeois* intellectual. He was certainly aware of the difference in temper and outlook between himself and the admired master. The famous words *Amicus Plato, sed amicior veritas* ("Plato is dear to me, but truth is dearer") – a classical expression of the scholar's search for truth, regardless of personal considerations – are a transformation of a *dictum* by Aristotle.

The philosopher's very extensive scholarly work was published about 400 years after his death, and the texts which were edited at that time appear to be notes taken by his pupils in the course of his lectures. The literary merits which are characteristic of Plato's writings are entirely absent from Aristotle's productions, which are mostly dry and rather dull. Repetitions and contradictions are fairly frequent.

Aristotle has written about literally everything which could be the object of human knowledge, in his days and for a very long time to come. Even today, ideas presented and discussed by Aristotle have assumed new importance. Thus, his analysis, in a short work referred to as *The Topics*, of the method of reasoning in such fields where exact, scientific knowledge is, for one reason or another, impossible to achieve, has not only attracted attention in continental jurisprudential writing after the second World War but also been recommended by several authors as a method to be adopted today.

That work which we shall first discuss in the present context, the *Politics*, was written, according to modern research, in the course of a long period, probably some fifteen years. It contains elements from different periods which have not been completely coordinated (as is frequently the case with Aristotle's writings). Students of Aristotle's thought agree that it is possible to find in the *Politics*, a slow but clearly discernible movement away from the positions adopted by Plato. There is, in fact, a marked difference from the beginning. The purpose of the work is another than that pursued by Plato in his *Republic:* Aristotle does not claim to present an absolute ideal for a state; he is out for something which can possibly be realized.

While Plato considered the laws and that political *régime* where they are predominant as a "second best" solution, adopted only because the very best – the rule of the wise as described in the *Republic* – was out of reach, Aristotle gives the laws, from the beginning, a decisive role. The Law, everybody's master without anybody being a slave, constitutes – according to a famous Aristotelian dictum – "a reason inaccessible to passions". The philosopher distrusts the idea that men, even the wisest men, can continuously exercise great power without serious inconvenients. The law reflects the experience accumulated by many people through a long time. It represents that empirically founded knowledge and wisdom which Aristotle considered more highly than analytical and speculative reason.

Aristotle also expresses a more nuanced view than Plato upon the law as an instrument of governing human relations. Unlike his teacher, he is not of the opinion that *society* and *family* can be treated in the same way by the legislators (the *individual* on the other hand, plays as insignificant a role in Aristotle's work as in Plato's). In politics, Aristotle says, we are dealing with relations between those who are *equals* in relation to each other. This is not the case within a family and for that reason rules which are intended and adapted for the intercourse of citizens at large cannot be used between the members of a household (which was, of course, in those days a highly patriarchal organization).

When Aristotle describes the relations within a state, as distinct from a family, as relations between equals, this does not mean that he would have represented egalitarian ideas in politics or economy. In this dispassionate and pragmatic observer's view, the question of division of powers is in the first place a search for an acceptable and accepted equilibrium, but this search, on the other hand, meant much more in his political theory than in Plato's, since the "state socialism" of the latter had no counterpart in Arisotle's writing. Consequently, the younger philosopher had to count with an uncontrolled emergence and growth of classes and groups, and consequently with conflicts of interest unknown in Plato's ideal society. The turbulent big city democracy, not to say mob rule, which had characterized Athens in the second half of the 5th century was as suspect in Aristotle's view as in Plato's. He found it difficult flatly to reject the claims of the well-educated and economically independent upper classes to be granted a measure of political influence exceeding the proportion that would follow from a mechanical counting of heads.

Aristotle does not give a clear preference to any type of ideal state, but it seems possible to conclude from his writings that he is in favour of a moderate democracy, a political system dominated by a strong and numerous middle class. The existence of this class and the large proportion of the population to which it is obviously assumed to correspond would seem to presuppose and imply relatively small differences in wealth in the society as a whole. Equilibrium between groups rather than absolute predominance for one or the other category was obviously what Aristotle preferred. He seems to have envisaged the role of the lower and lowest classes as a passive or negative controlling function intended to prevent abuses of power by the politically active upper classes. It is characteristic of his attitude in these matters that he preferred a state with a large agricultural population with little spare time for public affairs and little inclination to participate actively in politics. Such a state would obviously give the educated and leisured *élite* considerable leeway as a leading group, but at the same time there would be a certain measure of control over its use of that leeway.

In spite of the importance attributed by Aristotle to the proper distribution of power and influence among different groups of society, and to the relations between such groups, these questions do not loom large when the philosopher attempts to give a definition of the good state which means, in his view, a constitutional state. For the purposes of that definition Aristotle formulates three conditions, which the good state should fulfil: (i) it shall be governed *in the public interest,* not in order to favour any particular group or individual; (ii) public life shall be subject to *the rule of law* and not give room for arbitrariness; (iii) the citizens shall participate in public life *voluntarily,* not under coercion.

In one essential respect Aristotle's and Plato's theories of the state coincide: the former also deals exclusively with *pólis,* the Greek city state, although – or because? – he had witnessed, at close quarters, the effective government of a fairly large terriorial state, the Kingdom of Macedonia, and had also followed, at a distance, the founding of Alexander's huge empire. We do not know whether these examples of entirely different kinds of states served as negative examples, or whether Aristotle did not believe in their capacity to survive for a long time. It may be, and this is perhaps upon the whole the most probable assumption, that he considered the political system of Greece – which he held, without hesitation, culturally superior to all other nations – a goal towards which countries like Macedonia or the monarchies of the East would develop successively as their general cultural level was raised. Such a view would correspond to prevailing notions of "evolution" in the hellenistic world and a development along these lines took place, slowly and incompletely: under the successors of

Alexander, and even more after Rome had conquered the eastern Mediterranean basin, the "city," naturally grown or artifically founded, with its larger or smaller surrounding territory, became the standard unit of administration.

To Aristotle, the state is thus not a framework within which the good life can be lived. It is not an organization which makes it possible for individuals to plan their existence in the best possible manner. Participation in the properly organized state *is* the good life; the state is, as it were, its own, and the individual's highest, purpose. The very important limitation of the scope or Aristotelian political thinking which this implies has hardly been noticed until modern times.

Like Plato, but going further into details and subdivisions, Aristotle draws up a schedule for the classification of different forms of government; it is still used (monarchy and its negative version tyranny, aristocracy, or rule of the best, as distinct from oligarchy, rule of the few; democracy, or rule of the people, as opposed to ochlocracy, or mob rule). He also gives lasting contributions to political science by careful analyses of groups and factors of strength and weakness in the life of different societies. He discusses the relationship between politics and economy and outlines the division of tasks upon deliberating, executive and judicial functions and bodies.

In questions of the kind which are today considered to be "legal" in a narrow sense, Aristotle has not pronounced himself as extensively as in matters of broader political significance. That Aristotelian work which contains the philosopher's most clear and most elaborate discussion of such questions is the so-called *Nicomachean Ethics,* or *Ethics for Nicomachos* (Aristotle's son). According to modern research, it is a late work, possibly finished in Aristotle's last year.

Some features of particular importance in Aristotle's ethical teaching should be mentioned.

In the first place, Aristotle has taken over from the Sophists the distinction between *natural law* and *enacted, or positive, law,* but he does not analyse this dichotomy at depth. However, given his immense authority for at least a millennium and a half to come, the mere fact that he adopted and explicitly mentioned the two categories gave the distincion a weight which is today difficult to imagine. Some modern writers claim that Aristotle developed, in the course of his long career, from an attitude marked by strict and absolute ethical ideas, towards relativism, and that this meant a greater understanding and a higher appreciation of positive law. In order to grasp what Aristotle is likely to have meant by "natural law", we have to remember that *nature*, in the philosopher's thinking, has the character of a purpose-determined (and thus, in some respects, "rational") system, with an inherent urge for harmony and equilibrium. It is neither a dead and inert mass nor an "animated" nature in the religious (pantheistic) sense. Aristotle does not undertake any close analysis of "natural law;" he concentrates his efforts upon "positive" – or rather "society-related" – law, that body of rules which applies in human communities, more particularly in Greek city states.

With regard to positive law, Aristotle distinguishes between two kinds of "justice." The one we can call – using the Latin term which was adopted in the Middle Ages *(justitia distributiva)* – "distributive justice". By this concept, the philosopher meant justice in the distribution of desirable things – both property and, e.g., political power – upon the different groups, or individuals, of a given society. What justice demands, Aristotle stresses, is that the proper proportions be observed: the utilities should be shared according to the deserts and needs of the candidates, not mechanically according to the number of heads. Thus, the more competent citizen has a "just" claim to a larger share of political influence and honours than the less experienced or educated. The crucial point in this system would seem to be the treatment of wealth. Aristotle does not propose a "just" redistribution of property; at the same time wealth is one of the factors that give or may give, a claim to special political influence. The result if these ideas are applied to almost any given, historic society, will be a conservation of inequality.

The other form of justice discussed by Aristotle could be called "justice in exchange relations." It is traditionally termed "commutative justice" *(justitia commutativa)* and means, in short, that equal should be given for equal: an injury should be compensated with an amount corresponding to the economic loss, goods shall be paid for with a sum equal to their true value. This idea was to exercise a great influence in Roman law, particularly in private law, where we find principles dealing with unjustified gains, cancellation of contracts owing to gross disproportion between the obligations of the parties. The medieval doctrine of the "proper price" *(justum pretium)* was also based upon the notion of commutative justice.

Finally, among Aristotle's many contributions to the development of legal thinking, mention should be made of his doctrine of *equity* (Greek: *epieikeia,* Lat.: *aequitas*) as a corrective of strict statutory rules. That doctrine implies an unusually deep-going and realistic analysis of positive law as a set of standard solutions intended for average cases. If we compare Aristotle's short but incisive discussion of the "problem of the odd case," to which the legal rule fits badly, and an "equitable" solution is called for, with a famous passage, two thousand years younger, *viz.* Blackstone's, in his "Commentaries", it is striking how little, if any, progress has been made. It is a frequently made observation that – outside such fields of learning where progress in our knowledge of the facts has radically modified the situation – Aristotle's ideas and reasoning have remained "modern" and can still be used to an astonishing extent.

10. Cynics and Epicureans

Already in the days of Plato and Aristotle there had been philosophers who held that the good life was possible only outside – and far away from – public affairs. With the decay of city states, and their final breakdown as autonomous political units in the Hellenistic era, this attitude, which meant, according to a famous dictum of Aristotle, a life "for Gods or beasts," i.e. implied something profoundly inhuman, became more and more frequent. It expressed, obviously, both the homelessness created by the large territorial states and an attempt to find solutions to the intellectual and moral problems which they raised.

The most extreme among the schools of thought now referred to was the short-lived movement of the *Cynics* (from the Greek word for "dog": "dog-men"), who flourished in the third century B.C. The Cynics were wandering proletarian philosophers who preached complete independance in relation to property, marriage, family, citizenship but also such incorporeal goods as reputation, or theoretical learning. The main purpose of the endeavours proposed – but also realized – by these "drop-out" philosophers was a life in complete liberty. Among the Cynics, *Antisthenes, Diogenes* (the man with the barrel) and *Crates* were the most well-known. For reasons which need not to be developed, cynism did not give rise to any organized school of thought, and its influence does not seem to have been deep or lasting.

The third great school of philosophy (the two first being Plato's Academy and Aristotle's Lyceum) was founded by *Epicurus* about 300

B.C. and was called, after its founder, the *Epicurean* school. The term has frequently been misused, owing to misunderstandings concerning the message and tenets of Epicurus and his followers: "Epicurean" has often been used to denote a pure hedonist, a man exclusively interested in pleasure. The gist of Epicureanism however, was that true wisdom consists in avoiding pain, anguish, fear, and any kind of dependence. The similarity with the creed of the Cynics is obvious; in fact, Epicureanism is a less radical and less provoking parallel of Cynism. One inevitable consequence of Epicurus' teaching is that the wise man should avoid participation in public affairs and lead the life of a private citizen.

Epicureanism also meant answers to certain other questions of importance to the development of legal thinking. Generally speaking, this school was characterized by a deep-going scepticism. In nature, the Epicureans contended, the prevailing principle is that each being is out for advantages to itself. There is no "natural law." Rules are inevitably either conventions or devices by which those who framed the rules promote their own interests. Nor is there such a thing as absolute justice. The function of human societies is simply to create security for the citizens and the laws of the state are "just" as long as they serve that purpose effectively. Usually, the Epicureans tended to prefer a monarchic constitution with a strong and centralized government.

Even if Epicureanism did not exercise a lasting deep-going and concrete influence upon the development of law and legal thinking in the Ancient world, this school has been far from unimportant in a wide time perspective. Echoes from the sceptical and pragmatic attitude of the Epicureans with regard to the state and its function recur in the works of important modern writers, like, e.g., Thomas Hobbes 1588–1679, (cp. ch. 5, sec. 4 below). Another highly influential modern writer who was profoundly influenced by the Epicureans is the Frenchman Michel de Montaigne (d. 1592; cp.ch. 5, sec. 3). Upon the whole, the tenets and the underlying empirical observations, which are often of great acuteness, of Epicureanism have not seldon been adopted by, and provided arguments to, sceptical thinkers throughout the evolution studied in this book. In terms of practical attitudes and solutions, these tenets have frequently justified a conservative view without fanaticism.

11. The Stoics

Besides the teaching of Aristotle, *Stoicism* was undoubtedly the most influential and the most future-determining among the schools of thought that were founded in ancient Greece. The relationship between these two movements of ideas could perhaps be described as follows: Aristotle put a large and impressive arsenal of intellectual *tools* and analytical *instruments* – categories, concepts, terms, proposals for interpretations, classifications and divisions – into the hands of posterity; the Stoics gave Occidental legal thinking (and political theory in a broader sense) an ethical content which has played an exceedingly important role ever since.

The Stoic school – which derives its name from "Stoa poikile", "The many-coloured colonnade," at Athens where the followers of this school originally met for teaching and discussion – was founded by *Zeno* (d. 265 B.C.), a philosopher of Oriental origin, who gathered a group of pupils around him about the year 300 B.C. Among his successors, *Chrysippus* should be mentioned as a representative of the "older Stoa". *Panaitius* (d. 110 B.C.) played a decisive role in the development of Stoicism to that philosophy which more extensively and more deeply than any other school influenced the Roman aristocracy, its political leaders and its lawyers. Panaitius gave Stoicism – which had successively assumed a more and more esoteric character and recommended withdrawal from public affairs and, indeed, the world – that orientation towards practical problems and political action which the military commanders, politicians, administrators and lawyers of the rapidly growing Roman republic needed. *Poseidonius* from Rhodes (d.c. 50 B.C.) deserves to be mentioned above all because he had among his pupils *Marcus Tullius Cicero* (d. 43 B.C.), that most diligent, efficient and influential introducer and propagator of Greek philosophy and Greek culture in general. Under the heading "the younger Stoa", it is customary to gather those who carried on Stoic teaching and writing within the Roman culture: the statesman and writer *Seneca* (d 65 A.D.); *Epictetus* (d. 130 A.D.), who was born a slave in Asia Minor but became a highly influential teacher of wisdom and wrote a famous "handbook in the Art of Life" *(Enchiridion)*; finally the Emperor-philosopher *Marcus Aurelius* (d. 180 A.D.).

Although the Stoics also devoted themselves to problems in the fields of logic and natural science, their most important contributions are to be found in the field of ethics. Their principal question was how man should behave in order to achieve complete happiness. The answer most frequently given was that the solution is in finding full harmony with the "world soul" and the "world law". For it is a creed – basically a religious conviction – common to all branches of Stoicism that the universe is animated by a rational soul (Greek: *logos,* "the Word", or "the Reason"), which is essentially good. To lead the good life, to achieve complete happiness, means, in other words, to attempt throughout one's existence to translate, as it were, reason and goodness into action and behaviour: Thus the Stoics accepted from the beginning the idea of *a natural law on religious foundations.*

It is obvious that the Stoic doctrine, like any natural law theory of this description, carries with it a load of latent inherent contradictions which could at any moment give rise to criticism and controversy. The main theoretical objections – which recur througout the history of Occidental thinking into our days – may be shortly formulated as follows. If there is really a legal system, which is maintained by a good and rational being whose power is in principle unlimited, how can it be that we find everywhere injustice, violence, and social systems which are in blatant contradiction with goodness, justice, and reason? Shall the doctrine of a rational benevolent world order be taken to mean that existing conditions, such as they are, shall be accepted as expressions of that order? And if the state of affairs actually prevailing in the world is *not* accepted as expressing the will of Godhead, how can it then be said that this God (or "soul" or "reason of the world") is omnipotent; and, secondly, how can we obtain certain knowledge about Its will, i.e. of the precepts of natural law? Different attempts have been made, at different times, to solve these problems; we shall come back to them more than once in what follows.

Both the force and internalized religious conviction with which the Stoics expressed their ethical ideas under the name of "natural law" and the contents which they gave that body of norms are of great importance for present purposes. When compared with earlier schools of thought they undoubtedly represented a more broadly humanitarian and – to use the word in a somewhat anachronistic way – democratic stanpoint. According to the law of nature, they contended, all men are born *free and equal.* In the ancient world which was – albeit with very great variations from one state and one period to another – based upon slavery, this was obviously a highly radical and potentially subversive teaching. Aristotle, who may be said to express an essentially humane and enlightened attitude, does not hesitate to accept slavery as "natural". The position taken by the Stoics in this respect was important not least because it made one of the connecting links with Christianity when that religion became a social force to be taken into account.

The easiest and shortest way of describing the contents of Stoicism as a body of ethical precepts is to characterize it as *a doctrine exalting and sanctifying the notion of duty and the fulfilment of duties* in the most difficult conditions. This appealed strongly to the leading classes of Rome; they had received, as a venerable inheritance, a similar doctrine of duties, although exclusively related to the Roman Republic and devoid of any philosophical foundations. Stoicism, to put it cynically, made it possible for Roman noblemen and gentlemen to become Hellenistic "intellectuals" without incurring reproaches for that "softness" or "corruption" which had previously often accompanied any attempt to adopt more civilized habits of thought and attitudes.

Moreover, the Stoics taught *a general humanitarian and philanthropic attitude:* their precepts were not to cause injury to anyone, to redress whatever harm one has involuntarily caused, and to perform good actions whenever possible.

It should be underlined that as a creed for practical purposes, Stoicism could be read as pointing in two directions: towards more or less active work for putting the rules of natural law into practice in the world or towards a more passive and comtemplative attitude, implying the assumption that true wisdom, and harmony with the soul of the universe, consists in whole-hearted acceptance of the way things are. If the latter position was adopted – and this tended to be the case with regard to major social questions, such as slavery and misery in general, as opposed to the normal more narrow field of action of statesmen, generals, or landowners, where a both active and philantropic attitude was recommended – the radical and explosive elements of Stoicism did not obtain that broad political and social influence which could have been expected.

Chapter 2

The Romans

Selected Bibliography: A. Brimo, *Les grands courants de la philosophie du droit et de l'état*, 3ème éd., Paris 1978, pp. 27 ff.; G. Fassò, *Storia della filosofia del diritto*, vol. 1, 3rd ed., Bologna 1974, pp. 125–156; S. Iuul, *Grundrids af den romerske Privatret*, Copenhagen 1940; M. Kaser, *Das römische Privatrecht* (*Handbuch der Altertumswissenschaft* X, 3, 4); vol. 1. Munich 1955; Lord Lloyd of Hampstead, *Introduction to Jurisprudence*, 3rd. ed., London 1972, pp. 78, 92–96; K. Rode, *Geschichte der europäischen Rechtsphilosophie*, Düsseldorf 1974, pp. 41–51; F. Schulz, *Geschichte der römischen Rechtswissenschaft*, Weimar 1961; P. Stein, *Regulae juris*, Edinburgh 1966; I. Strahl, *Makt och rätt*, 7th ed., 1981, pp. 22–29; M. Villey, *La formation de la pensée juridique moderne*, Paris 1968, pp. 62–68, 446–480.

1. Introduction

If the selection of what should be presented and what could be left out in this short textbook had been determined exclusively by the intellectual originality and depth of a given civilization's contributions to the development of Occidental legal philosophy, Roman law would hardly have been able to claim a chapter of its own. Legal historians possess a vast and deep-going knowledge of the growth of Roman law in terms of concrete institutions and rules; they are less well-informed about the philosophical, theoretical and methodological ideas and principles adopted by the Roman lawyers. The term "lawyer" is used here in a narrow sense, excluding such politicians – usually with some legal training – as acted in the capacity of orators in court. The most famous of them all was Cicero, whose many works are a valuable source of information about, i.a., the state of the law in his time, but who was not considered a lawyer in the technical sense of the word.

As arguments *against* a very laconic treatment of Roman law, however, we must invoke not only the fact that this legal system reached a very high level in respect of substantive rules, particularly in the field of private law, and – above all – that Roman law was to exercise a decisive influence upon the development of Occidental law and, indeed, upon all aspects of public life, far beyond the limits of what we call "the law". One further reason for a fairly full treatment of the Romans in the present context is that when Roman law was rediscovered and made the object of intense studies in the high Middle Ages, from about 1100 A.D. onwards, the Roman sources of law and the Roman legal writers were granted a status of unique authority also in matters of legal philosophy. The rather meagre general statements on principles of law and justice, and the small number of dicta on the interpretation of statutes, which are found in Roman sources, above all in the introductory parts of the great codification *Corpus juris civilis* from the 6th century A.D. (v. sec. 3 below), consequently assumed a very great importance as points of departure for the work of medieval and modern European lawyers and, more generally, legal thinkers.

There is a general argreement on the assertion that from the 3rd century B.C., Stoic philosophy exercised a strong *general* influence on the Roman *élite* to which the lawyers belonged without exception. Scholars also agree that the intellectual methods and tools which Hellenistic science had created – within the framework of logic, grammar, and rhetoric – became at about the same time indispensable elements in the education of men belonging to the highest classes in Rome. Agreement ceases when we approach the more precise question of the concrete influence of Stoicism and, more generally, Greek science upon *Roman law* as actually applied – thus a body of solutions in specific cases, which must be distinguished both from philosophic discussions in Cicero's works and from general phrases about the purpose of laws, and similar questions, in the *Corpus juris*. According to some scholars there is sufficient evidence for the contention that Roman lawyers received, also in details, a deep-going influence from the intellectual world of the Stoa and from Hellenistic science. Others submit that this evidence is non-conclusive and stress emphatically the independence of Roman lawyers. It would seem, upon critical examination, that much of what was earlier considered to be expressions of Stoic influence has to be classified as ideological *loci communes* – very general and very vague dicta which were "in the air" and which cannot be interpreted as expressions of a real and serious exchange of thoughts – and the same cautious judgement undoubtedly has to be passed on many statements previously quoted with a view to proving that the principles and methods of Hellenistic logic were consciously and systematically put to use by the Roman lawyers. These – and this is a feature which must be stressed with some emphasis since it distinguishes Roman and Greek traditions in a highly important respect – were *professionals* and *experts* in the law of their country. This does not mean that they made a living as judges, attorneys or law teachers, but it means that they had, mostly from boyhood, gone through an informal but effective legal training, starting as a kind of pages, or gentlemen apprentices, attached to some eminent lawyer, in whose homes they lived and whom they assisted for many years. The training was an apprenticeship also because it was practically oriented; there was no theoretical, or academic, legal training, nor any institutions for that purpose, until the end of Antiquity (in the 5th and 6th centuries, the "law faculty" of Berytos, now Beyrouth, was particularly famous).

Another fact should be remembered when considering the attitude of Roman lawyers to Greek science. With few exceptions the leading lawyers belonged to the highest classes of Roman society. Rhetoric, a smattering of grammar, and some notions of both logic and grammar became routine elements of a Roman gentleman's education, but expert knowledge and "professional" work in these fields were matters not for gentlemen but for schoolmasters, frequently Greeks, slaves or recently emancipated. The tasks of the Roman aristocracy were to be found in law and statecraft. There is a clear anti-intellectual feature both in this general attitude and in the Roman view of law. To be a lawyer did not mean to use flawless logical conclusions, the sophisticated methods of interpretation invented by grammarians or the stratagems of orators; it meant exercising mature judgement, practical wisdom – *prudentia* (cf. "jurisprudence," "learning, or rather wisdom, in the law") – in individual cases, while taking into due account the position taken by earlier jurists in similar cases. The majority of active lawyers in the pre-Christian era were men of independent means who had made a political career and reached high office. They were not, and did not expect to be, paid for their advice to lawyers or litigants, or for their speeches for or against a party. The terms for a lawyer's fee – *honorarium*, which means "honorary gift" (Fr.: *honoraire*, German: *Honorar*) – still reflect this view of the relationship between counsel and client. In some countries, the claim for *honorarium* cannot be legally enforced; the fiction of a voluntary gift is maintained.

2. The Historical and Social Framework

The march of the little peasant republic in Central Italy from insignificance to political and military domination of the Mediterranean basin and most of the known Occident, and finally to breakdown must be considered one of the most remarkable processes in history. By the standards of the jet age, however, that process was a slow one. It may be divided, roughly, into four phases:
  (i) the monarchy and the early Republic (7th or 6th centuries–3rd century B.C.);
  (ii) the later Republic (3rd century B.C.–31 B.C.);
  (iii) the part of the imperial era known as the "Principate" (31 B.C.–284 A.D.);
  (iv) the part of the imperial era known as the "Dominate" (284 A.D.–476 A.D.).

The first period is characterized by the development and consolidation of the republican constitution and by never-ceasing wars with neighbouring tribes in central Italy. It is only towards the end of the period that Rome has fought her way to the leading position among these. It is in the early days of this heroic era – some time around 450 B.C. – that the *Law of the Twelve Tables* comes into existence. It is a codification of the primitive and formalistic rules that governed the life and doings of Roman citizens (just as the legal systems of the Greek city states were applicable only to those who enjoyed full citizenship). It was not a territorial body of rules but rather "bye-laws" for the individuals making up a certain hereditary community. We know far less about the Roman society of those days than about contemporary Greece; the sources are meagre. It may be taken for granted that the general cultural level was far lower than at Athens and Corinth. The earliest Rome was certainly an agricultural community, the mass of the population being composed of small freeholders. The state was led by a landowning aristocracy, which dominated the most important political body, the senate, the members of which were also preferred for high political office. The most influential posts were elective, and the period of mandate was one year. There are rules in early Roman law that reflect those struggles between the old aristocracy, the Patricians, and the mass of the people, the Plebeians, which loom large in the tales of Roman historians about the early period of the Republic.

These struggles – which need not be interpreted exclusively in the sense of class figthing; there may also be ethnical explanations – led to compromises and to a precarious but long-lasting equilibrium between the groups concerned. In the course of the centuries, a nobility *(nobilitas)* composed of both patrician and particularly successful plebeian families and honouring identic ideals of patriotism and public service came into existence.

The second phase covers the years of great and relatively fast territorial expansion. About the year 100 B.C., Rome holds sway over the whole of Italy, the French Mediterranean coast, territories in Spain, the North African coast, to the extent it is inhabited, from Gibraltar to Egypt, large parts of the eastern coast of the Mediterranean, most of the kingdom of Macedonia, including Greece. At the end of the period, in the days of the first Emperor *Augustus* (who reigned 31 B.C.–14 A.D.), the Alpine region south of the Danube, France, the Iberian peninsula, Egypt and the whole Near East lay under the sceptre of Rome.

This enormous development of military and political strength outside Rome took place at the same time as the Republic was shaken by increasingly violent internal strife, both between rival factions and individuals within the leading class, and between aristocratic and conservative groups on the one side, populist and even revolutionary elements on the other. This state of affairs, which degenerated at the end of the period into a permanent state of internal warfare, ruthless, cruel and destructive, came to an end with the dictatorship of *Julius Ceasar* (d. 44 B.C.) and, after the convulsions following upon his death by murder, the rule of Octavianus, called Augustus.

The turmoil of the last republican century was a symptom of more than conflicts between political parties. The conquest of the world had profoundly changed the social and economic structure of the once rural republic. That central Italian peasantry which had made up the hard core of the republic and, more conspicuously, of her victorious legions, had almost literally ceased to exist. Rome had become a very large city, with a mobile proletariat, living in the utmost squalor but ever ready to claim benefits in the form of bread and shows as payment for support in the daily streetfighting or for keeping quiet. The people of Rome gradually took free distribution of wheat, bloody circus games, and gifts in cash, as the natural tribute of rulers and ruled to the capital of the world. The Italian countryside had increasingly changed into a province of large estates *(latifundia)* where the agricultural work was performed by armies of slaves, war-booty from the frontiers but also, to a large extent, from the civil wars. A class of immensely rich merchants and financiers, who, like the mobs of Rome, profited from the City's political and military position to extort economic advantages from the conquered provinces had come into existence. Finally: the army, once consisting of citizens, sturdy peasants and townsmen, had become a professional army, prepared to follow their commander against his rivals and even against the lawful leaders of the Republic. In due time, the mercenaries – increasingly recruited from all parts of the Empire – were to learn that they could demand good payment for these services also from their commander.

The third period coincides, in its early phases, with Rome's greatest international expansion, in terms of both power and territory: Britain, large parts of Germany and of the mountains and plains north of the Balkans and the Black Sea, vast territories in Syria and Mesopotamia are added to the Empire. The conquered provinces, which had been ruthlessly looted and exploited by soldiers and governors in the first colonial era, were protected by the Emperors and got a more competent and less rapacious Roman administration. Traditional republican forms of government are still respected to the extent it is possible. The Emperors are not monarchs, they are *principes*, "the first" among citizens (the term "principate" is derived from this state of affairs). A high bureaucracy, still inspired with ideals of public service (and Stoic ideas) but less politically ambitious than the rulers of the late Republic, comes into existence, This period is the "classical" era in the development of Roman law. However, there are also dark elements in the bright picture of the Empire, and towards the end of the period, they grow more obvious and more destructive. To what extent the immense Empire is dependent upon the personal qualities of the ruling Emperors is demonstrated, in a frightening way, by the short and disastrous reigns of insane or incompetent rulers like Caligula, Nero and Domitian. In a state where all real power is concentrated in one person and his *entourage*, where active participation in public affairs – and consequently public spirit – decreases, the resulting lack of equilibrium, independence, and initiative in the large body politic becomes more and more obvious. As long as Rome's military strength is unimpaired, the bureaucracy and the army can mitigate the negative consequences of a bad reign for at least some time. Gradually, it becomes clear that the principal lever of power is the army; once this is understood, that body is no longer the mere lever: it is the centre of power. The period ends with half a century of chaos, the era of the "Soldier Emperors", rapidly nominated by their legions, as quickly lynched when payment is withheld or discipline enforced. Lack of economic equilibrium, rapid inflation combined with coin deterioration, low and sinking productivity – these, and possibly other, controversial or unknown, factors of social change inexorably erode the power of resistance of the Empire. Beyond the long frontiers, vital, curious, and rapacious new-comers are gathering: Germanic tribes, Persians, horsemen from the plains of Central Asia.

In the fourth period, the Empire gathers all her forces for a last show of strength. *Diocletian* (reigned 284–316 A.D.) reorganizes the State on new lines. As a display of what human energy, organization, and will to survive can achieve, it is a magnificent performance; yet it was doomed to fail in the long run. The first price that must be paid for efficiency and even more centralization is the sacrifice of republican forms of government: the Emperor is no longer the first citizen, but *dominus et deus* ("Lord and God"; the term "dominate" is derived from *dominus*). The State literally takes all the resources of the citizens in its service. The civil administration of the Empire becomes a huge tax-collecting agency; the money which does not remain in this apparatus is spent on the court and the army. The long-range development – marked by economic and cultural decay – is accelerated by wars, invasions, and internal strife. About 400 A.D., the Empire is divided into an Eastern and a Western part. Within less than a century, the latter collapses. In 476, the last Emperor of the West, Romulus Augustulus, is deposed, but already in 410, the catastrophe has made itself manifestly felt in the West: that year, Alaric and his Visigoths conquer and plunder the City of Rome. Contemporary writers echo the deep and lasting shock which this event means to the inhabitants of the Mediterranean world. The Eastern Empire survives for another 1100 years, with Constantinople as capital, an essentially Greek and Oriental state.

In the last two hundred years before the fall of the Occidental Empire, the civilazation and forms of social and cultural life which had been characteristic of the ancient Greco-Roman world and which had been adopted or imitated as the superior, "civilized" lifestyle throughout the Empire, had successively broken down, first in the peripheric areas, later even in the central provinces, and been replaced by a structure which is in many respects a forerunner of medieval, feudal, Europe. Urban life, which had been the ideal of the Greeks and which Hellenistic rulers and Roman colonial administrators had introduced throughout the Mediterranean basin and the Empire, gave way to forms of habitation where fortified manors, defended by more or less independent landowners with their retainers and neighbours, and fortified villages replace the open cities. Besides the decadent, impoverished, and doomed Roman state, the victorious Church more and more assumes – particularly after Christianity has become the state religion of the Empire (323 A.D.) and pagan sacrifices are prohibited in 394 – the function of carrying on and developing the intellectual and cultural heritage of Rome.

3. Sources for the Study of Roman Law and Legal Thinking

The first question to be considered, before we go somewhat more closely into the legal thinking of the Romans, is where we can find the expressions of that thinking. In answering that question, we have to make a clear distinction between the sources – statutes, decrees, decisions and works of legal scholarship – which we know were produced in the course of the almost 1000 years of legal development considered, and those sources which are available today. The distinction is more important with regard to Roman law, and Roman legal thinking, than in respect of any other field of ancient law, for as is well known (and will be developed more fully in a following chapter), Roman law – as it was then found – was considered, from the Middle Ages onwards, in some countries well into the 19th century, as a living, still valid legal system; like all legal systems in actual operation, it underwent successive changes to meet the needs of the times. It was in fact not until Roman law, as handed over by generations of lawyers and jurists, had been replaced by modern codifications that the texts of the Romans were released, as it were, from the burden of serving as a working legal system and came to be considered essentially as a *historical* phenomenon, a thing of the past. In the leading European countries that process took place between the middle of the 18th century and the end of the 19th; in fact, the year 1900 may be considered as the final point of this development, since on January 1, 1900, the new Civil Code of Germany entered into force, replacing either earlier local codifications or, in a large part of the then Empire, customary Roman Law.

(i) Although the history of Rome, both the mythical one told by ancient writers and that which emerges from the work of archaeologists and historians, begins at a much earlier date, the earliest document of Roman law known with some certainty is the *Law of the Twelve Tables*, which goes back to the early days of the Republic (c. 450 B.C.) and which was considered by the Romans themselves as the "fountainhead of all public and private law," as Livy puts is. There is not much point in arguing about the question whether the Law of the Twelve Tables should be described as a "codification," whether it simply restates customary law or whether it expresses an endeavour to realize a law reform. It is natural, considering the respect attached to this piece of legislation, and the energy with which the Romans always explored, explained and embellished their own history, that myths and legends were invented about the origin and elaboration of the Law. Among other things, it was claimed that the Commission entrusted with the drafting undertook enquiries into contemporary Greek reform legislation and even went to Athens to study Solon's laws on the spot. However that may be, the Law of the Twelve Tables is a highly casuistic (case-oriented, in contradistinction to generalizing, principle-oriented) piece of legislation without any attempt at a more elaborate or sophisticated systematization. Although quite detailed in some respects, it is far from complete; this would seem to imply a further argument in favour of the idea that it really restates customary solutions to particularly frequent, particularly important, or particularly controversial questions of law. The society reflected in the Law of the Twelve Tables would seem to have been – although this is a debated point – a fairly primitive, essentially agrarian and static community. Strict formalism, indeed ritualism – evidence of the religious origin and character of many legal rules and institutions – is characteristic of the law.

(ii) In the course of Roman history from the middle of the 5th century B.C. onwards, *legislation by the assembled people* becomes a generally acknowledged source of law, although there is still some controversy about the extent to which (or the time from which) it was at all held legally possible to modify the ancient law. The texts adopted by the people's assemblies were usually referred to as *leges* (laws), and it would seem that at least from the second century B.C. legislation became, as an eminent scholar puts it, a conscious instrument of legal innovation. This form of legislation survived until about the first century of the Empire (c. 100 A.D.).

(iii) A third source of law were the decisions of the Senate *(senatus-consulta)*, although it remained a disputed point in theory, if not in practice, whether this body had a formal right to do more than issue instructions for the elected officers who were the executives of the State. For all practical purposes, the decisions of the Senate were treated as valid law; in imperial times, from about 120 A.D., this became an officially acknowledged, in fact the usually adopted form for legislation; it survived until the end of the Third Century. From Augustus onwards, senatorial legislation really expressed the reigning Monarch's, not the deliberating body's views and intentions.

(iv) An original form of legal innovation which began to be practiced early in the time of the Republic is found in the so-called *edicts* of the highest officers of State, particularly the *praetors*, who were responsible for the administration of justice. It was an established principle of Roman law that these officers ("magistrates") had authority to issue what would be called today orders, or administrative regulations, within their field of competence. The praetor's edict was an order, issued at the beginning of each successive praetor's year of office, in which that official made known what actions he was going to admit and, if proved, sustain in his term of office. Originally, there was one praetor (elected, like all officers, for one year), but from the middle of the 3rd century B.C., another praetor was added with the special mission of administering justice in cases where one or both parties were aliens. Neither praetor had a legislative authority, but by making an extensive use of their right to regulate the forms of proceedings accepted in court, they did in fact create, besides the stiff and increasingly unsatisfactory rules of traditional law (*jus civile*, i.e. "the citizens' law"), a supplementary body of solutions which was given the name *jus honorarium* (or *praetorium*) and which, from the point of view of its function, comes quite close to *equity*, as a separate body of law supplementing the common law of England from the Middle Ages onwards. The *praetor peregrinus* ("strangers' praetor"), who was reponsible for litigation with elements of foreign law involved, obviously enjoyed much greater liberty in this respect than his colleague in charge of cases of purely Roman venue. The strangers' praetors developed, in fact, a set of rules largely based upon common sense, expediency, and fairness, which came to be known as the *jus gentium*, or "peoples' law", in contradistinction to the *jus civile* applicable to Roman subjects. The *jus gentium* thus became one of the mainroads along which enlightened contemporary thinking and evaluations – including, at least from the 2nd century B.C., some of the basic maxims of Greek, in particular Stoic, ideas – could enter into the system of Roman law.

The praetors were not, as is sometimes thought, judges in the proper sense of the word. Their function was, on the one hand, to keep control over the administration of justice, to issue and ensure the observance of the yearly edict, and to instruct judges, after a preliminary hearing, as to the handling of individual cases. The actual suit then took place before a court which was not (as far as private law is concerned) a people's court, but a one-man judge, or a small body of persons who were either legal experts or had access to the advice of such.

The most creative period of praetorial "legislation" was the late Republic. Most praetors, of course, took over the edicts of their predecessors, sometimes adding or subtracting some element of them. Under the Empire, praetorial initiatives became increasingly rare, and about 130 A.D. the content of the edict was fixed once and for all (the "perpetual edict," *edictum perpetuum*).

(v) From the point of view of quantity, the most important body of legal reasoning and legal solutions in ancient Rome were *the writings of lawyers*. In early Republican days, it was the task of the pontiffs, organized in "colleges," or corporate bodies *(collegia)*, to answer doubtful questions of law – very much as the most ancient Greek laws were in the hands of the aristocracy. In the second century B.C., however, non-pontifical, secular jurists appear on the scene – later historians name three of these early lawyers and state that they "founded the civil law." The activity of these jurists, whom we have characterized shortly in our introductory section above, essentially consisted in the giving of opinions on difficult points of law to magistrates, judges, and litigating parties. Opinions were collected into books and an enormous mass of legal writing came into existence.

When trying to understand and describe Roman legal thinking, the jurists – who flourished until the end of the Empire, although the last two or three centuries (from about 250 A.D.) witnessed, in this field as in others, a decline in creativeness – form the group which deserves the greatest attention. It is their response both to new intellectual developments, in particular the influx of Greek philosophy, which occurred about the same time as the secular jurists appear, and to changed social, economic and political conditions that ultimately gives Roman law its most characteristic features: its pragmatism and flexibility as well as its clearness and intellectual superiority to any previously known body of rules. It should be added that the contributions of the jurists are not evenly distributed over the whole field of law: private law and civil procedure dominate very clearly, whereas many areas of public law (including the rather neglected field of penal law) never became the object of the same intensive analysis and constructive development.

From the days of Augustus (beginning of the first century A.D.) it became customary that the Emperor granted to specially qualified jurists the "right to give opinions" *(jus respondendi)* and to deliver them by the Emperor's authority and under seal; this custom gradually disappeared in the years of decline of the third century. The second and the early part of the third century of the Christian era were the classical period of Roman jurists. In this period we find its greatest names: *Papinian* (d. 212 A.D.), *Ulpian* (d. 228); *Paulus, Modestinus*. By the latter half of the second century, a well-known writer affirmed that the opinions of the jurists were considered as authoritative sources of law. In fact, it was widely held that if the most distinguished writers were unanimous, their words had the same force as a statute. In case of disagreement, judges were free to choose.

It is obvious that in the course of time this situation could and would – particularly in a period when texts circulated only in manuscript copies – create a good deal of uncertainty and confusion as to the state of the law. The Emperors tried to meet the problems by ordering that some writings should not be used, whilst others should be preferred. Finally, in 426 A.D., the so-called Law of Citations was enacted. It gave special authority to five writers of the past (Papinian, Paul, Gaius, Ulpian, and Modestinus) and, subject to certain qualifications, to those earlier jurists who were cited by these. In case of conflict, the majority should prevail; in a situation with equal numbers on each side. Papinian was given decisive authority. The Law of Citations, an obvious emergency solution, was to remain in force for about a century. The last phase of the development took place in 534 A.D., with the enactment of what was to be the final statement of Roman law, Emperor Justinian's *Corpus Juris Civilis*.

(vi) Although the Roman Emperors were, with few exceptions, in a position to dictate the laws issued by the Senate, *Imperial legislation,* i.e. texts emanating immediately from the Emperor's chancery, became an increasingly important source of law already in the Principate. This legislation, for which the common name of *Imperial Constitutions* was early used, assumed many different forms: precedent--making decisions in individual cases *(decreta),* answers to questions of law submitted by officials or private parties *(rescripta),* administrative orders *(edicts)* or instructions *(mandata).* Although these texts did not, in actual form, assume the character of legislation in the proper sense, their validity as "law" was not questioned. In the later days of the Empire, the absolute Monarch also issued regular statutes.

(vii) Already in the fifth century A.D., attempts were being made to bring some order into the mass of "laws" claiming validity in the Empire. In fact, the Emperor Theodosius II issued an official code in 438. It was, however, Justinian, ruler of the Eastern Empire from 527 to 565 A.D., who finally succeeded with the formidable task of codifying Roman Law as a whole.

This is not the place to attempt even a summary description of the *Corpus juris civilis.* Possibly with the exception of the holy writs of the great religions, no other single book has been more extensively studied, analyzed, used, respected, criticized and commented upon. We shall have to confine ourselves to three items: its coming into existence, its composition, and the early history of its implementation.

The *Corpus juris* was the work of one of the most successful "Royal Commissions" in history; its chairman was Tribonianus. Modern scholarship confirms that the work was in fact performed in a few years. As originally issued in the years 533–534 A.D., the *Corpus* comprised three parts: a relatively short introductory treatise on Roman Law, intended for the use of students, *Institutiones;* the vast body of laws, essentially taken from the jurists' writings, known as the *Digest* or *Pandects;* the *Code,* which is made up of Imperial constitutions. To these three books were successively added the new statutes issued by Justinian and his successors (The Novels, *Novellae*). When putting together the Code and, to a greater extent, the Digest – which is thus really not a body of "ready-made" statutory provisions but a collection or quotations from the jurists (referred to by name under "sections" brought together according to subject-matter in the framework of a rough systematics) – Justinian's drafters made considerable changes in the original texts in order to "make them fit" in various respects, e.g. to eliminate contradictions, suppress matters considered to be antiquated or unsuitable, etc. These changes are known as *interpolations*, and much work has been spent both on tracing them and on restoring the original texts which went into the great codification.

Although Justinian's *Corpus* may be considered, in some respects, as the product of a period of decay as compared with the writings of the great jurists of the classical period, it nevertheless represents a work not to be mastered, let alone administered as a source of law, without great learning and great intellectual exertions. In the period of political decadence and, in the case of the Western half of the Empire, complete downfall, of social and economic stagnation and intellectual decadence in which the *Corpus juris civilis* was created, the implementation of the great codification in its original form was virtually impossible. In the Eastern part of the Empire, *Corpus juris* continued to be valid law, although mostly as found in drastically abridged and simplified Greek translations. In the West, where Germanic kingdoms had overrun the Empire, the Corpus served as a source of inspiration to several codes, in which the Germanic law of the conquerors was mixed with Roman law *(leges barbarorum)*, and was also used in abridged versions, as the law of the formerly Roman population of the new kingdoms. The original text, however, was in the course of time forgotten. It was to take about five centuries before – towards the end of the 11th century – a reasonably faithful version of the original was again established and made the object, first of academic study and then, in the course of time, of far-reaching *reception*, i.e. a reintegration as valid law both on earlier Roman territory and in large parts of Europe – in particular Germany – which had never been part of the ancient Empire.

(viii) The last source to be mentioned in this survey are *the writings of philosophers*. If this body of texts is mentioned after the others, it is because it is neither as rich nor as original as the works of the Greek thinkers. Just as we characterized Greek law as a law without a legal technique, it is tempting to describe Roman law as a technique without a philosophy. This is likely to be an oversimplified slogan, however. To what extent it is true remains to be discussed; the drastic formulation would nevertheless seem to have at least the pedagogic virtue of drawing attention to an important difference in what may be called the "intellectual climate" between Greece and Rome and to a difference in the emphasis to be put on different elements in the development of the two great civilizations concerned.

Even if Roman legal philosophy seems to us meagre in comparison with the Greek wealth of ideas, there are three reasons why some Roman writers in this field, or at least one – Marcus Tullius Cicero (d. 43 B.C.) – have to be considered in the present context. In the first place, Roman thinking enriched the then leading Greek school of thought, Stoicism, with a new and important element: a more pronounced orientation towards societal and practical problems. Furthermore, it was essentially *via* the Roman texts – and again, Cicero should be mentioned – that later Western legal thinking, before the revival of classical learning in the 15th and 16th centuries, could be influenced by the Greeks. From the downfall of the western Empire in the 5th century until the Renascence, Greek was, with few exceptions, an unknown language even among the most learned. Thus, Roman legal thinking came to determine the European idea of the Greek contribution, both by the way in which the Romans made their choice of Greek authors to be remembered and discussed, and by the way in which they presented them. Finally, throughout the Middle Ages, Roman law and legal thinking enjoyed a prestige and an authority which gave rather confused, or rather simple, statements by Roman writers an immense weight and influence in Medieval Europe; every word was studied and interpreted as a sacred text.

Of the original sources presented above, only a few have been brought down to later times. In many cases, we have to put up with fragments, and with more or less qualified guesswork about the contents of the texts concerned. Thus, the Law of the Twelve Tables has been reconstructed in part, by using fragments comprised in texts that have survived. Although there is much uncertainty about details, enough would seem to be ascertainable to convey a reasonably well-founded idea of the scope, purpose, and spirit of the codification. As for the other sources, it may be said, in a general way, that subject to three major exceptions, they are almost exclusively brought forward to posterity by the *Corpus juris civilis* which is, as already mentioned, essentially a body of quotations, of varying length, from the works of the jurists, including their more or less complete and faithful quotations from each other and from earlier statutes, provisions of edicts, etc. The three exceptions are, in the first place, those late Imperial enactments that are comprised in the *Codex* and the *Novellae*. Further, one single major work of a classical jurist, Gaius, was found relatively intact in an Italian monastery in 1816. It is called the *Institutes* (c. 160 A.D.).

However, it is not a typical representative of Roman legal writing since it seems to be intended to serve as a textbook, whereas the vast mass of books produced by Roman lawyers from the second century B.C. onwards was composed of opinions, i.e. expositions of individual cases, or groups of cases, with suggested solutions to the problems involved. In addition to Gaius' Institutes, two abridged fragmentary collections, commonly referred to as the *Rules of Ulpian* and the *Opinions of Paul*, have been handed down to our days. Finally, the texts of Cicero and other legal philosophers have been, with some exceptions, preserved throughout the Middle Ages.

4. The Contributions of the Philosophers

Compared with the Greeks, the Romans have added but little to the progress of analytical thinking in the field of legal philosophy. As already pointed out, however, not only the immense *authority* which the leading Roman writers came to enjoy, both by virtue of the political position of Rome from the second century B.C. until the breakdown of the Western Empire in the late fifth century A.D. and through the revival of Roman law, considered as the unique or at least the highest body of legal precepts valid for the whole of Western Christendom from the eleventh century A.D. onwards, but also the fact that it was for a very long time only *through Roman sources* that Greek thinking survived and was brought forward to posterity, give to the contributions of Roman philosophers and lawyers a weight which they would certainly not have carried otherwise.

The most important Roman writer, in this context, is *Marcus Tullius Cicero* (106–43 B.C.), a prolific author in many fields, one of the leading statesmen and public speakers of the last phase of Republican Rome, an eminently efficient introductor of Greek philosophy into Roman literature. Cicero was not a jurist in the narrow and technical sense of the word, but he had a legal education, and took a deep and active interest in questions of law. A member of the provincial Italian upper middle classes, he did not belong to the *nobilitas*, the politically leading Roman nobility, but yet managed – at the price of continuous intense efforts – to enter that milieu as a *homo novus*, "a new man", reached the highest dignity of Republican Rome, the consulship, and came to be considered as one of the leaders of the conservative party in the fierce struggles which marked the last century of the Republic. Ultimately, he paid for this success with his life: shortly after the murder of Julius Ceasar, the head of the "popular" faction in this struggle, Cicero was himself put to death at the order of Caesar's follower Mark Anthony.

Cicero has written a vast number of works in many fields of philosophy. Some of these are lost; it is particularly regrettable that his book on how Roman law should be transformed and presented as a "science" (or, as we would rather say today, as an "art") according to Greek patterns is no longer extant. Enough has been preserved, however, to give us a fairly precise idea of Cicero's legal philosophy and also of his views of legal reasoning. Many of Cicero's writings were composed, after the model of Plato, in the form of dialogues. The literary qualities of his work, although sometimes criticized as empty brilliance, have made him one of the Latin writers most intensely studied, and most widely imitated, in all Western countries and in most periods of later Western civilization.

Among Cicero's writings, the books *On the Laws (De legibus)*, *On Duties (De officiis)*, and *On the State (De republica)* are those most rewarding with regard to legal philosophy in the narrow sense, *On the Orator (De oratore)* is most fertile in respect of legal reasoning.

Cicero endorses, essentially, the Stoic idea that the world is governed by, and also reflects, a Divine Reason, a World Soul, which is at the same time the Supreme Good and the Highest God. Man's endeavour to reach the ultimate goal of existence, which is complete happiness, can be successful only by living in harmony with that Reason, whose dictates are the "eternal Law" *(lex aeterna)*. This attitude was expressed also by other Roman thinkers; mention has already been made of the statesman, playwright and philosopher *Seneca* (d. 65 A.D., put to death at the order of Nero, whose teacher he had been), of *Epictetus,* a former slave (d. 130 A.D.) and of the Emperor *Marcus Aurelius* (d. 180 A.D.). One obvious possible result of the attempt to obtain full harmony with the "World Soul" was complete passivity in political and social matters: true happiness and wisdom consist in accepting life as it is, since nothing can exist which is not – however hateful, unjust, or unsatisfactory it may seem at a first glance – "reasonable" because expressing the Divine Reason. Tacit acceptance of the facts of nature and of the society therefore expresses the greatest virtue. Cicero, however, was influenced not only by the Stoics but also by Plato, and

– it seems permissible to add – both his dynamic and energetic character and the unphilosophical but strong moral and intellectual Roman tradition with which he was imbued worked against this total acceptance of things as they are. Whereas in the pure Stoic doctrine, no limit can be drawn between that which *is* and that which *ought to be,* since it follows logically from the given premises that what exists is and must be upheld by Divine Reason, Cicero learnt from Plato that the Eternal Law is an *ideal,* is the pure and indestructible oroginal expression of something which, that is true, can be found by the exercise of right reason (for Cicero is a rationalist) but the appearances of which in the world of men and nature can be diluted, contorted and thus imperfect. Although Cicero, who was not a great logician, hardly seems to have been clearly aware of the contradiction between this idea and the tenets of Stoicism, he nevertheless introduced, by this Platonic element, a difference, or at least a possible difference, between that which is and that which ought to be: he avoided the risk of complete passivity following from pure Stoicism.

In trying to define the contents of the eternal unchangeable and universally valid law he is exalting, Cicero does not take us very far. The Eternal Law, that is a clear point, coincides with the law of nature. One element of its contents is equally clear – no one should do harm to others. Cicero gives this evident and time-honoured maxim a slightly different, more "social" turn: no one should disturb the social order. He adds, however, a second element which would seem to reflect, precisely, the Roman outlook: the Eternal and natural law requires all men to take *active part* in the life of the community to which they belong and in the interest of the public weal. By this principle of activity, Cicero breaks with the Stoic maxim of not questioning the society as it is.

Beyond the principle of active participation in public affairs and the rule of not doing harm by disturbing the social order, Cicero does not say very much of a concrete nature about the contents of natural law, except that he firmly believes that the traditional Roman constitution, as understood by the conservatives of his days, was (or at least could be, when put into operation by virtuous and enlightened statesmen) a perfect expression of the natural law. However questionable this standpoint may seem at a closer scrutiny, it nevertheless, by virtue of Cicero's immense posthumous authority, came to be widely adopted.

In one more respect, Cicero's contribution to legal thinking deserves a few words by way of commentary. Unlike Plato and Aristotle, the experienced Roman politician pushes the concept of "society" beyond that of the city state *(polis)*. In fact, Cicero operates with a whole hierarchy of communities. Starting with the smallest group, the family, he goes on to describe the next step, the State, then the larger community held together by a common language, next the human world community, and finally the highest level: the community mixing gods and men, who are all held together by common allegiance to the World Soul and the eternal law.

Cicero's ideas on reasoning and speaking can be left aside here – however influential later on, they never seem to have had a deepgoing effect upon the way in which Roman lawyers carried out their traditional tasks. In fact, it was not until much later, after the breakdown of the Medieval world, that Cicero's instructions for public speaking assumed a direct importance for legal argument.

5. A Legal Profession without a Philosophy

When characterizing Greek legal thinking, we called it a law without legal technicians. Applying similar criteria to Roman law and lawyers, it might seem justified, as already intimated, to speak about a legal profession without a philosophy of law. In fact, the most characteristic feature of Roman law in its heyday is its predominantly technical, "strictly legal" character. Those who like Cicero wrote about general problems relating to the Law, were not considered as jurists in the proper, narrow sense of the word. The true jurists were men who devoted themselves exclusively or essentially to the interpretation and implementation of the abundant source material in individual cases; they also sometimes acted as advisers or draftsmen in the creation of new rules, but as far as we know, they did not consider it part of their tasks to analyse the law from philosophical or other more general points of view. They did not observe and comment on the law from the outside, as a logician, a moralist, or a sociologist would do; they made the law work.

Another important dividing line, which we have also already hinted at, is that between law and politics. The political and constitutional history of Rome, while characterized by a marked continuity in many important respects – names, forms, and rites were often retained throughout centuries long after they had lost their original significance

– nevertheless implied dramatic and violent changes, with sometimes affected the very core of the society. There were long periods of internal strife and external crises which deeply affected the community. It is remarkable how little this dramatic history influenced the slow development of the legal system, in particular that of private law.

One of the most important lasting contributions of the Romans to the development of future Western patterns of society – a contribution that can be regretted and criticized but not denied – was the drawing up, and continued maintenance, of a dividing line between political and legal decision-making. Few societal features would seem to have contributed more to the fundamental stability – again a fact that can be criticized or praised, depending upon the observer's outlook and value judgments – of Western societies than the division of tasks between these two types of decision-making, indeed these two structures. One single example from the more recent past may be taken to illustrate the point. France underwent, in the 19th century, a political history marked by recurring political upheavals: Napoleon's Empire was founded in 1804, broke down in 1814, knew a short lease of life in 1815 to break down again the same year after the battle of Waterloo; the Bourbon Restoration came to an end by revolution in 1830; its successor, the July Monarchy, was overthrown in 1848. Three years of Republican rule were succeeded in 1851 by the Second Empire, which collapsed in 1870. Throughout this turbulent period, the Civil Code of 1804 – "the only true constitution of the country", to quote an eminent lawyer – remained essentially unchanged, as were basically the courts administering it; both expressed, and guaranteed, the fundamental stability of the deeper social structure of the community.

Had "the law" not acquired, as a result of the social engineering of the Romans brought forward through the centuries by a tradition founded upon, and strengthened by, their authority, its position as a special field of activity, distinct in principle from that of politics, the development would in all likelihood have taken a different turn.

What has now been said should not be exaggerated. The dividing line between law and politics was never absolute; it is continuously being questioned, modified, even eliminated in part. Other factors – economic, social, and moral – affect the relative stability, or aptness to change, of a given society. These factors also influence law and lawyers, and act upon their position, tasks, and habits of thought. Similarly, not even the most unphilosophic legal technicians can remain entirely outside the great intellectual and ideological movements of their time. The Roman lawyers, who with few exceptions belonged to the *élite* of the worldwide Empire, all came into contact, from their schooldays onwards, with the ideas prevailing in the Mediterranean world. And these ideas were, at least from the second century B.C., of Greek origin.

In the next section we shall deal with the influence of Greek thinking upon the more technical aspects of the lawyers' work: their habits of reasoning. Here, we shall discuss very briefly the impact of Greek philosophy, as directly imported from the sources or as conveyed by writers like Cicero, upon the *substance* of Roman law.

It has already been indicated above (sec. 3, under iv)) that the *jus gentium* developed by the *praetor peregrinus* was one of the ways along which modern ideas could enter into Roman courtrooms. However, the *jus civile* also developed, the praetor's edict as well as the jurists' opinions and Imperial constitutions being the chief instruments of change. When, in 212 A.D., by the famous *Constitutio Antoniniana* Roman citizenship, including allegiance to *jus civile* as the national law of Romans, was bestowed upon, in principle, all free inhabitants of the Empire, *jus civile* and *jus gentium* – the latter no longer being necessary – were merged; at that time, the difference between the two systems had decreased considerably.

The principal sources of information from which we can draw any conclusions about the "philosophy" of Roman lawyers in the above-mentioned narrow sense are statements in the *Corpus juris civilis*. In Book I, Title I of the Institutes, which has the heading "Concerning Justice and Law," and in Title II, which deals with natural law, the law of nations, and the civil law, these statements are explicitly attributed to their original authors. Some other evidence, of less importance, can be gathered from the *Corpus Juris*.

When Roman law was made the object of academic study in the Middle Ages, the statements thus put at the beginning of the Institutes and the Digest were quoted, admired, and interpreted with the greatest acumen. Looked at more closely, however, they hardly ever go further – in spite of sometimes great and suggestive formal brilliance, which has made them beloved quotations for almost a millennium – than commonplace expositions of current ideas about the exalted function of law and justice, about the fields of application of natural law, the law of nations *(jus gentium)*, and Roman civil law. The *Corpus Juris* was,

The Romans

after all, drafted in a Christian Empire, and thus the place of the Stoic "World Soul" is taken by Divine Providence. In short, the evidence in the field of legal philosophy that we are in a position to collect from the Roman jurists does not exceed, either in originality or in depth, the introductory flourishes that can be expected in textbooks which deal summarily with such airy matters, to hurry on to more substantial questions. We can conclude, not surprisingly, that the Roman lawyers were familiar with standard ideas of natural law and a natural justice, and that they held, essentially, such humane and enlightened views as were common stock in the ruling classes of the late Empire.

6. *Legal Reasoning*

It is noteworthy that whereas substantive Roman law belongs, since more than eight hundred years, to the most widely and intensely studied among all fields of human knowledge – indeed, there is certainly no single line in the *Corpus juris civilis* that has not given rise to at least one dissertation – the methods, and habits of thought, of ancient Roman lawyers have never been made the object of systematic study. In the 19th century, otherwise eminently fertile in Roman law scholarship, only one major contribution to this field of study may be registered: the great German jurist Rudolf von Jhering's *Vom Geist des römischen Rechts*, vol. III. An explanation of the silence of scholars, which has often been resorted to has been to, refer to the classicial Roman lawyers' repugnance to methodological theories and systems, indeed to any principles of a general scope, and to their preference for intuitive solutions. The classics, an eminent German expert says, developed no theory for the finding of law; they confined themselves to the development of an adequate technique. Lawyers arrive at the contents of the law by means of deduction from extant sources and other such material, but also by intuitive insight into the problems of cases, although that intuition was prepared by a close study particularly of previously decided cases. In case of need, the same authority adds, the classics made use of *interpretatio*, a construction of statutory texts that is based on common usage but which, from early days, makes an *extensive* construction, later also a *restrictive* construction as well as analogy possible.

One point seems clear: the Roman lawyers formulated, at an early date, maxims which show that they were fully aware both of the problems arising because the tenor and the intended meaning of a text do not cover each other (the *verba-sententia* problem) and of the importance of the linguistic context as a tool by means of which texts are understood more completely and more easily than if read isolated.

On the other hand, it seems equally clear that Roman lawyers themselves never developed regular *systems* for interpretation and other forms of legal reasoning, but confined themselves to the establishment of catalogues (as illustrated in Tit.I, 3 of the Digest).

It has been put forward that the "style of reasoning" of the Roman lawyers in the long period of development accessible to modern scholarship underwent different stages characterized, in particular, by different degrees of freedom in relation to the strict wording of statutory texts. From an archaic period of strict adherence to the letter of the law, particularly in the then wide field of sacral law, the lawyers, it is said, developed in the sense of greater freedom; towards the end of Antiquity, in the bureaucratic atmosphere characteristic of the centralized and theocratic late Empire, lawyers would have reverted to a narrow formalism. Further, it is claimed that different attitudes were adopted with regard to different sources of law. The greatest freedom reigned in the field of customary law and in those areas where legal solutions were essentially founded on the writings of private jurists, whereas the interpretation of formal enactments was more cautious.

Whereas the statements made so far would seem to be beyond controversy, a question which, although yet hardly sufficiently clarified by basic research, is highly disputed is whether and if so to what extent Roman lawyers were – in spite of the absence of evidence for the development of a system and a theory – influenced by the Hellenistic concept of science and, in particular, by the specific technique of reasoning characteristic of Greek rhetoric, including the so-called theory or doctrine of status. The question was raised, and answered with rather a provocative "yes," by a German writer, Stroux, in the 1920's. The greatest merit of Stroux' contribution may well be that it drew the attention of scholars to problems previously neglected and gave rise to a number of important studies.

The "theory of status", the elaboration of which is usually attributed to Hermagoras from Temnos (2 cent. B.C.) and which was taken up, i.e., by Cicero, can be described as an attempt to put into system the intellectual operations carried out by speakers when finding arguments for a given standpoint. One element in the theory of status was the analysis of different *status legales*, i.e. questions arising in connection with the interpretation of statutes. These were usually brought together under four headings: those relating to conflicts between *scriptum* (or *verbum*) and *sententia*, the letter and the intention of the law; further those relating to ambiguity in legal texts, contradiction between different provisions and, finally, problems concerning the use of analogy.

This is not the place to discuss at length the arguments for and against the contention that the technique of reasoning of Roman lawyers was influenced in a decisive and deep-going way by Greek rhetoric. As has been stressed by some scholars, sweeping answers to the question of that influence are of limited interest for an appreciation of the actual working methods of practising lawyers, since the theories of rhetoric dealt only to a very limited extent with the kind of questions lawyers normally dealt with. There are, upon the whole, reasons to warn against the conclusion that the term *interpretatio,* when used by Latin writers, stands for what we would call today "construction" or "interpretation", of statutes. Moreover, one has to remember that within the Roman legal world there operated at least two distinct groups of actors: the great orators, of whom Cicero was one, and the real lawyers to whom a man like Cicero did not belong. Evidence about the influence of Hellenistic science among orators is not conclusive with regard to the professional jurists. Nor would it seem justifiable to conclude that because the Greek influence on the level of general schooling and culture was avowedly strong within the class to which the jurists belong, this meant that the influence was deep, and went into details, in what may be called the technical aspects of the exercise of the legal profession.

On the strength of the most recent specialised research, it seems justified to conclude that so far, the discussion on this point has *not* basically modified the general characterization given in our introduction (sec. 1 above) and at the beginning of this section. Roman lawyers did *not* develop a doctrine of interpretation and reasoning which had the characteristics of a coherent and closed system. On the other hand, recent research has undoubtedly shown that the *catalogue of intellectual tools* used by these lawyers was more extensive than has been previously assumed and that there was probably a higher degree of *awareness* both of argumentative problems and of the fact that specific patterns of reasoning were applied than was earlier believed. By and large, it seems difficult to exclude the idea of at least some influence from Greek rhetoric. This conclusion is further corroborated by recent investigations (in particular by Horak, *op. cit.*) concerning the way in which Roman lawyers justified their decisions and opinions. The traditional view according to which they embraced a laconic method of reasoning, making use almost exclusively of the authority of earlier jurists' decisions, has to be revised considerably.

Chapter 3

The Emergence of Christian Thinking

Selected Bibliography: G. Fassò, *Storia della filosofia del diritto*, vol. I, Bologna 1966, pp. 157–224; F. Flückiger, *Geschichte des Naturrechts*, I, Zurich 1954; K. Rode, *Geschichte der europäischen Rechtsphilosophie*, Düsseldorf 1974, pp. 52–71; O. Schilling, *Die Rechtsphilosophie bei den Kirchenvätern*, in *Archiv für Rechts- und Wirtschaftsphilosophie* 16 (1922–23), pp. 1–12; W. Ullmann, *Principles of Government and Politics in the Middle Ages*, New York 1961; same author, *Law and Politics in the Middle Ages, An Introduction to the Sources of Medieval Political Ideas*, Ithaca, N.Y. 1975; A. Verdross, *Abendländische Rechtsphilosophie*, Vienna 1958, pp. 49–68.

1. Introduction

However rich in variants and nuances, the Greco-Roman intellectual world, with which we have so far been dealing, was characterized by considerable unity in basic ideas and concepts. Plato, Aristotle, Stoics, Cynics, Sceptics and Epicureans, Cicero, and the great Roman lawyers, could disagree on such fundamental matters as the ideal State, the good life, or the ultimate purpose of human existence, but they understood each other. Whether they spoke Greek or Latin, they possessed a common language of categories and arguments. Their terms of reference, including basic social structure and political experience, were essentially homogeneous.

This intellectual pattern of the western world was broken with the advent of Christianity. It is true that both Greece and Rome had known for centuries strong undercurrents of religious thinking and experience which pointed in the same direction – towards intimate personal religions with elements of mysticism and ideas about the survival of the individual soul – and it is equally true that many Oriental religions, where these elements and ideas were even more salient, were propagated in the Roman Empire. As already mentioned above, the yearning for a life transcending ordinary human existence, and the longing for some kind of mystical "salvation," were increasingly powerful elements in Hellenistic and Roman days.

Among the many creeds that saw the light of day in the Empire, however, Christianity – which is occasionally mentioned, in Greco-Roman writings from the first and second centuries, as an obscure, vaguely subversive and suspect Oriental sect among many – came out victorious and became, after some two centuries of intense propagation but also of persecution by the Roman State, the leading and, soon after, the official creed of the Ancient World. The reason why, and the means by which, this astonishing success could take place are questions which fall outside this survey; it should be noted, however, that the relative openness, the peace, the fairly efficient communications and the cultural unity which characterized the Mediterranean world of the early Empire were doubtlessly factors highly favourable to the propagation of the new religion.

Christianity introduced a number of ideas and concepts that had – and still have, whenever taken seriously – the effect of "problematizing" the very foundations of legal philosophy, till then a reasonably orderly branch of thinking, to the point of creating a set of perpetual insoluble paradoxes. We shall come back in due time to the most important problems created by the new creed, but some should be mentioned here, in order to give at least an idea about their radical character. To reason, experience, or whatever sources of knowledge ancient thinkers had referred to, Christianity added another, and supreme source: the direct *revelation*, transcending human understanding, of a personal God, who held the secrets of existence and chose himself which of them should be made available to mankind. The idea that human will, and human endeavour – albeit possibly weak and insufficient when confronted with supernatural or superior powers – were free agents, able to understand and to shape their world rationally, was rejected and replaced by the view that man, after Adam's fall, was the slave of death and sin, and that only *Grace,* a gift freely bestowed or withheld by God, could give him the light and the strength needed to save his soul. Even *"nature"*, where most ancient thinkers had found a rational order, indeed a soul, was contaminated by the fall of man: it was the realm of the Demon, of the "flesh," of sin and death. The State, which most Greek and Roman philosophers and jurists had celebrated as the exalted goal and purpose of human toil, was – at best – an indifferent external framework or a form of organization made necessary by the fall to check the sinfulness of men; at worst, it could be understood as the Devil's work, as no better than "a large band of brigands" (*magnum latrocinium,* as St. Augustine says).

These few examples are enough to show how problematic the task of legal thinkers had become when men attempted, in the new situation created by the advent of Christianity, to do what philosophers always have tried to do: to make things "fit," to obtain and to convey an intelligible and coherent view of the world, or at least of "their" part of the world.

2. The Jewish Heritage

Historically, the new religion was an offspring of Judaism, and some elements of Christianity cannot be understood without a reference to the religion, history, and thinking of the Jewish people, the "children of Israel".

That small nation which, after a prehistory of nomadic life in the desert, had settled in present-day Palestine probably in the 12th century B.C., had managed, through a history rich in suffering and turmoil, to maintain its national and, in particular, its religious individuality and originality. After a period of political stability and even greatness in the 10th century (Solomon), the Jewish State was split up into two, which in turn were conquered by the great Kingdoms of the East: the Assyrians in the 8th century and the Babylonians two hundred years later ("The Babylonian Captivity," 586 B.C.). The Persian King Cyrus allowed the Jews to return to Jerusalem (538 B.C.) and the Jewish people then shared the destiny of all territories east of the Mediterranean: they were ruled by Alexander and his Macedonian successors in the third and second centuries B.C., conquered by the Romans under Pompey in 63 B.C. Finally, after two bloody and unsuccessful revolts against Roman rule (66 and 115 A.D.), Jerusalem was destroyed and the Jews dispersed over the world.

Early Jewish religion, as still reflected in the Old Testament, possessed some particular features, foremost of which was its strictly *legalistic* character. Old Roman, and in all likelihood also early Greek, religion was also legalistic in the sense that decisive importance was attributed to the correct performance of such rites as offerings to the Gods. With the Jews, however, religion took the form of a regular contract ("the Covenant") between Israel's children and an all-powerful, jealous, and personal God, *Jahve*. To lead a righteous life, to be "just", meant in this perspective, to observe scrupulously the commandments of God and to obey His will; that was the human part of the contract – God's undertaking was to protect and favour his chosen people as long as they fulfilled their contractual obligations. The Law had been directly and physically handed over by God to the people of Israel, represented by Moses, on Mount Sinai. The normal sources of human knowledge had been set aside; God had revealed the Law in the Ten Commandments (to be found in the Second Book of Moses, *Exodus,* in the Old Testament) but also in a growing body of more detailed enactments in various matters (in the Fifth Book of Moses, *Deuteronomium*).

There is no need for much reflection to realise the fundamental difference between the Law of Nature – accessible to right reason and thus at least to wise and knowledgeable men – or indeed any immutable, universally valid and impersonal system of norms, as acknowledged by most educated Greeks and Romans – and the Jewish Law, dictated by an individual and highly personalized God. Nor was God's Law "universal": it was given to Israel's children exclusively, not to other peoples, the "Gentiles". Moreover, in the leading Greek interpretations of the world, God (or the highest God, Zeus or Jupiter) was *part* of the order of nature; thus, by exercising right reason, men participated in God's doing and thinking. Jahve had his existence *before* and *outside* the world, which was his personal creation. God could visit men, as He had done with the Patriarchs, the Fathers of the people of Israel, but men could no more participate in God than they could penetrate into his secret plans for the world. What men could do, to acquire merit in the eyes of God, was to observe in all details the law He had given them. Rational thinking was of no avail.

There are, in the writings of some of the great religious thinkers, preachers – and indeed poets – of Israel, the Prophets, expressions of tendencies that indicate the possibility of a development of this religion in new directions. The greatest of them all, Isaiah, foresees a future where the law and the word of God are disseminated to all peoples; other prophets speak about a time when the law is inscribed by God into the hearts of men, i.e. when it is no longer an external commandment to be honoured by external acts, but "internalized", transformed into an inward, personal conviction.

Strict legalism continued to be a predominant feature in Jewish religion throughout its development in the ancient world. However, just as yearning for a direct contact with a transcendent God, a faith which satisfies men's feelings, not only their reason or sense of justice, a collective or individual "salvation", and individual survival, becomes an increasingly strong element of all religions, and indeed philosophic speculations, towards the end of the pre-Christian era, so Jewish religion gives more and more place to similar elements. The chosen people waits for a Saviour, a "Messiah", who shall establish the Realm of God on earth. The Jewish ethos more and more becomes, as an eminent writer says (G. Fassò), an individual and mystic craving for internal identification with God, a yearning for "sanctity" rather than for the social – outward and community-oriented – virtue of righteousness.

This is the intellectual and religious climate in which Jesus from Nazareth sets out on his mission.

From early days, Jews had settled in other parts of the Mediterranean world; to the extent these Jewish communities mixed with other people – and that was inevitable in particular for those among them who did well economically and socially, – they met with the intellectual challenges and material temptations of the Greco-Roman upper classes. To these Jews, it became natural to compare their hereditary faith and thinking with the ideas prevailing among their new neighbours, and to look for similarities and possible compromises. Many of these Jews living outside Palestine became "hellenized." A well-known representative of this category is *Philo from Alexandria* (last pre-Christian and first Christian century), who developed, in a great number of works on philosophical subjects, ideas which come close to the rationalistic natural law theories of the contemporary Greek world: the law of Jahve, as handed over to Moses, is in Philo's view more or less identical with the law of nature of the Stoics.

3. The Specific Christian Message

Christ, in his own words, brings a "good message" (Greek: eu-angelion). It is not, however, a message about the establishment of a powerful and victorious Kingdom of God, nor – as many Jews had hoped – about the rebirth of a new and free Jewish State, where the Law of God would rule. The message of salvation brought by Christ concerns God's willingness to visit men in their hearts, if they search for Him, and to bestow upon them His grace, which will make them free from their burdens and grant their souls immortality. This salvation can be operated by grace, and by grace alone; it cannot be achieved by the "just according to the Law", however strictly he may observe the commandments.

Christ's message, as recorded in the New Testament, is no social philosophy. Nor is it a complete body of ethical rules for the individual. In fact, it defies any attempt at systematization. What the Gospels convey is the vivid, largely improvised, strongly personal, suggestive and highly effective preaching, on matters of particular religious importance, of an inspired and charismatic religious leader whose main concern is to show individual listeners the way to that mystic communion with God in their hearts that sole matters, because sole it can give them salvation. Jesus avoids to take position in such ethical questions as concern the "social," outward aspects of a life in righteousness. "Who made me a judge or a divider over you?" he asks a man who beseeches him to solve a dispute over an inheritance between the man and his brother (Luke xii, 13). When unavoidable he either gives short pieces of simple and straightforward advice, or finds his refuge in paradoxes tending to show the utter incompatibility between a true life in God and preoccupations with worldly matters ("Let the dead bury their dead", Luke ix, 60).

With regard to the secular society, Christ's preaching, as far as handed over to us, can be interpreted in two radically different senses, and since his words have been used for more detailed, energetic, and sometimes fanatic, interpretation than any other texts in the history of Western thought, both constructions have been tried repeatedly. On the one hand, there is much to be said for the view that Jesus treated State and authorities with complete indifference but also with total submission. "My Kingdom is not of this world", he says to Pilate, and he duly pays his taxes, with the word that Caesar should have his due – money – just as God should have His. The outcome, thus, would be passiveness. Moreover, Christ emphasizes that he has not come to abolish the Jewish Law – not one iota shall perish – but to complete it, i.e., internalize it, "inscribe it into the hearts" of the faithful. On the other hand, Christ sometimes expresses devastating criticism of Jewish legalism, and of the intellectually leading groups of the Jewish society, the Phariseans and those learned in the law. This criticism can be – and has been – interpreted as an exhortation to revolt, as revolutionary protests against the established social system and hierarchy.

Thus the two temptations that Christ's words could lead into were *complete passiveness* when confronted with the injustices of the world, or *a revolutionary breach* with existing societies. Neither attitude would seem to take into account the complexity and originality of Christ's teaching. As already stated, he endorses no social philosophy. His "good message" is of an entirely different character. However that may be, it is obvious that the new religion was difficult to reconcile with rationalistic natural law theories.

4. The Propagation of Christianity. Historical Background Facts

As already mentioned, the Mediterranean world was, from Hellenistic days at least, characterized by extensive religious syncretism: elements of various religions were mixed, and new creeds – generally with a tendency to develop mysticism and secret rites – were being propagated in addition to the official state religions of Rome, of the Greek city states, and of other old communities brought under Roman rule. In religious matters, the Romans were basically tolerant; the result of Roman conquest, in most regions, was that the cult of Rome, and of her rulers, with temples, offerings, in some cases a priesthood, were simply added to local forms of worship. Since polytheism was common in most parts of the ancient world, the obligation to pay lip service to, and participate in the cult of, these additional protective deities did not cause great problems either of a religious or of a practical or political character to the populations concerned. In the East, there was since times immemorial a tradition for deifying and worshipping kings and other rulers; in the poorer and culturally less developed Western provinces – Gaul (present-day France and Belgium), the Rhineland, the Alpine regions, Britain and the Iberian peninsula – the Roman way of life, acknowledged to be culturally and intellectually superior to local traditions, soon became fashionable with the upper classes, who tried to be as "romanized" as possible and accepted the cult of the goddess Rome and of the Emperor as part of the civilized patterns of behaviour they were aspiring to make their own.

The peaceful and, by the standards of the times, comfortable ways of communication made the circulation of ideas reasonably rapid and easy. Some additional factors were particularly effective in facilitating the penetration of new religious ideas. One was the Roman army, which from Augustus' days onwards was increasingly recruited from other parts of the Empire than Italy; the peripheral provinces, both in the East and in the West, contributed with large contingents of men (frequently accompanied by their families) to this mobile ethnic and religious meltingpot. Another – obviously of particular importance for the propagation of Christianity – were the colonies of Jews dispersed over the whole Mediterranean world. Finally, there was a general tradition of wandering teachers and priests of Eastern religions, who could count upon interested audiences in all the larger cities of the Empire.

Christianity spread quickly over the Mediterranean basin. In the New Testament – the Acts of the Apostles and Paul's letters – we can follow the missionary work that started soon after the death of Jesus, in the fourth decade of our era, and had great success, first in the East, but soon also in Rome. The new religion, which partook of the exclusive and intolerant attitude of Judaism with regard to polytheism and idolatry, soon ran into trouble with the Roman authorities, although extensive and systematic persecution was rare, except in some short periods. Suspect already by virtue of its denial of the value of the "world," and of its contempt of secular power and secular rulers (the historian Tacitus, in the first century A.D., refers to Christians as a suspect and subversive body of people) the new religion came into flat opposition to the Empire by the refusal of its followers to participate in the cult of the Emperor and the State. Major persecutions took place as early as the reign of Nero (about 60 A.D.), at the middle of the third century and towards the end of that century. Local Christian congregations were sometimes harassed, or even prosecuted, also at other times.

Nothing, however, could stop the new religion from spreading, and from organizing itself throughout the Empire. As early as the middle of the second century, to take one single example, we hear about a diocesan organization in the important city of Lugdunum (today Lyons) in central Gaul; a violent persecution about 175 A.D. does not seem to have broken that organization. In 177 a new bishop, St. Irenaeus – one of the most influential teachers of the early Western church – was active in Lyons, where he died, peacefully, in 202. A vast body of Christian writing in the field of theology and philosophy came

The Emergence of Christian Thinking

into existence from the first century onwards, showing that although the new creed found its first fervent adherents in the poor classes of urban populations, it also had a strong appeal to educated men, who thought it their task to defend it in learned works and to discuss its ethical and intellectual relations with traditional Greco-Roman philosophy.

Decisive dates in the history of Christianity are the year 312 A.D., when the Emperor Constantine the Great converted to the new creed and defeated his pagan rival Maxentius at the Milvian bridge near Rome (this was the occasion when the cross was used as the sign of the victorious army: *In hoc signo vinces* – "In this sign you shall conquer"); further, the following year, 313, when Constantine issued, at Milan, the "edict of tolerance," which recognized Christianity as one of the lawful religions of the Empire. Only seventy years later, in 383, the Emperor Theodosius I made the new creed the only legally recognized religion of Rome. Pagan religions certainly survived for at least another century, on the one hand among rural populations who continued to worship local deities, and on the other hand in the conservative Roman aristocracy, imbued with the great traditions of the City. However, the mainstream of Western thinking and worship had once and for all become Christian.

From the middle of the second century at the latest, it was a basic feature of the organization of the Christian Church that the senior priests of the city churches – known as "overseers" (Greek: episcopos) or "bishops" – exercized spiritual authority over the other priests and the congregations within their districts. Somewhat later, the bishop of Rome came to be acknowledged as the leader of the Church. The rise of the papacy in the West was probably to some extent facilitated by the splitting up of the Empire (in 395 A.D.) into a Western and an Eastern part, for the competing bishoprics of Antiochia, Alexandria and the new-founded Eastern capital, Constantinople (founded by Constantine in 330), all fell to the Eastern Empire. In the West, no other prelate could claim the same position as the bishop of Rome. From at least the great Church Council of Chalcedon (451 A.D.), the latter was generally recognized as the head of the Church, although his legal position and prerogatives never ceased to be subject to controversy in many details. Under the Pope, a network of organization – with church provinces, headed by archbishops, dioceses under the leadership of bishops, and parishes led by priests – came into existence.

Frequently, Roman administrative districts were used for the purpose of church organization.

The Church rose; the Empire declined, and ultimately fell. In 406–407 A.D., massive invasions of Germanic tribes overrun the weakened Roman frontier defence on the Rhine; in 410 Alaric's Visigoths conquer Rome. The fall of the Eternal City is a shattering experience to all contemporaries; in 429 the Vandals cross from Spain to North Africa; in 476 the last Emperor of the West is dethroned, and fifteen years later, the whole of Italy is under the rulership of Theoderic the Great, King of the Ostrogoths. Successful counterattacks by the Eastern Empire under Justinian, the Father of *Corpus Juris Civilis* (Emperor 527–565 A.D.) annihilate the Ostrogoths but produce no lasting results. The fall of the Western Empire is an irrevokable fact. On its territory, Germanic tribes establish their kingdoms in the 6th and 7th centuries: the Visigoths in Spain, the Franks and Burgundians in France and Western Germany, the Langobards (Lombards) in Northern Italy; in Britain and in Central and Eastern Germany, Germanic Kingdoms equally establish themselves, preparing soon to enter upon a scene which no longer coincides with the Mediterranean basin. Other newcomers, even further away, are organizing themselves: the Scandinavians in the North, and the Slavs in the East. Less than a century after the promulgation of *Corpus Juris,* that last great performance of Roman legal science, social engineering, and statesmanship, decisive events are taking place in the Arabian desert: a new religion is being founded by Mohammed; in less than another century it will deprive the Eastern Empire and the Christian Church of most of their territories east and south of the Mediterranean: in 711, the Arabs have overrun North Africa and deal the decisive blow to the Visigoths in Spain. Twenty years later, the Arab wave is broken by the Franks at Poitiers in central France (732 A.D.), but they retain Spain for another five hundred to seven hundred years.

What the Church lost in the South and in the East, was gradually compensated by what she conquered in the North and the West. As early as the fifth century, it was clear that the Church was more important than the rapidly declining Roman State not only spiritually; she was the only administrative organization that was at all viable. Her responsibilities, and her pretentions, grew in all areas. For three or four centuries, it was the Church alone that kept Christendom together, at least in some respects; she was the true heiress of Rome.

5. St. Paul and the Early Fathers of the Church

Above (sec 3 *in fine*) we mentioned *two temptations* that the original Christian preaching could lead into: complete passiveness before the sufferings and injustice of the surrounding world, or a violent, revolutionary breach with the society and institutions of the Empire. Neither tendency was unknown to the early Church, but neither was allowed to prevail. The rapidly growing new organization managed to find its way between the extremes.

From very early – in fact from the moment it was clear that Christ would not come back in the lifetime of the Apostles and that the faithful would have to live on in the world for a long time, perhaps for generations – the Church, as represented by her more perspicacious leaders, found herself confronted – consciously or unawares – with *three inevitable tasks:* (i) on the level of practical solutions, to define the relationship between Christians and a surrounding world which was, by definition, the realm of the Evil One or, at best, an indifferent and contemptible outward organizational framework within which the daily search for the good life had to take place; (ii) on the intellectual level, to define the relationship between Christ's teaching and prevailing contemporary creeds, theories, and doctrines; (iii) to find the forms of her own constitution as a permanent body.

There was no time to consider these questions at leisure, and in peace; some, at least the practical ones, had to be settled without delay, as conflicts arose. It cannot be expected, therefore, that the early leaders and teachers of the Church had much opportunity to weigh their words. Yet, given the immense authority which was later granted to the first generations of Church leaders – priority in time always supported *some* claim to preference, until recent days, and as regards Christianity, it was in the nature of things that the earlier a statement was, the closer in time to the authentic revealed word of God as preached by the Saviour, the greater its authority – the teaching, and the practical decisions, of these early churchmen were submitted to intense, recurring, and systematic efforts of interpretation, as if they had partaken of the special quality of the revealed word itself. Thus even the most summary, provisional, and sweeping *ad hoc* statement by the Apostles, or by the one we know best, St. Paul, has been made the basis of conclusions which are certainly, in many cases, far more deepgoing and far-reaching than the travelling Apostle, who had to make up his mind on thorny questions literally in any market place where he was preaching, can reasonably have foreseen. Therefore, what we really mean, when attributing an opinion or an idea to, e.g., St. Paul, is that there are, in the body of preserved Pauline writings, words that, when subjected to that kind of energetic interpretation, *may* yield the meaning attributed to them.

Paul, a Jew from Tharsus in Cilicia (Asia Minor), brought up in the creed of the most severe and legalistic school of Jewish theology – the Phariseans – was a young man when Christ was crucified. Originally he was a zealous enemy of Christianity, but a revelation made him an equally fervent Christian. He set out to preach the gospel; we can follow him in the Acts of the Apostles, on his missionary travels through Palestine, Asia Minor, Greece and finally to Rome, where he is traditionally reported to have suffered martyrdom for his faith. Paul's preaching can be followed in his letters, which make up a considerable portion of the New Testament.

Paul is in the first place a fervent, and tormented, religious personality. As a Pharisean, he had lived for, and by, the law. Converted, he excels in showing its insufficiency: what matters is the grace of God in men's hearts. The grace alone can give that faith, hope, and love of God and one's neighbour without which being "just according to the law," for all righteous actions, is of no avail. In the thirteenth chapter of his first letter to the Corinthians, Paul expresses, in glowing terms, the path that alone leads to salvation.

But Paul was not only an inspired preacher. He also had to take the burdens of secular leadership upon his shoulders. He had to negotiate with Roman officials and Jewish dignitaries. In his tracks, there grew up Christian communities, bodies of men and women living in the world, with rapidly growing external and internal conflicts; they turned to him for advice. For all his contempt of the world, Paul is no revolutionary. He repeatedly advises the Christians to respect secular authorities – to whom he seems to attribute not only negative functions but also the inescapable duty of maintaining order and repressing crime – and while he admonishes Christian masters to treat their slaves as brethren, he also tells the slaves to remain in obedience to the secular order and to obey their masters, whether Christian or pagan.

Paul's cautious approach to the established order was undoubtedly a fact of the greatest importance for the new creed's chances of spreading in the Mediterranean world, just as his – and, after some hesitation, the other Apostles' – willingness to admit non-Jewish proselytes to their embryonic "Church" was decisive for the prospects and propagation of Christianity: the opposite solution might have reduced that creed to one among several Jewish sects.

There are few reasons to believe that Paul had either time or inclination to give much attention to subtle and elaborate questions of legal philosophy. But there are, in his letters, words which came to mean very much for the approach of early churchmen to the "law of nature," as an essential element in the common Greco-Roman stock of ideas. In the letter to the Romans (ii, 14 f) Paul refers to the fact that the Gentiles, although ignoring the Law of Moses, exclusively given to the Jews, can perform "by nature," the works of the law, thus showing that the work of the law is "written in their hearts." This, no doubt, can be interpreted as an acknowledgment of a "law of nature," available to all rational beings *without* divine revelation, and thus serve as a bridge over to Greco-Roman thinking. That bridge came to be eagerly used by later Christian writers, who had an interest in bringing the suspect, obscure, and low-class new religion into at least some harmony with the prevailing ideas of educated Greco-Romans.

What these later writers, and even some modern scholars, seem to forget is, on the one hand, that the only concession to the idea of natural law that can be read into Paul's words is that if there is such a law, it raises its followers to the same level as Jewish legalism, repeatedly denounced by the Apostle as useless and leading to spiritual death, on the other hand that "nature," whether it be considered as a source of law or not, is invariably described by Paul as corrupt, by the fall of Adam, and indeed – as the Apostle writes in a famous passage – "sighing for redemption." For Paul, as for Christ, there is no "natural" bridge between God and His creation: both man and "nature" are *creaturae*, created beings, essentially and completely distinct from their Creator, whose grace alone can bring them into that mystic union with Him which is "salvation." Paul again and again repeats that if righteous deeds without grace were enough to save man's soul, Christ would have lived and suffered in vain. There can be no doubt that energetic interpreters of Paul's words *can* find support for the *concept* of some kind of natural law, but there is even less doubt that this concept, or rather this mere similarity of terms, in no way justifies the conclusion that the Apostle would have subscribed to ideas even remotely similar to Stoic or Ciceronian natural law thinking.

Another element in Paul's writings which was also energetically exploited by ingenious interpreters searching for bridges to Greco-Roman contemporary ideas and social realities is the cautious and not entirely negative approach to public institutions noted above. Could it be, these interpreters asked, that according to Christian thinking, "nature" means two distinct things, or rather, that there are two distinct phases in the development of the concept of nature? Before the fall of man, in the days of the Earthly Paradise, when God's creation was fresh and unsoiled, what was natural must be good (and this idea could be developed even further, by those eager to find parallels with Greek thinking: nature must be good, and indeed partake of God's nature); after Adam had eaten of the apple, "nature" shared man's corruption. That corrupt nature, it could be claimed, called for other devices to be kept in any kind of order; in the fallen creation, State, laws and such institutions as private property and slavery, could be considered as "natural" and defended as such. Consequently, there would be scope for *two sets of "natural" rules: the primary, or basic ones, which are valid in all circumstances, and the secondary, or relative ones, which presuppose the fall of man.* This is an idea recurring in the works of some early writers. It is mentioned here, not because there would be any support for it in Paul's letters, but simply because it provides an example of the wealth of subtle reasoning which could grow out of the rather meagre soil of the body of Pauline writings. What was important, however, for Christian thinking through centuries under the ever-recurring pressure of the, as it would seem, psychologically irresistible idea that there is, after all, some sort of "natural law," be it only a vague standard of common decency, which man can find for himself and apply – was the question *how complete* is the corruption of man and nature brought about by Adam's fall: is it total, as the most faithful and severe guardians of the Christian message proclaim, thus blotting out *any* memory of the idyllic order that prevailed in Eden, or is it only *partial,* as more optimistic and lenient theologians would pretend, so that human reason and human virtue may, with great exertion, ascend to *some* notion of it? The question may seem, today, a strange one, but it goes without saying that in centuries completely dominated or even merely influenced by Christian theology, the answer was of great importance for all fields connected with basic ethics, not least that of the law.

Two more remarks should be made concerning Paul's contribution to the future Western approach in matters of ecclesiastical law – a field of legal science which, in the course of the Middle Ages, was to exercise a deep influence on the development of secular legal thinking (just as ideas and principles of secular Roman law did from an early date have a strong impact on the law and legal thinking of the Church).

The notion of *"Church"* in Pauline writing has to be analysed with great care. It is essentially ambiguous. In some contexts, the word stands for the transcendent, mystical union of the faithful with, and in, Christ – a *Corpus mysticum*, or union which, literally, is neither of this world nor subject to time. However, the Church also means either a single local group of Christians – we should speak of a parish – or all these groups considered as a whole. There is some evidence, both in Christ's teaching, as recorded in the Gospels, and in Paul's letters, to the effect that the first Christians thought, and hoped, that Christ was to come back, now in His glory, in the lifetime of the first generation of faithful. It fell upon Paul, and other churchmen of his age, including of course, in the first place, the Apostles, to give to the "Church," in the sense of a body of believers, that minimum of organization and discipline which she required both in order to fulfill her spiritual mission – to gather the faithful in such forms as to give them access to the *corpus mysticum* of Christ – and in order to survive and grow in a hostile or at least suspicious surrounding society. As time passed, the eschatological element of Christian faith, i.e., the belief that the end of the world was close at hand, naturally passed more and more into the background; concomitantly, the need for a permanent organization with firm rules of all kinds increased. Two major preoccupations in Paul's teaching in respect of organization and outward discipline would seem to be, on the one hand, the wish to make access to the Church as easy to non-Jews as possible by reducing to a minimum those remnants of Jewish law that the Christians were to observe, on the other hand to endeavour to avoid scandal both in the surrounding Greco-Roman world and among local Jewish communities by imposing certain standards of behaviour at the meetings of the faithful. Paul's much-discussed and much-criticized words about the position of women in the Church may well be expressions of that cautious and diplomatic attitude in external matters.

The Christian theologians and philosophers of the first six or seven centuries of our era are commonly referred to as the "Fathers of the Church". The earliest from whom authentic writings of any importance have been preserved were active in the second century A.D. They wrote in Greek or Latin; there is a certain difference in what may be called intellectual climate between the two groups: the Greek Fathers tend to be more rationalistic, more speculative, and upon the whole more apt to confront Christian beliefs with traditional philosophical ideas and find parallels. The Latins are, generally, more cautious in this respect and tend to put more emphasis on practical questions.

The very voluminous body of writings of the Fathers of the Church (Patristics) cannot be discussed here; it is by no means homogeneous, and more than one of the once leading authors was, in his lifetime or afterwards, when the implications of his teaching became obvious, condemned as heretical, i.e., departing from the true Christian dogma. It should be remembered that theologians and philosophers in the first five Christian centuries covered very much ground and that a great many questions, arguments or objections which recurred centuries later were first formulated and tested in these years. Be it enough to say that although many of the early Fathers took a negative, or at least distrusting, attitude towards ancient authors and pagan ideas, there was upon the whole a strong tendency to reconcile Christian ideas with Stoic or Ciceronian natural law. The reproach was frequently made, against the latter, that it only took into consideration men, and human nature, as earthly beings and was therefore by definition insufficient; it was for Christianity to *complete* pagan natural law thinking by taking into account the soul of man.

Other, less controversial notions were to a large extent taken over by the Fathers, and thus incorporated, on the strength of their immense authority, into Christian thinking. The Aristotelian idea that man is by nature a "social animal" occurs in several patristic works. Technical terms, and concepts, were mostly borrowed from the ancient philosophers, and this taking over of words and phrases could sometimes lead to fairly radical consequences. Thus, the words "just", "righteous" and "righteousness" ("justice") were in Christ's teaching, as preserved in the Gospels, essentially names for an internal disposition, indeed for a state of religious perfection, or sanctity, far from the "social" connotation characteristic for Aristotle and other Greek thinkers. Although the Fathers generally stick to the meaning adopted in the Bible, some of them, probably under the influence of Greek writers, tend to give the word, again, a sense more close to that usually adopted in secular thinking. As a general proposition, it should be remembered that for a very long time – in fact well into this century – great importance was attached to terminology, to similarity of words, and to etymology as a source of explanation concerning the "original", or "real" meaning not only of words but also of the concepts and phenomena denoted by words. The fact that a technical term, or any word, from ancient philosophy, law, or religion, was taken over in early Christian writing – an event which was sometimes practically inevitable when a Greek or Latin word was required to render an utterance in the Eastern languages (Aramaeic, Hebrew) which were the original depositories of Christian teaching – could have very far-reaching consequences in later thinking.

A question of great importance that occupied the Fathers of the Church was how to look at the existing social system, in particular with regard to the very unevenly distributed property in land and goods and to slavery. We have already noted that St. Paul nowhere claims the abolition of slavery, and the same cautious attitude recurs in patristic writing. Just as the Stoics proclaimed that slavery was against the law of nature, which made all men free and alike, but had been introduced into *jus gentium* as a consequence of wars, so the Fathers stated that slavery was one of the results of the fall of man. As for private property, there would not seem to be any acceptable evidence for the Fathers condemning it as such (although there is strong evidence to the effect that the first Christians in Jerusalem lived in community of property), but they certainly stressed the moral obligation to *use* property and its proceeds for the common weal, and they also generally seem to have held that the existence of private property was a result of Adam's fall: like the State and other similar public institutions, the right of private property was necessary, as an element of "secondary" natural law. As for the State itself, it has already been mentioned that according to one wide-spread view it was also an institution of secondary natural law, thus "natural" only in the world corrupted by the fall of man. To a large extent, the question depends upon the definitions of "State" underlying the discussion of different authors: some stress the *community* aspect of the State – an aspect which could certainly be compatible with "primary" natural law; others refer, essentially to the State as a *coercive* mechanism, intended to keep the subjects in order; seen in that light, the State is obviously more likely to belong to the "secondary" phase.

Among the Greek Fathers, the greatest scholar, Origenes from

Alexandria (d.c. 250 A.D.), goes quite far in recognizing the basic identity of God's law and the law of nature; he speaks against the binding force of secular laws not compatible with these "unwritten" norms. In the Western Church, St. Ambrose, Bishop of Milan (d. 397 A.D.) develops the "social," outward-oriented character of Christian righteousness, which is at the same time the voice of uncorrupted nature, and stresses the need for *active* charity (as opposed to the passive acceptance of the Stoics) embodied in that notion. Ambrose, on the other hand, is one of the few among the Fathers of the Church who seems to have seen clearly the fundamental dilemma created, from a Christian point of view, by the recognition of a system of natural law: what is the use, and the necessity, either of the revealed Divine Law of the Jews, or – even more important – what need is there for "salvation", for Christ's sacrificial death on the Cross, if there already exists a body of law, accessible to human reason, which is sufficient to guarantee a righteous life and a peaceful society?

That obviously fundamental question escaped, upon the whole, unnoticed by the Fathers of the Church. It would seem, to quote a passage earlier in this section – and it is not the last time we have reasons to come back to this observation – that the idea of some sort of "natural law", be it only a vague standard of common decency, that man can find for himself and apply, is psychologically irresistible; as soon as the great religious revolution realized by the teaching of Christ had lost its first impetus, and the new creed had to be handled, as it were, as an everyday article for lasting mass consumption, Christian writers could not resist the temptation of abandoning both the complex, provocative and subtle psychological paradoxes of Christ's teaching, the Christian pessimism according to which man's "natural light" is not strong enough to show him the right way, let alone to make him follow it, and the even more uncomfortable idea that God's grace, the indispensible prerequisite for salvation, is given irrespective of merit.

These elements of the original Christian teaching were taken up, four hundred years after Christ's life on earth, by the greatest among Fathers of the Church, St. Augustine, with an eloquence and a vehemence that secured their survival, albeit somewhat mitigated, in the official creed of the Catholic Church, but also developed them so fully and clearly that whenever, in the course of later centuries, a Church reform or a religious revival took place – as would occur, quite frequently, when the original, exacting and provocative Christian message had been obscured by rationalism in the Church, or by the Church temporizing too smoothly with the world – St. Augustine was to be the authority invoked by reformers and revivalists. In this capacity, he has remained, and is likely to remain, one of the most influential *Doctores* as long as there is a Christian Church.

6. St. Augustine

In his person, Aurelius Augustinus unites the two most powerful intellectual elements of the late ancient world: the formal, literary and philosophical culture which was the Greco-Roman inheritance, and the Christian religion, as taught by the Latin Fathers. Although a fact of limited importance in this context, it should be mentioned that Augustine's attitude to the former of these two elements is likely to have been decisive for its survival: among the Christians of the first three centuries, it was a much-discussed point whether or not the whole apparatus of classical learning – including not only philosophy, but also literature, arts, and such areas of study as grammar and rhetoric – should be thrown overboard completely, as being expressions of wordly vanity, and thus perilous for Christian souls. St. Augustine took the position that the arts and the learning of the pagan world should be used in the service of the Church; had he decided otherwise, it is quite likely that little or nothing of the Greco-Roman inheritance would have been handed over to posterity.

Augustine was born in Tagaste in North Africa in 354 A.D. His life is well known to us: his autobiography, *Confessiones,* are one of the earliest literary documents of its kind which lay stress on psychological development. His mother, St. Monica, was a Christian, his father, a soldier, had remained a pagan. The young Augustine went through a number of religious experiences; his steady occupation, however, was with rhetoric, in which subject he was a teacher. Before the age of thirty, he went to Rome and then to Milan, where he came under the influence of St. Ambrose, who in 387 baptized him. Eight years later, he was called to the episcopal see of Hippo, in North Africa, where he was to stay for the remaining twenty-five years of his life (d. 430 A.D.).

St. Augustine has left a vast body of theological writing. His most famous works – besides the *Confessiones* (c. 397 A.D.) – are *De vera religione* (*On True Religion,* 390 A.D.), *De Trinitate* (*On Trinity,* 399–419

A.D.) and *De Civitate Dei* (*On the City of God*, 413–427 A.D.). As could be expected in a work of this size, scattered over some forty years, in many cases composed for short-term polemic purposes, it is not easy to draw out absolutely clear and consistent lines of thought – the less so since Augustine is at the same time a subtle thinker, a religious personality with a strong bend towards mysticism, and a polemist of almost fierce vehemence. Although he has been studied and analysed intensely, there is still no complete agreement on the interpretation of his ideas. We shall confine ourselves to two major aspects of Augustinian thought: his views of natural law, and his ideas about the State.

With regard to the first topic, it is important – and it would indeed seem helpful in order to avoid some of the controversy concerning the correct interpretation of Augustine's ideas – to observe carefully the chronology of the great bishop's works. For about 410 A.D., Augustine got involved in a polemic discussion which is one of the most important debates in the history of the early Church, which concerned, precisely, the dilemma we tried to characterize at the end of the preceding section and which forced Augustine to apply all his learning, intelligence, and christian zeal to the great questions of Divine grace and human perfection. It is in the writings posterior to that debate that we find the final, mature opinions of Augustine. His chief opponent in the great controversy was Pelagius, a British monk, who affirmed not only man's free will but also his ability to choose between good and evil and to achieve moral perfection without the intervention of Grace. Nature, and the law of nature, were in Pelagius' teaching basically good, as if the fall of man had never taken place. In short, the English Divine advocated theses which, if they were accepted, would have deprived the essential elements of Christian doctrine of their sense; Christ, as Paul put it, "would have lived in vain," were these ideas generally adopted.

Augustine launched a vigorous counter-attack, emphasizing the fundamental elements of original Christian teaching. He succeeded in having the Church condemn Pelagius' theses as heretical, but he was not wholly successful in convincing that body of the truth of his own so-called *doctrine of predestination,* i.e., the view that God alone, in his inscrutable wisdom, elects some humans for salvation, others for damnation; no regard is paid to merit, and no endeavour towards virtue and perfection can change God's will and plans. The Catholic Church chose a compromise between the Pelagian view and St.

Augustine's somewhat resigned, threatening and tragic preaching, but again and again in the course of history, Augustine found followers among the more severe schools of thought in the Christian churches.

Before the Pelagian controversy, Augustine makes statements about natural law which come quite close to Cicero's eternal law theories. However, in Augustine's thinking, the *lex aeterna*, which is Divine Reason, or God's Will, does not simply coincide with the law of nature, accessible to human reason, for the latter is only the more or less clear or corrupted imprint of the latter, as the wax upon which a real ring is pressed can render the seal more or less perfectly. The lowest stage of law, in the early Augustine's system, is the worldly law, *lex temporalis*, which has to conform to divine law.

After the conflict with Pelagius, Augustine takes, with great consistency, a position in which the idea of a law of nature, accessible to reason and capable of guiding man to the morally proper course of action, is rejected and replaced by the view that God's will alone decides what is right and what is wrong. It is only faith, expressing itself in Christian love, that can guide men to righteousness, and faith, in its turn, can only be the gift of God's grace. Fallen nature is unable to reveal moral truths.

Augustine's most important contribution to Occidental thinking in the fields of State and law is found in the great work *On the City of God – De Civitate Dei–* which resumes the ageing prelate's philosophy. An important source of inspiration to this great, learned, impressive but also difficult, indeed obscure, work, were contemporary political and military events – in particular the conquest of the City of Rome by the Visigoths in 410 and the devastations of the Vandals in Augustine's own North African diocese. These catastrophes give rise to the question what justification, and what value, the secular State could at all claim. Examining this question, Augustine is led to follow Roman history upstream, from contemporary disasters to the legendary beginnings; and everywhere, he finds violence, conquests, breaches of faith, internal strife – to such an extent that he puts the question whether the States of this world are anything but "large bands of robbers" *(magna latrocinia)*. Theoretically, Augustine would seem prepared to accept as justifiable such secular States as are permeated by Christian righteousness; if not, the worldly State, *civitas terrena*, simply belongs to the Devil. However, St. Augustine also discusses the City of God; basically, it is the *corpus mysticum* of the Church, the inward communion of Christians with their Saviour; in other contexts, the City of God certainly refers to the Christian organization on Earth, the Church. Since subordination to God's will is the condition which must be fulfilled for earthly States to be acceptable from a Christian point of view, the question arises whether the Saint means that secular societies should be in all respects subordinate to the Church. That was the interpretation advanced, in the high Middle Ages, by the Papacy and the Church in their conflicts with Emperors and Kings. It is difficult to say what was actually the opinion of Augustine on this point. Just as his "City of God" oscillates between a mystical concept and the living Church of Rome, so his worldly City can mean both an actual, concrete State organization and a state of mind, characterized by allegiance to the world, i.e., the Demon. But the secular State, as a body of men, has certain tasks: to maintain *peace* so as to allow people to practice their religion, and to survey good order and prevent sinful life. To the extent – difficult to ascertain, that must be stressed – Augustine at all recognizes a legitimate worldly state, the Saint's reasoning opens, for the first time, a way towards a distinction between such human duties as are imposed by the religious community, the Church, (with or without State support) and such duties as are of interest only for the City of God; in short, a rift between *positive secular law,* which is the State's domain, and the *moral law of the Church* appears for the first time in these Augustinian writings.

Augustine's ideas, and the relationship between God's State and the worldly State, are complicated further by the fact that he also sees the two bodies in a time perspective, which implies a struggle between them and the ultimate victory of God's State.

The fundamental ambiguity, both in basic terms and in more elaborate reasoning, between two concepts of "State" – a mystic-philosophic and a practical-historical one – does not increase the clarity of *De Civitate Dei*. The book was intensely read and interpreted from its appearance; it was frequently used in polemics, and the immense authority of St. Augustine was then exploited to the utmost. It is natural that it came to be a highly efficient weapon in the hands of the Church in her struggle for power with Emperors and Kings in the early and high Middle Ages. Generally speaking, it seems fair to say that *De Civitate Dei* is not only a magnificent piece of philosophic history-writing but also a gold mine of observations and ideas over a vast range of topics. But it is hardly a book that has contributed to clarify the legal-philosophical and political issues it deals with. Rather, it is responsible for confusion in several respects.

7. The Centuries of Transition

No period is completely empty, or uninteresting, in the history of the development of human ideas. It must be recognized, on the other hand, that between such phases in the growth of knowledge and understanding as the Greek fifth century, B.C., on the one hand, and the three or four centuries following upon the fall of the Western Empire on the other hand, there is a vast difference. The period 400–750 A.D. was undoubtedly one in which, silently and slowly but steadily, the ravaged, impoverished and isolated provinces of Western Europe recovered the strength necessary for new displays of economic, political, and intellectual grandeur. But from the point of view of legal philosophy, and more generally, legal thinking, the frequently used term "dark centuries" is upon the whole justified. A closer examination of chosen cities, or territories, at different times in these centuries would show us quite important variations – minor literary, philosophical, or artistic "renascences" occur locally, now and then, under the influence of highly varied favourable circumstances, such as temporary economic growth, the immigration of culturally creative refugees, the rise of a local intellectually active ruler or dynasty, or changes in the ways of international trade. (Let me illustrate my point with one single example: in the period 420–480, south-western Gaul, a province which, towards the end of that period, suffered particularly under wars and devastations, knew what has been called a "little Platonic renascence," due in all likelihood to the fact that an unusually great number of highly cultivated and intellectually interested aristocratic refugees from the North-East and other even more exposed parts of the Empire tended to gather there).

But nowhere, and at no time, did this period produce works that add anything substantially new, or original, to the capital of ideas gathered in the preceding millennium. The contributions for which we have the greatest reasons to be grateful are those of collectors, compilators, and lexicographers, who faithfully picked up, preserved, and brought forward to their successors such elements of ancient learning and writing as would otherwise have been irrevocably lost.

Mention should be made, here, of a few among those writers who thus kept learning, and philosophical writing of some relevance to legal thinking, alive through the dark centuries. *Boethius* (480–524 A.D.) and *Cassiodorus* (c. 490–c.580 A.D.) were both members of the Roman aristocracy, who rose in the service of the Ostrogoth kings then ruling over Italy; both rendered great services, and acquired immense influence on later Medieval writers, by carrying on important elements of ancient learning. Cassiodorus, commenting upon Paul, insists on the idea that kings got their powers from God (with the qualification, less frequently voiced, that only just commands by kings deserve obedience).

The Pope *Gregory the Great* (c. 540–604 A.D.) contributes, in his writings, to the survival of natural law thinking; he also supports the view that kings derive their prerogatives from God, subject to the standard qualification that unjust kings do not. *Isidore of Seville* (c. 560–636 A.D.) a learned prelate in Visigoth Spain, is another of the collectors and disseminators of ancient learning (works: *Etymologiae* and *Sententiae*): he develops a doctrine of the law of nature which is based upon – and mixes – elements of *jus naturale* and *jus gentium* as defined by the classical Roman lawyers.

The Carolingian Renascence – the progress made by arts and letters under the protection of the Frankish Emperor Charlemagne at the end of the 8th and beginning of the 9th centuries – is likely to be the most well-known and successful attempt to resist cultural decay in the dark centuries. Charlemagne tried to revitalize classical learning at the same time as he wanted to confer upon his new-founded Frankish Empire – he was crowned Roman Emperor by the Pope, in Rome, in the year 800 – some of the traditional dignity and splendour which was still attached to the idea of the old Roman Empire. Among Charlemagne's helpers and advisers in intellectual matters we find the learned Briton *Alcuin* (730–804 A.D.), a good latinist, and a prolific writer. Alcuin expresses a Christian natural law thinking without great originality but with a humane tendency which became of some practical importance insofar as it influenced Royal legislation intended to limit and ultimaltely abolish slavery. Natural law thinking is also found in the writings of another influential Carolingian churchman and scholar, *Rabanus Maurus* (776–856 A.D.). Finally, the learned Archbishop of Reims, *Hincmar*, adviser to the Emperors Louis the Pious and Charles the Bald, is of some interest because he stresses (although not consistently) the principle according to which legislation presupposes the consent of the king's subjects. This idea is very remote from the conceptions prevailing in the late Roman Empire, which gave the Emperor – *Dominus et Deus* – illimited powers of legislation. It is true that these powers were formally said to be derived from a *lex regia de imperio*, a piece of legislation by which the Roman people transferred, once and for all, its right to legislate upon the Emperor; but that *lex* was entirely fictitious – a last hypocritical bow from the absolute rulers of the Empire to the past glories of the popular assemblies of Rome.

When Hincmar of Reims stresses the importance of popular consent to legislation, he is not writing in the Roman tradition; his views are of Germanic origin.

8. The Germanic Element

Most of the barbarian tribes – in some cases, wandering Kingdoms – that overran the Western Empire in the course of the fifth century were of common stock; they belonged to the Germanic race. This is true of the Visigoths, who sacked Rome in 410, and then moved on through Southern France, helped the Empire against the Huns in 451, and finally settled in Spain, where the Arabs crushed them in the early 8th century. It is equally true of the Ostrogoths, established in Italy in the 5th and 6th centuries; almost exterminated by Justinian's troops in 563; of the Vandals, who settled in North Africa but were also crushed by Justinian; of the Langobards, who founded a Kingdom in Northern Italy towards the year 600; of the Franks, to whom fell present-day France, of the Burgundians in the Rhone Valley, the tribes that were to make up Medieval Germany, and the invaders of Roman Britain.

Did the Germanic elements contribute to legal thinking in a way sufficiently significant to retain us here? It should be said in the first place, quite emphatically, that there is plenty of evidence to show not only that the law meant as much, if not more, to the Germanic peoples as to the inhabitants of the Greco-Roman world. Moreover, there is also sufficient evidence to show that the Germanic peoples achieved a high level of legal development also where they did not come into contact with the Mediterranean civilization. Finally, it seems clear that on a number of important points, the attitude of these peoples to the law and to changes in the law was different from that of the Greco-Romans. Drastically simplified, the most important differences would seem to be the following two: (i) for a very long time, in particular in the case of those Germanic peoples which remained in their old territories or at least did not enter into direct contact with the Mediterranean world, it was held that "the Law" was an impersonal, unchangeable order, intimately connected with the life of the tribal community; the law was nobody's will, it was as old as the people, and no one had a right to change it; (ii) from the moment, and to the extent, changes of the law were admitted, they had to be approved by popular assemblies (*thing*), in principle by all free male adults. The King was a leader in war, and could be a leader in peace, but it was certainly neither his task nor his right to modify the law according to his own wishes.

These basic attitudes represent extremely important elements in European legal – and, perhaps even more, political, constitutional and ecclesiastic – history. This, however, does not necessarily imply that at the present juncture, they have a place in a history of legal thinking. For they were *attitudes* – possible to translate into words, as Archbishop Hincmar shows – not verbally developed bodies of principles, theories or rules. There was, in the early Middle Ages, very obviously a strong Germanic *influence* on legal thinking and legal solutions. But there was no such thing as a Germanic philosophy of law, and it would take a very long time before legal writers in countries with predominant Germanic tradition – usually reacting to what they considered to be "Southern," or "Roman" ideas and inventions – tried to formulate specifically "Germanic" ideas in questions of the kind we are dealing with here.

There is one more reason why the – verbally not very highly developed – Germanic elements did not find more energetic or clear expressions than, e.g., the opinions of Hincmar of Reims. That is the *revival* of the ideas of late Imperial Rome in matters of legislation. With the coronation of Charlemagne, it was widely held that the Empire had been restored, and to the Empire – as distinct from territorial kingdoms – belonged the prerogatives of the last, absolutist, *Domini* of Rome. After the decline and fall of the Carolingians, the Imperial dignity was conferred upon the German Kings. Otto the Great and his successors (c 950 A.D.); and Germany became the "Holy Roman Empire" – "of German nationality," that is true, but to medieval people, in particular medieval lawyers, the *political* unity of the West had been restored and with that, also the *legal* unity. We shall come back to this extremely important idea shortly. In this context, it is mentioned because it implied a powerful counterweight to the Germanic tradition.

Chapter 4

The High and Late Middle Ages

Selected Bibliography: A. Brimo, *Les grands courants de la philosophie du droit et de l'état*, 3e ed., Paris 1978, pp. 47–75; B. Brugi, "Il metodo dei glossatori bolognesi", in *Studi in onore di S. Riccobono*, Palermo 1936, pp. 21 ff; Fr. Calasso, *Medio evo del diritto*, Milan 1954; Y.C. Christie, *Jurisprudence, Text and Readings on the Philosophy of Law*, St. Paul, Minn. 1973, pp. 86–133; J.H. van Eikema Hommes, *Major Trends in the History of Legal Philosophy*, Amsterdam 1979, pp. 43–63; G. Fassò, *Storia della filosofia del diritto*, vol. 1, Bologna 1966, pp. 225–308, vol 2 Bologna 1968, pp.17–20, 77–91; J. Gaudemet, *La formation du droit séculier et du droit de l'église aux IV et V siecles*, Paris 1957; H. Kantorovicz, *Studies in the Glossators of the Roman Law*, Cambridge 1938; P. Koschaker, *Europa und das römische Recht*, 4 ed., Munich 1966; G. Otte, *Dialektik und Jurisprudenz. Untersuchungen zur Methode der Glossatoren*, Frankfurt am Main 1971; Piano Mortari, "Il problema dell'interpretatio juris nei commentatori", in *Annali di storia del diritto* II (1958), pp. 29–109 (Milan); K. Rode, *Geschichte der europäischen Rechtsphilosophie*, Düsseldorf 1974, pp. 67–91; Fr. K. von Savigny, *Geschichte des römischen Rechts in Mittelalter*, 2 Ausg., Heidelberg 1834–1851; M. Sbriccioli, "Politique et interprétation juridique dans les villes italiennes au Moyen âge", in *Archives de philosophie du droit* XVII (1972), at pp. 104 ff.; S. Strömholm, "Juristerna och tolkningsläran," in *Ideer och tillämpningar*, Stockholm 1978, pp. 81–106; same author, "Liljorna i Bologna", in *Svensk juristtidning* 63 (1978), pp 419–434 (Stockholm); J.W.F. Sundberg, *fr. Eddan t. Ekelöf*, Stockholm 1978, pp 39–73; M. Villey, *La formation de la pensée juridique moderne*, Paris 1968, pp. 104–272; A. Verdross, *Abendländische Rechtsphilosophie*, Vienna 1958, pp. 68–81; W. Ullman, *Law and Politics in the Middle Ages*, Ithaca 1975; Sir P. Vinogradoff, *Roman Law in Medieval Europe*, 2nd ed., Oxford 1929.

1. Introduction.

It is only in the most elementary textbooks of European history that the period commonly referred to as the "Middle Ages" appears as a monolithic block of time, with a clearcut beginning and an equally clearcut end. For the purposes of *political* history, the fall of the Roman Empire in the West (476 A.D.) is a reasonable starting point, but as already pointed out above, that date is far less useful when trying to draw a justifiable dividing line between the "ancient" and the "medieval" world in other respects: thus, e.g., the social and demographic structure characteristic of Greco-Roman antiquity, where towns, and town life, constituted the cultural, religious, commercial and political centers of the community, had at that date already been declining for centuries in the West and had gradually been replaced by forms of organization that are usually considered as typical for "medieval" feudal society: the fortified manor, occupied and defended by a great landowner, becoming more and more an essential basic element of the community. The religious structure and organization of Christendom was also "medieval" for at least a century before the end of the Western Empire. On the other hand, Greco-Roman culture survived, in the central parts of the Empire, long after Rome had fallen. And some elements of "medieval" civilization which we consider to be particularly typical do not really appear until half a millennium later: the crusades, the universities, the free cities, the leading position of the papacy, the specific life-style of chivalry.

It is even more difficult to find a generally acceptable date for the *end* of the Middle Ages. No doubt, a number of very important events took place between 1450 and 1550 A.D. – geographic discoveries that would fundamentally change the world conception of Western Europeans, the Copernican revolution in science, the Reformation, which put an end to the religious unity of the West, the invention of the art of printing – but on the one hand, it was to take a very long time before most of these events had a noticeable impact upon the everyday life of Europeans; on the other hand many economic, social, and cultural changes had been prepared, and had successively taken place, centuries before in the most advanced parts of Europe. There is a very great difference between these and the pheripheric areas, such as Scandinavia and North-Eastern Germany. Russia remained, essentially, outside the Western community throughout the Middle Ages.

For present purposes, the terms "High" and "Late" Middle Ages are used to denote, without any pretention to exactness, the period 900–1500 A.D.

It should be strongly emphasized that although there are some particularly important common features which justify us in discussing that period under a common name – the most important one being the existence of a *corpus Christianum,* the religious unity and the relative political unity of Western Christendom – even these features were continuously changing. There is, particularly in Protestant countries, much prejudice about the gloomy and fanatic uniformity of the Middle Ages in particular with regard to religion.[1] It is too often forgotten that in the span of time proposed above, the Catholic Church underwent changes that were just as dramatic, if not more, than in the last five centuries: from deep decadence in the 9th Century, the papacy, and the Church throughout Europe, rose to a never since rivalled position of intellectual splendour and political power in the 12th and 13th centuries; the crusades were but one expression of its strength; at the same time, the rise of the new mendicant orders – Franciscans and Dominicans – show that the virtues of humility and self-imposed poverty were not lost. Already at the beginning of the 14th century, a new period of decadence made itself felt; it led to the Great Schism, with several popes and antipopes fighting each other, and the "Babylonian Captivity" of the papacy at Avignon. In turn, this development gave rise both to local reform movements and to heresies but also to great councils of the Church held at Constance (1415 A.D.) and Basle (1431 A.D.).

In the field of ideas, including that of legal thinking, the High Middle Ages reconquered from oblivion two great sets of intellectual tools that were to shape Western Europe, and all countries and civilizations partaking of the European heritage, according to their pattern. These sets of tools were Roman law and Aristotelian philosophy. Both became more or less completely accessible to scholars in the course of the 12th century; both were received, with enthusiasm, as revelations from a world of a higher order: The term "renascence", which means "new birth", is just as apposite for this period as for the "revival" of secular classical learning three hundred years later. Of the two, Aristotelian philosophy was, in the course of the centuries, ousted from its position

---

[1] Mr. Jingle's reaction to the medieval castle of Rochester, Ch. Dickens, *Pickwick Papers*, ch. 2 (p. 82 in the Penguin edition of 1982) admirably resumes the vulgar 19th and 20th century Protestant view: "glorious pile – frowning walls – tottering arches – dark nooks – crumbling staircases – old cathedral too – earthy smell – Pilgrims' feet worn away the old steps – little Saxon doors – confessionals like money-takers' boxes at theatres – queer customers those monks – Popes, and Lord Treasurers, and all sorts of old fellows, with great red faces, and broken noses, turning up every day – buff jerkins too – match locks – Sarcophagus – fine place – old legends too – strange stories: capital. . ."

as the philosophy of all higher learning; Roman law survived, and still does, to a very great extent, although in many fields, its influence is no longer seen or recognized. One reason is simply ignorance; another is that the principles and solutions of Roman law have been modified, renamed; in some cases the word "rechristened" is particularly adequate, for one of the most important roads along which Roman legal science penetrated into the medieval and modern world was precisely the Law of the Christian Church, canon law. From the middle of the 12th century – some fifty years after *Corpus juris civilis* – the ever-increasing body of ecclesiastical law was made the object of systematic study and analysis. Methods, concepts, terms and indeed complementary solutions, principles and attempts at systematization were largely taken from the Roman lawyers; no other tools of similar quality existed. The Church lawyers – "Decretists" or "Canonists" – were philosophically schooled theologians, quite frequently with a much better theoretical training than contemporary secular lawyers. Moreover, the condition, and the laws, of the Church were subjects much more controversial than Roman private law. And just as, in modern times, armaments and wars tend to promote, with particular efficiency, scientific and technological progress, in the same way the brisk climate of controversy tended to sharpen the tools of thinkers and practitioners on both sides. Much later European constitutional and political debate had its roots in the way medieval Church lawyers used concepts, ideas, and formulae of secular Roman law as arguments in ecclesiastic controversy.[2]

2. Some Historical Background Facts

Between us and the Ancient World, there is the broad gulf of the "Dark Centuries" – not only an intellectual rupture, but also one of extensive physical destruction. Much material has been lost. In spite of wars and revolutions, no such breach separates us from the Middle Ages. The mass of available relevant material, although meagre in the first centuries, grows quickly the more we approach modern times. This

---

[2] This topic, which cannot be explored in the text, is dealt with briefly, but in a particularly convincing manner, in B. Tierney, *Religion, Law, and the Growth of Constitutional Thought 1150–1650*, Cambridge (Cambridge University Press) 1982.

means, for the purposes of this book, that we have to stick, more narrowly than when dealing with Antiquity (where, also, more general background information could be expected to be necessary) to the actual topic of our study: legal thinking. The delineation of that field is by no means easy: it is seldom enough to deal only with "the law" in the narrow technical sense given to that word today. There are vast areas, bordering on "general" philosophy, political science, sociology, and indeed theology, which cannot be left completely out of view. Political, social, economic and cultural history is obviously no less important for understanding fully medieval legal thinking than for following the growth of Greek, Roman, and early Christian thought; but all these branches of history – better known than with regard to the Ancient World (at least so we hope) and more complex, because closer to the eye and therefore visible in their various national ramifications – must either be left out or dealt with in a sweeping fashion that is unsatisfactory but inevitable.

The two leading actors on the scene of medieval Western Europe, from the 8th century onwards, were the Emperor and the Pope, each at the head of a unique organization: the Roman Empire and the Catholic Church. There is no need to point out the basic difference between these two bodies – when meeting, they embodied the still well-known concepts "State" and "Church" – but some points must be made as to their relative importance, strength, and claims in the medieval setting.

The "Empire" undoubtedly existed, but it existed on two levels; there was – and in the course of time turned out more and more to be – a considerable gap between them. Ideologically, the Empire was Rome resurrected: through the revival of the Imperial dignity under Charlemagne and later the German Kings of the house of Saxony, the *Imperium Romanum,* temporarily in abeyance, had come to life again; that State comprised the whole of Christendom (or at least the Christian Occident; the relations with the Christian East are a complicated matter which cannot be dealt with here), and was, simply, the only imaginable form of State for the Christian World until the end of time; it was also, as a matter of course, a legal unity; its legal system was Roman Law. But ideology aside, on the level of physical realities, the "Empire" was far less impressive. In terms of political and military power, it was composed of those territories where the King of Germany held sway: modern Germany, the Alpine countries, the Netherlands, parts – frequently varying parts – of Eastern France and Northern Italy. Within these vast territories there were provinces that "really" belonged to the Emperor – provinces where he was the hereditary ruler – others which, in the course of a rapid feudal dissolution, had other "direct" hereditary rulers but paid homage to the Emperor as their Suzerain; and finally a third group essentially composed of ecclesiastic fiefs (Archbishoprics, Bishoprics, Monasteries), which were of particular interest because they could not, by definition, become hereditary and the holders were thus appointed by the Emperor. In the course of the period now considered the forms for electing the Emperor were stabilized; seven of the territorial rulers of the "physical Empire" became electors; the Emperor was invariably taken from the great hereditary princes. From the end of the 13th centuries he belonged, with few exceptions, to the house of Habsburg, which had most of its inherited principalities in Austria, then a part of the Empire. The territories here described as the "physical" Empire did not, of course, coincide with the ideological Roman Empire; for most practical, including legal, purposes they were, from the late Middle Ages, the only "Empire" that existed. It retained its stately name, "The Holy Roman Empire of German Nationality" and its ruler claimed, still for some time after the end of the period, superior rank in relation to other worldly rulers.

These other rulers – and here we have to simplify drastically – were the Kings of the growing national monarchies: France, England, Portugal, the other kingdoms of the Iberian peninsula (later to be united into Spain), Bohemia, Hungary, Poland, and the distant Scandinavian monarchies, Denmark and Norway, Sweden (with Finland). The claims of these sovereigns were increasingly difficult to reconcile with the idea of an Empire comprising all Christendom; in the case of the northern and eastern monarchies, the idea was particularly difficult to accept since none of these kingdoms had ever belonged to the ancient Roman Empire. But even in the former provinces of that State, the increasingly powerful rulers, while paying, for the better part of the Middle Ages, some lip-service to the Emperor's claims of hierarchic superiority, were really completely independent in all matters of any importance (including that of waging war against the Emperor, when circumstances were held to call for it).

Like the Empire, the Church existed on different levels: in the first place, of course, ideologically, as the *corpus mysticum* of Christ but also, more tangibly, as a body of religious and, to an increasing extent, legal precepts and doctrines; further, as a complex hierarchical organization with the Pope as its undisputed head, archbishops, bishops, chapters, deans, parish priests and, besides the regular clergy, the monastic orders, some of which counted thousands of members all over Europe. The organization was kept together by Christian doctrine, canon law, and the general principle of obedience to hierarchic superiors which was an essential part of church discipline and which gave the highest dignitaries a great religious and political power. The religious power, in fact, did not only extend to the clergy and the orders; laymen also professed allegiance to the Church at least in matters that concerned basic religious tenets and the conduct of Christian life. In even more concrete terms, the Church also held great economic power; its wealth was essentially based on its right of taxation but also on land ownership or feudal land tenure; this in turn meant jurisdiction and direct power of command, in the capacity of suzerain, over great numbers of people. In terms of discipline and efficiency the Church was, with the exception of periods of decadence, superior to secular States, including the administratively week Empire. Churchmen were, at least until the middle of the period considered – when university-trained lawyers began to fill Imperial, royal, and princely government offices – better educated than their lay counterparts. There were always tensions within the Church: between the bishops and the Pope, between the regular clergy and the monastic orders, between prelates and parish priests. Heresies were seldom completely eliminated. Upon the whole, however, the Church was, throughout the period, the most powerful organized body in existence.

Considering their basically different tasks and claims, there was room both for the State, in particular the Empire, and for the Church. In the most flourishing periods of the Middle Ages, they cooperated peacefully. But their spheres of action and interests were close enough for conflicts to occur quite easily; indeed there were large overlapping areas. To the extent Church and State collided in matters concerning the salvation or damnation of souls, it was obvious, under the basic assumptions upon which medieval society was founded, that the claims of the Church had higher priority than those of the secular State. It was equally obvious – let us remind, here, of the unsolved conflict illustrated by St. Augustine's *De Civitate Dei* – that the Church could in fact legitimately claim leadership in vast areas of public policy. To these possible conflicts should be added those which could arise from the fact that the Church was a large landowner and holder of fiefs and, concomitantly, the fact that secular rulers, the German Emperor more than others, had a particularly strong interest in these ecclesiastic fiefs, since the nomination of their holders (based on their non-hereditary status) was one of his few remaining means of keeping together and controlling large states, like the Empire.

One of the great controversies that divided the Europeans of the High Middle Ages – and that ultimately caused incurable prejudice to both parties involved – was the "Investiture Contest". It concerned precisely the Emperor's right to appoint (to grant "investiture" to) the prelates who were, by virtue of their ecclesiastic office, holders of large Imperial fiefs. The Emperor's interest in these nominations was obvious; it was equally obvious, however, that from the point of view of strict Church law, this was an intolerable interference by the secular powers into ecclesiastic affairs. In terms of practical solutions, the Emperor was often best served by warlike and worldly-minded prelates; their appointment and activity could no doubt be in the interest of both State and people, but the Church had other criteria for eligibility to high ecclesiastic office. In the period of weakness and decay that had characterized the Church in the 9th and 10th centuries, the strong Emperors of the Saxonian dynasty had had their way; with Church reform and more active Popes, the question was brought to a head. In the second half of the 11th century, Emperor Henry IV and Pope Gregory VII were soon engaged in a lengthy conflict, which gave rise to much polemic writing where the claims of both parties were critically examined. At first, the Pope's weapon – excommunication – seemed successful: Henry submitted, in 1077, to penitence (the famous "march to Canossa"); once absolved, he took up the battle again. The conflict, which outlasted the lives of the two original opponents, did not lead to definite victory for either.

A hundred years later, a conflict arose between the Pope Boniface VIII and King Philip of France. Times had changed; the King managed to mobilize popular opinion on his side – a strong nationalistic element is already visible – and the conflict ended with total failure for the Pope, who was in fact made a prisoner for a short time by the officers of the French Crown. This controversy, like the Investiture Contest, gave rise to much polemic writing; it gave the

French King's Roman-law-trained civil servants an opportunity to state a number of important points concerning the relations between State and Church (and between the national monarchies and the Empire).

Important, for our purposes, because of the intense and fertile polemic activity they initiated, are also the "Great Schism" of the 14th and 15th centuries and the Councils of the Church in the late 14th and early 15th centuries. In the course of these, theologians and ecclesiastic lawyers, confronted with the problem of Church government in crisis situations with competing Popes, or no legitimate Pope at all, formulated principles of constitutional law, some of which survived and were used through centuries, e.g., in the internal conflict between King and Parliament in 17th century England.

On the level below Emperor and Pope, the leading persons on the medieval scene were the rulers of the kingdoms and principalities which emerged from the turmoils of the dark centuries and gradually developed through periods of feudal disintegration which differed greatly both in intensity and in length, from one part of Europe to another, into the national states of modern Europe, First, there was France, which became slowly, under royal leadership, a *political* unity in the course of the 12th to the 15th century but did not achieve *legal* unity until the reign of Napoleon I, in the first years of the 19th century. England, conquered by the Normans in 1066, had a shorter way to go before national unity was achieved; in the 14th and 15th centuries, England seriously threatened France. In Germany, the real winners, while the Empire struggled for at least a nominal survival, were the local princes: Austria, Bohemia, Bavaria, Saxony, the Rhine principalities, and in the East, Brandenburg, that was ultimately to become the most powerful of them all, under the name of Prussia. Medieval Germany expanded towards the East, moving the frontiers of Slav states until, at the end of the period, the Kingdom of Poland temporarily stopped the expansion; the German Emperor also held large Italian territories, while the rest of the Appennine peninsula was split up into small principalities – the Pope's domains being among the larger ones – and free cities. The reconquest of Spain from the Arabs was completed, slowly, towards the end of the period considered here, and the Kingdoms of Aragon, Castille, Leon, and Portugal became important members of Western Christendom. Late, poor, and peripheral members of that great family were Denmark and Norway, both unified Kingdoms from about 900, and Sweden, which emerges as a political unity in the 11th century, and soon after was to conquer and christianize Finland. In the South-East, the Kingdom of Hungary becomes, after 1000, the outpost of Catholic Europe against invaders from Asia. Greece and Asia Minor remain under the still surviving Roman Empire of the East (conquered by the Turks in 1453).

If the last centuries of the Ancient World were a long period of decay in most respects – including both culture and economy – the period from about 800 onwards is one of expansion, improved agricultural methods and results, increasing population, and intensified trade. By 1100, Europe, which had been threatened for half a millennium by the Arabs, strikes back: the Crusades are not only an expression of religious zeal, they also show that Europe had recovered sufficiently to grasp the initiative lost with the decline of the Roman world. A catastrophe which does not hit Europe only and which profoundly affects all areas of life was the Great Plague, or Black Death, which ravages whole provinces and cities in the decades round 1350; those parts of Europe which suffered most lost between one-third and half their population in a few years.

In retrospective, compared with modern development, the medieval world was, in spite of all the dramatic events that took place, a world of slow change. Everyday life in the countryside – and the vast majority of people worked for their scarce daily bread in the country – was seldom greatly affected by political changes. Scientific discoveries and ensuing technological changes, the two factors that are likely to have meant most for the radical transformation of the world since the latter half of the 19th century, hardly played any role at all; the results of slowly improved agricultural techniques showed themselves, essentially, in the increased capacity to feed a growing population – but always close to the starvation level.

3. The Contributions of Early Scholastic Philosophy

The bases of all higher education and intellectual culture in the Middle Ages had been laid in the days of the late "real" Roman Empire; the curriculum of studies hammered out at that time survived in those medieval institutions which were, in the period now under consideration, to develop into the first European universities. That curriculum comprised throughout the Middle Ages and well into the 18th century, the so-called seven "liberal arts." The three elementary arts, known under the common name of "trivium," comprised grammar, dialectics (corresponding, essentially, to the modern subject of logics) and rhetorics – a subject the core of which can be described as the art of persuasion (Cicero's *De inventione* being a standard textbook) but which included many old and new disciplines, such as forensic speech, letter-writing and similar branches of practically oriented "creative writing." In addition to the *trivium*, advanced students were taught the *quadrivium*, or the four "higher" liberal arts: arithmethics, geometry, astronomy, and music. The methods of teaching were lectures, where the masters commented upon classical texts, and disputations, intended to give the students an exercise in logical reasoning: problems were formulated, arguments for and against proposed answers were analyzed, and solutions were given. These methods, obviously similar to traditional legal reasoning, were undoubtedly apt to promote critical judgment; it should be stressed, however, that among the two acknowledged ultimate sources of knowledge – reason *(ratio)* and authority *(auctoritas)* – the latter, which might be based upon the Bible, Roman law, or the "Philosopher," Aristotle, held a dominant place. The purpose of learned discourse was not primarily to arrive at new knowledge and certainly not to undermine or even question authorities; it was to show the coherence and consistency of the traditional truths laid down in the authoritative sourses.

The intellectual tools used in this activity – in contradistinction to the stock of knowledge to which scholars could resort – were, essentially, the principles of Aristotelian logic. In the early Middle Ages, only the elementary parts of that body of laws for correct reasoning were known; in the 12th century, to a large extent by the intermediary of Arab writers, the more advanced parts of the "Philosopher's" writings in this field (as well as other Aristotelian works) were made accessible to scholars. Plato was less known, except through other writers, in the Middle Ages; at least one of his dialogues, *Timaios*, which exposes a complex and suggestive philosophy of nature, exercised a considerable influence upon some thinkers throughout the whole period.

The philosophy – indeed the whole scientific activity – of medieval schools and universities is commonly referred to as "Scholastics;" in the course of time, that term has acquired a somewhat deprecatory connotation. Although the system and methods of medieval university scholarship could undoubtedly lead into "disputation rage" and an exaggerated faith in barren logical subtility, Scholastic thinking achieved remarkable and lasting results in many fields. As a very general characterization, it may be described, with few exceptions, as a rationalistic school of thought, with a sometimes naive belief in the possibility to arrive at certain knowledge by the exercise of human reason. There can be no doubt about the strong, indeed decisive impact of Christian faith on Scholastic philosophy; it is just as important, however, to stress the fundamental importance of the Greco-Roman, rationalist undercurrent in the works of the leading Scolastics. The strongest evidence in favour of that contention is the importance attributed by these scholars to *the concept of natural law*. It is true that there was always a pretty strong fraction of philosophers who took a voluntaristic, rather than a rationalistic, view of the *lex naturalis:* they describe it as the will of God, as expressed in the Holy Scriptures. The adoption of the term "law of nature", however, illustrates the strength of the Greco-Roman tradition to which the Scholastics gave, in fact, a lease of life through a period in which strong counter-influences might otherwise have seriously threatened its survival.

Among early Scholastic philosophers, mention should be made, here, of four. *Pierre Abélard* (d. 1142), a scholar of the young university of Paris, was above all a logician; according to tradition, he took a naive pride in the possibilities of that science. Abélard is of interest here primarily because he would seem to be the first who uses – in a short passage where he gives a clearly rationalistic definition of the law of nature – the term "positive law" *(jus positivum)* to designate manmade rules. Abélard was an eager reader of Plato's *Timaios*. The influence of that dialogue – passing, since it was frowned upon by the Church which, not without reason, found traces of pantheistic heresies in the works of contemporary Platonists – is more strongly marked in a somewhat later writer, *William of Auxerre* (d.c. 1231) who operates a distinction between a "most universal," a "more universal," and a "special" natural law, the first being valid for all things, the other one for all living beings, the third for beings endowed with reason. A similar hierarchy reoccurs in the works of the English philosopher *Alexander of Hales* (d. 1245), the first European to make use of the recently "re-imported" parts of Aristotelian philosophy; he also draws a distinction between the implementation of natural law before and after the fall of man. At the same time, however, Alexander subscribes to the Aristotelian idea of a purpose-oriented "nature" – a basically optimistic idea which is far from the Jewish-Christian view of a creation contaminated by original sin.

Albert the Great, who taught at Paris and Cologne (d. 1280), has a right to be remembered because he was St. Thomas' teacher, and because he made decisive contributions to the introduction of Aristotle in the European learned world. Albert gives a special position to the law revealed by God in the Old and New Testaments, but he acknowledges a natural law which is the law of human reason and thus accessible to human understanding; the idea – sometimes voiced in Roman writing – that the natural law be based upon human *instincts* is rejected by Albert.

4. St. Thomas of Aquino

St. Thomas (1227–1274), of the noble house of the Counts of Aquino in central Italy, spent his whole life, from the moment he entered the Dominican order, in studies, teaching and scholarly writing. He was a pupil of Albert the Great in Cologne and Paris; for some time, he was Albert's successor on his Parisian chair of theology. Thomas spent his last years in Naples. Contemporary sources agree in describing him as a man not only of the greatest learning and scientific acumen, but also of a saintly character and deep personal piety.

Thomas is the author of a vast body of scholarly writings, of which his great *Summa Theologica* is the largest and most important work, both in general and for present purposes. Two other works should be mentioned: his commentaries on Aristotle's Ethics and Politics, and the short treatise in political science (or rather political ethics) *De regimine principum.*

Thomas is – to attempt a rough introductory characterization – an Aristotelian, a rationalist, an optimist and – perhaps the most noticeable quality in a modern reader's eye – in spite of his unworldliness, a man of admirable good sense, sound practical judgment, and moderation. The last-mentioned virtues are not without some connection with his preference for Aristotle, for whom these qualities were also typical.

The medieval thinker's Aristotelianism is evident not only in his frequent references to "the Philosopher", or in his doctrine of natural law – of which more will be said shortly – but also, and perhaps most fundamentally, in his adoption of the old Master's idea that nature, and everything in nature, has a goal and a purpose (entelechy), towards which the whole creation is thus continuously striving. In the case of the only species of beings endowed with reason – mankind – this goal-orientation, which in the case of other entities assumes the form of blind, instinctive growth, and activity, becomes a moral obligation to strive for self-perfection; that state, in the case of man, created after God's model, is the greatest possible similarity to God. In this idea, Thomas' Aristotelianism merges with his deeply personal, almost mystical piety.

The fundamental element in the complex, yet clear and well-structured "system of laws" which Thomas studies is the "eternal law", *lex aeterna,* which is identical with God's wisdom; that wisdom enlightens and leads God's will: whereas men's desires can be in conflict with their reason, will and insight are one in God – and constitutes, at the same time, God's "great plan" for the universe. God (and those to whom he has given the secret) is alone in possession of full knowledge about the *lex aeterna.*

However, a fraction of the eternal law is accessible to man, by virtue of his reason. That fraction Thomas calls "natural law" *(lex naturalis)*; it is thus not a subordinate, or "secondary", legal system in relation to the eternal law – it is an integral part of that more comprehensive body of rules.

What is the content of the natural law? What concrete rules can man formulate on the strength of his innate rationality? There has been considerable discussion concerning the specificity of Thomas' *lex naturalis.* Until quite recently, it was held by most Catholic scholars that the great theologian had envisaged a body of highly detailed, and at the same time immutable rules, in short a more or less complete "code of natural law". Modern scholarship tends to interpret Thomas in a different way: the law of nature, according to this view, which would seem to be supported by a considerable weight of evidence, has a very sweeping and general character; it is really a set of *goals* that men should try to attain rather than a body of precepts. *What course of action* the natural law prescribes in a given factual situation is thus a question that can be answered only upon examining carefully the individual conflict, and weighing the opposing interests and values. Guidance for the substantive evaluation is found in the *"natural inclinations"* of man; the instrument with which the evaluation is performed is *human reason.*

The "natural inclinations" are divided into a hierarchy of three: at the bottom, we find the instinct of self-preservation, which man shares with all entities; next comes the disposition for sexual intercourse and the rearing of offspring, natural to man and animals; finally, the third and highest stage reserved for man alone, as a rational being, is represented by the inclination to know God and to live in society. It follows from these definitions and from Thomas' general approach to the law of nature that whereas the fundamental elements of natural law – that one should do the good and shun the evil, and the principles of evaluating goals and inclinations – are universal and unchangeable, individual solutions may differ from one case to another. Rules can and should be considered only as standardized average solutions.

Within the general framework of the *lex aeterna*, of which the *lex naturalis* is a fraction, Thomas operates with another partial system, the "divine law," *lex divina*. This body of law, which has been characterized by modern scholars as "God's positive law," has two essential characteristics, which distinguish it from the law of nature: first, with regard to *substance*, it comprises those rules which are necessary for man's salvation, for the fulfilment of his *religious* duties; it regulates his activity as a citizen of the Kingdom of God, in contradistinction to his duties on the human and societal level, which are laid down by natural law; secondly, with regard to *form*, and *sources of knowledge*, the divine law is *revealed* in the Bible; otherwise it would not have been accessible to man, whose unaided human reason cannot penetrate into the mysteries of religion.

By introducing the notion of divine law, Thomas meets some of the most serious objections raised, from the days of St. Paul, against the possibility of reconciling the assumption of a natural law with such basic Christian ideas as that of God's grace, and Christ's work of redemption, being necessary for man's soul to be saved. Natural law, in Thomas' system, shows man the way to a righteous life on earth, a socially acceptable *secular* behaviour; for the completion of man's destiny on the *supernatural* level, God's grace is indispensible.

The last, and lowest, level in the hierarchy of legal systems established by St. Thomas is the "human law", *lex humana*, or "positive law" which, in order to be valid, has to be in conformity with the natural law (and, of course, the divine law); a positive enactment contrary to natural law is no longer law, Thomas affirms, in a famous passage – "it would be a corruption of law." The invalidity of unjust human laws is not total, however: in some cases, says Thomas, it may be preferable to obey an unjust law to avoid another evil, viz. public scandal. Basically, human law can be related to natural law in three ways: it can constitute a simple *conclusion* drawn from a natural law rule; it can give more *precise contents* to a general norm belonging to the law of nature; finally, it can be *added* to the body of rules existing in the law of nature, and thus fill out lacunae in that law, for the good of mankind. It should be added that it is in this context that Thomas deals with private property, which had caused early Christian thinkers considerable problems: private ownership was introduced, "by way of addition", since the law of nature knew only community of property. With Thomas, we are back at the Aristotelian idea that "justice" is basically a *social virtue* – it is exercised in relation to others, not as an element of intimately personal religion.

Upon the whole, Thomas is keenly aware of the societal function of law – of its character of *collective* solution of problems. The common weal *(bonum commune)* is a concept which, in his writings, gives legitimacy to human legislation and, consequently, draws up the limits of that legitimacy. "Common weal" is a battered expression, much abused by politicians and other wielders of power. Thomas is not of opinion that collective interests were *ipso facto,* by the sheer superiority in numbers of the collectivity, superior to individual interests. On the contrary, the *bonum commune* is defined as such public rules and institutions as are indispensible for individuals to achieve the moral goals set out for them. Thus, it is for the community to create the necessary framework of the good life, not to dictate or interfere with that life as such.

5. Later Scholasticism

St. Thomas was, and remains, the great "classic" of medieval religious and philosophical thinking, in the same way as Virgil is *the* classic *par préférence* of Roman poetry: they both represent a height of achievement and a harmonious blending of qualities that, as is generally felt, cannot be equalled, let alone surpassed, in that particular field.

The late Middle Ages is a period of intense intellectual activity in many fields. The serene harmony between Christian faith and Greco-Roman rationalism was, as classicism always is, a passing moment. New trends made themselves felt. Already towards the end of the 13th century, the Augustinian challenge, with its emphasis on God's will as the sole source of law, and its rejection of rationalism, was taken up by several important theologians and philosophers.

The three cornerstones in the reaction against Aristotelian and Thomist thinkers were *voluntarism, nominalism,* and *empiricism.* Voluntarism, i.e., the idea that all kinds of law including natural law, to the extent that concept is at all accepted, is an expression of will (Latin *voluntas*), not of reason, is heralded by the English Franciscan *Roger Bacon* (1212-c. 1292), whose most important contributions to philosophy concern natural philosophy but who also taught in the field of ethics. According to Bacon, there was no other "natural law" than that found in the Bible; thus natural law is revealed, and, Bacon adds, it can only be revealed to one single person, the legislator, whose commandments should neither be criticized nor even analyzed. Bacon is thus a forerunner of what was later to be called positivism: there is no other law than the *jus positivum* (on the term, cp. sec. 3 above), which has been enacted by some superior authority. A similar attitude is taken by another thinker, also a friar, and also of British origin, *John Duns Scotus* (c. 1270–1308), who rejects the Thomist assertion that God has issued to precepts of the Decalogue because they are good; according to Duns Scotus, the Ten Commandments are good because they express God's will. The only fetter upon the free exercise of the divine will is that it cannot contradict itself logically; it is, however, free to modify the contents even of its own basic precepts. There is, however, in Duns Scotus' writings, a certain hesitation before the most radical consequences of the theologian's own statements. Thus, he recognizes that the Ten Commandments are "obvious" principles of conduct, and his notion of "right reason" as guidance to morally acceptable behaviour retains at least something of the rationalist optimism and belief in man's ability to find ethical principles for himself.

The most radical critic of classical Scholasticism in our field – and a radical and fertile thinker in other domains – was the English theologian *William of Occam* (c. 1290–1349), whose extreme position with regard to the idea of natural law cannot be understood without at least a short reference to his commitment to the two other basic philosophic doctrines mentioned above: nominalism and empiricism.

Nominalism (from the Latin word *nomen,* "name") is, drastically simplified, the view that the general concepts under which we gather the individual members of a species, class, or group – e.g., "dog", denoting all animals answering to a certain description; "good", to classify a group of actions – have no independent existence of their own; they are nothing but "names", which man, in accordance with certain conventions, invents for the convenience of philosophic discourse. Reality, in the nominalist view, is nothing but the sum of individual things observed in nature. The opposite school are the *realists* (from Latin *res*, "thing"), according to whom general concepts have in fact a kind of existence of their own. *Empiricism,* frequently (but not by virtue of any logical necessity) opposed to *rationalism,* is the attitude, or view, according to which actual *experience* (usually, but not necessarily, by means of perception by the senses) is the unique, or at least the essential way of knowledge.

Occam, whose discussion of the notion of natural law is far from clear, takes a firm stand on an essential issue: the only source of law is God's arbitrary will; what He will, is just, however shocking it may seem to man; what is against His will is unjust, however attractive or even evident that course of action may seem from the point of view of human rationality. Reason does not in any way legitimize law of any kind; nor is it accepted as a means of obtaining knowledge about any law, "natural" or other. Knowledge about God's will can only be empirical knowledge of God's commandments. All "natural law" – for Occam cannot do without that time-honoured term – can be found, explicitly or implicitly stated in the Holy Writ.

By insisting upon a complete separation between human reason on the one hand, God's will on the other, Occam foreshadows both those future schools of thought that make a clear-cut division between the field of scientific knowledge, which is the domain of reason, and that of religious faith (and which consequently make the latter inaccessible to rational analysis) and, at a somewhat greater distance, those thinkers who study law as an entirely man-made, secular and basically arbitrary institution.

Occam is important for future legal thinking also in another, more technical respect. As has been shown by the French writer M. Villey, Occam – in one of the many controversies where that intensely active man took part – has contributed decisively to the development of the notion of "(subjective) right." In a quarrel concerning the very substantial wealth of his Order, the Franciscans, he develops, with great acumen, the difference between various kinds of rights, depending upon their actual contents, and the distinction between the factual "use" of the gifts bestowed upon the Franciscans – a use which could be without difficulty reconciled with the poverty to which the Order and its members had pledged themselves – and formal "rights" in the property concerned. There was nothing to prevent that, e.g., under a will or a gift, these two elements were separated and granted to different beneficiaries. Both by his subtle distinction between the "right as such" and such elements of a given legal situation as had earlier not been, as it were, "broken out" from the total position of, say, ownership, and by the way in which he outlined a systematization of private law with the different "rights" as essential elements, Occam is a pioneer (for a long time unnoticed) in legal science.

Voluntarism and nominalism – catchwords of a development which meant, in a wider perspective, the end of Scholasticism as a recognized "science," blending Christian theology and secular philosophic rationalism – were not the only schools of thought that were represented in the universities of the late Middle Ages. Rationalism not only defended itself in many quarters but also, in some cases, moved its positions forward, far beyond the limits set by St. Thomas. *Gregor of Rimini* (d. 1358), a pupil of William of Occam, elaborated a distinction between the "indicative law", the sole task of which was to *describe* rightful and wrongful actions, thus to fulfill an entirely "theoretical," or "rational" function, and the "imperative law" which contained one single command: to obey the indicative law. By this device, the law as "reason", expressed in the *lex indicativa,* and the law as pure volition, the *lex imperativa,* could survive, as it were, side by side.

Thomist rationalism survived (although neither alone nor free from attacks) as the standard school philosophy of Catholic theological studies; in that function, its position has been reinforced, since Thomism has been formally declared the official philosophy of the Catholic Church.

A first Thomist "renascence" took place in Spain in the 16th and early 17th centuries. Although this means breaking the chronological limits of the present chapter, it seems appropriate to deal briefly with the Spanish development in this context.

Rationalism carried far beyond Aristotelian and Thomist positions is voiced by *Fernando Vasquez,* whose work *Controversiae illustres* (1559) operates with two "layers" of law besides the positive legislation of individual States: the original *jus gentium naturale,* which came into existence with the creation of man and coincides with his "right reason" – considered, however, not as a general standard, but rather as an ability to pass sound pragmatic judgements on the social utility of actions and states of affairs – and the *jus gentium secundarium,* a set of rules based upon humanity's common experience and common practical needs. Vasquez' contribution to legal thinking is important also because he formulated a fairly comprehensive list of what may be called "human rights" derived from natural law and gave an unusually clear, narrow and lucid definition of the tasks of the State. Vasquez may be considered as one of the founders of that school of modern natural law thinking which broke away from the religious foundations of earlier doctrines to found its tenets essentially or exclusively upon pragmatic common sense.

More in line with original Thomist legal philosophy is the teaching of the Salamanca professor *Francisco de Vitoria* (d. 1546), who deserves attention also as one of the founders of modern public international law; his most famous contribution in that field is the work *Relectio de Indis,* where he claims, for the non-Christian peoples of the New World, the right to be treated as independent nations with the same legal position as Christian States. Vitoria's legal philosophy comes close to that of Thomas; "nature" has a divine purpose, and it is for "reason", enlightened by God's grace and revelation, to try to find, and realize in action, that purpose.

The last great Spanish thinker who can still be considered a follower of original Thomism was *Francisco Suarez* (1548–1617), who has equally acquired merit particularly by putting that philosophy to extensive use in the field of public international law, where he attempts to establish principles based upon the common weal of humanity as a whole.

Although the Spanish writers now mentioned never obtained the same recognition, as "fathers of the law of nations", as the Dutch jurist *Hugo Grotius* (cp. ch. 5 below), – two of the reasons being no doubt, that Occidental Christendom had already been split up by the Reformation, and that for centuries to come, the Protestant part of Europe, where Grotius belonged, advanced in power and intellectual influence at the expense of the Catholic South – there are reasons not to forget these last original representatives, in legal philosophy, of the homogeneous Greco-Roman-Christian world to which they still belong, together with Aristotle, Cicero, Augustine and St. Thomas. The

Reformation was the first, and one of the most important, blows that were ultimately to break that world into pieces.

6. The Glossators

The history of legal thinking is hardly – is in fact far less than the history of substantive law and legal institutions – a field characterized by sudden and dramatic events. Yet, there are exceptions. The most remarkable one would seem to be that development – we are in fact entitled to speak about a revolution – which took place in the town of Bologna in the last decades of the 11th and first decades of the 12th century.

Some time at the beginning of that period (the official chronology indicates the year 1088), a university graduate in "the Arts" (today we would say philosophy) called *Irnerius* began to lecture on the *Corpus juris civilis* of Justinian. For about one century and a half, Irnerius and his successors, called the *glossators* – among whom we mention five: the "four doctors" Bulgarus, Martinus, Hugo and Jacobus, all of them teaching at Bologna in the 12th century, and Accursius, the last great glossator, active in the 13th century – lectured and, as a basis for their teaching, wrote increasingly detailed, subtle and learned notes, so-colled *glossae*, on the interpretation of the text of the *Corpus juris*.

This peaceful activity merits the dramatic name of revolution for many reasons. For the first time after the fall of the old Empire, *Roman law* was studied in the original texts, and was studied for its own sake, not as an element in the teaching of rhetoric. For the first time, a free institution of learning opened its doors to the world at large: the European, and consequently also the American, *university* was born. Bologna, the first of these seats of learning – soon to be followed by Paris, Oxford, Cambridge, and others – grew at a rate which would be impressive even today: half a century after Irnerius commenced his teaching, there were about 10,000 students in the city; among these, there was a large proportion of mature men in good, sometimes even high, positions in Church and State. A few generations later, the scene of Occidental public life had acquired a new actor, who was to remain on the scene; and who still does: the learned, *university-trained lawyer*. Finally, the revival of the study of Roman law at Bologna, and the explosionlike propagation of that study and that law throughout Medieval Europe, exercised a decisive influence on the frame of mind of the modern Occident: it developed, to an extent unknown in any other comparable civilization, *legalistic, rationalistic,* and *formalistic* patterns of conflict-solving, decision-making, acting upon people's behaviour, arguing, writing, and even thinking, in matters public and indeed, very largely, also private.

To quote an eminent German scholar: the jurisconsults of Bologna "were the first in Europe who learnt, from the great Roman lawyers, the art of solving the vital problems of human coexistence not as prisoners of irrational customs or by violence but through an intellectual discussion of the isolated legal problem and in accordance with a general rule laid down to solve the problem as such. This new claim of the lawyers has made the public life of Europe legal and rationalistic until our days. . . By establishing a rational principle which took – at least *inside* States – the place of violence in settling human conflicts, legal science has created one of the most essential prerequisites for the progress of culture in the material sense, in particular of the science of administration, of the rational economic society, and even of the mastering of nature by means of technology which is characteristic of the modern era."[1]

This is not the place for a general description, or analysis, of the contribution of the Bolognese school of law, and of other medieval faculties, to the general development of law in the West. That subject belongs to legal history rather than to historical jurisprudence. What is of interest here are two elements in the work of the Glossators: their basic legal philosophy, to the extent they had any, and their methods of legal reasoning, in particular of statutory interpretation.

It would not seem to be unfair to state, very briefly, that the mastering of the Justinian text gave the Glossators enough work. They had neither the inclination nor the ability to develop, in addition to the arduous task of understanding and exposing, a legal philosophy of their own. They took what they found in the *Corpus juris,* and that, as we have already stated (ch. 2, sec. 5), was essentially a collection of commonplace expositions of current ideas about the function of law and justice, and about the fields of application of natural law, the law of nations (in the Roman sense: *jus gentium*), and Roman civil law.

However meagre the philosophical fare thus offered to the first generations of medieval lawyers, they received it with veneration. It

---

[1] Fr. Wieacker, *Privatrechtsgeschichte der Neuzeit,* 2nd ed., Göttingen 1967, p 69.

should be remembered that in the Middle Ages, the two commonly recognized sources of knowledge were *reason* and *authority*, the latter source being, in the first place, God's revealed words in the Bible. Roman law, as handed down in the Corpus juris, could of course not claim to be a revealed legal system in the same way as the Decalogue. Nevertheless, once reconstructed and reconquered, the Justinian text in its heavy majesty seems to have been regarded with a respect which comes quite close to that bestowed upon a Holy Writ, and in actual fact, it was treated very much in the same way. Its authority was never questioned; the task of the interpreter was to use all his learning and cleverness for the purpose of understanding and of making the sometimes fairly obvious contradictions "fit." This complete and unquestioned authority of the Roman material is one of the foundations of all medieval legal science: the task of reason, i.e., for all practical purposes, logic, was not to question or to criticize – it was to create good order, and if possible an overview within a ready-made, sacrosanct and eternally valid body of rules. At Bologna, legal science became *dogmatic* in the same way as theology; it is not fortuitous that the term "dogmatic," which has in most other contexts a slightly pejorative ring, as well as the word "doctrine", became and still are neutral and frequently used terms in Continental legal science.

One prerequisite for the authoritative character of the Justinian codification has already been touched upon (sec. 2 above): the conviction that the *Roman Empire* had been called into life again, that it embraced the whole of Christendom, and that consequently, Justinian's law was unquestionably valid as the law of the land. It was in the nature of things that the legal scholars of Bologna were, and remained for a long time, particularly strong and convinced advocates of the Emperor's claims. Irnerius, the founder of the school, seems to have paid for his allegiance to the secular head of State with a period of excommunication. And at the famous Diet of Roncaglia, in 1158, the great "four doctors" unanimously supported Emperor Frederick Barbarossa's claim that he had a right of taxation over the – otherwise already almost independent – cities of Northern Italy. Later on, however, with the decline of Imperial power in Italy, the lawyers took different sides in the lengthy and increasingly confused controversies between Emperor, Pope, and city-communes. However, the strong emphasis on a centralized State, with unlimited power, which was an essential element in the heritage from the late Empire, and clearly expressed in the Corpus juris, became an integral part of the "political philosophy" of the legal profession. It is needless to add that these ideas were just as welcome in the chanceries of kings, princes, prelates and free cities as they were with the German Emperor: in fact, the State conception of the late Empire, developed and glorified by the learned jurists, became one of the most powerful intellectual arms with which national rulers fought feudal lords, assemblies of commoners, and other elements that made opposition against the modern bureaucratized and centralized State in its early days. We shall see in what follows, however, that Roman law could also offer arguments for constitutional rule – but these were neither as close at hand nor as clear as the arguments for autocratic rule.

If such were the lessons of political philosophy given by the glossators, the question should be asked whether, and if so, to what extent these ideas were reconcilable with the natural law philosophy predominant among theologians and philosophers at the time when the school of Bologna was founded and went through its first triumphant century. It is obvious, by way of answer, that no opposition between Roman law and the law of nature was felt to exist throughout the Middle Ages. It should be remembered, in this context, that the late Roman law studied at the first law faculties was at least formally and superficially Christian, and that it was at any rate strongly coloured by stoic natural law thinking. In fact, the university-trained lawyers, from Bologna or elsewhere, who returned to their countries of origin, with sometimes indeed chaotic legal systems of mixed Germanic and Roman origin, considered themselves as the spokesmen of a rational "law of nature." The Roman law taught at the universities seemed vastly superior, not only from an intellectual, but also from an ethical point of view. Roman law was claimed – and the first to support that pretention were obviously the lawyers – to be *ratio scripta*, "written reason," i.e., according to most contemporary philosophical doctrines, a codification of the rationalistic law of nature.

The methods of reasoning of the glossators still remain, to a large extent, unexplored by modern research. It was only quite late that these questions began to attract the interest of scholars. One of the reasons for this may be that the technique of the early medieval jurists was so generally adopted – although, obviously, successively modified – by later generations of lawyers that it was very largely taken as a matter of course; it became an everyday tool, and nobody took much

The High and Late Middle Ages

interest in underlying theoretical assumptions. Another probable reason for the neglect of scholars may be that from the Renascence onwards, legal philosophers and lawyers taking a special interest in methodological questions (as opposed to practical lawyers, who went on using and perfecting the tool) tended to look down upon medieval law, its scholastic character, subtle distinctions, and sometimes exaggerated logical niceties; it was not considered a subject deserving serious study. It was only with the advent of historicism in the 19th century that legal scholars began to take a scientific interest in the working methods of their colleagues in the 11th, 12th and 13th centuries.

Any discussion of medieval legal reasoning must be based on a realistic appreciation both of the "external" aspects of their work – what kind of writings did they purport to produce and for what purpose? – including quantitative aspects. What the first three to five generations of European legal scholars actually did was to write commentaries on *Corpus juris* texts, literally in the margin of these texts. After a couple of generations, a competent law teacher would start, when discussing a given passage in the *Corpus,* with his predecessors' commentaries, ending by adding his own criticism and suggestions. A good illustration of the quantity of work thus performed is offered by a famous early manuscript in a library in Munich. On 416 pages, this manuscript contains not only the Justinian text but also between 30,000 and 40,000 items of commentary, ranging from very short notes to lengthy *exposés*. In some pages, the text is surrounded by close to 300 such notes. Another example, which conveys an idea of the amount of work performed by the glossators is the *arbor actionum* ("Tree of actions") of the 12th century law teacher Johannes Bassianus, who elaborated a table comprising – in two large handwritten pages – a network, or rather a kind of "chessboard," with 180 boxes. Using a system of symbols of his own invention (based upon the letters a-m, to which were added one to four dots in different positions and combinations), Johannes describes 169 different forms of action known to Roman law; modern scholars have made the computation that if the information thus pressed into the two pages were written out in full, the system of symbols would correspond to some two thousand sentences, many of them quite complicated.

As their name indicates, the glossators devoted their efforts to "glosses", margin commentaries. It is true that in the very voluminous

– and still to some extent unexplored – mass of texts from the 12th and 13th centuries, there are writings that express at least some ambition to carry the work further, to formulate more general rules, to combine and to systematize. The lengthy notes on particularly difficult or important passages tended to grow into independent treatises. Upon the whole, however, this development did not go beyond a trend increasing in force. Towards the middle of the 13th century, something like a crisis of overfeeding in legal science occurred. The basic work – the interpretation and analysis, section by section, of the *Corpus juris* – had been performed. Practical needs and new intellectual developments called for a complete reorientation of the work of legal scholars. At that time, the last great glossator, *Accursius,* merged and presented, with his own work, the contributions of the glossator school in what came to be known as the "Standard Gloss" *(Glossa ordinaria);* this immense textbook became, in practice, more influential than the Justinian text itself. Courts and jurists tended to use it for centuries as a combined statute book and textbook.

As for the methods of reasoning adopted by the glossators, it would seem to be clear that 12th and 13th century lawyers did not establish, and did not attempt to establish, complete "systems" for that activity which held the undisputed central position of their work: the interpretation of statutory texts. They confined themselves to making up non-systematic, enumerative catalogues of admitted interpretation procedures. To the extent methodological questions were at all deliberately taken up for treatment in their own right, isolated examples were discussed and opposing solutions were compared, taking into account their respective practical drawbacks and advantages. In these discussions we already find, in fact, both many or most of the problems debated ever after, and much of the still used terminology in the field: the relative weight of *words* as opposed to *intentions,* the use of extensive and restrictive interpretation and of analogies.

A major question concerning the methods of reasoning of the glossators upon which modern writers are in disagreement is whether these early legal scholars were using only that rather primitive logic (dialectics) which had been carried on, in unbroken tradition, as an element of the *trivium* programme, by the compilers of the dark centuries from the late Empire, or whether they had also adopted at least the elements of that more sophisticated Aristotelian logic which had been successively rediscovered and reconquered in the course of a long development essentially terminated in the early 13th century and which had characterized Scholastic thinking in its heyday and thus given decisive impulses to all later European philosophy. Research carried out in the last ten to twenty years would seem to support strongly the view that some methods characteristic for Scholastic dialectics – such as the frequent and highly developed use of classifications *(divisio)*, specific techniques of definition, and a manner of arguing based on Aristotle's doctrine of "topics," – played an increasingly important part in the writings of the glossators. One of the leading scholars in this highly specialized field of research, G. Otte, resuming his results, has pointed out that the glossators represent an intermediary stage between the scientific – "geometric" or "axiomatic" – methodology of later legal reasoning, and the older tradition based upon the ancient art of rhetoric. Rationalistic natural law thinking as well as later Roman law methodology (from the 17th century onwards) tried to make room for legal reasoning among the natural-science-oriented, or rather mathematical, branches of science. They endeavoured to find and define basic legal concepts which should bring the small, partial systems of legal concepts together into all-embracing systematic structures – if possible into one single great system. The next step was to formulate general propositions applicable to the whole area covered by the basic concepts and to derive all specialized propositions from these generalities. The glossators – and indeed, as we shall soon show, also their successors, the commentators – were obviously still very far from that development.

The question of the philosophical foundations of early medieval legal reasoning may seem, at first, both remote, narrowly technical, and of small importance from a theoretical and – even more – a practical point of view. It is submitted that precisely because so much of the methods of reasoning adopted by the early university teachers in law and university-trained jurists quickly and unnoticeably grew into silently accepted, seldom taught and seldom criticized habits of the legal profession, the basic theoretical assumptions upon which these methods were founded – deliberately or, more probably, without much conscious reflection – are essential for understanding many problems concerning legal reasoning (and, indeed, legislative technique) which have retained their practical importance to this day. If, as the best evidence now tends to show, the glossators worked with Aristotelian logic, it must be remembered that that science was *not* designed to meet the needs of practical decision-making but had been elaborated for the purposes of theoretical analysis. The theory and practice of syllogism as the major form of correct conclusions which was adopted by the glossators and brought forward to posterity without any critical discussion tended, well into present days, to hide from lawyers the fact that they are engaged in practical decision-making, inevitably based upon evaluation, not in the testing of the correctness of propositions about facts nor in the complete and consistent classification of such facts. The Aristotelian theory of definitions, and the procedure consisting in systematizing concepts and objects in sharply delimited classes characterized by specific class-determinative attributes also became, and remained until recently a straitjacket which made it particularly difficult to handle facts which were likely to be more profitably studied in terms of "type," or "model," cases, connected by transitional, or intermediary, cases without clearcut limits between them.

7. The Commentators

In philosophy, the late Middle Ages brought important changes: Aristotle's and St. Thomas' rationalism gave place to the radical voluntarism of Bacon and Occam; the rift between faith and reason which was ultimately to destroy the well-ordered universe of classical Scholasticism (as early Christianity had destroyed the rational Greco-Roman world, and St. Augustine had destroyed the sunny and placid rationalism that had again grown strong in his days) was becoming wider and wider, although still not apparent to most observers.

There was no corresponding break in the development of legal science. The glossators had brought their contributions; Occidental lawyers now mastered, in all its details, the Justinian codification, as good craftsmen master their tools. The task of the already highly influential legal profession was now to put the tools to active use, in particular to find, on the solid foundations of Roman law, solutions to the conflicts and problems of their own world. That activity, in turn, presupposed an effort to put Roman law rules into a larger systematic context, to draw general principles out of the scattered dicta which were still predominant in Justinian's Code, to transplant viable Roman private-law solutions into other fields, to invent or improve the conceptual apparatus needed for handling the legal tools.

It is common to use the terms "commentators," or "postglossators," for those lawyers who, from the middle of the 13th century to the end of the Middle Ages, carried out the task just outlined. The revolutionary or "explosive" era of European legal science was over. The university-trained lawyers had conquered their positions as a leading element both in government offices, in courts, and in council chambers. Roman law was gradually becoming – by a remarkable process commonly known as "the reception" – the law of the land in the German Empire and in some other areas. Roman law was being taught at a great number of universities, from Prague in the East to Oxford in the West, and from Uppsala in the North to Coimbra in the South. Some of the founders of late medieval legal thinking – in addition to the philosophers and theologians we have already mentioned – were Frenchmen, but the most eminent ones were still Italians, such as *Bartolus of Sassoferrato* (1314–1357) and *Baldus degli Ubaldi* (1320-c. 1400).

Among the pressing needs which the commentators had to meet, a particularly important one was to find solutions to the legal problems arising from the existence not only of national states completely independent of the Empire in all practical respects, but also of smaller unities, such as the Italian (later on German and Flemish) free cities; all of these issued their own laws, competing with the Justinian codification. This was essentially a political question; from the discussions, still technical in appearance, of the relationship between imperial and local legislation emerges, still embryonic, the modern international law concept of "sovereignty." The notion of "jurisdiction" as a name for political and legal power, in contradistinction to ownership or other private-law positions, similarly emerges from the complicated web of feudal legal terms and ideas.

As for the *philosophical* aspects of late medieval legal science, what has been said of the Roman lawyers and of the glossators remains true: the commentators were essentially technicians, although they were called upon, more frequently than their immediate predecessors, to use their art in issues with broader implications. "Lawyer", and "philosopher," or even "legal philosopher," were already two distinct specialized professions.

The characterization given above of the methodology of the glossators would seem to remain essentially valid also for the commentators (and indeed, for many practitioners of the legal craft well into the 18th and 19th centuries). They did not invent a complete system for the interpretation of texts, which remained their most frequent and cherished occupation. No doubt, they developed and refined the logical apparatus for the scholarly treatment of law, i.e., for the presentation in treatises of vast masses of rules and for the handling of individual cases; the art of making subtle distinctions and finding subdivisions reached peaks unknown in the past. On the other hand, they did not in any decisive way abandon the commentative method in order to present or discuss rules in the framework of extensive, logically structured "systems". The "axiomatic" stage of development (p. sec. 6 above) was still far away. Nor did the commentators suffer considerations of a systematic or logical kind to influence the treatment of cases with the use of authoritative texts.

Four characteristics, a modern writer says, were particularly typical for interpretation in the period of the commentators. In the first place the techniques of interpretation were *open*, i.e., the list of accepted interpretative procedures was never closed; secondly, there was a strong tendency to organize the different procedures in hierarchic order; thirdly, to each procedure, or "trick," corresponded – as equally possible – its opposite; at last, interpretation was carried out, and conceived of, in the traditional and well-known form of argumentation.

The openness is well illustrated by the frequently used lengthy – indeed, never-ending, and therefore elusive – lists of procedures, each of them provided with a special, although not necessarily very clear, name: *correctio, abrogatio, declaratio, expositio, additio, derogatio, prorogatio. . .*" No wonder that one of the leading commentators, Baldus degli Ubaldi expresses an attitude of doubt, or even resignation: "This term, "interpretation", is ambiguous in our legal language."

Against this background it may be said, without undue cynicism, that the arsenal of interpretative procedures inherited from late antiquity and further developed by scholastic university men had at least one clear function: to *legitimate* the one or the other decision, as obtained by means of "legitimate" arguments or models of arguing known under the name of "interpretation". This description is not unduly cynical, for it must be remembered that the lawyers did not enjoy complete liberty: they were acting, normally, against each other, and had to convince other lawyers; standards of professional competence were undoubtedly important correctives. Moreover, the above-mentioned tendency to organize arguments and interpretative procedures in hierarchic order also offered at least some protection against pure arbitrariness.

Practical reasons forced the commentators both to develop the concepts of legal science beyond what was needed to master the *Corpus juris* and also to create more sophisticated lists of interpretative procedures. One of these practical reasons was that they found themselves in a far more complicated situation, with regard to the sources of law, than did their predecessors. For besides – in principle below – Roman law, which was frequently described as the *"general"*, or *"common"* law *(jus commune)*, there grew up an extensive body of *local* law. Such law had, of course, always existed, but with the emergence of the national states and of free cities and similar political units, that claimed sovereignty within their territory, the problem of the relationship between Roman and local law became more accute. We shall not deal here with the solutions suggested to deal with the question. Suffice it to say that no *theoretically* satisfactory solution was found or could indeed be found. What is of particular interest for present purposes – it provides a good illustration of the methods of work and habits of thought of the commentators – is that they discussed at length, item by item, whether and to what extent the interpretative procedures, and the hierarchy of such procedures, applicable in the implementation of the Roman law texts possessed the same validity in respect of local laws. It was, in particular, the legislation – in the form of *statutes* – of the progressive and highly developed free cities of Northern Italy that was made the object of this careful analysis.

Towards the end of the period we are now dealing with, the first systematic treatises on the art of statutory interpretation are published in Italy: the scattered discussions of this art in glosses, commentaries, and treatises had come to make up a sufficiently voluminous body and the arguments put forward had become so complex – at the same time as a stabilization and normalization had taken place – that the field was ripe for specialist treatment. At the end of the 16th century, these existed a substantial body of monographs on the interpretation of statutes, or even on some special element of that art. These works, although in many cases both interesting and valuable, resume the time-honoured maxims of interpretation elaborated in the course of five centuries; they do not attempt to analyze critically or to reform the interpretative theories, methods and procedures generally adopted by lawyers. However, the very idea of describing in detail, and with an effort at systematization, the interpretation of the law certainly reflects, as a specialist has put it, a need for critical reflection on the basic conditions of intellectual activity.

It should be added, by way of conclusion, that although medieval legal science spread rapidly over Europe, there remained some countries which retained – largely because of their peripheric location or old-fashioned structure and culture – considerable independence in relation to the Roman law and the theories and methods connected with it. This "originality" does not mean, of course, that the countries concerned would have developed original patterns of legal thinking for themselves, and even less that they would have created their own philosophy of law. On the other hand, what was certainly looked upon by medieval lawyers – in most cases rightly so – as backwardness and lack of legal culture, could give pre-Roman, Germanic elements of legal thinking a chance of survival which did not exist in the more central, and more deeply Romanized, parts of Christendom.

Originality of the kind now referred to could be claimed by Scandinavia, in particular Sweden; it is not by chance that Sweden and England are the only two countries where parliamentary institutions have been functioning, without interruption, from the high or late Middle Ages onwards. In these countries, the Germanic idea that the law of the land was essentially a body of immutable customary rules, binding upon the King as well as upon the subjects, seems to have possessed greater strength and to have survived essentially intact (although in these early days rather as an attitude, or an implicit assumption, than as an explicit doctrine), whereas the autocratic ideology of the late Empire, according to which the Prince is above the law, exercised a powerful influence in most European countries. Neither Scandinavia nor England produced, in the Middle Ages, any writing that can claim the rank of contributions to legal philosophy, but it should be noted that already the earliest writers on the English common law – Glanvill in the 12th, and Bracton in the 13th century – insist on the validity, as legal rules, of the customs of the land. Bracton goes further; although deeply influenced by the glossators, whom he quotes freely, he goes out of his way to refute the Justinian maxim "what pleases the prince, has the force of law;" it is only what the King has decided with the council of the magnates of the realm that can claim this dignity. Indeed, the King's own position comes from the law; and law is necessary for a state in the proper sense to exist.

8. The Canonists

From quite early days, the Church was a law-producing body. And unlike the Roman Empire, the law of which was found, frozen as it were, in the *Corpus juris* – however energetically Frank and German kings and Bolognese lawyers claimed that the Empire was still alive – that body went on issuing new provisions adapted to the changing needs of the times.

The most important form of ecclesiastic legislation were the so-called *decretal letters* or decretals (*epistola decretalis*) of the successive Popes. The oldest extant letter of this kind dates from the end of the 4th century. The decretals are strong evidence both of the early monarchic ambitions of the Papacy and of the influence exercised by the administrative and legal tradition of the late Empire upon Church government: the decretal letter goes back, in form and function, to the rescripts, or letters, of the Roman Emperors. The papal decretals were, from the beginning, acknowledged in principle as law by the Western Church, whereas the East refused to grant them that status. Other important sourses of ecclesiastic law were the decisions of councils, royal ordinances and decrees dealing with Church matters (in particular the so-called *capitularia* of the early Frank Kings).

Private collections of those texts which were considered to belong to the body of valid Church law – including a couple of famous forgeries, such as the Pseudo-Isidorian Decretals from the 9th century, aimed at strengthening the position of pope and Church as against the secular powers – had been circulating for several centuries when an Italian monk, Gratianus, who taught ecclesiastical law at Bologna, gathered and edited, about 1140, the collection originally called *Concordia discordantium Canonum* (*Harmony of discordant canons*); it soon was to be called simply the *Decretum*.

Canon law continued to grow; indeed, it still grows as the Catholic Church changes. Additional collections of texts have been added to Gratianus' original edition. However, already in his life-time, a school of canon law came into existence at Bologna, besides the school of secular Roman law. The canonists took their place, as learned specialists, in medieval society. If the Roman-law trained secular jurists rapidly became, as a body, highly successful and influential, the same judgment is true – possible even more true – about the canonists. From about 1200 onwards, for about 300 years, a great proportion of the Popes were ecclesiastic lawyers, and legislation became, for centuries, one of the foremost occupations of the papal see.

It is hardly an exaggeration to say that the medieval Church – reflecting, like so many other bodies and institutions in the later Middle Ages, the immense intellectual impact of Roman law – completed, with the rise of the canonists, a development towards extreme legalism which had already been foreseeable in earlier centuries. It is significant, an expert says, that the first decretal in the *Liber Extra,* an official collection, or "law-book," issued in 1234, fixes the contents of Christian faith in terms of law.

Church law reflects, more explicitly and more clearly than secular legislation – for the learned theologians that were experts in canon law cared rather more than their secular brethren for ideologies and doctrines – the development not only of religious, but also and particularly, of political and constitutional ideas in the Middle Ages (and onwards). A notable feature is the conciliar law, i.e., the texts produced by the great Church councils convoked in the early 15th century to put an end to the Great Schism and to decide on Church government in a situation when the papacy did not function properly. This body of Church law expresses radical ideas about the people's political and legislative sovereignty and also about the Church as a corporation (this is where Roman private law principles offered solutions of great importance for further constitutional debates). Upon the whole, the great era of the canonists (coinciding roughly with the years 1150–1500) can be considered as unique in the sense that there has hardly been any other period in Occidental history when an intellectual *élite* has exercised such a continuous, massive, and direct influence upon a great center of political power; scholarship and power never worked so closely together for such a length of time; in fact, brilliant canon law scholarship *meant* power. Our picture of medieval legal thinking would not be complete if the existence, special features, and influence of canon law were not briefly mentioned.

With regard to *teaching methods* and *legal reasoning,* the canonists borrowed whatever they needed from the secular Bolognese jurists. It cannot be denied, however, that – living in contact with the ever-developing living body that was the Church, and called upon to produce ideologically and practically acceptable solutions to the problems involving that body, both internally and in relation to the world outside – the canonists, who usually had a solid theological training, soared higher than their secular brethren.

If the canonists were inventive and acute thinkers in constitutional matters, they were less original and less creative with regard to *legal philosophy* in the narrow sense of the word. Gratianus endorses, obviously without giving much attention to the problem involved, different and contradictory theories of natural law in the short passages he devotes to this kind of questions. As a general statement, however, it would seem that the canonists had a special preference for the *rationalistic* variants of the neutral law doctrines.

Chapter 5

The Transition to the Modern Era (1500–1650)

Selected Bibliography: A. Brimo, *Les grands courants de la philosophie du droit et de l'état*, 3ᵉ éd., Paris 1978, pp 76–116; G.C. Christie, *Jurisprudence. Texts and Readings on the Philosophy of Law*, St. Paul, Minn. 1973, pp. 133–158, 292–357, 872–918; J.H. van Eikema Hommes, *Major Trends in the History of Legal Philosophy*, Amsterdam 1979, pp. 69–81; G. Fassò, *Storia della filosofia del diritto*, vol. 2, Bologna 1968, pp. 7–160; Lord Lloyd of Hampstead, *Introduction to Jurisprudence*, 3rd ed., London 1972, *passim*; P. Koschaker, *Europa und das römische Recht*, 4th ed., Munich 1966; S.F.C. Milsom, *Historical Foundations of the Common Law*, 2nd ed. London 1981; K. Olivecrona, *Rättsordningen*, 2nd ed., Lund 1976, pp. 21–34; V. Piano Mortari, *Aspetti del pensiero giuridico del secolo XVI*, Naples 1970; K. Rode, *Geschichte der europäischen Rechtsphilosophie*, Düsseldorf 1974, pp. 92–116; G.H. Sabine, *A History of Political Theory*, 3rd ed., London 1952, pp. 285–437; S. Strömholm, *Idéer och tillämpningar*, Stockholm 1978, pp. 107–119; J.W.F. Sundberg, *fr. Eddan t. Ekelöf*, Stockholm 1978, pp. 77–115; A. Verdross, *Abendländische Rechtsphilosophie*, Vienna 1958, pp. 81–110; M. Villey, *La formation de la pensée juridique moderne*, Paris 1968, pp. 273–427, 481–707; Fr. Wieacker, *Privatrechtsgeschichte der Neuzeit*, 2. Aufl., Göttingen 1967, pp. 152–248.

1. Introduction

In those days when history – both as a general discipline and as a specialized study of the development of different human fields of activity – put more emphasis upon a neat classification of periods, and clear dividing lines between them, the term "modern" came to be applied to those events which took place from about the year 1500 onwards. In many branches of science, in fact, "modern" was used, and is to some extent still used, as the opposite of "ancient;" thus, the Middle Ages were also included. In other contexts, to be "modern" means, really, to date from the last few years, indeed even from that last period of one year which is called a "season." Since the latter usage is far more widely spread, students entering the world of learning are frequently astonished to find how generously the exclusive quality of "modernity" is thereby granted to ideas, institutions and indeed men.

The Transition to the Modern Era (1500–1650)

Although most historians of today are likely to agree that their predecessors were somewhat rash in accepting an interpretation of history which attributes "modernity" to everything which slow-moving time places after the year 1500, neither the date nor the term are arbitrary. From the early 16th century, a number of new elements are simultaneously present on that part of the Occidental scene which is of direct or indirect interest for present purposes. "New," in such contexts, is always a highly relative quality; some of the elements just referred to are clearly "new" in the simple sense that they did not exist in any form earlier – this is true both of the great geographic discoveries and of some scientific knowledge – others are "new" inasmuch as they represent the fully developed, "ripe" stage of the growth of phenomena that had existed before: this applies, e.g., to the national state, to the cultural movement known as the Renascence, and to religious schism.

To speak about the simultaneous presence of several new elements of interest to our subject is another way of expressing that the scene, being more crowded, has become more complex and more difficult to survey. This is not simply a result of those optical laws which make objects observed at close quarters look bigger than distant things, and which allow us to see more details when close to the thing observed (although these laws *also* apply, of course, and make the historian's task even more difficult). Both the growth of material culture, viz. a larger production of physical things, including men; the greater density of problems, conflicts, or simply "events," which is inevitably caused by more men and more property; the increasing mass of knowledge; and finally, as a result of all this, the growing output of ideas with some claim to our interest – for response to new experience is one of the main sources of legal thinking (tradition, or even routine, being another, that is true) – all these factors make it necessary not only to be even more selective, in this and the following chapters, than we have been in the preceding chapters with regard to what can be dealt with and what cannot.

The simultaneous presence of *surviving* ideas with *new* thinking which was, and remains, characteristic of Occidental legal theory undoubtedly constitutes a good reason for organizing the study of "modern times" in this field according to schools of thought rather than in a chronological order and thus to follow, as one line, "natural law thinking" from the Renascence to the present day, and to give the same treatment to "positivism" and other schools with a common basic outlook. Other principles for the arrangement of the matter under consideration here could also be attempted: a case could probably be made for both nationality and religion being used as criteria of classification.

In spite of these considerations, we choose to give chronology the first place as organizing principle; other criteria may be useful for subdivisions. Our reasons are essentially three. Legal thinking, or at least new and original legal thinking, we have already stated, is a response to new concrete experience, and although there are wide differences between the moment when such experience calls for a reaction in the culturally, economically, or socially most advanced societies, and the day when it is felt with similar strength in lagging and peripheral *milieux,* relative contemporaneity would nevertheless seem to guarantee a minimum of common inspiration, and knowledge about such common elements seems to be of crucial importance for understanding: in fact – and this is of course a personal and subjective standpoint (but one which *has to* be taken, and formulated) – their common experience of the world outside is likely to create more important uniting links between a late 17th century rationalist like John Locke and a Catholic thinker from the same period, like the French lawyer Jean Domat, than would their common allegiance to some basic tenets (of which little more than the *name* may have remained indentical) between Locke and a 20th century advocate of a secular natural law-theory, or between Domat and a spokesman of Neothomism. Secondly, by grouping the partisans of this or that school together, regardless of the passing centuries, and by making the development of their common ideas the Ariadne thread of the study, the historian incurs the risk of stressing unduly, to the detriment of important nuances, a few features in the thinking of the authors concerned, and of establishing both lines of continuity and common features which are, upon closer scrutiny, artificial. Finally, there is the obvious and yet treacherous risk of committing anachronisms: words remain, their content changes; problems lodged under this or that heading today were unknown yesterday – the heading stood for something entirely different.

Thus, a chronological order which is flexible enough to account for the relativity of the concept of simultaneousness seems to furnish, albeit both old and conventional, the best principle for organizing our study.

Although "the law" becomes an increasingly specialized activity in

The Transition to the Modern Era (1500-1650)

the course of the modern era – and should consequently become easier to study as distinct from such branches of thinking and knowledge as economy, ethics, or political science – the inevitable task of drawing a reasonable dividing line between that which does concern us here and that which, however interesting, important in itself, and related to the law in substance, must fall outside the heading of "legal thinking" becomes increasingly difficult to perform in a satisfactory manner. The study and practice of law was never a selfcontained activity, though it can certainly claim to be one of the oldest reasonably well-defined intellectual pursuits. For a long time, in fact, the study of the law represented the only higher – i.e. systematically studied, analysed and taught – training of a mixed theoretical and practical character; in all those contexts where the terms "administrative", "social," "political" or even "economic" are used today, lawyers had to meet emerging needs, and apply their tools. The birth and growth of new specialized sciences in the fields thus designated, and in others, meant that lawyers were relieved of some of their responsibilities, but it also meant that new knowledge of relevance to law and legal scholarship, at any rate to general legal thinking, was being accumulated with increasing speed.

The choice of such elements of religious, philosophical, and political (including economic) thinking that have to be at least briefly mentioned – were it only because without a reference to them, the legal philosophy of a given period would be incomprehensible – cannot be made without some arbitrary decisions. Nor can the choice of that which is held to *be* legal thinking and should be treated accordingly, as distinct from that which merely *concerns,* or *influences,* such thinking from the outside. What would seem essential, in a work without any claim to expert knowledge, is that the important elements – men, ideas, debates – are mentioned, accounted for as briefly as can be, and assessed in respect of their impact upon legal thinking. Whether these elements are treated as *part* of legal thinking as such or as merely *instrumental* to its development is an essentially terminological question.

2. Some Historical Background Facts

The political scene of Europe, the leading characters of which we described in the barest outlines in the preceding chapter (under 2), did not change beyond recognition in the period now discussed, but it underwent great and to some extent dramatic changes.

The Transition to the Modern Era (1500–1650)

In the first place, the world had become much larger than the known universe of the Middle Ages. After decades of expeditions along the West Coast of Africa, the Portuguese rounded the Cape of Good Hope (Bartolomeu Dias, 1487, and Vasco da Gama, 1497), and started founding trading posts in the Indian Ocean; in 1500 Cabral, also a Portuguese, set out eastwards on a voyage that brought him to Brazil. Half a century later, a trading station was founded in Macau in China. In 1492 Columbus' first voyage brought the Caribbean islands under the Crown of Spain; later Spanish explorers and conquerors extended these modest colonies into a vast Central and South American Empire. In 1519 Magellan, sailing down the Eastern coast of South America, rounded Cape Horn. Dutch, English, and French explorers, missionaries, soldiers and merchants started the exploration of North America; in the Indian Ocean, the Dutch soon ousted the Portuguese in most important places and founded a colonial Empire that was to last until after the Second World War.

Not only did the great discoveries change the map of the world. They also profoundly affected the balance of power in Europe. The Mediterranean basin, which had been the center of the Greco-Roman world and had remained through the Middle Ages the principal connecting link between Europe and the trading routes from the Far East and Africa, could no longer maintain its old central position. Economic and political power shifted nortwards and westwards. The Italian cities, which had held a very strong position in world trade by virtue of their links with the East, were reduced to a secondary place, and for similar reasons the cities of Southern Germany lost in importance compared with those of the North and the West. For almost a century, Spain, united into one monarchy, was to become the strongest economic and military power of Europe.

It would certainly be an exaggeration to believe that the expeditions to far-off continents – mostly undertaken om a modest scale, by small ships manned by handfuls of adventurers – changed abruptly either the everyday life of Europeans or prevailing ideas and attitudes. Gradually, however, effects beyond the level of the military and financial power structure and beyond geographical knowledge made themselves felt. The precious metals imported from the colonies in quantities earlier unknown hastened the development of a monetary economy and caused inflation, a development that contributed to disintegrate feudal society, based as it was on personal services and

The Transition to the Modern Era (1500–1650)

dues in kind. The winners of this process of social change were on the one hand the national rulers, particularly in the West, who found themselves in possession of cash incomes and could thus hire standing armies and maintain an efficient administration, on the other hand merchants, and manufacturers, who developed a system of pre-industrial capitalism. The most conspicuous losers were the feudal nobility, to the extent that class did not participate in the exploitation of the new economic possibilities or rally with the monarchies. Successively, in a slow process with great variations from one country to another, modern "bourgeois" Europe, with strongly centralized States, which had ambitions going far beyond the peace-keeping, law-administering aims of their medieval predecessors, came into existence. For centuries, the eastern part of the Continent – roughly from Poland eastwards – did not participate in this evolution. In this increasingly mobile world, technical, including military, and administrative efficiency became of paramount importance in the political struggle for power. A particularly striking example is the case of Sweden. That kingdom emerged from the Middle Ages as one of the poorest and most remote and backward states of Europe, with about one million inhabitants. After less than a century of intensive administrative reform and organization on all levels, ranging from education and ecclesiastical organization to military tactics and equipment, the small Kingdom of the North entered (in 1630) the Thirty Years' War in Germany and conquered a position as one of the great military powers in Europe which it was able to maintain for almost a century, until it was (about 1720) outweighed by sheer numbers in a conflict which brought the Russian Empire into the European scene for good.

Among the losers was the Emperor. The idea of Christendom being one single state, the Roman Empire, had to be given up in the face of political realities; in spite of repeated attempts to reform the constitution of the Holy Roman Empire of German Nationality, that body had sunk into complete political insignificance before the end of the Middle Ages. The power of the Emperors, who since the 14th century had with few exceptions belonged to the house of Habsburg (as the case was to be until the ultimate dissolution of the old Empire in 1806), was founded on their position as hereditary rulers of Austria, Bohemia, Hungary, and – in the former half of the 16th century, when Charles V (d. 1557) ruled over a monarchy "where the sun never set"

– also Spain and the Netherlands. In Germany, the Habsburg Emperor was only the first and greatest among territorial monarchs; hundreds of other rulers, ranging from powerful Electors, Dukes, Landgraves and Margraves with vast and well-administered territories to impoverished "Knights of the Empire," ruling over a couple of parishes, or "Free Imperial Cities" with a few thousand inhabitants, were for all practical purposes unlimited sovereigns each in their own lands. In Italy, the same situation was prevailing; with the exception of a few larger principalities and free cities, the confusion and the decadence of political power was even more marked in the old centre of the Empire.

The great rival of the house of Habsburg was the French monarchy, which under a series of strong rulers, assisted by an increasingly efficient and powerful civil and military administration – where the lawyers played a decisive part – had managed to eliminate the threats of English invasion and of the great feudal rulers dividing the country into independent territorial principalities. By 1500, France was the largest and most ambitious single member of the European family of states. For cultural, political and military purposes, it was a unified country, on the way to becoming a highly centralized bureaucratic state. The economic and judicial unification of the country was still to be achieved; it was not performed until the great Revolution. England, although perpetually engaged in warfare with its northern neighbour, Scotland, and already burdened with the problems caused by her imperialist policy in Ireland, was in many ways more efficiently centralized than any continental state. Under the energetic and forceful monarchs of the house of Tudor (1485–1603), England developed considerable economic and political strength. The victory of the English navy over the great Spanish armada in 1588 marked, more clearly than most other signs of the times, the shift in power from Southern to North-western Europe, in spite of the increase of wealth and power which the creation of a colonial Empire had given Spain. In 1603, the Anglo-Scottish strife came to an end through the personal union of the two Kingdoms under the first ruler of the house of Stuart.

The Scandinavian Kingdoms – at this time only two: Denmark with Norway and Sweden with Finland – underwent, on a smaller scale, a development similar to that of France and England.

Among the losers of the period was also the Papacy. Not only had the rulers of the national States, although still members of Roman

The Transition to the Modern Era (1500–1650)

Christendom, successfully opposed, since the early 14th century, papal claims to leadership in political matters. The decisive blow came with the movements for Church reform that finally led to the irrevocable splitting up of the unified medieval Occident into Northwestern Protestant, and Southern Catholic Europe. Reform movements, as well as heresies and socially and politically tinged rebellions against Catholic Church government, had taken alarming proportions in many parts of Europe (Wycliffe in England, Jan Hus in Bohemia) from the 14th century onwards, but the Church had so far been able to repress them with the help of the secular powers. The movements initiated by Martin Luther in Germany (1483–1546; the "ninety-five theses" published in 1517), Jean Calvin in Geneva (1509–1564) and Ulrich Zwingli in Zurich (1484–1531) might well have come to the same end if these reformers had not, at an early stage, found secular authorities which for various reasons were willing to support them. The political strength and the institutionalization thus lent to the reform movements also contributed to their breaking completely with Rome and setting up Church organizations of their own. State-protected established Lutheran churches soon came into existence in Germany and in the Scandinavian Monarchies (which still have established episcopal national Churches of Lutheran creed). The headquarters of Calvinism became the Republic of Geneva, but Calvinism also became the basic doctrine of the established Church of England; this branch of Protestantism was also victorious in the Netherlands and rallied strong minorities of the population in parts of France. Zwingli's predication remained, essentially, a local Swiss phenomenon.

The splitting up of the once homogeneous religious community of the Middle Ages was an event of immense importance for the intellectual and political – some scholars also claim for the economic – development of Europe. Not only did the mutual intolerance of the opposing parties, Catholics and Protestants, lead to a century of bitter religious warfare. It may, of course, be asked with regard to many of these wars whether religious disagreement was the essential cause of conflicts or a pretext covering other motives (and adding, this is a point on which there can be little doubt, a particular ferocity to the fighting). In some cases, the Reformation had, at first, scanty popular support; in England and in the Scandinavian monarchies, the most active supporters of the movement were the Kings and the nobility, who could profit from it by laying hands on much of the vast land holdings of the

Church. Gradually, however, the religious differences led to deepgoing differences in general attitudes and outlook. The Catholic Church energetically organized itself for counter-attack (the "Counter-Reformation"), and many of the abuses which had been violently denounced by the Reformers were in fact abolished. Upon the whole, the new national Protestant Churches tended to come under very heavy influence from the state; at times, they were not far from becoming just another centralized bureaucratic institution, whose function was to maintain religious discipline and uniformity in the national state. In some countries, learning and higher education suffered very heavy blows for a long time: the weak, State-dependent, and impoverished Protestant Churches could no longer support the learned institutions which had, in the Middle Ages, been very largely protected and maintained by the Church. The spirit of controversy, which engaged much intellectual energy in the first century and a half after the Reformation, was in some respects a negative factor. Religious strife menaced the very existence of the French monarchy for a period of some thirty years (1560–1590), and in England, dissent in religious matters combined with constitutional issues remained a conflict-generating factor from the middle of the 16th century until the Glorious Revolution (1688). Germany, finally, suffered repeated religious conflicts throughout the 16th century and had to support, from 1618 to 1648, the horrors and devastations of the Thirty Years' War, which considerably retarded the economic and cultural development of the country as compared with its neighbours.

On the other hand – now as in the Middle Ages – controversy also brought an element of intellectual stimulus. Religious minorities claimed freedom of worship. The collapse of the monolithic medieval civilization raised new questions about the relationship between Church and state. The coexistence of states with full sovereignty and different creeds (like the confrontation with non-Christian states in the colonies) called for new solutions. The complex and powerful movement of ideas known as the Renascence gave birth to a revival of classical learning, including direct contact with Greek thinking, which had previously been known essentially through Latin intermediaries.

3. Major Trends in Religious, Philosophical and Political Thinking

Although it is undoubtedly correct to state that in a long range perspective, the development of ideas in the period now considered meant a deep-going and – so far – irrevocable reduction of the importance of *religion* as an element in Occidental thinking and, more generally, intellectual, cultural and societal life, it vould be false to believe that the religious bases of Western societies were eliminated overnight and replaced by secular philosophy. The popular idea that the Renascence period was one of joyous paganism is essentially false. Even apart from the basic sociological fact that religion maintained its fundamental place in the beliefs and everyday life of the overwhelming majority of Europeans at least well into the second half of the 19th century, Western philosophy and legal philosophy did not break either with Christian dogma or with the underlying assumptions about the origin, nature and structure of the universe and of society. In fact, the Reformation gave new life to problems which had been debated in the days of the Fathers of the Church but had been pacified, as it were, by the temporarily successful attempts of medieval theology, in particular Thomist Scholasticism, to establish harmonious and intellectually acceptable compromises between Christian doctrines and Greek rationalism. In many respects, the Reformation implied a "reactivation" of religion as an all-permeating element of human life; at the same time, however, some of the most important results of centuries of painstaking efforts to reconcile Athens, Rome, and Jerusalem were swept aside by the Reformers.

By far the most important and most spectacular among these results was the Catholic Church, as it emerged from the High Middle Ages: an organization which had managed to cast much of the Christian message into a rational legalistic mould and to express essential parts of that message in terms of actions and rites comprehensible to the masses; in short, to make that salvation, in the form of eternal survival and union with God, of the individual soul which was the ultimate goal of the Christian religion and the ultimate reward it offered to the faithful, a collective and indeed to some extent, an "administrative" affair. This was, by and large, an immense achievement. But a price had had to be paid: the Church had not been able at all times and in all circumstances to avoid the risk of becoming – to use an expression which may seem crude but is chosen to illustrate drastically, not to caricature – a monopolized, strictly legalistic salvation factory. The Reformers reopened the discussion initiated, more than a millennium earlier, by St. Augustine. They placed man, alone, in front of God; *salvation,* in their preaching, *became an individual question;* no body, however perfect, could or should interfere, let alone claim a monopoly in organizing collective salvation; God's grace alone, sensible in the heart of men, could save sinners.

Although new ecclesiastical organizations – hardly less eager than the old Church to make religion a legal and an administrative matter – soon came into existence in those parts of Europe where the Reformation was successful, the impact of the revolt was nevertheless immense. The question of spiritual life and death had become the object of an individual decision. None of the new religious bodies could claim that which was the principal strength of the Roman Church: unbroken historical tradition going back to the first Christians. However solidly built, the new Churches were new structures; at the utmost they could pretend to be *reconstructions*. Decisions on the contents of Christian faith had been passed by contemporary individuals, alone or in assemblies. The generally accepted definition of catholicity, formulated in the early fifth century by Vincent of Lerinum – that which has been believed *always, everywhere,* and by *everybody* – was no longer, and could no longer be, maintained by the new Churches. Men had taken their religious destiny into their own hands. The power of anonymous tradition was irremediably broken. The impact of that event in a great number of respects can hardly be exaggerated. In the present context, we confine ourselves to pointing at five particularly important aspects of the religious revolution brought about by the Reformers.

In the first place, an element of *arbitrariness* had been introduced in a domain where strict discipline – both intellectual and hierarchic – had previously reigned, or at least been considered as a supreme value in itself. The Reformers, of course, never realised and never admitted that they had assumed arbitrary powers for themselves or their followers: they all in good faith claimed to have rejected arbitrary innovations in the Christian Church. Their good faith cannot change either the facts as such or their consequences. The growth of heresies and of sects on a low intellectual level in the wake of Protestantism is evidence enough.

The Transition to the Modern Era (1500-1650)

Secondly, by stressing the individual character of man's adhesion to a religious creed, they – also involuntarily, and also in good faith – contributed to widening *the gap between religious faith and scientific knowledge* which the voluntarism of the late Scholastics had opened: the more private, the more essentially personal religion is, the less it is accessible to objective knowledge – the essence of which is intersubjectivity – and to rational analysis.

A third aspect of the religious revolution is the underlying *democratic assumption:* if salvation or damnation are fundamentally individual issues, every man or woman, however ignorant and however low in the social hierarchy, has – to put it in terms of political and legal science – a right of vote on the issue. And if the most important of all questions is thus left by God with all human beings for their discretionary decision, how can anyone claim that the poor or the ignorant should be excluded from participation in the far less important decisions which concern human affairs? Pushing the point further: does not this power of individual decision given by God even to the humblest indicate that their voice – and vote – has the same weight as that of the high-born, the rich, or the learned? Neither of these latter has been entrusted with a more important choice than that which concerns his own salvation.

In the fourth place, the very notion of "authority" – as a source of knowledge, and as an argument for obedience – had suffered a severe blow. Of the two notions appearing so frequently in Medieval reasoning – *auctoritas* and *ratio* – only the latter remains unchallenged. This change, which is to produce, in due time, its effects in legal philosophy, also gives rise to a question: who or what can *justify,* or *legitimize,* solutions of social problems if authority is gone?

And, finally, if religion is a matter for individual decisions, it is essentially a matter in which *a far-reaching right of privacy* can be claimed. This consequence – and its secondary effects in the legal sphere – took a long time to come to the fore. Nevertheless, in the long-range perspective, it was to provide arguments both against state interference in religious matters, against organized churches as such, and against public worship in any form. Combined with the other elements discussed here, it contributed to widening the gap between religion – utlimately, a matter for individual intimate feeling – and scientific knowledge and research.

This is not the place to go more profoundly into the teaching of the Reformers. There were, and still are, considerable differences, going far beyond mere nuances, between Lutheranism and Calvinism (we can refrain from dealing with Zwingli who, upon the whole, is more close to Luther than to the French Reform leader). Luther, basically, represents the Augustinian standpoint – which was also, in this particular respect, that of late medieval voluntarism – that God's sovereign will and grace alone decide of the salvation or damnation of man. The official Church, at that time, had moved far, in practice if not in doctrine, towards Pelagianism; pious deeds, and obedience to the Church, were held to be efficient means of obtaining salvation.

Luther energetically rejected legalism in all forms. The true Christian is and should be *free* in relation to the law; salvation is a gift from God; "righteousness," in Luther's language, as in Paul's, is an inward disposition, a state of perfection or holiness. Although Luther's language is not always clear, it is obvious that in the field of religion, he leaves no room for a "natural law," let alone a body of precepts accessible to human reason unaided by the revelation. "Natural law" – for Luther admits the existence of such a body of rules, and in fact recommends Aristotle and Cicero as authorities – is an entirely "worldly" concern. Religion, in Luther's thinking, which on this point comes close to primitive Christianity, is essentially non-legal. This fundamental standpoint, however, leads Luther, who was an eminently practical man and who saw clearly the need for a firm social and political organization, to an attitude which is very far from that of St. Augustine. Luther emphatically stresses the necessity of human laws, and human authorities, for the maintenance of peace, and for keeping men, irremediably corrupted by original sin, to the outward observance of Christian virtues. Thus the state, when maintaining order, is serving God, and the subjects of the state are under a duty of obedience which is of religious origin. Since, at the same time, Luther would have as little as possible of an autonomous ecclesiastical law and Church organization – he had seen enough of both in the Roman Church – this aspect of his thinking became particularly important as, in several German states and in Scandinavia, national Churches were established under royal and princely domination. Lutheranism, in stressing the religious duties of secular rulers, also seemed to give some legitimation to their interfering in Church affairs.

Jean Calvin's religious thinking is also voluntaristic and Augustinian; he goes further than Luther in preaching the doctrine of predestination: the salvation or damnation of each single individual is the outcome of

The Transition to the Modern Era (1500-1650)

God's inscrutable decision; good deeds do not affect it; faith alone, a gift of God, works that union with the Divinity which gives eternal life. Like Luther, Calvin is far from the Scholastic theories of a natural law based upon human reason; like Luther, he stresses the legitimacy of secular powers, and the duty of obedience they can claim. It was certainly of great importance, however, that the "secular powers," in Calvin's experience, are represented by the burghers leading the republic of Geneva, and the religious community he had himself founded there; they were not autocratic kings or princes.

In spite of the great similarities between the doctrines of the two most influential Reformers, they and their followers undoubtedly represent what may be called highly different intellectual and religious climates. To make the point clear by drawing caricatures: Luther became the prophet of loyal, silent and obedient *subjects* of strong, paternalistic states; Calvin became a teacher of independent, critical, perpetually arguing and eternally oppositional *citizens*. The last attempt at a characterization is particularly doubtful with regard to the Anglican Church, which presents – both in its articles of faith and in its conservative maintenance of Church rituals abhorred by radical Calvinists – many similarities to the episcopal Lutheran established Churches in Scandinavia. By and large, however, Calvinism, and the numerous sects grafted upon the austere teaching of the Reformer of Geneva, became the religion of civic freedom *par excellence* A great German scholar (Franz Wieacker) rightly says that the "climate" of the precursors of *modern rationalistic natural law theories*, which were to become the basis, in legal philosophy, of the 18th century Enlightenment, of the American and French Revolutions and, in a still larger perspective, or 19th century liberalism, was "the salt wind of the high seas, where liberty is defended against the minions of absolute monarchs." This description may seem to imply a contradiction; we noted that Calvin was just as reluctant as Luther to recognize a law of nature based upon reason. This, however, did not remain true with regard to his followers. In their fight for religious liberty they needed natural law; so they invented it. Let us repeat, at this juncture, an observation which has already been made twice in this book: "the idea of some sort of 'natural law', be it only a vague standard of common decency, that man can find for himself and apply, is psychologically irresistible." Just as the early Fathers of the Church, as soon as the great religious revolution realized by the teaching of Christ had lost

The Transition to the Modern Era (1500–1650)

its first impetus, moved towards Greco-Roman ideas of a rationalistic law of nature, so the legal thinkers, who set out to create a philosophy of law that both corresponded to the creeds of the Reformers and met the practical needs of the new, divided and much larger world of the 16th and 17th centuries, could not do without some kind of natural law. In fact, already Luther's faithful friend and disciple *Filip Melanchton* (d. 1560), a learned humanist, expressed ideas which come quite close to the rationalistic natural law conception of classical scholasticism.

* * *

In the field of *philosophy*, and of *general intellectual development*, the period now considered is less original than in the domains of theology and political science (to the latter discipline, we shall revert shortly). The Renascence was not essentially a philosophical movement; in the universities, Scholasticism, in its late, refined but somewhat sterile form, lived on as the official "school philosophy"; in Spain, as we have already mentioned, "neo-thomism" flourished and gave birth to important theological and philosophic writings. In some *élite* circles, Platonism was revived and played a considerable part. The enthusiasm for ancient literature among classical scholars and a small but growing "educated general public" was accompanied by a corresponding contempt for the allegedly barbarian and "Gothic" Latin of the Middle Ages. The writings of the commentators were frequent targets of derision among the humanists. Although the Renascence was essentially a movement within the domains of arts and letters in the broadest sense of these words, and basically foreign to legal science, its influence was strong enough to give rise to a new style in legal writing: particularly in France and in the Netherlands, "elegant jurisprudence" – a school which gave particular attention both to the pedagogic and systematic arrangement of Roman law textbooks and to the classical purity of the Latin in which they were written – took the place of the traditional "Italian style" *(mos italicus)* of the late commentators.

Towards the end of the period now under consideration, powerful new currents in scholarly thinking, connected both with the rise of natural science and with the rationalistic philosophy of René Descartes, gave new impulses also to legal philosophy. However, the results of this development did not make themselves strongly felt until the latter part of the 17th century. Mention should only be made here of the conservative scepticism of the great French philosopher *Michel de Montaigne* (d. 1592), who frankly declared that what was called "law of nature" was nothing but human convention, and of the equally sceptic attitude, both to natural law and human laws, which was adopted from entirely different, deeply religious points of departure, by a later French thinker, *Blaise Pascal* (d. 1662), who had been converted to Jansenism, an influential and oppositional Augustinian revival movement within the Church of France.

Finally, an isolated but influential English thinker should be noticed. *Francis Bacon's* (d. 1626) fame is more closely connected with the philosophy of science, where he is the first great representative of English empiricism, but Bacon, who held for some time the office of Lord Chancellor, also wrote several works on law and legislation in a spirit of positivism which did not appeal very much to his contemporaries but were to influence later English thinkers, e.g. John Locke. Bacon also proposed, without success, a codification of the laws of England.

* * *

The religious struggles of the period discussed here were mostly interwoven with political and also social controversy. It was a period of great fertility in the domain of *political thought*. Besides what may be called the "official" Church reform movements – those initiated by Luther, Calvin, and Zwingli, supported by secular rulers, and leading to the establishment of lasting ecclesiastic organisations in Northern and Western Europe – there arose, particularly at the beginning of the period, numerous sects, some of them with radical egalitarian ideas, which were considered as heresies not only by the old Church but also by the new establishments and by the holders of political power. Some of these movements, supported by the poor classes of the community, led to open rebellion against the existing social order. They were mostly suppressed with the utmost brutality, but vague ideas and ideals of total equality and community of property survived, as secret undercurrents, sometimes coming to the surface in connection with political, economic and religious crises.

The foundations of 16th and 17th century political thinking had been laid in the late Middle Ages; to this inheritance was added the wealth of political experience and theories of the Ancient World, which the revival of classical learning made directly accessible to contemporary Europeans. The Greco-Roman influence was exercised on different levels: outside the world of learning, where Greek and Latin texts were studied with enthusiasm both by philosophers and by historians and linguists, that influence, transmitted by a growing body of translations, frequently had a literary rather than a theoretical character. Thus a famous biographical work, the *Parallell Lives* of the Greek statesman and writer Plutarch (d.c. 125 A.D.; French translation by Amyot in 1559 and English translation by Sir Thomas North in 1579), in which the "Republican virtue" of Greek and Roman heroes was celebrated, came to exercise a deep-going influence upon generations of young Europeans and provided, by example, rather than by theory, the ideological foundations of opposition against absolute monarchy and bureaucratic administration.

The medieval bases of Renascence political thinking have already been briefly mentioned above (ch. 4, secs. 7 and 8). To a large extent, what would today be called "political" questions were discussed in legal terms, particularly with a view to solving two sets of problems: first, the increasingly obvious discrepancy between the claims of the Empire, and of Imperial law on the one hand, the rapid development, in fact, and growing pretentions, in law, of sovereign states on the other hand; secondly, the principles of Church government in the long period of schism and constitutional strife in the Church of Rome in the 14th and 15th centuries. The discussion of these problems, and the solutions proposed, enriched with the direct contact with the Ancients, were the bricks with which modern political philosophy was built.

The absolutistic claims of secular rulers had been formulated quite early in the Middle Ages. They are voiced, e.g., in *Egidius Colonna's* (d. 1316) famous work *De regimine principum (On the Rule of Princes)* from about 1300; similar ideas were expressed at about the same time by *Dante Alighieri* (d. 1321), who still dreams of a universal monarchy, the resurrected Roman Empire. Half a century later *Bartolus of Sassoferrato* (cf. ch. 4, sec. 7) develops the notion of sovereignty, based upon the concept of jurisdiction – the public authority exercised within a territory – while still reserving supreme power, on a higher level, for the Empire. Shortly before 1400, *Baldus degli Ubaldi* (cf. *loc. cit.* above) deduces the autonomy and sovereignty of states from the law of nations, *jus gentium*, which thus assumes, in Baldus' thinking, at least

The Transition to the Modern Era (1500–1650)

a part of that character of "public international law" that has later become its principal denotation. Baldus also laid the foundations of modern *private* international law by distinguishing between the "personal law" of a citizen – which follows him wherever he goes – and the "real law" which is applicable to property and is the law of the place where the property is located. Radical support for the claims of the secular state – in the sense of each territorial or local organization that does not recognize a superior – is found in the *Defensor pacis (The Defender of Peace)* of the influential polemist *Marsilius of Padua* (d.c. 1342), a work which expresses a strict positivism: human laws are commands, provided with sanctions, issued by a sovereign, whose legitimacy is based upon popular consent.

Both the absolute independence of the individual state, envisaged as a *de facto* centre of power, and the complete separation between secular government and positive law on the one hand, natural law and religious ethics on the other hand, are affirmed by *Niccolò Machiavelli* (d. 1527) in his famous – and frequently misunderstood – book *De Principe (On the Prince)*. Law in fact, in Machiavelli's view, is one among several instruments in the service of political power; the detention and exercise of that power are the supreme goals of the leader of the state. Machiavelli's book, where he coolly discusses the use of violence, treason, and perjury as methods of political action, exercised a profound influence on his contemporaries; it reflects, but it probably also strengthened, the lawlessness and brutality of the struggle for power in Renascence Italy and also in other parts of Europe in the last phase of the feudal society and the early years of centralized national states. It should be added that Machiavelli neither attempts to justify, from a moral point of view, the methods he discusses nor glorifies them as such. However, the fact that he quietly demonstrates the efficiency of immoral actions *as means* without condemning them have made generations of readers take him for a spokesman of applied immorality in public life. Many Renascence monarchs and politicians read Machiavelli's "De principe" as a textbook in the art of governing and imitated the acts, frequently used as illustrations, of the immoral Italian adventurer Cesare Borgia, a Pope's son who managed, with brutal and treacherous methods, to establish himself as a territorial ruler and to maintain himself, for a short time, in that capacity.

The importance of such isolated works as that of Machiavelli should not be exaggerated. Although the period we are discussing here was undoubtedly one of great and deep-going changes, these were neither revolutionary neither – applying modern standards – very rapid. The social framework within which changes took place was too solid to be torn down in a short time, and that framework – including such institutions as assemblies of magnates, guilds and corporations, Cathedral chapters and Church councils – embodied political, constitutional and legal experience which had been gathered for centuries, painstakingly studied, analysed, justified and attacked with the time-honoured tools of Roman and Canon law concepts and less explicit but in some cases strong elements of Germanic and feudal legal thinking. Modern research tends to show convincingly the basic continuity of Western political thought from the High, or even Early, Middle Ages into the modern era. Thus the idea, forcibly expressed in the legal texts of the last century of the Ancient Roman Empire, that the prince was above the law and that his will was a source of law, had coexisted for centuries with the opposite view: that the prince held his office by the people's will, by virtue of their mandate, and under the law; in fact, even the late Emperors had had recourse to the fiction that the Roman people had formally transferred their power of legislation to the Emperor, and in the Digest itself it is stated that laws are binding because the people accept them.

The Roman – private – law of associations and Roman rules on delegation of authority had been heavily drawn upon, for centuries, by Canonists in their attempts to reconcile the elements of papal absolutism and Council constitutionalism in the Church. Problems of majority rule had been similarly explored by Canonists when discussing the decisions of collective bodies. To take one concrete example[1] illustrating the process which an isolated phrase in classical Roman law could undergo: in the Justinian Code, the sentence *quod omnes tangit, ab omnibus approbetur* ("What concerns all should be approved by all") refers to decisions by *co-tutors;* in the course of the Middle Ages, this phrase, vested with the immense authority of Roman law and handled with the subtle and fertile inventiveness of lawyers, grew into a constitutional principle, applied to general councils of the Church, to Italian minicipalities, and – in Edward I's election writ, 1295 – to the Parliament of England. In short: the glosses, commentaries, treatises,

---

[1] From B. Tierney, *Religion, Law and the Growth of Constitutional Thought 1150–1650*, Cambridge 1982, pp. 24 ff.

The Transition to the Modern Era (1500–1650)

and polemical writings of the Middle Ages already contained – referring to social realities close and well-known to 16th and 17th century thinkers – a rich arsenal of ideas and concepts which could be used, with greater or smaller adaptations and amendments, to the new or changing situations and problems of their world.

From the general political and constitutional discussion of the period now under consideration (in contradistinction to the legal debate in a narrower sense) we shall mention three examples, two from France and one from Germany. The English development, which presents some original features, will be dealt with below (ch. 6, sec. 3); it came to a provisional end with the Glorious Revolution in 1688 and is most properly discussed in the light of that event.

The French 16th century, as already indicated, was a particularly troubled period. At the beginning of the new era, the French monarchy emerged, politically strong, from the last struggles with feudalism and engaged, with mixed success but without serious defeat, in fighting for European leadership with the House of Habsburg in Italy. From 1560 to 1590, religiously inspired civil war almost overthrew the Monarchy; the last ten years of the century were a new period of recovery and consolidation. Although frequently obstructed or threatened, a main line of development is visible: the growth and slow consolidation of the centralized bureaucratic Royal administration at the expense of feudal and provincial particularism. The wars of religion had obvious constitutional aspects; sharp-eyed contemporary polemists were not late to realize this.

Jean Bodin (d. 1596) was a lawyer and follower of the school of "elegant jurisprudence" in the spirit of Renascence humanism; he had, like many of that school, the ambition of presenting Roman law in a clear systematical arrangement and in pure Latin. His best-known work, however, is *Les six livres de la République* (*Six Books on the State*, 1576) – a lawyer's attempt to draw up, with the concepts and terms of legal science, a system of political theory. Bodin develops with logical rigour a theory of *sovereignty:* the state, he contends, has an absolute power over its subjects, and that power is not limited by any law. The state alone can issue laws, without being bound by them, and laws, in fact, are nothing but the sovereign's commands. This radically voluntaristic and positivist doctrine – which would seam to correspond to the wishes of many Frenchmen, at that time, to strengthen the Monarchy and thus enable it to put an end to the cruel and devastating civil war between

Protestants and Catholics – is mitigated, in form rather than in substance – by a reference to "the laws of God and of nature"; this concept would seem to go no further than to God's explicit commandments and thus covers an area which is essentially narrower than the "natural law" of the Stoics, Cicero, and St. Thomas.

If Bodin defended Royal absolutism, the contemporary so-called Monarchomachs (Monarchy-fighters) attacked the King's power in the name of popular sovereignty. The vast body of polemic writings referred to under this heading is mostly of small interest for present purposes; it is more violent than convincing. Among the Monarchomachs we find, however, at least one famous lawyer, to whom we shall revert shortly (sec. 5 below): *François Hotman* (d. 1590), a fervent Calvinist but also a distinguished representative of the school of "elagant jurisprudence." Hotman contends – referring to the Germanic origins of the French (Frankish) state – that the Kingdom of France had never been an absolute monarchy and that it still was subject to constitutional rules which made the consent of the people (expressed by the Estates General, a representative assembly of clergy, nobles and the "Third Estate", which had come into existence in the Middle Ages but was convoked by the Kings's will) the condition of legitimacy of all political power. In fact, Hotman claimed that the assembly had inherited from the old Frankish assemblies the right to elect and depose kings. In another work emanating from the Monarchomachs, the anonymous treatise *Vindiciae contra tyrannos* (*Claims against the Tyrants*, 1579) the idea of popular sovereignty is also developed at length. Kings, it is contended, are the servants of the law and thus subject to them; it is only in primitive and barbarian states that kings are absolute rulers. The author of the Vindiciae further introduces the idea of a *social contract* as the legitimating basis of the state; this contract, however, is of a fairly special character, since it is in the first place – in the spirit of Calvinism, largely inspired by the Old Testament – a contract between God and the King; the people guarantees the latter's compliance with the terms of the Covenant and thus, indirectly, acquires contractual rights and duties in relation to both God and the ruler.

Another early expression of the idea that the State is founded upon a social contract is found in the writings of the German lawyer *Johannes Althusius* (d 1638). He is influenced by the late Spanish Scholasticism which was based upon St. Thomas' natural law thinking, and he writes in conscious opposition to Bodin. Althusius represents a curious mixture of medieval and modern ideas. Thus he operates with a classical natural law concept of religious origin; that law is binding upon all, rulers as well as ruled. On the other hand, he stresses energetically the principle of popular sovereignty. The King, in his view, is merely an "administrator". He does not enter into a social contract with the people as an equal contracting party but holds his office by virtue of a mandate. Althusius is a precursor of modern political thinking in particular because he stresses the need for a fundamental law, a constitution, which draws up clearly the limits of governmental power.

4. The Rise of Secularized Natural Law: Grotius and Hobbes

The two highly influential legal thinkers brought together in this section – the Dutch lawyer, polyhistor and diplomat (in the service of Sweden) *Hugo Grotius* (1583–1645) and the English scholar *Thomas Hobbes* (1588–1679) were contemporaries and dealt to some extent with similar problems. In so doing, they made use of, and contributed decisively to developing, the concept of natural law. Beyond this, they had little in common. Grotius is often described as the founder not only of modern, non-theological natural law theories, but also of the discipline of public international law; it is frequently added that he is the father of a clearly *rationalistic* branch of natural law thinking. Hobbes founded no school; yet his profound scepticism and gloomily pessimistic views on the realities of political and legal institutions remained for a long time – indeed still remains – a challenge for all those who try to convince others and themselves about a more idyllic interpretation of the social facts of state and law.

Hugo Grotius (Huigh de Groot) would seem to provide a particularly striking illustration of two trivial but not unimportant observations of universal validity in the history of ideas, viz. that the personality and position of a thinker may be just as important for the success of his ideas as their contents, and further, that the literary and stylistic qualities of a writer may be just as decisive for his influence on future developments as the originality of the message he conveys. This is not to say that Grotius was a mere compiler or just the elegant, and therefore successful, propagator of other people's ideas. The breadth and depth of his intellectual culture, and the skill with which he develops his theories are beyond doubt. As for originality, however, it is equally beyond doubt that he drew heavily on the work of earlier natural law philosophers and theologians, in particular the Spanich theologians, canonists, and jurists of the 16th century who pursued St. Thomas' tradition of blending Greco-Roman and Christian thinking into a harmonious whole, strongly tinged with rationalism and optimism. Grotius, in fact, openly recognizes his indebtedness to the great Spaniards, and quotes them frequently.

Grotius became, in his youth, something of an internationally famous wonderchild, a prodigy of learning in all fields. At the age of seventeen, he was made a doctor of laws at the university of Orléans, at that time one of the greatest centres of legal science in Europe. He made a brilliant political career in his homeland, the Netherlands, but fell upon hard times when his party was defeated, fled to France, where he was well received but found no employment suitable to his ability; then, for eleven years, he was the Ambassador of Sweden to the French court. He died after a shipwreck on the German coast. He was a prolific writer. His most well-known works were a treatise on Dutch law, the polemic pamphlet *Mare liberum* (*On the Freedom of the High Seas*, 1609), where he lays the foundation of the basically still valid doctrine of the supranational status of the Oceans; and finally *De jure belli ac pacis libri tres* (Three Books on the Law of War and Peace, 1623), his greatest work, where he develops both the principles of a universal law of nature and, on that basis, a body of rules of public international law.

As we have indicated above, the moment for presenting these solutions was singularly well chosen: after the breakdown of the homogeneous world of the Medieval Occident, where Church and Empire held, at least in theory, an undisputed position of leadership, after the discovery of new Continents, with non-Christian states that could not be fitted into the traditional patterns of legal relations, Europe, and the world, urgently needed a new consensus on at least some basic principles of law. To obtain that consensus, the proposed legal solutions had to fulfil a number of – essentially negative – conditions: they could *not* be founded on, or even be too closely related to, any single one of the competing religious creeds; *nor* could they be based on the now discredited fiction of a political unity under the aegis of the Empire. In positive terms: to be universally acceptable, the proposed body of rules must correspond to commonly held convictions – which meant that they could neither be openly opposed to religious beliefs common to all Christians nor imply such radical political, social or cultural assumptions as went against the interests and ideas of ruling groups and classes – and they must also be compatible with the level of scientific knowledge and general intellectual development of these groups. One particularly strong element in the intellectual culture of Europe in the late Renascence was the knowledge of, and veneration for, the literature and the law of classical Antiquity. Elegant Latin prose, well-chosen quotations and evidence of solid classical scholarship would give added persuasive authority to any work submitted to the educated public. Another element of contemporary culture, still confined to an *élite*, but of growing importance, was interest in, and respect for, mathematics and natural sciences; the age of Descartes and Newton was close at hand. Grotius's writings admirably fulfilled all these conditions. He was, in the first place, a believing and pious Christian (Calvinist) – a quality that does not prevent him, as St. Thomas's example should be enough to prove, from undertaking the construction of an essentially "secularized" natural law. Politically, he was – as his position in the political struggles of the Netherlands shows – a conservative. He possessed great and extensive learning, which he both showed and used in his works.

Man, in Grotius's view, is basically both *social* and *rational*. Natural law is the body of precepts which man's rationality shows him to be necessary for social life. They are, however, also prescribed by God. What makes the Grotian concept of natural law "secularized" if compared with, e.g., the teaching of St. Thomas, would seem to be the categorical way in which he affirms the *objective necessity* of the precepts of natural law, in particular the fundamental maxim that "contracts should be kept" *(pacta sunt servanda)*: it simply could not be otherwise, he affirms, and it would be the same even if "we supposed – the which cannot be said without the gravest impiety – that God does not exist, or that he does not care about human affairs." In another famous passage, he states that not even God can modify the natural law: "Just as God cannot make two by two anything else than four, he cannot make that which is intrinsically evil anything else than evil." This obviously amounts to saying that in one sense at least, *reason* – or rather *logic* – is stronger even than the Maker of the universe, who is bound by the "laws" (in the sense of the natural sciences) of His own creation. These ideas, which have sometimes been interpreted as evidence for the fundamental independence of Grotian natural law from religious foundations, *need not be considered anti-religious;* similar expressions had occurred in medieval legal philosophy. Indeed, Thomas himself had affirmed, although in different terms, that God cannot act against the natural law because in Him, will and reason coincide and thus He cannot wish anything that is not rational: "To say," Thomas writes, "that justice depends upon (God's) will alone amounts to saying that Divine will does not follow the order of wisdom, and that is blasphemy". Grotius's idea is obviously far from clear: it leaves open such difficult problems as the Dutch jurist's view upon the creation of the universe and God's role in that process and in the further development of the world. A cautious interpretation should, in my view, make halt before the difficulties arising from the quoted passages: in the absence of conclusive evidence about Grotius' thinking on such other basic questions as could serve to enlighten his reasoning on the points now mentioned, definite conclusions cannot be drawn with any certainty. Grotius was not a logician, nor had he the ambition to build a complete and all-covering system of propositions: the possibility of his ideas containing internal contradictions cannot be excluded.

In fact, modern scholarship has shown that on another fundamental point, Grotius is really oscillating between a non-theological and a theological standpoint. Reason, we explained above, shows man the rules necessary for life in the society. That life corresponds to man's social nature and instincts. But then the question arises what makes "nature" and "instinct" *binding*. It is only if there is a binding obligation to lead a certain kind of life that the precepts dictated by reason, as means to achieve that life, can claim, in turn, to *be absolutely binding*. For however necessary they may be for achieving in the most rational way a given purpose, they obviously could – and indeed *would* in all likelihood – be otherwise if alternative purposes could be pursued. It is difficult to avoid the conclusion that a social existence is, for Grotius, not merely a form of life dictated by man's natural instincts but also an existence man is bound to lead by God's will and command. It is only in this way that the empirical, sociological observation that men prefer living together assumes the status of *law*.

The basic tenet of natural law, according to Grotius, is thus that "contracts should be kept." This principle serves to explain, and give legitimacy to, *human laws,* for Grotius like many of his contemporaries accepts the idea of a social contract. The contents of that covenant could vary from one state to another – Grotius refrains from developing any preferences in this respect (undoubtedly one of the reasons why his teaching could be universally accepted) – but the basic reasoning is clear: what makes the social contract binding is the *pacta sunt servanda* axiom; once the contract concluded, laws enacted under it are also binding upon the parties concerned.

Grotius repeatedly affirms that the fundamental rules of the law of nature (on the level next below the general *pacta sunt servanda* maxim) – respect for the property, or rather, more generally, "sphere of rights," of others, duty to render other people's property to them, duty to comply with contractual obligations, duty to accept penal responsibility – are matters of *knowledge, not of will*. They are obvious, and by exercising right reason, all men will find them. The author has not the ambition to build a complete system of detailed natural law rules – that was to come in the following generations of natural law thinkers – but he draws up some principles which were to be of immense importance for future development. Some of these should be briefly mentioned; a full discussion of them belongs to other branches of legal science. Grotius' greatest contribution, from a practical point of view, consists in the laying down of a body of rules on the relations between sovereign states in peace and war; the starting point of his reasoning was that since no social contract has been concluded between states, they are subject to natural law, and their acts should be judged accordingly. War, e.g., was just (*justum bellum*) only as a measure of legitimate self-defence or enforcement of rights that could not be defended otherwise. With regard to warfare, Grotius pleaded – invoking the law of nature – for its humanization, e.g., in the treatment of civilians and prisoners. There are also, in Grotius's works, important contributions to many private law questions; on these points he was to exercise a deep-going influence on the Continental development of the doctrine of property and – in particular – contract. Given the decisive importance of the latter concept for the whole of Grotius' legal thinking, he studies at depth the notion of "declaration of will" and the consequences of contractual obligations.

If philosophical originality were the exclusive, or the foremost, criterion of the importance of legal theorists, Thomas Hobbes would undoubtedly be considered more important than Grotius. In many respects, it would be more appropriate to deal with Hobbes's thinking in the following chapter, and to give him the position of a pioneer of "modern" (this time, "modern" by virtue of the content of his ideas, not merely his place in history) philosophy of law and state. Hobbes had in fact made the personal acquaintance of those French *élite* milieux where Pascal and Descartes moved and from which decisive impulses to modern scientific thinking emanated. Unlike Grotius who, in these respects, stands firmly on traditional ground, Hobbes not only professes a radical materialism, a mechanistic view of the world, and a pronounced nominalism, but also presents an unusual mixture of a strict empiricism – ruthless observation of facts viewed with disillusioned but also suspicious, indeed timorous eyes is at the root of his theories – and of a rationalism coloured by his close contacts with, and interest in, mathematical science.

Hobbes, the son of a poor Church of England clergyman, lead the life of a teacher and scholar; at an early date, he came into the service of the earls of Devonshire as a private teacher and remained a retainer of the Cavendish family for most of his life. He also had contacts with the court of Charles I and Charles II and was a supporter of the royal cause in the contests between these monarchs and Parliament; for a number of years, under Cromwell's protectorate, he lived in exile in France. He has written a number of smaller treatises on questions of political science and law, but his greatest and most influential work is *Leviathan* – published in English in 1651 and in Hobbes's own Latin translation in 1668 – which has been called the first great work of modern political theory. It is only logical, against the background of his fundamental ideas, that he was severely critical towards contemporary English common law theories, which tended to deduce the validity of that body of essentially customary (i.e., in this context, judge-made) law from its foundations in human reason, viz. from its essential compatibility with a rationalistic law of nature.

Hobbes's originality, and independence from earlier authorities, is noticeable already in his basic assumption concerning the nature of man: whereas Aristotle and most thinkers after him, e.g. Grotius, had attributed to man "a social nature," Hobbes considers him to be *antisocial*, the slave of voracious and destructive passions.

Hobbes has been sometimes described as a representative of "naturalistic" natural law theories (cf. ch. 1, sec. 1 above). This description is basically misleading. In "nature" – the situation extant before the creation of states, there reigned, according to Hobbes, "natural rights," but that concept has nothing to do with a *normative system*: it simply means that there was nothing to prevent men from following their instincts and appropriating whatever their appetite urged them to lay hands on, including the goods and, indeed, the persons, of their fellow men. The "natural rights", thus, are nothing but the name given to the *de facto* possibilities of action in a lawless situation. The state of nature, in Hobbes's view, is a war of all against all *(bellum omnium erga omnes)*. In these circumstances, man's life is – as the philosopher grimly says – "brutish, nasty and short". Man realizes that in his own interest he has to refrain from the exercise of his "natural rights" and enter into a contract with his fellow men, whereby they all promise on the one hand to "lay down" as much of their liberty of actions as is necessary for the maintenance of peace, on the other hand to obey a ruler. In this context, Hobbes's rationalism becomes evident; reason is the source of "natural law" (as opposed to the natural rights just mentioned) inasmuch as it both demonstrates the necessity first of coming to terms at all with other men in order to draw up "convenient articles of peace" and also indicates with mathematical precision, the course of action conducive to peace and order. It is clear, however, that this "natural law" is no more a body of *norms* than were the "natural rights": it is in fact a body of "laws" in the sense of the natural sciences, i.e. essentially descriptions of empirical observations. They are, as Hobbes himself indicates "mere conclusions and theories relating to that which leads to the conservation and defence of oneself".

Not only is this "natural law" not a body of binding precepts; it is not even sufficient to ensure compliance with the terms of the social contract. Reason, in Hobbes's pessimistic view, is not strong enough to keep man's antisocial passions at bay. These must be fought with another passion, of the same strength. That is fear. Social peace is guaranteed by fear of the omnipotent state, which Hobbes describes as a sort of organic entity, infinitely stronger than individuals, and by necessity provided with unlimited rights of legislation and, more generally, command over the subjects. The only limitations to that right are, on the one hand, that the state cannot require a subject to lay down his life without defending it – it was, after all, for the preservation of life that the social contract was concluded and the state established – and on the other hand that the state is in fact successful in maintaining social peace. Failure in that respect amounts to a breach of the contract on the ruler's side. That ruler, in Hobbes's system, can be a single individual or a body. What is essential is the ruler's efficiency. Among the tools the ruler can, and indeed should, use for his purposes is a State Church, which is considered precisely in this light: as one more among the instruments of power. Nothing shows better the religious indifference of Hobbes's thinking.

Hobbes may be described as the first writer to advocate a radical and uncompromising positivism. We have already noticed that neither the "rights" existing in the state of nature nor that "law of nature" which showed men the consequences of not keeping peace have a normative character; they belong to the realm of facts, not to that of rules. The only *legal* rules Hobbes recognizes are those laid down by the state, and these have their binding force and normative character exclusively from the fact that they are the commands of the sovereign. In fact, Hobbes goes as far as to state that without, or outside, the state the terms "justice" and "injustice" are devoid of sense. It is for the state to declare certain actions licit and others illicit. And it is only by virtue of the law-making act of the ruler or rulers that the maxims of "natural law" – which were previously nothing but "theorems" – assume the character of "true law."

It need not be said, here, that Hobbes's legal theories never achieved great popularity, and that reproaches for exaggerated pessimism, for cynicism and lack of piety were brought forward from an early date. Hobbes did not found a school of followers. However, by his logical strictness and unflinching realism, Hobbes has made one of the lasting contributions to legal thinking.

5. Legal Reasoning in the Renascence Period

As has already been mentioned (cf. ch. 4, secs. 6 and 7 above) the methods used by lawyers in their everyday work did not undergo drastic changes in the Middle Ages; the foundations laid by the glossators remained essentially valid throughout the period, although towards the end of the 15th and at the beginning of the 16th centuries, several treatises on legal reasoning, particularly on the art of interpretation, were published in Italy. Nor did the increased need for general concepts and principles, whereby the strictly case-oriented solutions of ancient and early medieval Roman law could be made useful for new situations and new problems, lead to a thoroughgoing systematization of the large body of rules handled by the commentators and the canonists.

The Transition to the Modern Era (1500–1650)

The vast majority of legal writers and practitioners in the period now under consideration continued to use their tools essentially in accordance with the methods elaborated by their predecessors. Bartolus of Sassoferrato is quoted as a leading authority throughout the period and beyond it. There were, however, exceptions. We have already referred to the emergence, in France and the Netherlands, of the so-called "elegant" school of legal writing (sec. 3 above) which, inspired by the ideals of the Renascence, attempted to break with traditional legal science and give to that branch of study a new, intellectually and philosophically more satisfactory, orientation. These attempts can to some extent be considered as forerunners both of the rationalistic jurisprudence of the 18th century and of that systematic restructuring of Roman law upon which the great 18th and 19th century continental codifications were to be based. These elements of Renascence jurisprudence therefore deserve a brief discussion.

A strong current in Renascence humanism leads back, beyond the late Roman authorities which transmitted ancient thinking to the Middle Ages and deeply influenced the intellectual culture of that period, to Platonism and Stoicism. With regard to the latter school of thought, great attention was paid not only to the Greek philosophers who founded and developed it, but also to Cicero, whose works became again, at this time, the acknowledged ideal of Latin prose and who exercised, for that and other reasons, a deep and lasting influence upon the European learned world. Several writers working in the spirit of Renascence humanism restated Cicero's claim that legal science ought to develop into an *ars*, a methodically studied and systematically presented body of scientific knowledge. The building of a logical structure of rules was held preferable to the piecemeal interpretation of isolated provisions; general principles and great lines of thought were sought for rather than the scholastic analysis of single points of law. The adoption of Platonism made lawyers emphasize the existence of a general idea of justice, of which the various detailed rules were only examples and illustrations; the Stoics had always insisted upon the need for logic and systematics in all scholarly activities, and this claim was now put forward by Renascence lawyers. In this spirit, the French jurist *Duarenus* writes, in the introduction to his *Commentaria* (1559) that he purports to divide into its logical components and present according to the demands of a true art, all that which Tribonianus had put together, without order, under the two headings of Pandects and Institutions.

Another important French jurist, *Hugo Donellus* (Hugues Doneau, d 1590), was among the first to attempt to present the whole body of Roman private law in a systematic order based upon the nature of the rights conferred by law upon a person. In a simplified form, his systematics was as follows:

Quod nostrum est
(That which belongs to us)

Quod vere et proprie nostrum est (That which is truly our own)		Quod nobis debeatur (That which is due to us)	
In persona cuiusque (With regard to our own person)	In rebus externis (In outward things, i.e. the law of property)	Ex contractu (By virtue of contract)	Ex delicto etc (By virtue of a tort, etc.)

The success of Doneau's and other Renascence lawyers' attempts at a rational systematization was neither general nor immediate. In France as in the Netherlands, they undoubtedly contributed to found a tradition of legal writing that survived, unbroken, through the following centuries. In Germany and Italy, medieval traditions still held their own; however, in the course of the 17th century, German lawyers – mention should be made of the great scholar *Hermann Conring* (d. 1681) and of *Samuel Stryk* (d. 1710) – developed under the influence of "elegant" jurisprudence, a technique of legal study and presentation that became known as *usus modernus* ("modern usage"), where some of the claims of the Renascence pioneers were satisfied. Italy and Spain remained for a very long time conservative, and England had already chosen its own, original way in the field of legal writing (although an influence from Continental legal science was never wholly absent).

It should be added that both "elegant jurisprudence" *(mos gallicus)* and German *usus modernus* had an essentially practical orientation. Lawyers like Duarenus and Donellus organized their material in what they conceived to be a clear and logical order, and they had the ambition of proceeding from general principles to specialized rules (the latter being, essentially, those which the commentators had elaborated in their adaptation of Roman law to modern needs), but they did not try to create complete systems in disregard of the realities of the complex body of rules inherited from late Roman law.

In the fields of legal reasoning and statutory interpretation, two representatives of Renascence jurisprudence shall be briefly dealt with here.

François Hotman (Franciscus Hotomanus, d. 1590) has already been mentioned as one of the French "monarchomachs" (sec. 3 above). He was a militant Protestant and a prolific writer. His work *Jurisconsultus sive de optimo genere juris interpretandi* (1559) is an ambitious – although neither revolutionary nor wholly original – treatise on statutory interpretation; after a reasoning section of some two hundred pages, he gives – in another hundred pages – a list of examples, where his maxims of interpretation are applied to selected passages from the *Corpus juris civilis*. Hotman divides – in accordance with a by then firmly established tradition – interpretation into three branches: grammatical, dialectic and legal. Grammatical interpretation, which serves to clarify obscure expressions or to amend corrupt texts, represents the first stage. On the chapter of dialectic – or, as it is more frequently called, logical – interpretation, Hotomanus follows ancient authorities, and divides it into *constructio* (putting together), *partitio* (splitting up into elements), and *divisio* (organizing into groups). Among these three procedures, he concludes that only *partitio* (which is a Latin translation of the Greek "analysis") is useful for lawyers, since it is only the systematic breaking down of a problem into its components that can give "true knowledge" about the matter under consideration. As for the specifically "legal" techniques of interpretation, Hotomanus presents a list of essentially well-known situations rather than to suggest a systematic approach: there are conflicts between strict law and equity, there are ambiguities of various descriptions, and there are unclear isolated terms. Like his predecessors, Hotomanus thus enumerates typical problems instead of trying to find general formulae or to organize the matter into a systematic structure.

Donellus' treatment of the problems of interpretation in his *Commentarii de iure civili* (1589) is too complex to be dealt with in detail here.[2]

---

[2] For a detailed analysis, see Strömholm in 22 *Scandinavian Studies in Law*, pp. 213 ff (1978), at pp. 223 ff.

The Transition to the Modern Era (1500–1650)

Basing his discussion on the fundamental conflict between *scriptum* and *sententia* – the literal wording and the intention of the law – he proceeds to analyse various situations where a "restrictive" (narrowing) interpretation is called for, cases where an "extensive" construction is necessary, and finally problems caused by obscurity in the text. Although Donellus is convinced – as lawyers were to be for at least three more centuries – that the problem of interpretation is exclusively a linguistic one, he is nevertheless clearly aware, without being able to state it explicitly, of the basic fact that the principal function of laws, and consequently also of their handling under the name of interpretation, is to solve social conflicts and meet human needs rather than to provide lawyers with opportunities for learned or logical exercise. Although inevitably caught in the traditional conceptual apparatus developed by his medieval predecessors and in the fiction of the all-knowing and all-wise legislator, Donellus understands the special position of legal hermeneutics, dictated by its specific practical purposes and needs. It is not astonishing that considerations of legislative policy and social expediency are referred, in his analysis, to two all-embracing concepts: that of the legislator's will and that of equity. Under these two headings, he finds ample and sufficient space for most of those reasonable and relevant evaluations that lawyers of today would account for openly.

Chapter 6

The Era of the Rationalistic Law of Nature (1650–1789)

Selected Bibliography: B. Ahlander, *Om rätt och rättstillämpning*, Stockholm 1952, pp. 19–40; A. Brimo, *Les grands courants de la philosophie du droit et de l'état*, 3ᵉ éd., Paris 1978, pp. 87–142; G.C. Christie, *Jurisprudence. Texts and Readings on the Philosophy of Law*, St. Paul, Minn. 1973, pp. 158–236, 357–459; J.M. van Eikema Hommes, *Major Trends in the History of the Philosophy of Law*, Amsterdam 1979, pp. 83–184; G. Fassò, *Storia della filosofia del diritto*, vol. 2, Bologna 1968, pp. 163–365; Lord Lloyd of Hampstead, *Introduction to Jurisprudence*, 3rd ed., London 1972, *passim*; S.F.C. Milsom, *Historical Foundations of the Common Law*, 2nd ed., London 1981; K. Olivecrona, *Rättsordningen*, 2nd ed., Lund 1976, pp. 21–34; K. Rode, *Geschichte der europäischen Rechtsphilosophie*, Düsseldorf 1974, pp. 117–129; G.H. Sabine, *A History of Political Theory*, 3rd ed., London 1952, pp. 438–521; S. Strömholm, *Idéer och tillämpningar*, Stockholm 1979, pp. 36–53, 68–80, 91–99; Same author, "Legal Hermeneutics – Notes on the Early Modern Development", 22 *Scandinavian Studies in Law* (1978), pp. 213–241; J.W.F. Sundberg, *fr. Eddan t. Ekelöf*, Stockholm 1978, pp. 77–115; A. Verdross, *Abendländische Rechtsphilosophie*, Vienna 1958, pp. 110–136; M. Villey, *La formation de la pensée juridique moderne*, Paris 1968, pp. 552–579; Fr. Wieacker, *Privatrechtsgeschichte der Neuzeit*, 2 Aufl., Göttingen 1967, pp. 249–347.

1. Introduction

In the introduction to the preceding chapter, we have justified the principles adopted for organizing our materials and dividing our presentation into chapters: a rough chronological order has, in spite of strong arguments for a different approach, been chosen. It is sufficient, here, to refer to that discussion; only a few remarks should be added by way of characterizing, in general terms, the period now under discussion (1650–1789).

The more one studies the richly orchestrated development of legal philosophy, and legal thinking in general, the more one tends to think in terms of long, complicated and sometimes bewildering periods of preparation, shorter "peaks" – classical periods, where some features emerge, in full strength and maturity, as dominating voices, temporarily reducing other elements to a second place – and "postclassical" periods, or, as some would perhaps say, periods of decay, characterized by the breaking down (which mostly means a less spectacular critical elaboration in details) of the leading themes and ideas, growing complexity and transition to a new "preparative" period. It is only too easy to argue that this thinking is based upon illusions, or optical errors which consist in understanding, or explaining, historical events and situations in terms of what followed – as if, e.g., the heyday of natural law in the 18th century, or the short-living triumph of the liberal society in the 19th, provided "keys" whereby such developments as constitutional thinking in the debate over Church government in the 15th century, or the voluntarism of the late medieval Scholastics could be "understood", or "explained", as "preparations" for later currents of thought.

This naive view upon history, sometimes referred to in an Anglo-American perspective, as "the whig (i.e. liberal) interpretation of history," has flourished, in particular, in periods characterized by a firm belief in the idea of linear progress in all fields of human activity. Objectively, there is of course no such thing as "periods of preparation": each part of history has a right to be heard and understood, on its own terms, as a phase – arbitrarily singled out for observation – of an uninterrupted work with problems then felt to call for solution. If one single factor had to be picked out, as a general characteristic of the process we are studying here, the best choice would undoubtedly be *continuity*: to the extent "explanations" are useful elements of the study of history – and since this is not the place to deal with the epistemological question of what "historical understanding" means, suffice it to say that without *some* kind (out of many possible approaches) of "interpreting" which goes beyond the mere registration of facts, that study would be a sterile occupation – it is certainly by the *past*, not by *later* developments that a given phenomenon is best understood. The use of the intellectual tools handed over from earlier generations to emerging new situations and new needs, and the ensuing continuous adaptation of these tools would seem to be, essentially, the most salient characteristic of the development we are studying.

Nevertheless, if provided with due reservations, the idea of a movement – preparation, classical period, transition – would seem permissible and indeed helpful in organizing the presentation of the past. The late 12th and the 13th centuries can justly be described as a period of harmony, dominated by a few dominating mature trends. The span of time from the middle of the 17th until the end of the 18th century can be envisaged in the same fashion – in spite of very clear signs of dissolution, decay in some respects and fresh starts in others towards the latter half of the period – as one of the classical phases of what may be called preindustrial "Old Europe". Political, social and economic tensions, although accumulating, were not strong enough to break through the complex, illogically built but still viable framework of the Occidental monarchies that had emerged from the turmoils of the late Middle Ages and the Reformation. Religious controversy had ceased to be a primary source of open strife. Many attempts have been made to define the elusive concept of "classicism". A minimum of harmony, or at least of peaceful coexistence, between the strongest political, social, economic, religious and, more generally, intellectual forces at work is certainly required. An additional ideological criterium, however, would seem to be an explicit *awareness* of that equilibrium, a reasoned satisfaction with its blessings, and some belief in its duration.

The last decades of the 17th and the first decades of the following century witness, particularly in the intellectually leading Occidental power, France, the emergence and growth of an extremely important attitude, which can legitimately be considered an expression of such an ideology: the *idea of progress*. The view according to which history is a steady march towards greater and greater perfection would seem to be, insofar as the Occidental world is concerned, one which gradually came into existence – as a more or less generally held conviction, entertained with sufficient consistency and persuasiveness to serve as a basis for serious human acting, indeed for the organization of society (as opposed to temporary or individual outbursts of satisfaction with the present state of things) from the last decades of the 17th century onwards. Although this conviction – strongly expressed in the work of the possibly most influential of all 18th century writers: Voltaire – soon gave way to a more nuanced view at least among more thoughtful observers (including the ageing Voltaire himself), it nevertheless became part of the average stock of prevailing ideas of modern Europe for a very long time. In Antiquity, philosophers had tended to stress the cyclical character of the process of history: "golden ages" were succeeded by periods of decadence, leading

The Era of the Rationalistic Law of Nature (1650–1789)

through catastrophe to new starts. Christian thinkers mostly considered secular history as a march not towards perfection but towards the Last Judgment. The idea of continuous progress was essentially new. Many factors contributed to this optimism: by and large, life in Western Europe had become easier for large groups of the population; there had been long periods of at least local and relative peace and prosperity, and even the recurring wars had to some extent become less ferocious; the administration of centralized states appeared, when compared to earlier periods, efficient, enlightened and able to create a security of life and limb formerly unknown; science, including medical science, and technology had made some progress which, although very modest by modern standards, affirmed man's relative control over nature and promised to extend that control. It had been the firmly rooted habit of educated Europeans to consider the Ancients as the old and wise masters; now, reversing that attitude, the more logical idea emerged that Antiquity was the childhood of humanity and that it was modern man, by virtue of the experience gathered in the course of centuries and of his increased scientific knowledge, who represented maturity and wisdom.

Once established as a general attitude, the idea of progress represented an immensely important change in the way of looking upon society as a whole, and law as an element of that society. As would become apparent before the end of the 18th century – the great French Revolution being the principal evidence – relative satisfaction with slowly improving conditions was not to stop for a long time those who considered the path of history as the road towards perfection, a view previously reserved for utopists and the followers of small sects. In the Middle Ages, and beyond, major law reforms had mostly been presented – such was the strength of belief both in the basic immutability of the law and in the perfection of ancestral custom – as a *restatement*, an elimination of pernicious innovations introduced as a result of man's corruption and decadence. The need for slow adaptation to new needs was sometimes recognized, that is true, but the idea of large-scale change, and of the use of law as an instrument of such change, was essentially foreign to the majority of both lawyers, political leaders, and people in general. The rediscovery of Roman law and its intellectual impact had strengthened the general respect for ancient law; at the same time, Roman rules partook of the general veneration for the Ancients. Their instrinsic rationality was hardly ever doubted.

The Era of the Rationalistic Law of Nature (1650–1789)

The slowly spreading belief in progress – in the Golden Age as a future, not a past, state of humanity – eroded the position of Justinian law as the last word of legislative wisdom. The delicate balance between *authority* and *reason*, *auctoritas* and *ratio*, which had characterized so much of earlier European thinking, changed; in some intellectual *milieux*, the change was rapid.

In the introduction to the preceding chapter, we mentioned the incipient specialization of different fields of knowledge, the increasingly clear line of demarcation between legal thinking and such disciplines as political science, and the consequent need (dictated also by the practical necessity of keeping our survey reasonably manageable in terms of breadth and size) for concentrating more strictly upon those sectors of European thinking which can be described as *legal* in a modern, technical sense. These remarks have an even greater claim to validity with regard to the period now under consideration. To *political science*, as a specialized discipline, albeit still largely operating with concepts borrowed from Roman and Canon law, should be added, from the latter half of the 18th century, the systematic study of *economics*.

For the reasons thus indicated, most major contributions to general and political philosophy will be briefly mentioned, in the present chapter, as part of the general intellectual background against which the development of legal thinking has to be considered. Three exceptions will have to be made from that principle, however: special sections will be devoted to the thinking of John Locke, Charles de Montesquieu, and Jean-Jacques Rousseau, although neither of them can be considered a legal philosopher in the narrow acception of that concept. Their ideas were of such fundamental importance for later legal thinking that it would be misleading to relegate them to a mere background position.

It follows both from the emergence and growth of a specialized "political science," and from the increased specialization of legal studies as such (were it only owing to that vastly expanded mass of legal rules in new fields of human activity which was one of the consequences of the development of the modern bureaucratic state) that the domain of legal philosophy in the strict sense, tends to become a narrower and more technical branch of science than in those earlier periods when lawyers had described their craft as *notitia rerum humanarum atque divinarum* ("knowledge of things human and divine"). In fact, whereas legal science had been from its origin in ancient Rome an essentially "exporting" discipline, lending from its rich arsenal of ideas, concepts, solutions and terms to other, younger and less well-established fields of study and reflection, the "terms of trade" in this mutual exchange tend to change towards the end of the period now discussed, although that tendency does not become clear until the following period, the 19th century: jurisprudence is becoming an "importing" science, borrowing from the more generalistic empirical social sciences ideas, patterns of thought, and analytical concepts that are subsequently processed into concrete legal solutions. Compared with the contributions of Descartes, Locke, Montesquieu, and Rousseau, legal philosophy, in the strict sense of the word, in the late 17th and in the 18th century appears fairly bleak, and lacking in originality. This development, which has continued with increasing obviousness in later times, is nothing the student of legal philosophy should spill tears for. The lawyers' plight is shared by the representatives of most old sciences, which once could lay imperialistic claims to vast areas of knowledge, then sparsely populated and extensively farmed, which are now centres of intense specialized scientific activity.

2. Some Historical Background Facts

There may seem to be a built-in paradox in the fact that the era of rationalistic natural law theory, a period when many a peaceful law professor, forgetting the world around him, taught his students ideal rules, firmly put together in ideal axiomatic systems, coincides with the era when Royal and princely absolutism was the clearly dominating constitutional system of the vast majority of European states. In Europe, only England and Sweden, and to some extent the Netherlands, presented a different picture. Absolutism, however, appeared to many or most, among them the great Enlightenment prophet, Voltaire, as the inevitable means of securing internal peace, rational policies, and a competent public administration, just as despotism had been greeted by a majority in ancient Rome as the only possible way out of civil war and political chaos. It should be remembered, however, that in actual fact, the allegedly absolute power of European rulers was in most countries of the West (as distinct from the emerging great Eastern power, Russia, where oriental despotism prevailed, mitigated only by inefficiency and the despots' fear of being murdered) a highly relative position: ancient custom, innumerable remaining and jealously guarded feudal rights, still powerful religious habits of thought and behaviour, the increasingly influential public opinion and strong social conventions of the *élites,* and finally occasional outbursts of popular discontent – formidable at a time when an efficient police had not yet been invented and both the means and the methods of rational police operations on a large scale were unknown – were as many obstacles in the way of absolute rulers. It was for later centuries to learn how whole populations can be governed with some efficiency completely against their will. The "despots" of the 18th century had to master the art of compromise; their rule was very largely based upon at least passive consensus.

France was the leading power. Her *grand siècle* did not last for a full century, however. Already at the death of Louis XIV in 1715, and even more markedly after the Seven Years' War (1763), it was clear that the French "classical" period we tried to define in the foregoing section was over, that her political and social framework was no longer considered as instrumental to progress, and that the maritime, commercial, colonial, and soon also industrial strength of England – hardly less ridden by social problems – gave the latter country a more solid position of power. Spain rapidly sank into poverty and relative political insignificance, although the vast colonial Empire was still held, and still sent its gold to Madrid. Italy was, as it had been, divided; poor, corrupt, but intellectually and artistically creative, the country became the goal of incipient international tourism. In Germany, equally divided, the Imperial House of Habsburg still wields the greatest power, based on its hereditary possessions in Austria, Northern Italy, Bohemia and Hungary; after the defeat of the Turks at Vienna in 1683, Habsburg expands towards the South-East; in the North-East, the Kingdom of Prussia, the most striking example of the efficiency of the "modern," strictly centralized and disciplined administration and war machine, develops, by internal reforms and territorial conquests, into a great European power. Sweden, having been for about one century (c. 1630–1721) a vast Empire, with possessions all along the southern coast of the Baltic (Estonia, Livonia, parts of Pomerania) is reduced to a second-rate power; its place as the leading military power of the North is taken by Russia. The Kingdom of Poland, victim of Swedish, later of Russian, Prussian, and Austrian aggression, finally ceases to exist as an independent State at the end of the period (1792), and is divided between the three last-mentioned powers.

The Era of the Rationalistic Law of Nature (1650–1789)

Throughout the period, the European expansion in America, Africa, and Asia continues; the struggles between the candidates for European supremacy now take place on the high seas and in the colonies almost as much as on the traditional battlefields in Flanders, the North Italian plains, central Germany and on the Rhine. Successive peace treaties in 1713, 1747, and 1763 affirm the leading position of England, at the expense of France – which loses Canada in 1763, after which time the North American continent is, with few exceptions, English-dominated territory – of Spain and Portugal, which retain only their Ibero-American possessions, and of Holland, which keeps, however, vast colonial holdings in the Sunda Islands. From the middle of the 18th century, England is, directly or indirectly, in control of most of present-day India and Pakistan. Economically and culturally important trade relations are established between Europe and the Chinese Empire.

The unprecedented success of Europeans overseas are due neither to superiority in numbers nor – as the case was to be in the 19th and 20th centuries – to superior scientific or technological skill. The keyword would seem to be – much as when Alexander's Macedonians and Greeks swept the Near East and when the Roman legions conquered more densely populated, culturally equal or even superior states in the Mediterranean basin – rational organization and strict discipline (in addition to considerable ruthlessness). Clive's handful of redcoats at Plassey (1757) – farm hands and jobless apprentices recruited from England's illiterate proletariat – were neither braver nor better equipped than the large army of the nawab of Bengal, but they were severely, indeed brutally, drilled professionals in the art of manoeuvring in closed order in the field, just as Charles XII's 8.000 Swedes at Narva (1700) beat 80.000 Russians by virtue of competent staff work, careful planning, rational organization and strict collective and individual discipline. "Rationalism", pushed to mathematical precision, was not merely a formula expounded by teachers of law or philosophy or a slogan adopted by enlightened rulers and their ministers; it was an attitude which gradually and deeply permeated European public life and professional and business activities. Political, military and economic success overseas and at home, combined with slow but uninterrupted scientific and technical progress contributed to enhance the prestige of rationalism, to strengthen the belief in progress by the exercice of right reason and rational methods in all

The Era of the Rationalistic Law of Nature (1650-1789)

fields, and also to create a feeling of superiority in relation to other civilizations, in which other, as it seemed less viable, ideals and patterns of organization were predominant.

A factor of great importance for the future of the Occident was the American Revolution (1776) and the creation of a new state, with a Republican federal constitution and based upon some of the leading principles both of reformist natural law thinking (the freedom and equality of all men) and of contemporary constitutional ideas (in particular those of Montesquieu). The new Republic also strongly appealed to, and reinforced, the enthusiasm for Antiquity, and for Roman republican and civic "virtue" as understood in the second half of the 18th century. Another element of European thinking in the late 18th century, which ran contrary to the prevailing dry rationalism but also contributed largely to make the new-founded United States an ideal with a great power of attraction, was the glorification of nature, natural life, and the innocence and purity of "natural man" – the noble savage, introduced in particular by Rousseau – as opposed to the artificial and rigidly conventional life-style of the old world; the insurgent American colonists were seen, particularly in France, as representatives of a powerful revolt of "nature" against the wicked and tyrannic rule of the King of England. As envoy of the insurgents in France, the knowledgeable, practical, and astute Benjamin Franklin made great success in high society as a true and "natural" philosopher. Both into the American Declaration of Independence (1776), the Federal Constitution (1787) and several State constitutions – all of which documents were the works of highly cultivated men, frequently lawyers, who had little in common with "noble savages", declarations, and lists of human rights were inserted, essentially in keeping with the natural law thinking of the time.

The American example exercised a considerable influence upon large groups of the French social and intellectual *élites*. When in the 1780's, it became increasingly obvious that the French monarchy and its state organization were unable to find adequate solutions to the political, social and economic problems of the country, and when the King finally convoked the medieval representative assembly of the Kingdom, the Estates General (clergy, nobility and the "third estate") which had not met for more than 170 years, that example gained – for some time at least – in practical importance. Although the deepest underlying causes of the great upheaval which started in 1789 were

The Era of the Rationalistic Law of Nature (1650–1789)

to a very large extent problems related to state finances, taxes, and the whole socio-economic structure of the country, claims for personal and political freedom and for equality in principle were to constitute, in the early phases of the Revolution, the basic reform demands of the leading groups. At the very beginning of the revolutionary process, which was to demolish, in a few years, both the Monarchy and most traditional institutions of France (including, for about a decade, the Catholic Church), a Declaration of the Rights of Men and Citizens was adopted by the National Assembly that had soon taken the place of the Estates General. In that declaration, which has remained part of French constitutions since then, the philosophy of radical natural law thinking is developed at length. The liberty and equality of all men is affirmed, and it is stated that the purpose of human society – which should be based on the doctrine of popular sovereignty and express, in its laws, the "general will" of the nation – is to protect the natural and imprescriptible rights of man: liberty, property, and resistance against oppression. Freedom of opinion, religious belief, and expression is guaranteed, and some basic tenets of criminal law, intended in particular to offer protection against the arbitrary infliction of punishment for acts not punishable when committed, are explicitly formulated.

In its later course, the Revolution gradually degenerated into dictatorship and a bloody terror régime, until, after a decade, it found its end – not unlike similar upheavals in ancient and modern days – in the military dictatorship, and later, the Empire, of a military and political genius and adventurer, the Corsican artillery officer Napoleon Bonaparte.

Among the most important achievements of the period now considered in the political and legal field are a number of great codifications, which express both the basic elements of natural law thinking – or, more exactly, of such thinking grafted upon modernized Roman law – and the systematic and pedagogic preoccupations of that school of legal philosophy. Three of these codifications should be mentioned here: the Prussian Civil Code *(Allgemeines Landrecht)* of 1794, the French "five great Codes" of the first decade of the 19th century (in particular *Code civil*, 1804; the others were the Penal Code, the Code of Commercial Law, the Code of Civil Procedure and the Code of Penal Procedure), and the Austrian Code of Private Law *(Allgemeines Bürgerliches Gesetzbuch)* of 1811. The French and Austrian Codes are still

The Era of the Rationalistic Law of Nature (1650-1789)

in force, whereas the Prussian Code was, in most respects of any importance, replaced in 1900 by the General German Code of Private Law *(Bürgerliches Gesetzbuch)*. Although there are great differences, both in systematics, legislative technique, and substantive contents, between these Codes – that of Prussia, in particular, reflects the structure and ideals of the autocratic state of Frederick the Great – their common inspiration in the law reform movements, and general philosophy, of the era of rationalistic natural law is obvious. We shall return, in due course, to some aspects of the codification movement.

One last remark about the great Codes: they were ambitious attempts to cover the whole area of law concerned, and they were exclusively applicable to their respective national territories. National and provincial Codes had existed earlier, through the Middle Ages onwards (e.g., the Swedish Rural Code of 1350; the still valid Danish and Norwegian National Codes of 1683 and 1687, respectively, and the Code for Sweden and Finland, 1734, equally still in force), but *legal science* had been international, and in that science, Roman law had dominated. With the great Codes from the years around 1800, the teaching of law, as well as legal scholarship and research, became for the first time in the history of Europe essentially confined to national systems in the major European countries. It is one of the ironic – and tragic – elements of modern European legal history that the final outcome of the teaching of a *universal* natural law was the establishment of a narrow legal nationalism which still subsists and which a century of comparative law studies and efforts at international harmonization has only partially managed to break.

3. Major Trends in Religious, Philosophical and Political Thinking

It would be grossly misleading to contend that from the middle of the 17th century, *religion* was no longer one of the foremost preoccupations of Occidental thinking; the description given in ch. 5, sec. 3, above of the development in the era of transition (1500–1650) remains true also with regard to the period now under consideration. Western Europe and America remained, throughout the period, essentially Christian, and repeated revivalist movements both in the Protestant world and within the Church of Rome produced deep and lasting effects not only upon the everyday life of all classes of society but also upon all branches

175

of the social sciences, including legal theory and legal philosophy. On the other hand, the rift between religious and scientific thought, which had been opened already towards the end of the Middle Ages, was successively widened. Arguments taken from religious faith and dogma frequently recur in the jurisprudential writing of the period, but even where such arguments are more than conventional lip service to established religion – and it should be remembered that in most countries, Protestant as well as Catholic, strict ecclesiastical censorship often made such lip service necessary – they are, mostly, no longer *necessary,* or *integral,* parts of the ongoing discussion. With many exceptions, that is true, Occidental thinking in the fields which interest us here is basically secularized.

Among the exceptions which deserve a short discussion, the survival and development of Catholic natural law thinking in *French jurisprudence* is of some interest. Above (ch. 5, sec. 3) we mentioned Montaigne and Pascal, who both arrived, from radically different points of departure, at a deeply sceptical and relativistic view upon the idea of a universal and immutable law of nature. Montaigne and Pascal were not lawyers, however, and their attitude, however influential as a general trend, was not typical for the lawyers of their own and the following period. The leading legal writer of the French classical era, *Jean Domat* (1625–1696) – a close personal friend of Pascal, and like him a staunch supporter of the Jansenist reform movement that had, throughout the 17th century and beyond, a strong appeal to the French intellectual élite – bases his great work *Les loix civiles dans leur ordre naturel (The Civil Laws in their Natural Order)* on religious and political foundations which can be most adequately described as Neothomist; no opposition between Christian faith and rationalistic natural law reasoning can be found in this treatise, which was to serve as the starting point for that systematization of Roman and French law which was developed and refined by – equally Catholic – 18th century writers and ultimately adopted in the *Code civil* of 1804.

If traditional religious thinking thus remained powerful among Catholic lawyers, religious controversy had a fundamental importance for the development of *English legal thinking* throughout the 17th century. Since other elements, in particular constitutional theories, are even more important in the long and violent debate that accompanied the deeply troubled but also highly creative century of the Stuarts

(1603–1688), we shall come back to the English scene at the end of the present section.

As for *philosophy*, and *science in general*, two major trends, which are intimately linked with each other and which are both immensely influential for the future of all theoretical thinking in the West, not least for the development of natural law theories, should be discussed briefly.

The Copernican revolution in science had taken a long time in penetrating the minds of men. Ancient and medieval scientific ideas survived, even in the writings of highly educated, and otherwise "modern," scholars well into the 17th century. In the universities, the ancient conception of the universe, and of nature, held its own for a long time, in spite of the contributions of such scholars as Galilei, Bruno, Bacon, and Pascal. Slowly, however, a new view of the world penetrated and replaced the medieval outlook, which still made the Earth the center of the universe. One of the great achievements of the 17th century was to organize international communication in the learned world, the "Republic of Letters," far more efficiently than before; new discoveries rapidly became known throughout Europe; scholars organized themselves in Academies and other learned societies. Progress was particularly marked in the fields of mathematics and physics. *Sir Isaac Newton* (d. 1727) laid the foundations of a new, mechanistic view of a universe subject to rigorous, mathematically calculable laws. As already mentioned, this meant that for the first time in the existence of man, a strong faith in the possibility not only of *knowing* but also of *mastering* physical nature came into existence and gave increased strength to growing optimism and belief in human progress.

Somewhat earlier, the Frenchman *René Descartes* (Cartesius, d. 1650), the founder of modern analytical geometry, brings about what may justly be called a revolution in philosophy. Earlier thinkers had parted – whatever conclusions they ultimately drew from that starting-point – from the certainty that the observable world around them was basically "real" (although that "reality" might be, as in Plato's thought, of an inferior or derived kind, as distinct from the world of ideas) and that their task was to understand and interpret the situation of man in, and in relation to, that reality, where his place was given once and for all. Descartes throws this certainty overboard. He parts from the only absolutely safe object of observation: the thinking individual himself. Since man, or rather the individual "I", performs the act of thinking, he *must* exist: *cogito, ergo sum* ("I think, therefore I exist"). As for the rest of the world, it has to be constructed, as it were, parting from that sole vantage point, and using the only safe methods available: human reason operating upon a minimum of inevitable axioms with the methods of a kind of general mathematics. The world, then, is no longer the sum of a set of practically indefinite observable realities; it is the body of conclusions obtained by means of the logical operation of the mind; in short, it is an artificial system. The last-mentioned term is fundamental: it is not "the world" that imposes upon the observer, by means of his perception, its own structures and laws; what structures and laws there are, are the results of the operation of the mind. To "know" the world means to have constructed, by exercise of reason under its mathematical laws, a complete system. Although this idea could not, for many practical reasons, penetrate immediately – or, indeed, ever penetrate completely – into such eminently practical activities as the work of lawyers, it gave a decisive impetus to the old idea, found in Cicero and some Renascence writers, of constructing bodies of legal rules into clear and consistent hierarchic structures, proceeding from the general to the specific. Cartesianism is one of the major sources of inspiration both of the notion of legal "systems" as such and, more particularly, of the movement of codification we have already mentioned. Both Catholics, like Domat, Protestants, like Pufendorf, later German natural law writers (v. sec. 4 below), and numerous philosophers are deeply influenced by Descartes' bold rationalism.

Among "general philosophers" active in the earlier part of the period considered here, three should be mentioned. The Dutch Jew *Baruch Spinoza* (1632–1677), an isolated thinker, abhorred both by the Jews and the Christians of his time, developed a pantheistic system. In *"God, or Nature" (Deus sive natura)*, the ubiquitous power that permeates the universe, there is no difference between that which is, and that which ought to be: God's order prevails, and whatever exists is thus "necessary." Every living being, including man, has as much "right" as it has, by nature, power to act; the "law of nature" coincides with that which actually occurs. To be subject to, or obliged by, another's "rights," simply means to be subject to that other person's physical power. Thus Spinoza's "law of nature" comes close to that of Hobbes: it has no ethical contents. Men come together in societies exclusively for practical and egoistic reasons; rationality leads them to the State, and that body has the function to assure, to the extent it is compatible with its task of securing peace and security, the free development of its citizens. Thus Spinoza arrives at conclusions radically different from those adopted by Hobbes: he is in favour of the greatest possible freedom and also of a democratic form of government.

Gottfried Wilhelm Leibniz (1646–1716) was a universal genius; he made a career as a scholar, a courtier, and a diplomat, and wrote profusely in philosophy, jurisprudence and international law, political science and mathematics. One of his ambitions was to treat legal problems with mathematical methods and to teach law in the same way (the treatise *Nova methodus discendae docendaeque jurisprudentiae, A New Method for Learning and Teaching Law,* 1667). Although Leibniz himself insisted on his traditionalism, and on the Christian inspiration of his views upon law – which are expressed in many of his writings from various periods and cannot easily be brought into a consistent system – he belongs, by virtue of his method and general outlook, to the rationalistic school of natural law. This is visible in particular in his recurrent and energetic attempts to cast legal science and legal teaching (of contemporary *Roman* law, not of a hypothetical "natural" law system) into the mould of a hierarchic system of simple rules, free from exceptions and capable of answering all questions. Leibniz was also a convinced advocate of codification.

Giambattista Vico (1668–1744) whose originality and profundity have been more and more acknowledged in later years, spent his life as a professor at Naples, where he taught philosophy and law. Among his many scholarly works, the *Scienza nuova prima* (full name: *Principi di una scienza nuova in torno alla commune natura delle nazioni, Principles for a New Science concerning the Common Nature of Nations,* 1725; new ed. 1744) reflects his mature thinking. Vico is one of the pioneers of historicism; his "new science" purports to combine history and philosophy in such a way as to avoid the naive, ahistorical rationalism of the Enlightenment period. Law, in Vico's view, represents the blending of universal and immutable principles with the empirical facts of history, which may seem arbitrary and irrational but is nevertheless permeated with rationality. An eminent expert in Roman law, Vico finds in the basic institutions of that body of rules expressions of a general natural law. Thus unlike the majority of philosophers and jurists of his time, Vico does not "construct" the law of nature as a system entirely independent

The Era of the Rationalistic Law of Nature (1650–1789)

of positive law but rather as a set of principles underlying the laws of historically given societies and becoming evident when these systems, in their development, are compared to each other.

An optimistic belief in reason, and in the progress of mankind as a result of its application not only to scientific but also to social, economic, and political problems were the chief characteristics of the later part of the period now considered – the era of Enlightenment. Another element, closely related to this basic conviction, was deep distrust, and indeed contempt, of all those political, social and religious institutions, customs, and beliefs which had their roots in the "dark centuries" of the Middle Ages and could not be rationally justified. The Church, in particular the Catholic Church, was one of the main targets of the Enlightenment philosophers. While the early representatives of the movement, such as the French writers *Bayle* (d. 1706, the author of a great encyclopedic work, *Dictionnaire historique et critique*) and *Fontenelle* (d. 1757, a popularizer of Copernican and Cartesian thinking), still acted with great caution, the later "philosophers", *Denis Diderot* (d. 1784), chief editor of the great *Encyclopédie* (1751–1772), *Voltaire* (d. 1778), who was the most influential of them all, and the mathematicians *d'Alembert* (d. 1783) and *Condorcet* (d. 1794), criticized openly, sometimes with great vehemence, the institutions of their time from the point of view of radical rationalism. The French Enlightenment writers were mostly not deep or original thinkers; their talents often consisted in, and their great influence was based upon, the journalistic gift of popularizing eloquently and suggestively ideas taken from others and of applying such ideas to problems and situations with which their readership was likely to be acquainted. Thus such notions as innate human rights, liberty (of expression, of religion, of trade) and equality, which had their origin in earlier and contemporary natural law thinking, became, through the "philosophers," effective political slogans. In the same way, Voltaire and others (mention should be made, in particular, of the Italian nobleman and administrator Marquess Cesare de Beccaria, d. 1794, whose short treatise on penal law, *Dei delitti e delle pene, On Crime and Punishment,* was an extremely influential contribution to the humanization of criminal procedure and of criminal sanctions) managed to create a wide-spread public opinion against the brutality and irrationality of contemporary criminal law.

One "general philosopher" from the later part of the period we are now dealing with is worthy of special mention, although he did not exercise a very great immediate influence (the treatment of two other thinkers who wrote much of their most important works before 1789 – the German Immanuel Kant and the Englishman Jeremy Bentham – is postponed to the next chapter, since their ideas are essential for understanding the 19th century development). *David Hume* (1711–1776), a native of Edinburgh, where he spent most of his life, got into personal contact with the French Enlightenment when, at the middle of the 1760's, he worked as a secretary to the British Ambassador in Paris. For a short time he was the host of Rousseau, then a refugee in Britain. He wrote several works of great originality and depth, among them *A Treatise of Human Nature* (1739–1740), *An Enquiry concerning Human Understanding* (1748), and *An Enquiry concerning the Principles of Morals* (1751). Hume is a radical empiricist, and a sceptic. His theory of knowledge and of action makes him a particularly effective critic of some of the basic tenets of contemporary natural law thinking, among them the doctrine of the social contract, What ultimately dictates man's answer to ethical, including legal, questions, Hume contends, is the pleasure or the pain which a given state of affairs causes him. This does not mean that Hume excludes the possibility of disinterested, or philantropic motives playing an important part in answering such questions, for the pleasant or unpleasant feelings can be caused not only by what affects an individual himself, physically and immediately, but also by the exercice of his faculty of *sympathy*, or participation in the reactions of others. It follows from this view of the foundations of ethics that *reason* – which the prevailing contemporary natural law writers made the basis of the law of nature – is unable to determine the direction of human will and thus also to determine moral attitudes. What is "right" or "wrong" is decided by feeling, not by reason. The role of reason is merely to demonstrate the proper, or most practical, way to achieve the goals fixed by feeling. Human ethical attitudes – "virtues" – are either the natural results of feeling and passion or the secondary, or derived, conventions adopted in order to avoid the mischief flowing from the conflicts of passions, in particular with regard to the insufficiency of those objects which are desired by all men. To solve conflicts in the latter respect is the task of justice. It is part of Hume's empiricism that he rejects both the idea of a primeval state of nature and that of a social contract: the former, he says, is a "philosophical fiction", since man has always lived in some kind of society, be it only the family group, and has thus always been taught some code of social behaviour. "Natural law", in Hume's thinking, is simply the body of precepts which must be ovserved for the society to survive, and since men frequently prefer the immediate satisfaction of their desires without heeding the anti-social and destructive consequences of such behaviour in a long-range perspective, a government is necessary to force them to observe social utility, as expressed in legal rules. Obedience to the State is thus not a result of contractual obligations; it is a necessity for human survival.

We need not follow here the development of *political science* and political thinking in the period 1650–1789. Some of the most influential writers – Locke, Montesquieu, and Rousseau – made contributions to legal theory in a narrow sense which justify a somewhat more detailed treatment below (secs. 5–7). Important trends of Enlightenment political theory – in particular the tendency to analyse and present the law in terms of *individual rights,* frequently envisaged as imprescriptible "natural", or "innate", human rights – are expressed also in the works of the spokesmen of rationalistic natural law in the field of legal science (sec. 4 below). Other trends – *humanitarianism* and *criticism* of the constitutional, social (and religious) legacy of earlier periods – have already been mentioned. A particular feature of late 18th century political thought, which may seem to be in opposition with the general idea of progress, is the strong attraction exercised, by ancient, Greco-Roman political institutions and ideals. The stern "Republican virtues" of the Ancients were celebrated throughout Europe, but in particular in the active and ledading circles of the French Revolution.

In the field of political thought, three topics must be briefly addressed, however, before we conclude the present section: English constitutionalism, the emergence of American political thinking, and the birth of economy as a specialized branch of political science.

In an earlier part of this survey (ch. 4, sec. 7) we have mentioned briefly some original features of English legal writing in the Middle Ages (Glanvill and Bracton). The profound originality of English legal thinking became even more stressed in the course of the late Middle Ages and the Renascence period. Since political and constitutional aspects were to assume, in a critical period of the English development, a particularly great importance, this may be the proper place to make a few further remarks on the evolution of English legal thinking in the 17th and 18th centuries. One of the explanations of English originality

The Era of the Rationalistic Law of Nature (1650-1789)

is undoubtedly that English legal debate from an early date assumed a more technical and less "philosophical" character than on the Continent. Although Roman and Canon law was taught in the universities, judges and practitioners – reasoning in the framework, and with the technical terminology, of the common law, as a body of national positive law – and not law professors became the protagonists of the scene of English legal thinking.

Whatever may have been the indirect intellectual influence of Continental writing (and of the very few English legal writers who, like John Fortescue, d. 1476, translate local customary law into the language of contemporary natural law terms), English lawyers remained apprentices and masters of the *craft* of the law as applied by the national courts. The basic idea that the common law of the Realm is supreme, and also binding upon the King, prevailed even under the monarchs of the Tudor dynasty (16th century), although they were, for all practical purposes, as powerful as their contemporary Continental counterparts (this doctrine of the common law is thus expounded by, e.g. Thomas Smith, d. 1577, in *De republica Anglorum, On the State of England*).

With the accession of the Scottish House of Stuart to the throne of England, the traditional doctrine was put to new tests. Opposed both by Catholics, who had strong support paricularly in the old aristocracy, and by radical Calvinist sects, "the Puritans," recruited essentially among the rising middle classes, the Stuarts insisted on the divine rights of Kings and tried to make themselves independent of the increasingly unmanageable Parliament. In ecclesiastical matters, the Dynasty favoured, and found support in, the established (Anglican) Church of England which the radical Calvinists found too "popish" both in doctrine and in rituals. Questions of faith, and of Church government, became inextricably interwoven with political and constitutional issues. These preoccupations are reflected in the influential treatise *Of the Laws of Ecclesiastical Polity*, by the churchman *Richard Hooker* (d. 1600), who defends the established Church – with arguments coming close to the natural law theories of St. Thomas – but also insists on the binding character of a social contract under which popular consent alone legitimates the power of Kings. Among the supporters of the first Stuart monarch, James I, we find Francis Bacon, who wanted to reduce the power of judges and codify the law of England. The great champion of the common law in the early part of the 17th century was the Chief Justice of King's Bench, *Edward Coke* (d. 1634), whose *Institutes of the Laws of England* proclaim both the supremacy of Parliament as the law-giving body of the Realm and the sanctity of the common law, which in Coke's presentation assumes a place and dignity similar to that given by his Continental contemporaries to the concept of natural law: the common law is, like Cicero's natural law – to which Coke refers – right reason, and no single individual, not even the King, can set it aside. This exalted common law comprises, in Coke's view (which retains undoubtedly, in this respect, an element of medieval and feudal conceptions), not only private and penal law, but also the law of the constitution, as developed in English practice from the *Magna charta* of 1215 onwards.

The violent struggles between King and Parliament led to civil war in 1640, to the execution of Charles I Stuart in 1649, to the military dictatorship of Cromwell, to the restoration of the Stuarts (Charles II) in 1660, and finally, to the victory of constitutionalism over Royal aspirations in the Glorious Revolution of 1688, which ultimately established the English constitutional and legal system, so much admired by Continental Liberals throughout the 18th and 19th centuries. In the course of these decades of turmoil, polemical writings were produced in great numbers from both sides. On the side of Parliament, mention should be made of *John Selden* (d. 1654) who argued against the claims of Roman law to be recognized in England and who developed a system of natural law on the basis of the Old Testament. Radical Republican and egalitarian ideas on Scriptural and natural law foundations were voiced by the left wing of the Puritans, the "Levellers"; their message was too clearly opposed to the interests of the most powerful sections of the English society to rally much support, but their eloquent pleading for liberty and, in particular, equality, as innate human rights was to remain a challenge until modern days. Politically, if not socially, radical ideas were also put forward by the poet *John Milton* (d. 1674), who defended the execution of Charles I and pleaded for freedom of expression, by *James Harrington* (d. 1677), who expressed Republican ideals in his utopian work on "the commonwealth of Oceana", and by *James Tyrrell* (d. 1718), who introduced Continental natural law ideas into the English debate. The most influential writer among those who rejected the claims of the Stuarts was John Locke, to whom a special section is devoted below (sec. 5). On the side of the dynasty we find Thomas Hobbes (ch. 5,

The Era of the Rationalistic Law of Nature (1650-1789)

sec. 4 above) and also Sir Robert Filmer, whose *Patriarcha* (*The Patriarch*, 1680) derives the claims of Kings from the paternal authority of Adam.

The colonization of North America was a venture undertaken, with various degrees of success, by many nations, and by many groups of people. The French, the Dutch, and the Swedes held smaller and greater possessions on the new Continent, but the European nation which ultimately came to set its seal, in a decisive way, to the moral, intellectual and legal development of North America were the English. After the French had lost Canada (1763), the whole North Eastern part of the country was in English hands. After the American Revolution, the United States were to continue the conquest by acquiring Louisiana from France, California from Spain, and Alaska from Russia.

The English settlements in North America were far from uniform in social and political structure; they were also different in ideological respects. Whereas the northern part of the American east coast, with Massachusetts as the centre, was dominated by Puritans and other oppositional elements, who had emigrated to escape from persecution under the Stuarts in the early 17th century, the southern colonies, such as Virginia and North and South Carolina, were peopled in the latter half of the century by Cavaliers; large tracts of land were granted by Royal charter to members of the nobility and gentry. The Puritan settlements, peopled by sturdy and uncompromising nonconformists, who considered themselves – not without reason – the salt of the earth, developed theocratic communities, with representative assemblies, not unlike the régime established by Calvin at Geneva. Thus, an unbroken tradition of constitutional principles and constitutional experience came into existense.

In fact, the "Pilgrim Fathers," who sailed from Plymouth to Massachusetts in 1620, provide one of the few examples of a community founded on an explicit "social contract", which was signed on board the "Mayflower" before the colonists went ashore. Similar covenants were made in some other colonies, later to become states in the Union (Rhode Island, Connecticut). In all of them, the idea that popular consent is the essential legitimation of the state is strongly emphasized, and this idea survived when, after the Restoration, Royal Governors were appointed in the colonies. The settlers could also draw on the elements of constitutional law inherent in the common law of

England, which was the legal system retained by them; and on those constitutional ideas in the field of ecclesiastical law which had been developed, on medieval bases, in English religious controversy from the 16th century onwards. These elements, combined with ideas from Samuel Pufendorf (cf. sec. 4 below) are visible in the works of early American writers, like *John Wise* (d. 1725, author of i.a., *A Vindication of the Government of New England Churches*).

Thus, when after the middle of the 18th century, the tension between the English Government and the colonies grew, essentially over issues concerning taxation, into open conflict, the Americans were ideologically prepared. The intellectual *élite* of the North American settlements were also acquainted with contemporary Enlightenment thinking, in particular with the works of Locke and Montesquieu (cf. secs. 5 and 6 below). The element of rationalistic natural law is thus evident in the first American declaration of rights, that prepared by George Mason and adopted by the representatives of Virginia in 1776, shortly before the Declaration of Independence of the thirteen insurgent States at the beginning of the war of liberation.

From the middle of the 18th century, *the science of economics* becomes a specialized discipline, breaking out from the common field of political and philosophical reflection on human society. The "father of political economy," *Adam Smith* (1723–1790), a compatriot and contemporary of David Hume, starts his career as a moral philosopher of the empirical and utilitarian school of thought. In France, the Physiocrats, headed by the philosopher *François Quesnay* (d. 1774), who also wrote on natural law, reflect the emphasis which many Europeans of the late 18th century – Rousseau being the most radical and most famous among them – tended to put upon "Nature" and upon the need for man to conform to what is "natural." The Physiocrats celebrated agriculture as the sole producer of real wealth, as opposed to the crafts and to trade, which had been exclusively encouraged and protected by the national States in the preceding era (the period of mercantilism).

The Physiocrat movement, as well as contemporary literary and artistic fashions – the German *Sturm und Drang*, with its accent upon spontaneousness, nature, and the freedom of the creative genius, the increasing interest in "Gothic" architecture and medieval ballads in England, and the rise of a non-classical, sentimental, *bourgeois* drama in France – would seem to express a growing weariness with the all-permeating rationalism, felt to be dry and stifling, and a craving for patterns of thought and of life more apt to satisfy man's irrational but deep-rooted need for feeling and imagination. The long, strenuous and strictly disciplined school day of the West is approaching its end; the evening, and the feast of the Romantic revolution and its aftermath – that feast of dreams and imagination, feeling and folly, revolution and catastrophes – is close at hand.

4. The Heyday of Rationalistic Natural Law Theory

"Rationalism", in the sense of strong faith in the ability of human reason both to find the bases of a social order and to develop and maintain the rules expressing that order, is – as we have already stated with regard both to ancient and to medieval thinking – by no means an invention of the 17th century. It may well be described as one of the fundamental, ever-recurring attitudes of mankind to the basic problems of legal philosophy. What justifies us in treating rationalism as a specific and characteristic feature of 17th and 18th century thinking are essentially two features in the legal theory of that period: on the one hand, the impact of Cartesian philosophy (and, to a lesser extent, Newtonian mechanistic thinking), which tended to transform the theoretical exploration of the field of law (as any similar intellectual pursuit) into the construction – using as much as possible the principles underlying mathematics, or rather analytical geometry – of complete systems rather than the observation of facts, and on the other hand, the increasing independence of these systems in relation to Roman law. In fact, it came to pass that the borderline between law and ethics – at all times a problematic line of demarcation – was almost completely deleted. Lawyers build up and taught, on the basis of their axioms, new systems of rules which reflected their ethical ideas rather than any body of positive law. This tendency varied considerably in strength from one writer to another, and from one time to another. We shall only deal, here, with three representatives of rationalistic law theories, all of them Germans: Pufendorf, Christian Thomasius, and Christian Wolff. None of them is a radical representative of the two features defined above.

Samuel Pufendorf (1632–1694), a professor at Heidelberg in Germany and Lund in Sweden, later Swedish and finally Prussian Historiographer Royal, was one of the most famous and successful writers of his times. He may justly be called the first theorician of law to attempt

The Era of the Rationalistic Law of Nature (1650–1789)

the establishment of a natural law system based exclusively on reason. Pufendorf's rationalism should not, however, be understood as an uncritical acceptance of a mechanistic or materialistic explanation of legal or ethical rules. He was, from an early period, influenced by the original German philosopher *Weigel* (d. 1699), who drew up, more clearly than had been done before, a distinction between the physical world, which is entirely mechanistic and of which man, as a biological entity, is a citizen, and the moral world, characterized by man's free will and by the existence of ethical norms.

In his voluminous writings – among which it is sufficient to mention here two: the book *De iure naturae et gentium* (*On the Law of Nature and of Nations*, 1672) and the last treatise on legal philosophy – *De officio hominis et civis iuxta legem naturalem* (*On the Duties of a Man and Citizen under the Law of Nature*, 1673) – Pufendorf parts from two basic notions, viz. *imbecillitas,* the weakness and helplessness which makes man dependent upon his fellows, i.e. upon society, and *socialitas,* the urge to participate in, and not disturb, social life. Whereas the former attribute is "natural" in the sense that it is a condition for biological survival, the latter cannot be understood as a binding precept without recourse to God's will: by creating man as a social being, God has imposed "sociality" upon him as a commandment. In giving this religious explanation to the first axiom of natural law, Pufendorf is close to Grotius, whereas the notion of *imbellicitas* recalls Hobbes' thinking. The German writer's acceptance of the religious foundations of law are equally obvious in his tripartite division of the sources of knowledge about legal precepts: God's revelation teaches man his duties as a Christian, the commands of lawful rulers lay down his civic duties; reason, finally, makes apparent the tenets of natural law, which embody the general duties of all men. At the same time, Pufendorf emphasizes, on the level of general principles, the conformity of natural law with Christ's teaching. Thus, different from Hobbes, Pufendorf gives natural law a validity of its own, due not only to the necessity of peaceful coexistence for survival but also to its ethical contents.

The fundamental principle of the rational law of nature is, according to Pufendorf, that man should develop and maintain whatever serves the purposes of life in common. Pufendorf's view of human life is essentially *social,* not individualistic. From this principle, four subordinate rules are deducted: no one should inflict injury upon another; all men should be treated as equals in rights; men should make themselves useful to their fellow men as much as is in their power; all voluntarily assumed obligations should be honoured. By means of a distinction between "absolute" and "relative", i.e. historically given, norms of natural law, Pufendorf manages to find room, in his system, for many institutions of his time, which would otherwise be difficult to reconcile with the principles he develops.

As would appear from what has been said, the bricks with which Pufendorf builds his system are not, as was the case with some earlier writers (e.g. Donellus, cf. ch. 5, sec. 5 above) and with most later representatives of rationalistic system-builders, the *rights* of man under the law of nature, but his *duties*. Thus the duty not to harm others is the foundation of the law of torts, and the duty to help one's fellow men is used to lay down public law principles on assistance to the poor.

Pufendorf does not claim that his natural law is a complete and effective legal system, since it does not contain sanctions; by stressing the need for coercion – and here he falls back upon the Hobbesian position – Pufendorf cannot do without the State, and when it comes to the relationship between natural and positive law, he proclaims the absolute rule of the latter. The law of nature cannot even be invoked as an argument against tyrannic or manifestly unjust rulers. It is of small avail that rulers are exhorted to realize in their laws the principles of natural law: in the end, Pufendorf shows himself a child of the era of absolutism, Thus, although he was to exercice an influence on such radical writers as John Wise in New England (cf. sec. 4 above), Pufendorf cannot be counted among those natural law theoricians who prepared the ground for 18th century reformist constitutional thinking. His greatest importance has to be sought elsewhere: in the clear and convincing exposition of a logically consistent and hierarchically structured body of norms, going from the general to the specific. By virtue of this contribution to legal science, Pufendorf came to influence deeply the great codifications of the 18th and early 19th centuries.

Christian Thomasius (d. 1728) was for a long time a highly considered and influential teacher at the University of Halle in Germany; he was originally a disciple of Pufendorf, but in the course of his development he came increasingly under the influence of Hobbes and of Locke. Thomasius was an active and undaunted Enlightenment lawyer: he fought for a humanization of criminal law and criminal procedure; he criticized effectively the belief in witchcraft and the burning of witches, which was then still practiced in many parts of Europe; he advocated

The Era of the Rationalistic Law of Nature (1650-1789)

consistently the freedom of religion, and he ridiculed the slavish acceptance and sometimes pedantic study of Roman law as a supreme expression of legal wisdom. He was an early admirer of the life-style and attitudes of French Enlightenment, and an eclectic but effective vulgarizer of rationalistic natural law thinking rather than an original scholar. In his theoretical writings (*i.a., Fundamenta juris naturae et gentium, Foundations of the Law of Nature and of Nations,* 1709) he affirms energetically the supremacy of human will over reason, and of pragmatic utility over other ends of laws. Thomasius indeed blends a voluntaristic view upon the law, understood above all as a body of commands, and a rationalism which is used to organize and structure a "natural law" which ultimately boils down to a set of pragmatic ethical precepts. Thomasius's greatest contribution to legal thinking may well be that he operated, more consistently than any earlier writer, a fundamental distinction between the domain of ethics, which is essentially of a private character, a tool in the pursuit of private, utilitarian happiness, and the field of law, characterized by the social, inter-subjective nature of its commandments and by the need for coercion as an indispensible part of any legal system.

Like Thomasius, *Christian Wolff* (d. 1754) although not a major or original thinker, was a highly influential writer, who treated a vast number of philosophical questions. His master was, in most respects, Leibniz. The title of his greatest work in the field of legal philosophy – *Jus naturae methodo scientifica pertractatum* (*The Law of Nature Treated with Scientific Method,* eight volumes, 1740-1748) – is significant for his interest in the method rather than the matter of legal philosophy. The natural law is described as at the same time natural, since it is rooted in the essence of men and things, and divine, since God as creator is its remote cause. The fundamental precept of this law is that men should perform all those actions which tend to perfect them and refrain from those which work against that perfection; from this axiom, Wolff deduces, by logical operations, a vast body of general and specific precepts. Unlike Thomasius, he does not draw any dividing line between law and ethics; unlike Pufendorf he organizes legal rules according to rights, not duties, and he emphatically stresses the perfection of the individual as the ultimate goal of legislation at the expense of the collectivity. Upon the whole, Wolff – who exercised considerable influence on the codifications of the late 18th century – may be the most representative among Enlightenment writers in our field.

In addition to the legal scholars presented above, mention should be made of a few minor but in their time influential writers, were it only to show the extent and the international character of the natural law school of the Enlightenment. The French Huguenot *Jean Barbeyrac* (d. 1744), a translator and follower of Pufendorf, wrote the history of ethics and of natural law thinking; he was the first to attribute to Grotius that position as "founder" of the modern law of nature (the man "who broke the ice", is Barbeyrac's famous formulation) which could undoubtedly also have been claimed by the Spanish Neothomists. The Swiss writer *Burlamaqui* (d. 1748) was also an admirer of Pufendorf, but his theory of the social contract, obviously inspired by the Republican ideals of his hometown, Geneva, forebodes the analysis of another citizen of Geneva, Jean-Jacques Rousseau (cf. sec. 7 below). Another Swiss, *Vattel* (d. 1767), contributed to vulgarize Wolff's teaching in the French-speaking world; however, his most important contributions were in the field of public international law.

5. John Locke

Some thinkers, frequently the most original ones, are recognized and come to exercise an influence *in spite of* the conditions and ideas prevailing at the time they wrote, whilst others achieve eminence *due to* the immediate positive reaction of their contemporaries. John Locke (1632–1704) was of the latter kind. He was very much the man of the moment. His influence on Occidental 18th century thinking was immediate and immense. This is not to deny the depth and breadth of his thinking. Of middle-class origin, born and educated a Puritan, he studied at Oxford, cast his lot with the Ashley family and shared the fortunes of the later Earl of Shaftesbury under the Restoration – including a sojourn in France in the 1670's and six years of exile in Holland under James II. He followed William of Orange back to England after the Glorious Revolution and held high office until he retired, a few years before his death.

Locke underwent, under the influence of Oxford friends and later readings and acquaintances, a successive development from the strictly voluntaristic Calvinism in which he had been brought up towards an independent attitude in which rationalism and empiricism are mixed. The growth of his mind and thought can be followed more closely in some works from his youth which have only recently been published; these writings show the influence which Hobbes exercised upon him in the earlier stages of his development.

Locke's greatest contribution to general philosophy falls in the theory of knowledge; his most famous work is *An Essay concerning Human Understanding* (1690), where his empiricist ideas are developed. In the field of political and legal theory, *Two Treatises of Government* (published in 1690 but written some ten years earlier) is his best-known work. Among his recently published books, written in the 1660's, mention should be made of a volume of essays on the law of nature and a work on religious toleration. In what follows we shall only deal, however, with the products of his mature thought.

In *An Essay concerning Human Understanding,* Locke develops a consistent empiricist theory of knowledge: the human soul is, originally, a sheet of white paper, upon which experience inscribes true knowledge by a laborious process, in the course of which the perceptions of the senses in the form of direct observations, and in the form of intellectual operations – which are the stored results, as it were, of previous observations – cooperate to build up knowledge by successive comparisons between "ideas," i.e. conceptions of reality, which are either retained as being consistent with the accumulated experience based upon previous observations, or rejected as being inconsistent with it.

If Locke is thus a radical empiricist in his epistemological writings, his theory of law and state is essentially rationalistic. He firmly believes in a natural law which coincides with human reason. Like many other writers, he operates with the concept of a "state of nature," but this state, in Locke's version, is different, on at least one highly important point from that described by Hobbes. Whereas the latter considers the state of nature as a war of all against all, Locke describes it as a situation characterized, above all, by freedom and equality. The decisive difference is one of fundamental human attitudes rather than of theoretical concepts: Hobbes, in his profound scepticism, believes that men are the slaves of their blind and greedy passions; Locke, on the other hand, takes a more optimistic view of mankind; in his "natural state" reason, i.e. the law of nature, is a stronger force than passion. Since reason is obvious and intelligible to all, the natural law reigns, and under that law, men are free both to act and to do what they like with their property, and they are all equal. Reason teaches them not

The Era of the Rationalistic Law of Nature (1650–1789)

to cause injury to each other. In Hobbes's analysis, reason is strong enough to make men realize that a state organization is necessary for survival – and that only the strongest, indeed the most totalitarian organization that can be set up is required to curb the passions and to inspire that fear which is the most, if not the only, efficient means of keeping peace. Locke does not deny the importance of greed and lust, but his belief in the strength of reason, laying down the precepts of natural law, prevails.

Both Hobbes and Locke operate with the idea of a social contract. In the case of Hobbes, the necessity of that act need not be further explained. In the case of Locke, on the other hand, it may be asked why "natural man," enjoying the benefits of freedom, equality and various rights – including, as a particularly important one, that of property – ever entered into a state which could add little to his felicity. For Locke (like Hobbes) does not recognize, as did Grotius and Pufendorf, either an instinctive human *socialitas*, i.e. a yearning for life in common, or a religious or ethical duty to form societies. Pleasure and pain are the ultimate motives of human action in the English empiricist's view. Another question is, of course, whether Locke really believed in the historical reality of the state of nature and of the social contract. As for the latter problem, it would seem safe to say – although the question is not an easy one – that Locke did *not* believe in a historical situation where men would have lived outside any form of community but that, on the other hand, the social contract presented to him the character of historical authenticity.

The motive, according to Locke, which prompted men to form societies by means of a contract, was that however pleasant life in the state of nature might be, it was after all precarious. Whenever litigation arose, there were no fixed and generally acknowledged laws, and there were no impartial umpires to settle them. The need for well-defined and universally known standards of behaviour and for impartial judges are, in Locke's thinking, the only reasons why men should enter into the social contract.

The different intentions of the contracting parties obviously exercise a decisive influence upon the contents of the contract. Hobbes' "natural men" say, to the sovereign established by that contract: "Give us peace and security, lest we perish, and we hand over all power to you forever." Locke's men in nature say: "Let us agree upon those rules which are necessary to protect our natural rights, to settle disputes among us, and to give us impartial judges." Nothing more is necessary, nothing more is intended; it is part of Locke's rational law of nature that no one can, without his consent, be deprived of any element of his natural rights. The function of the state, under Locke's contract, is to maintain the law of nature. That law – which, in Hobbes' analysis, did not really exist (except as a sort of law of the jungle) in the state of nature – continues to govern men, and human society, after Locke's contract has been concluded, and it is not merely the explicit terms of the covenant but just as much, indeed more, the law of nature which define the limits of state authority and the tasks of the state. The essential function of that body is to adjudicate impartially and in accordance with the law of nature upon such litigation as arises in the society.

The highest power given to the state is that of legislation, but legislative power is, as would appear from our definition of the contract, by no means unlimited. It is subject, in the first place, to the law of nature, and to the purpose for which the contract was made. Thus legislation has to respect absolutely the individual rights of freedom and of property. To serve its purpose, it must be embodied in clear, fixed and publicly promulgated laws consistent with these rights; it may not be delegated to, e.g., administrative bodies. The exercice of public power, be it in then legislative or the executive branch of government, is thus really nothing but a mandate, a trust, from the members of the society. In case of breach of that trust by the state and its organs, the members are free from their undertaking: they have a right of "appeal to Heaven" – i.e. to revolt – and they become again, as in the state of nature, their own judges. This was precisely, in Locke's interpretation, what occurred in the Glorious Revolution of 1688, when James II and the Stuart dynasty were overthrown. Locke provides an effective justification for the revolution, and for the Bill of Rights, which the new King, William of Orange, accepted before he was admitted to the throne.

The notion of property, which plays such an important part in Locke's definition of the natural rights, means more than ownership in physical objects. It sometimes stands for the whole sphere of an individual's vital interests, including life and freedom. However, it *also* means proprietary rights, and it is beyond doubt that in giving the right of property such a prominent place as a natural right, Locke appealed strongly to the interests and ideas of the emerging English middle

The Era of the Rationalistic Law of Nature (1650-1789)

classes, who were at this time becoming politically, socially and economically as important as the traditional aristocratic ruling class. The place of property in natural law had been hotly disputed since antiquity; early Christian thinkers had been hostile to it, some medieval Scholastics had admitted it, not without hesitation, as a part of natural law; upon the whole, however, it had never held a predominant place. Locke firmly placed property among the essential rights of man, and he justified this standpoint at length, deriving property from labour. This part of his thinking was to prove immensely important in the following centuries, as is apparent, in particular, from the prominent place given to the right of property in declarations of rights and liberal constitutions from the late 18th century onwards.

On a more general level, another aspect of John Locke's contribution to Occidental legal thinking may be of even greater and more lasting importance: he is the first, or at least the first internationally known, writer to lay down, clearly and precisely, the principles of a society based, in all exercice of public power, and in all details, on the rule of law. It is true that many before him, from Plato and Aristotle onwards, had emphasized the importance of laws as the foundations of the good society, and it is equally true that at least from the revival of Roman law studies in the Middle Ages, legal arguments had been predominant in political, constitutional, and indeed ecclesiastic, controversy throughout the West. However, Locke's forceful, consistent, and persuasive plea for a society where even the legislator has to act within fixed well-defined limits which guarantee respect for private rights and liberties had such a strong appeal that it matured, in a relatively short time, into a lasting fundamental element of Occidental ideology. Sometimes the genius of a broadly influential writer can make already extant disparate fragments and isolated ideas chrystallize, as it were, into a clear pattern. That was what happened with the idea of the "Law-State", the *Rechtsstaat*, in Locke's works.

Finally, when discussing the organization of the public powers created by the social contract, Locke stressed the importance of a division between the legislative power, representing the people, and the – in principle subordinate – executive authority (King, or Government). Although he did not elaborate upon this principle, it was to exercise a deep-going influence, in particular through the intermediary of Montesquieu.

6. Montesquieu

Charles de Secondat, Baron de La Brède et *de Montesquieu* (1689–1755), commonly referred to by his last name, was by training and by profession – for the short time he exercised one – a lawyer, but his greatest contributions to Occidental thinking fall essentially in the realms of political science and of sociology; he can in fact claim the rank as one of the earliest pioneers of the latter discipline, although it would take at least another century before it developed into an independent branch of science. However, as a writer both on questions of constitutional law and theory and on problems concerning the relationship between law and society, he has exercised such a deep-going influence also on the development of legal thinking that he deserves a place of his own in this survey.

Montesquieu was a member of that class of the French society which had, since the high Middle-Ages, provided the monarchy with its most efficient and faithful servants, first in the struggle against the great feudal rulers and later in the organization of the judicial and administrative apparatus that was to rule France until the Great Revolution and, indeed, to a very large extent survive into the Napoleonic era and beyond. This class, and in particular its higher section, to which Montesquieu belonged, had been richly rewarded by the Kings and had gradually ascended, under the name of *noblesse de robe* ("nobility of the robe", i.e. the garment worn by judicial officers) to a position of wealth and prestige comparable to that of the old feudal nobility (*noblesse d'épée,* or "nobility of the sword") and to a power which largely superseded that of the old *élite*. Montesquieu, at the age of 27, inherited the high post as President of the *Parlement,* or provincial Court of Appeal, of Bordeaux, but he soon left this office and lead the comfortable but studious existence of a private scholar, living from independent means. Attracted to the gay life of Parisian society after the death of Louis XIV (1715) he made himself famous throughout Europe by a satirical word, the *Persian Letters* (1721), which was published anonymously; the secret was not very well kept, however. The book contains a highly critical description of French social life, manners, and public affairs described by a fictitious diplomat from Persia. After years of study, including a two years' visit to England (1729–1731) Montesquieu published *Reflections on the Rise and Fall of*

The Era of the Rationalistic Law of Nature (1650–1789)

the Roman Empire (*Considérations sur les causes de la grandeur des Romains et de leur décadence,* 1734) which equally became rapidly famous; it is an original and penetrating study of the factors which contributed to the expansion of ancient Rome and to the decline and ultimate fall of that state. Montesquieu's preoccupation with the deeper causes of historical development and with the interaction between laws and public institutions on the one hand, the surrounding social and cultural structures on the other hand, make the book a pioneer work, although the author displays a good deal of carelessness in matters of scholarship and although, obviously, the means and methods available for an enquiry of this kind were still primitive. In 1748, Montesquieu published his most famous and influential work, *De l'esprit des Lois (The Spirit of Laws)* which immediately gained great influence on political and constitutional thinking in the Western world. The most well-known and lasting tribute to that influence to this day remains the Constitution of the United States, but elements of Montesquieu's thinking were, and still are, noticeable in many constitutions in the world.

The *Persian Letters,* still an amusing book, full of pertinent observations and caustic remarks, reveals a profound scepticism; the comparisons between laws and customs in France and the East which the fictitious Persian observer frequently makes give the author many opportunities to criticize the idea of a universal natural law. The ironic stress laid upon the role played by convention, and indeed fashion, similarly implies criticism against the notion of eternal and immutable legal principles. Thus, already in this early work, Montesquieu expresses that belief in the *relativity* of social structures, institutions, and convictions which was to be the basic idea explored, developed and put into system in his scholarly writings. Other important elements of Montesquieu's thinking which are already visible in the *Persian Letters* are his inclination towards a pragmatic and empirical approach to the study of law and state. Unlike the orthodox representatives of Cartesian rationalism (which otherwise, in many respects, still influences his method of reasoning), he tends to take the social system as he finds it, for granted instead of building systems upon axioms or such theoretical assumptions as a social contract. In the great work on the Roman Empire, we find the same tendency to go from facts to ideas, and to attempt to find causal explanations of political and constitutional (and – to a lesser extent, since the topic is not of immediate interest to him in that context – also legal) facts and developments in given, and changing, social conditions in the broadest sense.

In *The Spirit of Laws,* Montesquieu starts with a famous definition of the concept of laws as "the necessary relations which are derived from the nature of things." It should be noted, in the first place, that there is no space for a normative, or ethical, approach to the notion of "laws" in this description. The "laws" the author refers to are social facts and not, at least neither necessarily nor exclusively, expressions of moral standpoints. It should further be made clear that when Montesquieu speaks about "the nature of things" he does neither, as is amply demonstrated throughout his work, refer to "nature" as opposed to "society" nor think of a given prehistorical state of affairs. "Nature", in Montesquieu's view, includes not only such elements of the outward framework of human societies as climate, soil, geographical conditions, but also – and indeed predominantly – both such historically developed factual elements as customs, public institutions, class structure, economic activities, and also such ideological elements as religion, historical examples, and prevailing interpretations of the past. These, all taken together in their complicated interaction, where physical nature is one factor among many, make up "the nature of things" and form that *esprit général,* or "general spirit" which permeates the laws of the society.

Whenever Montesquieu refers – as contemporary conventions would have it – to "natural law" as a body of precepts detached from a historically given society (and he sometimes does, for this cautious observer of social realities is by no means out to engage in a theoretical controversy which he would in all likelihood have considered as futile) he always takes good care to make it clear that he is speaking about something which is hypothetical, not real. When, after the publication of *De l'esprit des lois,* he has to defend his work against criticism, he becomes in fact more explicit on this point and states that "natural man," in the sense of man living in a presocietal "state of nature" is an unrealistic supposition. Moreover, he also makes it clear that the scientific study of the laws of human societies cannot confine itself to examining those true laws of nature to which man, like all beings, are necessarily subject, but must also take account of the fact that man, as an intelligent being, to a large extent creates his own laws, which may frequently violate those of God but must nevertheless be closely studied, i.a. by legislators, since these man-made laws, bad and contrary to the demands of physical nature as they may be, are nevertheless elements of that "general spirit" which makes up a nation's "nature" and thus contribute to delimit those "necessary relations" which a competent legislator has to observe.

When discussing more closely the legislator's task, Montesquieu insists on the necessity of reason and of rational acting. Again, however, reason does *not* mean an organ by which lawgivers are made able to find, and to lay down, those rules which are in harmony with an abstract standard or rationality, logically derived from one or a few inevitable axioms. Reason, in Montesquieu's language, here stands on the one hand for applied common sense – for the choice of the best means towards an end, which is precisely a legislation in harmony with the historically given "general spirit" of the nation. On the other hand – and this is part of the general intellectual climate of the Enlightenment – Montesquieu certainly also means, in this context, that new laws should be as "rational" as possible in substance and contents, i.e. practical, efficient and generally "sensible," free from arbitrariness, unnecessary cruelty and superstitious elements. In that pedestrian sense, Montesquieu acknowledges a "general human reason," of which, as he says, the political and civil laws of all nations ought to be special applications.

A few words should be devoted, by way of conclusion, to Montesquieu's immensely influential constitutional ideas and to his views on legal reasoning. In the former respect, two main sources of inspiration would seem to have exercised a decisive influence on the French philosopher. Although, as already mentioned, Montesquieu was a highly privileged member of a class that had contributed more than any other to the formation of the French state as it then was and had been richly rewarded for its work, he shared, from his early life, the aristocratic opposition against Royal absolutism in which, from the later years of Louis XIV's reign, the judicial and bureaucratic nobility had joined forces with progressive elements of the feudal aristocracy and the intellectually leading stratum of the "Third Estate". In this opposition there were elements both of aristocratic class egoism and of genuine concern for freedom, for the rule or law, and for a competent handling of state affairs, and not least state finances. The other great source of inspiration was admiration for the English constitution, as it had developed after the Glorious Revolution (1688) and been expounded in the writings of John Locke.

In the case of Montesquieu, this influence was strengthened by his own years of study in England. On these bases, the French writer drew up that famous tripartite system of checks and balances which was so much admired by his contemporaries and so diligently put into practical legislative action by constitution-makers. Montesquieu recommended a system comprising a strong legislative power for which, obviously, the English Parliament had served as a model; an executive power, equally strong but acting under the laws laid down by the legislature; and finally an independent judicial power, which should guarantee the exact and unbiased application of laws.

The history of the influence of English thought and English institutions on Continental thinking is largely one of fertile misunderstandings. It may well be asked – and the question had been intensely debated – whether and to what extent Montesquieu really understood the constitutional and political realities of early Georgian England. The relationship between the Crown, the Cabinet, the House of Lords and the House of Commons was certainly far more complicated than in his schematic analysis, and the consequences of the emerging party system seems to have escaped him. Similarly, the role of the judiciary in the common law system hardly corresponds to the functions Montesquieu attributes to that body.

Montesquieu's discussion of the tasks of the courts – which shows that he had not been able to discover the fundamental law-making activity of common law judges – is a remarkable exception to the otherwise realistic and pragmatic outlook of the great Frenchman and shows to what extent Montesquieu, although himself a lawyer, was caught, in those areas which were not at the centre of his sharpsighted analytical interest, in the naive rationalism of the Enlightenment period. The judge, he flatly states, should be only "the mouth that pronounces the words of the law". Thus adjudication should be strictly reduced to a mechanical application of laws which should be so clear as to call for no interpretation. It is superfluous to demonstrate how far this judicial automaton was from English judges, but it is worthwhile to mention that owing to the great influence of Montesquieu, this highly unrealistic idea of judicial decision-making and the interpretation of statutes became, albeit for a short time, a creed of legislative reformers, i.a. in revolutionary and Napoleonic France, and was to create ideological obstacles, for a long time beyond that period, to a realistic study and evaluation of the creative function of judges.

7. Rousseau

Even more than the work of Montesquieu, the vast body of writings of the Swiss vagabond, musician, polemist, writer, literary lion, misanthropist, utopian and – beyond reasonable doubt – genius, *Jean-Jacques Rousseau* (1712–1778) falls outside the area of legal philosophy and theory in a strict sense. For reasons identical to those accounted for above, however, some attention must be paid here to certain elements in Rousseau's thinking.

Rousseau, stemming from a small bourgeois family in Geneva, was almost thirty and had already behind him an eventful, sometimes parasitic, wandering life, mostly spent in modest employments or unorganized but passionate studies, when he established himself in Paris as a musician, a composer in a small way, and a writer on music. In 1750, he wrote, within the framework of a contest organized by a French provincial Academy, at Dijon, a prize essay on the question whether the progress of arts and sciences had contributed to the felicity of mankind. His answer was a thundering "no". Paris society, which had initially dazzled and attracted him, had gradually come to frighten and repel him. This non-conformist attitude, in addition to a highly personal and suggestive literary style, and many deep and acute observations, was enough to make the obscure Swiss immigrant famous. Fame followed Rousseau for the rest of his life, but fame did not bring him either happiness or a stable situation. He continued his career as a critic of contemporary civilization in a great number of important works.

France was at this time, in practice if not in form, prepared to tolerate even far-reaching and sharp criticism of established political, social and – with somewhat more caution – religious principles, but that toleration had certain limits; some discretion was demanded. Rousseau, an egocentric with strong exhibitionist inclinations, refused to follow the subtle rules of the game, and thus could not in the long run avoid a persecution which, by modern standards, was inefficient and mild. From the age of fifty onwards, he led the life of a refugee, in Switzerland, England (where David Hume offered him hospitality) and France. Noble and powerful patrons protected him; he was consulted as a wise man, on the ideal constitution of new states; but embittered and increasingly paranoid, he soon tended to be involved in personal conflicts with protectors and neighbours and had to move on. Towards the end of his life, he came to some rest, engaged in botanical studies and autobiographic writings.

Among the many works, and many original ideas, of Rousseau, we can only deal, here, with one; for present purposes *Du contrat social* (*On the Social Contract*, 1762), is the most important contribution of that philosopher. The key notion in all Rousseau's thinking is "nature." Whatever is good, pure, healthy, and constructive, is "natural," whatever is morally bad, unhealthy, artificial, is a result of human society and cultural development. Everything, Rousseau says in a famous passage, is good when leaving the Creator's hands, everything degenerates in the hands of man. There can be no doubt that Rousseau was a profoundly religious man, and some of the finest pages in his later writings express a deep and intimate, almost mystical devotion, a trusting belief in the Creator; although this belief, coupled as it is with Rousseau's exaltation of "nature," sometimes assumes a pantheistic character – the Supreme Being expresses itself everywhere in His creation – there are also personal elements in it: God is undoubtedly expected to give a special, and understanding, hearing to the individual Jean-Jacques Rousseau. On the other hand, religion does not come in either as a factor of theoretical or explanatory significance in the philosopher's thinking, nor does it greatly affect his views upon laws and society. There is no need, therefore, to go more deeply into Rousseau's religious ideas. A question that calls for some attention, on the other hand, is whether he considered the state of nature, that state of purity, innocence, and spontaneous generosity, as a historical fact. It seems certain that this was not the case, although Rousseau depicts the lost Eden of mankind in glowing colours, The "state of nature" is, in his reasoning, a "model" – a term of comparison by means of which the corruption of actually existing societies is more clearly brought out. But it is also a possibility, a state of bliss which man can attain, provided he organizes society in the proper way. In one respect at least, Rousseau seems to consider the happy nature as a fact, or as based upon a factual situation of great practical importance: he obviously thinks that the earth is sufficient to feed all without conflicts and without a need for special incentives or special organization. There is nothing to show that he assumed, as did Locke, a body of rationally, ethically or religiously founded natural law which would be operative, and recognized, in the state of nature. It is consistent with Rousseau's cult of spontaneity, and his hostility to whatever can be described as an artefact, a product of social and cultural development, that he is, in a general way, distrustful and negative towards legal rules. It seems likely that he did recognize some kind of basic precepts, but these would seem to be either of a "naturalistic" character (the instinct of self-preservation) or of a vaguely religious kind (a duty of pious adoration of the Creator and of nature) or possibly both.

The real fall of man, the breakdown of human happiness, in Rousseau's view, was the establishment of private property. The true founder of civil society, he says – in one of these striking and suggestive formulations which contributed to make his message so effective – was the first man who enclosed a piece of land and who said: "This is mine," and found people stupid enough to believe him. For the institution of property meant the end of equality between men, made human beings ambitious, avaricious, and low, and gave rise to ever-recurring strife and turmoils. To put an end to this, laws were established, but these laws were the works of those who had made use of the establishment of property to become rich and powerful; whilst limiting and regulating internal warfare, they fixed inequality and put the majority of mankind into chains. In his uncompromising rejection of the historically given society, and his firm belief in the goodness of nature and "natural man," Rousseau refused to find in the building of human communities any growth of real values; that "culture," and "progress," which the Academy of Dijon had expected to find glorified when organizing its essay competition on the question whether the progress of arts and sciences had contributed to the felicity of mankind were to him nothing but elements of that corruption which had started with the institution of private property.

The task, then, of philosophers and of political leaders, according to Rousseau, was to find the way back to nature, to give man, as it were, a new chance, and to restore those "natural" – if not juridical, at least ethical – rights of which he had been deprived by society, as it had developed in the course of history. This is the task Rousseau sets out to solve in his *Contrat social*.

This time, Rousseau seems to be speaking about a contract, which is in some sense "real", a covenant upon which the society ought to be based, although it is highly unclear whether he really expected or proposed the actual conclusion of such a contract in some future society. It is, however, a contract of a highly special character: it implies, in Rousseau's description, a collective act by means of which all men *give themselves up* – emphasis should be put on this term, for unlike the social contract described by Locke, which was the result of a bargaining where a minimum of powers were handed over, on trust, to the collectivity, Rousseau's contract means a complete, unreserved and irrevokable giving up of the persons and property of the participants – not to a ruler, or a state foreign to themselves, but *to all the members of the community*. Thus, Rousseau reasons, when concluding this true and beneficial social contract, men give up themselves to themselves, since they are obviously parts of "all," and consequently do not sacrifice anything but retain, in their capacity as members of the collectivity, the gift which they had made. In the society founded upon this social contract the natural rights of freedom and equality, suppressed by the earlier society, would resurrect, as it were, and now in a legal form, as *civil rights* guaranteed by the contract and the society it has created.

There is no need to point out the logical and practical difficulties raised by the idea of a "contract" of the kind proposed by Rousseau. The fundamental ambiguity of an act whereby men give themselves up both to themselves and to others becomes obvious when Rousseau goes on to discuss how the society thus created operates and how it expresses its volitions and decisions. What legitimates the state organization and its acts, Rousseau says, is the "general will" *(volonté générale)*, i.e. the will of the collectivity as such. This will, however, should be distinguished from the "will of all" – the sum of individual volitions in the society, which may, obviously, be varying and even conflicting. The "general will" is the *true* will of the society. The only way of ascertaining that will, in a society characterized by total equality, must be to consult the majority. In this, there is nothing astonishing or objectionable, but Rousseau, in his wish to demonstrate the legitimacy of his society – and in his firm belief, as it turns out, in the goodness of man once returned to nature and in the impossibility of real conflicts within that framework – introduces arguments which are as specious as the idea of man retaining himself while handing himself over to all. The possible objection that the majority may oppress the minority is met by the contention that those whose individual volitions do not coincide with the collective will, duly established and ascertained, have no valid reasons for complaining: what happens is that they are *forced* to accept the "general will," and that will being the true will of all, it is also their will, since they are parts of "all". Thus they are "forced to be free".

The notion of *volonté générale* comes back when Rousseau discusses the laws or the new society. The general will is the fountain of all laws, and these must thus, by definition, be just, since they are based on the true will of all, and since no one can do harm to himself; consequently, as a member of the collectivity – one out of the "all" – he does not and cannot suffer injustice from the laws. Moreover, being expressions of the general will, the laws of the true society are in accordance with reason.

Rousseau's philosophy of law and state implied practical consequences which are not likely to have been clear to the philosopher himself, but which emerged in the later phases of the French Revolution, upon which Rousseau exercised a profound influence, and in other societies of Rousseauan inspiration, i.e. societies with a Socialist or Communist ideology. The idea of a complete surrender of the individual to a collectivity guided by an infallible "general will" left no room for an individual sphere of liberty withdrawn from the power of the state or, more generally, the collectivity; thus the civil rights restored by the true social contract tended to become delusive; the right of liberty was obviously eroded by Rousseau's tampering with the concept of freedom in his discussion of collective decision-making. Moreover, the identification of the positive law of the Rousseauan society with justice and reason meant the absence of any body of valid "natural law" besides the law of the state and thus excluded any appeal by the individual to standards not adopted by the majority. Gradually, Rousseau's dream of a society where men were no longer "in chains" turned out to provide the justification of societies far more totalitarian and less respectful of individual rights than any absolute monarchy of the 17th and 18th centuries.

8. Legal Reasoning in the Era of Rationalism

Legal reasoning, as distinct from the philosophy of law, is part of the practitioner's craft. There are reasons to expect, therefore, that this part of jurisprudence, which developed slowly but steadily on the foundations laid by the medieval lawyers and had reached, towards the end of the Middle Ages, a stage where specialized treatises were felt to be necessary, responds to changes in the field of theories only if, when, and to the extent, such changes have a noticeable impact on the way in which the day-to-day work of judges, attorneys, and scholars in the various fields of positive law is performed.

This expectation is verified by the development of the methods of legal reasoning in the 17th and 18th centuries. In fact, the slowness of that development would seem to illustrate a trend which is of some importance for a proper understanding of the evolution of legal thinking in a larger perspective. One of these trends is growing specialization within the field of legal scholarship in the large sense. The great medieval lawyers, like the Roman jurists, had been, to use a somewhat simplified formula, their own philosophers to the extent they felt the need for a body of theoretical propositions in and about their work. Many ideas certainly penetrated from the outside – from scholastic theology and philosophy – but upon the whole, lawyers were enough "generalists" to cover for themselves, on the basis of the common stock of principles and ideas which were part of the ancient inheritance, many or most of the general theoretical problems pertaining to their science. In fact, legal scholarship was still, as we have already pointed out above, an "exporting" science, providing categories, concepts and solutions, to the emerging specialized study of constitutional and political problems.

With the growth and development of natural law thinking, in particular from the moment that branch of teaching and writing parted ways with Roman law studies, a growing rift came into existence between legal science as a "technical" discipline and legal theorizing, which was frequently more oriented towards ethics or political science. As a result, "true" lawyers tended to concentrate their efforts more to the study and solution of problems of positive law – paying lip-service to or giving shallow summaries of prevailing general theories or ideologies in prefaces or introductory chapters. At the same time, the theoricians, notably those who taught natural law as an independent subject, tended to make less extensive use of positive – i.e., in most parts of Europe, Roman – law. To an increasing extent, the teaching of the natural law thinkers, however admired and influential on a general level, contained less and less materials that could be used by practising lawyers. The latter were left with their texts and their problems. Cartesian reasoning could only in an indirect way help them in their tasks, and the logical system-building of some natural law teachers was simply incompatible with, or at least impossible to use in, a work that

The Era of the Rationalistic Law of Nature (1650–1789)

had to be performed on the basis of the sometimes chaotic body of Roman and medieval rules, royal legislation from the modern era and the rapidly increasing output of administrative regulations that was one of the results of centralized bureaucratic states with unlimited ambitions to regulate commerce, manufactures, agriculture and indeed private habits of consumtion, lodging, and life in general.

The "law" – as a sociological reality – in 1750, or even 1700, was something completely different from what it had been in the Middle Ages or in Antiquity. There was undoubtedly a need for general principles concerning its interpretation and application, but to most lawyers, the casuistic methodological precepts of the commentators, as developed in a growing body of mostly traditionalistic textbooks, are likely to have been far more helpful than the sweeping deductive methods of rationalistic theoricians, few of whom cared to go into the technical aspects of legal work. It is only towards the end of the period now under consideration – i.e. at a time when natural law thinking, as represented by, e.g., Pufendorf (who was, it should be added, enough of a "technical" Roman lawyer to be to some extent useful, and quoted, in practical contexts), had begun to have an impact upon legislation, particularly in the codifications of the late 18th century – that we can notice more clearly the effects of rationalism, otherwise than as a general style, and attitude, in works on legal reasoning.

The 17th century textbooks in this field are still very much of the traditional character, although sometimes embellished by what may be called Baroque ornaments of learning and eloquence. A good example is V.V. Forster's *Interpres sive de interpretatione libri duo (The Interpreter, or Two Books on Interpretation,* Wittenberg 1613), who devoted lengthy passages to the use of arithmethics, geometry, physics, medicine and indeed metrics for the purpose of interpreting Roman law.

Later 17th century writers were mostly less exuberant, but they did not depart noticeably from the traditional patterns framed by the commentators. Baldus and Bartolus are still frequently quoted as great authorities.

To the extent 18th century writers on theoretical questions dealt with statutory interpretation and legal reasoning, they mostly expressed a naive belief in the possibility of expressing legal rules with perfect clarity. Natural law – which is, in these contexts, a new name given to the notions of "equity," "justice" or "fairness" referred to as last resources in case of doubt by earlier writers – is sometimes invoked as a convenient way of escaping from difficult problems of interpretation. More often than not, writers refer alternatively to the *ratio legis* and to natural law as supplementary sources of law without attempting to discuss the precise relationship between the two concepts. This is likely to be a reminiscence of the traditional attitude of Roman lawyers, who usually assumed that the Imperial legislator – Justinian – was all-wise and all-rational, so that the purpose of his laws must coincide with reason and justice. Some Enlightenment writers were profoundly suspicious of any interpretation at all; the judge should apply the law literally, that was all. Any attempt to go further was an illegitimate usurpation of the function of the legislator. This highly naive idea was, naturally enough, in great favour among absolute rulers; it occurred, in fact, that kings who promulgated new codes issued explicit prohibitions against "interpretation." It is more astonishing to find that both Montesquieu and Beccaria, in the 18th century, share this view of the judge's work. It recurs in the French Revolution; for a short time, the so-called *référé législatif,* or referendum to the legislature – i.e. a duty for judges, when in doubt about the interpretation of a statutory text, to submit it to the lawgiver for an answer – was part of French law (as the King of Denmark, a century earlier, had ordered his Supreme Court to consult him in similar situations). An element in this general distrust of judicial interpretation among writers and rulers was the idea that precedents should not be granted any authority; creating and following precedents was held to imply an usurpation of legislative powers by the judiciary. It even happened that the use of earlier decisions as precedents was formally prohibited.

As a good example of the development, among lawyers in the narrow and proper sense of the word, of the theory of statutory interpretation at the end of the period here considered, when rationalism had come to exercise an influence upon legislation, we can take the exposition of a German writer, Christian Friedrich Glück, author of a highly considered textbook of Roman law (*Ausführliche Erläuterung der Pandecten nach Hellfeld,* 2nd ed., 1797).

Glück's fairly extensive discussion of legal hermeneutics presents, in particular, three salient features. On the one hand, he refrains from using much of the subtle network of divisions, subdivisions and corresponding theoretical concepts which had been elaborated by medieval lawyers and brought forward. systematized, and developed into even nicer ramifications by the Pandectists of the 16th and 17th centuries. In this sense, Glück's work carries the marks of the less rigid approach, more conscious of questions of legislative policy and social considerations, which had grown slowly, side by side with the never abandoned Scholastic and exegetic tradition, in the course of the 18th century. On the other hand, Glück is still faithful to tradition to the extent that he systematizes the hermeneutic problems. Finally, his general outlook is traditional throughout: the task of the interpreter is to find the legislator's will. That "Sinn des Gesetzes," or *sententia legis*, which is the ultimate object of his efforts is nothing but precisely this. The law is, in its entirety, a consistent volition.

The point of departure of the intellectual process of interpretation, according to Glück, is to ascertain with a maximum of precision the sense of individual words and to find their reference to those underlying concepts which common usage and the linguistic context assign to them. Since, however, men are, as experience shows, unable to say just as much or as little as they want to, this semantic investigation must be completed by an inquiry into the *ratio* of the piece of legislation concerned or into the true intention of the lawgiver; in this process, it is important not to confound the *immediate* intention embodied in the text under consideration with more remote purposes. In other words, as Glück stresses emphatically, it is only the linguistic context in a narrow sense, other pieces of legislation in related fields of the law, and historical evidence concerning the actual legislative procedure that can be consulted. In particular, Glück warns against the perils following from an unlimited resort to what is believed to be "equity," besides the ascertainable purpose of the statute.

Among systematic novelties in relation to earlier hermeneutic writings we may note one, of small substantive importance, viz. the division of interpretation into two main groups, "legal" and "doctrinal" interpretation. The former expression refers, in the first place, to so-called authentic explanation of the law, i.e. statements by the legislator himself about the true meaning of the text. However, Glück makes the term "legal interpretation" cover also what he calls "usual interpretation", a concept which corresponds closely to what today we call case law. Here, Glück's exposition reflects a development and a set of problems, of which lawyers had become increasingly conscious in the 17th and 18th centuries, when – frequently in connection with reforms and with the establishment of permanent and specialized supreme courts independent of the sovereign's person – the legitimacy and usefulness of precedents had been discussed, although with few clear results.

It is under the heading of "doctrinal interpretation" that we find, in Glück's exposition, those questions and that apparatus of concepts which had been developed by earlier writers; to some extent, the terminology has changed. The essential dividing line is drawn between "grammatical," or "philological," interpretation, on the one hand, and "logical", or "philosophical" construction, on the other, although it is stressed that for practical purposes the division cannot be maintained with full clarity, since a purely grammatical interpretation which considers merely words and phrases and neglects the legislator's intentions, is described as an abuse. Glück rejects the idea of a third form of interpretation, called "political," The purpose of such a method was, according to its advocates – and we here find a clear expression of the increasingly independent attitude of 18th-century lawyers towards ancient and early medieval authorities – to find out "whether and to what extent those laws which we are making use of are adapted to the situation prevailing today and to the constitution of our own time and are thus capable of being used or whether that is not the case." Such investigations are frequently necessary, Glück admits, but the task remains part of "philosophical" or "logical" interpretation.

With regard to grammatical interpretation, Glück establishes a number of rules, based upon common-sense observations; the basic principle is that what should be determinative is, in the first place, prevailing usage at the time of the actual drafting, in the second place, the technical language of lawyers.

The most characteristic element in Glück's discussion of "logical", or "philosophical" interpretation is the persistent endeavour to establish coherence and consistency both within the individual statute and within the legal system at large. In this perspective, the triad of concepts which played a predominant part in many earlier writings, viz. extensive, restrictive, and declaratory interpretation, occupies a modest place in the reasoning; these concepts are used, as it were, as secondary heads of classification, intended to denote the final results of what is really in substance one unitary process of interpretation, the main feature of which is the effort to maintain the harmony and rationality of the system. In the framework of this informal discussion of the problems involved, the author also deepens the analysis of the concept *ratio legis;* he draws a distinction, on the one hand, between the true and deep social need which a piece of legislation is intended to meet and the more accidental and superficial immediate reason for legislative intervention, and on the other, between the nearest and essential motives and the more remote or secondary reasons for the legislator's action.

Chapter 7

Towards a New World: the 19th Century

Selected Bibliography: B. Ahlander, *Om rätt och rättstillämpning*, Stockholm 1952, pp. 41–107; A. Brimo, *Les grands courants de la philosophie du droit et de l'état*, 3ᵉ éd. 1978, pp. 143–325; G.C. Christie, *Jurisprudence. Texts and Readings on the Philosophy of Law*, St. Paul, Minn. 1973, pp. 459–601; H. Coing, *Grundzüge der Rechtsphilosophie*, 3. Aufl., Berlin 1976, pp. 35–54; J. Dalberg-Larsen, *Retsvidenskaben som samfundsvidenskab*, Copenhagen 1977, pp. 109–251; H.J. van Eikema Hommes, *Major Trends in the History of Legal Philosophy*, Amsterdam, New York and Oxford, 1979, pp. 165–228; G. Fassò, *Storia della filosofia del diritto*, vol. 2, Bologna 1968, pp. 387–410; vol. 3, Bologna 1970, pp. 11–230 (G. Fassò's third volume also exists in a French translation, Histoire de la philosophie du droit. XIXᵉ et XXᵉ siècles, trad. par Catherine Rouffet, Paris 1976, v. pp. 1–167); K. Larenz, *Methodenlehre der Rechtswissenschaft*, 5. Aufl., Berlin, Göttingen and Heidelberg 1983; P. Stuer Lauridsen, *Retslæren*, Copenhagen 1977, pp. 61–90; Lord Lloyd of Hampstead, *Introduction to Jurisprudence*, 3rd ed., London 1972, pp. 152–177, 183–224, 335–342, 354 f., 561–584, 630–636, 654–657; K. Olivecrona, *Rättsordningen*, 2nd ed. Lund 1976, pp. 34–71; E.W. Patterson, *Jurisprudence*, Brooklyn 1953, pp. 376–464; K. Rode, *Geschichte der europäischen Rechtsphilosophie*, Düsseldorf 1974, pp. 130–168; G.H. Sabine, *A History of Political Theory*, 3rd ed., London 1952, pp. 522–664; S. Strömholm, *Rätt, rättskällor och rättstillämpning*, 2nd ed., Stockholm 1984, pp. 78–86; J.W.F. Sundberg, *fr.Eddan t. Ekelöf*, Stockholm 1978, pp. 150–182; A. Verdross, *Abendländische Rechtsphilosophie*, Vienna 1958, pp. 136–168; Fr. Wieacker, *Privatrechtsgeschichte der Neuzeit*, 2. Aufl., Göttingen 1967, pp. 348–468.

1. Introduction

Dividing a continuous development into sections, and trying to justify the principles adopted for that exercise by means of sweeping "portraits" of the "period" or "epoch" thus delimited, in order to show their specificity in relation to other segments of never-stopping time – although this is a highly doubtful and essentially ungrateful part of the historian's task, it is nevertheless inevitable. Completely arbitrary divisions and subdivisions would obviously be a greater nuisance; it seldom occurs that the principles put into practice, however well-founded they may seem to the writer who chose them, are so obvious to others that they speak for themselves and need no justification; finally, although intellectually suspect (because they can hardly ever be either proved or disproved and appeal to essayists rather than scholars), some kind of individualizing "portraits of periods" would not seem to be utterly useless. There is an obvious need for tools and instruments enabling us to grasp such elusive objects as blocks of time. This is true particularly about a non-specialized textbook, in a field which cannot be expected to be well-known to the reader, or surrounded by well-known areas.

Advancing, as we do, in chronological order, from the distant to the more nearlying past, it seems reasonable for a history of legal thought (ending, for reasons set out in the preface in 1900) to give the 19th century a chapter of its own, were it only because after a couple of decades of that century, legal philosophers could, for the first time in history, indulge in their interests on board fast ships without sails or in even swifter horseless carriages; they could walk down gas-lit, later on electrically illuminated, streets which would have seemed as bright as day to their 18th century predecessors; at the end of the period, they could speak to each other, *viva voce*, across hundreds of miles; if they fell ill, they could count upon medical science to relieve them from death and pain with a chance of success infinitely greater than ever before. In the multi-secular contest between man and nature, man seemed to have got the upper hand at last; in an increasing number of essential respects, man could command nature according to his wishes.

In the leading Occidental countries, it could also seem, at times, as if the problems of social organization, cooperation and control had found lasting solutions, at least in terms of peaceful coexistence in crowded communities, law and order; towards the end of the century, hygienic, sanitary, social and economic conditions, including a minimum of security against starving to death, had been improved beyond what had ever been thought possible. Yet, it is clear that there was, in the whole Occidental world, a growing discrepancy between man's command of nature, which developed triumphantly and uninterruptedly, including improved techniques of destruction and devastation, and man's command of himself and his fellow men. Social and political unrest, to a considerable extent as a response to the dramatic changes in living conditions which resulted from the industrial revolution, social strife, lack of consensus on the basic principles of social organization, and a permanent and serious risk for violent outbreaks were endemic in many or most Occidental countries for longer or shorter parts of the century, on an unprecedented scale. In many countries, such outbreaks did come to pass: throughout Europe in 1848, in France in the wake of the lost Franco-German war (1870–71). For wars did not belong to the plagues from which men were relieved by science and technology. On the contrary, war – which had tended, in the 18th century, to become a pursuit of relatively small professional and highly disciplined armies, according to rules of international law and custom which successively improved the conditions of the civilian population – had become, with the French Revolution and the introduction of compulsory military service in many countries, a matter for whole populations.

These are features in the portrait of the 19th century which are visible even at a very great distance. We shall come back to some of them more specifically. For present purposes, it is necessary to discuss somewhat more fully three trends of development which are of a less general nature and more specifically connected with the development of legal thinking.

There are many possible ways of characterizing legal theory in the 19th century; within a wide range, one may be as good as another. In the present writer's view, however, the most characteristic general feature is *ideological homelessness*. In fact, the whole 19th (and, indeed, to a very great extent, 20th) century development could be described as a sequence of attempts to answer the pathetic question: *what can we do now that natural law is dead?* Not all lawyers, not even all legal philosophers, put that question; to many of them, the law of nature remained, explicitly or implicitly, the base of their concept of a legal system. But the vanguard of Occidental theorists – and for present purposes, we have to follow the vanguard, while reminding our readers of the fact that the battles they fight may not even be perceptible to the main body of lawyers until decades later – thought, after the critical onslaughts of, in particular, Hume (cf. ch. 6, sec. 3, above) and Kant (cf. sec. 5 below), that the idea of a law of nature could no longer be maintained. Theoretical refutation was not alone to discredit natural law thinking; the *naiveté* and complete lack of understanding for historical, geographical, and social relativity which had been displayed, not least in the course of the French revolution, by natural law advocates of Rousseauan inspiration, and the abuses, excesses, and brutalities which had been committed and defended, by enthusiasts for "natural" equality and "fraternity" had also contributed to render the notion of a law of nature inacceptable to the European intellectual élites in the early 19th century. One particular element of 18th century natural law thinking – the concept of "social contract" was more discredited than others in Europe (but not in America).

It is probable that in the heat of polemics, the opponents of natural law theories did not realize, at first, what they had lost. We have seen, in earlier parts of this book (cf. ch. 3, sec. 6; ch. 4, sec. 4; ch. 5, sec. 4) with what tenacity the idea of a law of nature has not only held its own but also managed to come back, after the heaviest blows, dealt with the greatest strength. It was incompatible with the basic tenets of early Christianity; we find it, more or less clearly, already in the writings of the Greek fathers. St. Augustine tried to demolish it; it comes back, triumphantly, in Scholastic thinking. The Church reformers were essentially hostile; yet, Calvinistic and Lutheran natural law philosophy is just as strong, in the 17th and 18th centuries, as the corresponding Catholic thinking. It would indeed seem that the idea of a body of basic rules, which are immutable, ubiquitous, established by the Creator (or at least, if a religious explanation of existence is avoided, contemporary with Creation) and the content of which can be ascertained by all men of good will and common sense, belongs to the most deeply rooted, most firmly held, and most commonly accepted ideas of mankind in the field we are studying. No other concept in the realm of legal theories can claim a position even remotely similar to that held by natural law.

This is easy to understand if we consider the questions with which the collapse of natural law thinking confronted legal theorists. In the first place, they had to find a base of *legitimation* for law as a system of social constraint. They also had to find foundations for the law's claim to be *binding* on men. Furthermore, they must justify, rule by rule, the *contents of law* as they found it, or conversely invent (and give motives for) *new rules* if they found the prevailing ones inacceptable. They also must *delimit* law as distinct from other bodies of rules. All these were tasks which the Natural Law had performed, in one short formula.

The legal thinking of the 19th century is best understood, as a whole, against this background. It is a quest for an acceptable successor to the old now dethroned king: the law of nature.

That quest is not successful. Moreover, it is carried out – this is my second point – under circumstances and upon conditions that make the Grail-seeking legal thinkers feel their homelessness even more acutely than if they had had to cope with the break-down of secularized rationalist natural law alone (secularized, for to the extent the law of nature was conceived of as theologically founded, as was the case, e.g. in Catholic confessional teaching, it remained, of course, unquestioned as much or as little as the creed of which it was part). For, *on the one hand,* in those earlier periods when the law of nature had been more or less wholly abandoned, it had been replaced by other ideologies with equal or similar pretentions to general validity and explanatory value, mostly by some school of religious voluntarism. Now, it was replaced by nothing, or rather, by theories of far more modest pretentions, precarious status, and limited explanatory value. In fact, the continuous dwindling in scope and lowering in explanatory ambition of legal theories (both claimed by optimists to be redeemed by the increasing *solidity* of the ever narrower and ever more trivial conclusions) may well be considered the most significant general feature of the development of legal thinking from the early 19th century onwards. That feature is more and more accentuated in the course of the present century.

On the other hand, the quest for a successor to natural law theories in the 19th century took place in intellectual surroundings which made legal thinking appear more desperate, desolate, and destitute than ever. For concomitantly with that quest, two lines of development were making rapid progress, to the confusion and dismay of the representatives of many traditional academic discipline, including law (not to speak of theology). The 19th century was, as already intimated, the period when man's relationship with nature assumed, at last, a new character; man took a firm command in a great number of respects. This was made possible through the rapid progress of the natural sciences in all fields. To each technical innovation, there corresponded one or more scientific discoveries. Within the framework of the traditional universities, legal philosophers (as distinct from the students of substantive law, that indispensable and developing tool of social organization in the industrialized world) were –, or could at least be considered, or consider themselves, as – fighting a losing battle in

Towards a New World: the 19th Century

the vicinity of laboratories where triumphs were celebrated every day. In addition, however, even closer – literally next door to the faculties of law – new branches of research, theory-making, and writing came into existence: sociology, anthropology, ethnology, in short, all those disciplines which can be brought together under the heading of empirical social sciences. We shall return somewhat more specifically to certain developments in these areas (sec. 3 below). Be it enough to say, here, that the new fields of knowledge, and the new methods of research combined with the natural sciences to constitute a formidable challenge to legal philosophy.

It is important to stress that, then as now, developments of this kind did not occur over night; the intellectually lazy could ignore them with impunity for a long time, – old men could die in peace; their successors took the new scenario for granted.

It is equally important, however, to stress that what thus happened, peacefully, was little less than a revolution to those concerned. The "law" in a wide sense, as an academic discipline, had for times immemorial offered the only course of study which purported to give, and gave, some knowledge about the actual running of human societies. The university-trained lawyer had been, with two other, far more specialized experts, viz. the medical man and the soldier, the only actor on the scene of the European *ancien régime* who had had some professionally based claim to the most prestigious, influential and wellpaid posts of numerous and growing central and local bureaucracies. This claim remained valid for most of the 19th century, but economists, social scientists, and engineers tended to encroach upon what had been the lawyers' enclosure since the High Middle Ages. This development to some extent contributed to make legal thinkers even more conscious of the crisis they were facing.

The third and last among the trends of development, in the 19th century, which would seem important enough to call for a brief discussion already at this stage is more difficult to seize in a formula than the quest for a successor to natural law and the challenge of the successful natural and social sciences. It relates to the concept of law as such, and to the relationship between the law and the community. It is not one single and uniform trend but rather a number of developments, some of them contradictory. Their combined impact is not easy to define; it meant, however, for all practical purposes, a profound change in the status and substance of that which legal philosophers without changing their terminology continued to call "the law."

From the earliest days of Occidental legal thinking, some human and social relationships had been "legal," others had fallen outside that category. Aristotle is clear on this point, and so were the Roman lawyers and the Scholastics. Upon the whole, there had been a broad and usually tacitly accepted consensus about the scope and function of "the law." That scope and function had been widened enormously, albeit only on the strictly theoretical level, by the partisans of rationalistic natural law in the 17th and 18th centuries. They had constructed vast and all-embracing "legal" systems which included, notably, also such relations as had earlier been treated as clearly "non-legal." This was not only due to moralizing and systematizing zeal. To some extent, it was logically inevitable, for the rationalists built up "systems" the legitimation of which could not be found in Roman or other *auctoritas,* but only in *ratio,* or reason, and this meant, i.a., that deduced from a handful of general, or at least very wide, axioms as they were, they simply *had to* be general in scope: the only legitimation that could be claimed for them was their logical infallibility and consistency. Making exceptions, and ruling out cases or groups of cases, would amount, under these premises, to arbitrariness, and that was clearly something which treatise-writing professors, unlike the Emperor Justinian, could not afford.

One result was that the area covered by "the law," in 17th and in particular 18th legal philosophy, had increased very considerably and embraced, in particular, matters which had previously been referred, by most writers, to the realm of ethics. It is true that 19th century writers very largely reacted against this, and restored – in some cases rather too strictly – a clear dividing line between law and morality (to be again blurred, or at least significantly modified, in 20th century legislation in such areas as social welfare law, criminal law, consumer protection, and, at least as an attempt, fiscal law), but they could not refuse to receive, as a result of the previous development, a vastly increased domain under the name of "law."

One particular aspect of that inheritance haunted them, at least on the Continent: the idea of "the law" as an all-embracing and logically structured system. There was of course, in the first place, a strong intellectual appeal in that notion; to many lawyers it seemed to provide the answer to the challenge of the natural sciences and the empirical social sciences. The "law," it could be claimed, was as vast and as objective a realm as physical nature; there were, in fact, "natural laws" in their field as much as in that of scientists; a vast apparatus of precise and refined concepts was as necessary for legal discourse as when describing and analysing nature; finally, the intellectual operations by which legal problems were solved were basically of the same character as the corresponding activity in other sciences. In the second place, the idea of "the law" as a complete system, from which solutions could always be drawn, however specific, odd and seemingly new the questions put to it would be, corresponded to strong ideological and practical needs.

For although Rousseau's ideas of the law as *volonté générale* had hit upon much criticism, and had been discredited by the excesses and abuses of the French Revolution, and although many leading European states remained, for all practical purposes, more or less absolute monarchies well until the middle of the 19th century, yet there can be little doubt that there was more and more support for the idea that *legislation* – as distinct from the exercice of public authority in other forms – needed at least some form of approval, consent or participation, of the people. Even in otherwise despotically governed states, various forms for such participation in legislation were invented, and as the century advanced, the legislative process as a specific public activity and decision-making procedure developed along essentially similar lines in the majority of European states. There were all sorts of exceptions, interruptions and derogations, but upon the whole, there can be no doubt that the principle according to which full-fledged "law" ought to be enacted only on the strength of some kind of parliamentary deliberations and decision was gaining ground steadily.

Concomitantly, in the same vein, as a fruit of 18th century Enlightenment ideology, as a reaction against the arbitrary exercice of power of absolute rulers in the 17th and 18th centuries, the ideal of the rule of law, the *Rechtsstaat*, steadily and rapidly gained ground. Practically, this meant that all exercice of public power and authority, in order to be legitimate, must be based upon the precepts of the law. This claim for "legal support" (to translate clumsily but literally an old Swedish term, which expresses the principle, *laga stöd*) was, naturally, especially strong with regard to interferences with the citizens' personal liberty and proprietary rights. The notion of "human rights," which had been developed by the 18th century Enlightenment philosophers and the natural law writers in the same period, and which had been adopted, i.a., in the North American and French Declarations of Rights (1776 and 1789), exercised a strong influence in this area.

A corollary of the idea of civic participation in the legislative process was, at the beginning of the period, considerable mistrust against law-making by courts, in the form of precedents.

In a situation where, on the one hand, formal "law" was held necessary for all such decisions by public agencies or officers as concerned the citizens, and, on the other hand, the making of new law was a complicated political process, the outcome of which could not always be foreseen, it is not unnatural that the notion of the complete and coherent "legal system," in addition to its intellectual attractiveness to legal thinkers, presented allurements of a more practical order; if able to find solutions to all emerging problems in the law as it stood, lawyers retained much of the power and influence which they otherwise incurred the risk of loosing. Although not explicitly stated, this may have been an argument of some importance also for legal theorists.

It should be added, finally, that the idea of the all-embracing legal system was, in the 19th century, far less of a myth than it had been a hundred or a hundred and fifty years earlier, when natural law writers developed their vast structures of ideal rules, deducing them from a handful of axioms. For in the 19th century, several influential Occidental states were provided with impressive codes of laws, such as the Prussian Civil Code of 1794, the French *Cinq Grands Codes*, 1804–1811, the foremost being the *Code civil* of 1804, which was introduced and remained in force in large areas of Western Germany until 1900, and the Austrian General Civil Code of 1811. These codes were more or less strongly influenced by 18th century natural law thinking; the ideal of consistency and completeness, at least in principle, is clearly a heritage of the natural law era. In addition to this, the 19th century, although unable to compete with the 20th in this respect, was a period of intense and extensive legislation. As the century advanced, the ideal of the *Rechtsstaat*, dominated by the rule of law, was completed, and to some extent replaced, by what might be called the predecessor of the modern welfare state: a – by modern standards modest – *Sozialstaat* which tried to remove or mitigate some of the most obvious negative consequences of the industrial revolution and to create a minimum of social security to the poor classes. This

– and the increasing administrative and military apparatus in all fields – gave rise to an ever-growing body of legislation. Again, the 19th century may be considered as the humble overture to the stormy full-orchestra piece of the 20th. Yet, there can be no mistake: the tune is the same; it is already "modern."

2. Some Historical Background Facts

Although this is a statement that hardly influences the present book, which by definition deals primarily or exclusively with Western Europe anyway, it is nevertheless important to remind ourselves by way of general characteristic of the now no longer obvious fact that the 19th century was the European century *par préférence*. North America was heading, with increasing strength and speed, for an equivalent or superior position in terms of economic and political power, but at the end of the century, the United States still had a fairly long way to go, as compared with Western Europe as a whole. In terms of cultural achievement, including legal theory and near-lying fields of science, the outcome of the comparison is even more obvious, throughout the century, although America was already making independent and valuable contributions and could claim an honourable position among the advanced nations. In relation to the rest of the world, the European predominance, which had been prepared, and made great progress, since the great discoveries about 1500 (cf. chap. 6, sec 2), became complete in the 19th century, when Europe literally divided between her leading powers such territories as were without a state organization strong enough to defend themselves and had not already been conquered, or taken under protection, by European powers. In the 16th, 17th, and even 18th, centuries, European colonialism had mostly fought, as it were, on equal terms with indigenous princes or tribes; superiority in organization and discipline had been Europe's "secret weapon." In the 19th century, the phenomenon later to be called (in a similar, although slightly different, context) "the technological gap," with regard to arms, transports, and equipment in general, gave the Europeans an increasingly growing, and ruthlessly exploited, superiority.

Thus, with great efficiency, mostly with equally great brutality, in fierce competition between her nations and business interests, and with an initially extremely modest but growing dose of religious and cultural missionary zeal, Europe, for better or for worse, created a "world community" which, unlike the *orbs* of the Romans, and the "inhabited world" of the Middle Ages, was no longer a small spot of light surrounded by dim *terrae incognitae* but did in fact embrace the globe. By 1914, that community was fairly well-established; its peripheric members, and "lesser breeds," could take their seats – to the extent they were not invited to join the actors – and witness how their masters and betters set about demolishing the proud tower that was Europe with an efficiency quite equal, and a speed many times superior, to what had been displayed in building it. The performance was not lost upon the audience.

The statement that the 19th century was the century of Europe must be subject to further qualifications: it was the century of Northern, and Northwestern, Europe – of that part of the Continent which faces, and copes with, the North Atlantic. The 18th century had been the French *siècle*; it started with Louis XIV's star at its highest point; culturally it remained French although the political decline of that country was becoming more and more obvious. The immense explosion of vitality, in all fields, which characterized the revolutionary and Napoleonic era certainly created the impression that France hed kept its position. The greater strength of England, and of united Germany, became more and more obvious, however. From Waterloo onwards, there can be little doubt about England's place on the international scene; from 1870–71, Germany can contest claims of superiority in political and economic strength from any other nation, and at the same time, the British economic leadership is silently and peacefully, but efficiently and with increasing speed, threatened by the United States. Just as the "French century" is the period where the position of France is, outwardly, more splendid than ever while silently undermined, in the same way, the "British century" is the period in which Britain, with all the outward appearances of an unbreakably solid wealth, power, and splendour, is gradually overtaken by the protagonists of the next act.

The two World Wars have to some extent concealed, or made at least Englishmen and Americans forget to what extent the 19th century was, from the beginning, not only – we shall come back to that – the British but, particularly in intellectual matters, also *the German century*. When the great national States of Western Europe emerged, in full glory, from the 16th century onwards, divided Germany had been lagging; the 30 Years' War (1618–1648) dealt a terrible blow to the country; it took a century to recover. In the fields of science and learning, Germany had, of course, always held her own. From the mid-18th century onwards she conquered a place in the sun in European literature and general culture. Goethe gave lustre to the decisive phases of this development; from the 1780's, a European "great tour" could not avoid Weimar (an earlier compulsory station, Voltaire's Ferney, was empty since 1778). By 1810, German philosophy, and romantic literature, although fighting against the reluctance of Englishmen and Frenchmen to learn other people's languages, had conquered a position of European leadership. A smattering of German, and a short stay at some German university to imbibe the most profound truths of the reigning philosopher, became in the course of the century fairly common dishes on the menu of the British *élite;* America followed suit; France was more reluctant.

If we insist on questions of political, economic, and intellectual supremacy which in themselves have little to do with legal thinking, it is because some knowledge of that kind of, let us call it, practical inter-European sociology, attributing greater or smaller importance to different schools or writers, is indispensable to make and justify a correct, or at least rational, choice of items to be treated from the rapidly growing wealth of intellectual production. For from the early 19th century – with the great national codifications – onwards, legal philosophy tends to become more and more national, indeed nationalistic. Since most well-organized states felt it their duty, in the course of the century, to maintain a full range of professorial chairs in all or most subjects known to the civilized world, since the holders of these chairs were strongly encouraged to produce a vast amount of learned writings (in fact, they would not get at the chairs, if they had not already published volumes), since a great proportion of those productions lacked all real intellectual independence and originality but frequently enjoyed great prestige in the author's own country, were compulsory reading for the state-conducted or state-supervised examinations mostly imposed upon Continental universities and thus constituted sources of an uninspired and unrevealed but fairly efficiently maintained legal state religion, it is good to know at least the outlines of a map showing the intellectual landscape of Europe, its high peaks and swampy valleys. Throughout the century, Germany could show, in competition with England, the most impressive range of peaks.

Towards a New World: the 19th Century

The 19th century started with great turmoil, French revolutionary armies, soon under the leadership of a young Corsican soldier of fortune and of genius, pouring out of the young republic and overrunning, again and again, Austrians, Prussians, Russians, Swedes – but never the English. The slogans of liberty, fraternity and equality make many heads turn, throughout Europe, but the more Imperial – and imperialistic – Napoleon and his French Empire become, the more contributions they extort from conquered provinces, the more members of the Bonaparte family are placed upon old or new thrones, the more even young Europeans begin to doubt the value and practicability of the revolutionary catchwords, and – the most lasting result – the more strongly they feel that their heart is with their own people, their own language, their own history (and, in a country where Napoleon never succeeded – Spain – their own religion).

When, in 1815, the dust rises from the Napoleonic battlefields, a tired Europe, led by English tories, Austrian reactionaries, with Prince Metternich as the most prominent statesman of the day, equally reactionary Prussians, a Czar, Alexander I, who dreams of a religiously founded chivalrous fraternity of European monarchs, is prepared to go back to order, as it was before the Revolution. France, exhausted, accepts. It is the period of the "Holy Alliance" – the Czar's dream – and of massive reaction throughout Europe.

By European standards, a peaceful century follows. There are few major conflicts, none on a European scale: in 1848, in the wake of the revolutionary movements of that year, there was fighting in Italy, where unsuccessful attempts were made to oust the Austrians, in Hungary, against the Habsburgs, in Slesvig, between Germans and Danes; at the middle of the 1850's, the Crimean war engaged France, England, Turkey and the Italian Kingdom of Sardinia against Russia for a couple of years: the war was a bloody affair, but essentially carried out by professionals, and far off. Five years later, the Austrians were at long last thrown out of Italy, with French assistance, and the rulers of Sardinia became kings of a united Italy. In the mid–60's, Prussia beat Austria, and turned the Habsburgs out of that family of states which five years later, in 1871, after a victorious war against France, agreed to form the German Empire, a union with the King of Prussia as Emperor. For the rest of the century, there was peace in Western Europe – a peace period of unprecedented length, a "long golden afternoon" which was to last until August, 1914 (the period 1763–1792 is frequently described, by contemporary memorialists, in the same glowing colours).

Optimistic writers of secondary school textbooks in history frequently pointed out, as late as the 1930's, that after 1870, Europe had come to a state of rest and harmony (the events of 1914–1918 being described as a regrettable accident) because the problem of *nationality* had found its proper solution in most of the Continent, and the great powers had obtained their so-called *natural frontiers*. Austria-Hungary was the great exception, as was subdued and divided Poland; that is why trouble started there. We need not criticize this naive standpoint. What is important is that *nationalism,* which turned out to be reconcilable with all political colours, from the blackest reaction to the reddest radicalism, was in fact one of the strongest determining forces in so far as practical politics were concerned. All other ideologies tended to be swept aside by nationalism in conflict situations.

Another movement which seemed irresistibly strong, and which also made other ideas yield in acute crises, was *imperialism.* There were, of course, nuances between Whigs and Tories in handling Indian problems, as there were nuances between French conservatives and radicals with regard to North Africa and Indo-China, but hardly any political party or movement was prepared to give up, in principle, imperialism as a practical line of action, and not even such a forceful statesman as Bismarck – one of the very few who harboured genuine doubts about the blessing of colonies – could prevent his country from joining in the race for African territories (and paying an enormous price, in terms of moral, men and prestige, for very little).

More or less stealthily, and on the strength of a great number of misunderstandings and errors, enlightened 18th century Europeans, in particular French Liberals, had admired England: her relative political freedom and religious tolerance, her wealth, civic spirit, and capacity of mobilizing resources in times of crisis. The bright image was somewhat blurred by the English politics, warfare, and general attitude in the conflict with the American colonies; it was severely damaged by Tory politics in the first two decades of the 19th century. Yet, Waterloo – far better known than Peterloo – was in some way considered the confirmation of the admiration and hopes attached to England. After 1832, with Parliamentary reform and the emancipation of Catholics, England seemed to fulfil the great expectations which liberal Europe had put in her. There was no lack of dark pictures from mines, factories, and slums. Yet, there can be no doubt: the 19th century was the English century also because the *élites* of Europe considered her the most advanced and the most promising country. The growth of the Empire, the mostly peace-promoting activities of the Royal Navy – such was its prestige that even the most doubtful debt-collecting raids against weak exotic republics were held to lay down, by means of new precedents, the international law of nations – the aloofness of Britain in Continental conflicts, her firmness to Russia, Austria and other reactionary powers, all this gave Victorian England not only a political, but also a moral *place à part*.

France, on the contrary, went through an ungrateful period: the euphoria of the Revolution and the unreal splendour of Napoleon's ten imperial years, 1804–1814, were bought very deerly. Revolutions succeeded each other. The reactionary Bourbons were ousted by the July Revolution in 1830, the *bourgeois* monarchy of Louis-Philippe of Orléans was overturned in 1848, the first President of the short-lived Second Republic, Prince Louis-Napoléon, made himself Emperor, Napoleon III, in 1851, by a well-prepared *coup dÉtat;* in 1870, ignominiously defeated by the Germans in the shortest, but most bloody, of Europe's great 19th century wars, he fell, and in spite of Monarchist majorities in Parliament, France settled down to her unglamorous but hardworking Third Republic, which not only continued the colonial policy of Kings and Emperor in North Africa but also vastly extended the French possessions in Central Africa and created an Indo-Chinese colonial Empire. The revolutions, obviously, expressed something deeper than constitutional quarrels: both in 1848 and in 1870, the short "political" phases of the revolutions overturning Louis-Philippe and Napoleon III respectively were followed by passionate, cruel, bloody and, in both cases, brutally repressed upheavals by the Paris proletariat – attempts at social revolutions in the spirit of socialism and communism. In spite of these movements, for the repression of which the provincially recruited army could always be trusted, France showed a very great social stability. The true constitution of France, an eminent lawyer wrote in 1904, was not any of the successive documents known under that name, but the Civil Code of 1804, the great private law codification of Napoleon, summing up the principal results of the great revolution to the extent they were generally and lastingly supported by the *bourgeoisie* and the great rural majority of 19th century France. The stability of private relationships,

Towards a New World: the 19th Century

in the first place family relations, and of the strictly centralized and well-organized civil and military administration gave France a tenacity in all her crises and catastrophes which astonished foreign observers. Napoleon had done very much to tidy up the German scene – in 1806, the Holy Roman Empire of German Nationality ceased to exist, the last Emperor, of the House of Habsburg, assumed the title Emperor of Austria, a number of Electors, Margraves, Princes or Dukes were promoted to completely autonomous Kings (Bavaria, Wurtemberg, Hanover, Saxony), or Grand-Dukes (Bade, Mecklenburg, Saxony-Weimar), and some 300 secular or ecclesiastical rulers became subjects of these greater potentates or were simply swept away. Napoleon ousted, the bigger animals of prey kept their booty. Although reactionary in principle, the new-made Kings and Grand-Dukes did not restore any territories to the former owners. A loose German Federation was created; rivalry between Prussia and Austria deprived this attempt at unification of all its significance; it was only in the realm of economy that any real progress was made. The revolutionary year 1848 shook the reactionary German states profoundly; in Austria, where the revolutionary movement assumed a social character in Vienna, and a nationalistic colour in Hungary, the Habsburgs could hold their own only with Russian help. The German states, where the revolution essentially remained a liberal and *bourgeois* affair, mostly bought their peace with some kind of more or less half-hearted and mostly not very liberal constitution. After a few years, in Austria as well as in the rest of Germany, reaction was again victorious.

This was of fundamental importance for the future. The liberal *bourgeois* had not managed either to unify Germany or to give her, or her still numerous States, a "modern" constitution. It was for one of the monarchies, the most militarized and bureaucratic (but not necessarily reactionary) of them all – Prussia – to carry out the work of unity under the leadership of a highly gifted but also highly traditionalistic *Junker,* Otto von Bismarck-Schönhausen. In 1866 Prussia, in a dazzling campaign of few weeks, defeated Austria but claimed no territory: the real fruit of victory was that the Habsburg monarchy left the German question to Prussia alone and concentrated her energy on the South-East of Europe, the unruly corner of the Balkans, where the Habsburgs were to meet their and Europe's destiny in 1914. When, in 1870, a conflict between Prussia and France became inevitable, the other German states sided with Bismarck. The new

German union, the Second *Reich,* which was proclaimed in the Palace of Versailles in 1871 after France had been totally defeated, was a union of kingdoms, grand-duchies, principalities, and a handful of free cities. The Emperor, King of Prussia, was only *primus inter pares,* and the other states retained a far-reaching autonomy. Yet, from now on, Germany was no longer a chaotic mixture of independent states, that could be played out against each other by foreign powers; there was one single Germany, and it was the strongest military and political unity on the Continent. The aristocratic, military and bureaucratic tradition of Prussia stood out as victorious where liberalism had been too weak and this fact tended to give Imperial Germany her specific character and atmosphere in many respects. Two lost Great Wars have contributed to make caricatures of the Second *Reich* more wide-spread than true portraits. While caught, in some important and, as it would turn out, fatal aspects of public life, in a network of dangerous militaristic and nationalistic traditions (shared, to a greater or lesser extent with most Continental powers), Germany was not only a constitutional state, it was also a *Rechtsstaat* – the rule of law prevailed; freedom of expression like most other essential freedoms were respected – and, finally, a progressive state in terms of social policies and incipient welfare legislation.

Sorely tried by never-ending quarrels between her many "unredeemed" nationalities and by hostility between the two leading ethnic groups, the Magyars of Hungary and the Germans of Austria, the battered Habsburg monarchy not only survived, to the indignation of liberals and nationalists, but flourished economically and profited now and then from the weakness of the Ottoman Empire to snatch a piece of land in the unruly Balkan peninsula, where, over the heads of newborn local small states, Habsburg met another fisher in troubled waters: Russia. A competent and decent administration, the economic advantages of a 50 million inhabitants' national market covering the whole Danube valley and a highly developed multinational cultural life with Vienna as its centre were the blessings bestowed by the Habsburgs upon their halfhearted or reluctant subjects.

Southern Europe went on loosing ground, culturally, economically and in terms of political and military power. The Iberian peninsula spent its 19th century with internal throat-cutting, miscarried constitutional experiments and general decay. The colonial empires of Portugal and Spain were drastically reduced when, in the 1820's, Latin

Towards a New World: the 19th Century

America revolted against their European masters and set up a number of independent republics. Portugal retained her possessions after Spain had lost most of hers, but neither of the civil-war plagued Iberian kingdoms had the strength to take an important active part in the 19th rush for new colonies.

The most spectacular progress made in the South was the long-dreamt of unity of Italy, which became a reality when in 1861 a Parliament, convoked to Turin, the capital of the liberal Kingdom of Sardinia, offered the throne of Italy to Victor Emanuel, King of Sardinia. In 1870, when Napoleon III could no longer protect the Pope, Italian troops entered Rome, which became the capital of the new monarchy. In spite of great concessions to Catholic interests, Pope Pius IX and his successors refused to accept the situation, signed all documents "imprisoned in the Vatican" and took a hostile attitude to the Italian State. In spite of great and fervent patriotic enthusiasm, the task of merging provinces which had not been united since the 6th century and which were highly different in all respects proved a very heavy assignment. Although hampered by these difficulties, Italy claimed a place among the great powers of Europe, maintained a strong army and pursued an active colonial policy. Here, as in Germany, it was, after all, a King, his great Minister – Count Camillo Cavour – and his army that had been successful where generations of grandiloquent liberal intellectuals had failed.

Among the smaller nations, the Kingdom of the Netherlands, created after the Napoleonic wars, was divided for good, in 1830, into the Netherlands and Belgium. In the North, Sweden lost Finland, an integral part of her territory since the early Middle Ages, to the Czar; by way of compensation, Norway was cut off from her four hundred years' union with Denmark and reluctantly handed over to Sweden in 1814. The highly unhappy marriage ended in 1905, peacefully but after a great expense of harsh language.

A world map from the year 1900, using different colours for the different powers, creates the impression of a Europe-owned world. The large surfaces allotted to the United States and the Chinese Empire are the principal exceptions. At a diplomatic conference in Berlin in 1884, what then remained of Africa was divided up between the European powers, the King of Belgium being given the Congo as a personal possession. After that, there were few areas in the world which could not be attributed to one or the other Occidental State or at least to their "spheres of interest." The pink colour mostly used on Continental maps for the British Empire competed with the green or yellow of Russia; the latter covered the largest coherent surface, but the former – adding British India, Burma, Australia, New Zealand, Canada, Egypt, to South and East Africa – seemed to hold a firm grip over the whole globe. France, with North and Central Africa and Indo-China, came next; Portugal and Spain, with patches of their old empires, the Netherlands with Indonesia, Belgium with the Congo (handed over to the Kingdom of Belgium by the King), Germany with an ungrateful piece of East Africa, and Italy with troublesome territories in northern and eastern Africa, followed suit on a smaller scale.

In one part of the world, Europe had not only refrained from expansion but had retired continuously: in North America. The young United States, originally thirteen small predominantly English colonies on the eastern coast of the continent, had grown with tremendous speed. By occupation – frequently combined with highly leonine treaties with the aboriginal Indian populations – purchases from France and Spain, conquests from Mexico and treaties with England about the Canadian border, the Union had reached its present frontiers in 1853. In 1867 Alaska was bought from the Russian Empire. In 1800, the United States had counted some four million inhabitants. In 1840, there were 14 million; in 1860 that figure had been doubled, and in 1880 the number exceeded 40 million. At the turn of the century, the Union accounted for 67 million, more than any of the Occidental great powers. Immigration from Europe answered for most of the increase. In spite of the very great economic, cultural and social problems which the enormous immigration from all the countries of Europe was bound to raise, and in spite of the devastating civil war, 1861–1865, the United States quickly developed into a great power with an economic potential which already in 1900 surpassed that of any single European power. Intellectually and culturally, the Union presented – as could be expected, given in particular the different levels of literary and general culture among the immigrants – a highly uneven picture. However, a basic American cultural identity developed with astonishing speed.

Within the political framework, outlined here, the Industrial Revolution took place, modifying beyond recognition the conditions of those concerned. It had started in England, in the latter half of the

18th century; by 1850, it was largely completed in England, while it had made only slow and partial progress in many other European states. That year, Great Britain produced roughly half the world supply of iron and more than two thirds of the supply of cotton fabrics. Considerably more than fifty percent of all tonnage on the high seas sailed under British flag. For a long time, the economic activity and the wealth of Britain were considered as almost miraculous. In some areas, such as northern France, Belgium and the Netherlands, the Rhineland and the Ruhr district in Germany – areas which had strong mercantile and pre-industrial traditions – a similar development took place, although decades later and initially on a smaller scale.

By the end of the 19th century, industrial processes had to a very large extent replaced older methods in the manufacturing of goods throughout Europe, and more or less pronounced forms of capitalist economies were prevailing. It would, however, be an error to believe that "industrialism," with its consequences for living conditions in general, social structure and attitudes, permeated western Europe as a whole by 1900. The traditional rural community was still predominant, or at least considered as the "normal" state of affairs, in most parts of the European continent. This is of some importance in the present context, for towards the end of the 19th century, the question arises, in the public debate in some countries, whether the existing private law systems, including such fairly recent codes as the French *Code civil* of 1804, were adapted to the needs and interests of the then quickly growing population of industrial workers; it was in fact asked whether the law did at all concern this new class. For the law, critics contended, dealt at great length with property, of which the working class had little or nothing in excess of necessary household goods of the simplest description. It dealt with marriage and matrimonial property, with filiation and legitimacy, wills, inheritances, the administration and distribution of estates, with rights in land, etc. The proletariat, some critics contended, simply never got into contact with the law, except in the form of military legislation (since they were welcome as canon fodder under the compulsory military service systems that existed in virtually all Continental states), of the slowly growing social legislation, and of course, if they were unlucky, of penal law. Private law was for the property-owning classes.

It is difficult to formulate a well-founded standpoint on this criticism. No doubt, in some parts of Occidental Europe, the "new state," with all it stands for, in terms of both welfare and deepgoing interferences with matters which the citizens had previously had to (or been allowed to) settle by themselves, had made its first timid appearance at the end of the 19th century. Education, public health services, social insurance and old age pension schemes were, in the most advanced societies, matters of public concern in the last one or two decades of the century. Upon the whole, however, the 19th century represents, when compared with the present situation, a period of transition, with still very strong features of the old world and some vigorous elements of the new.

3. Major Trends in Religious, Philosophical and Political Thinking

There can be no doubt about it: throughout Europe, the early 19th century is a period of *religious* revival; it develops into an epoch strongly marked by religious preoccupations, taken most seriously. Of course, the vast majority of Europe's population had remained profoundly and sincerely Christian throughout the preceding era. The unbelief disseminated by the Enlightenment movement had not penetrated very deeply (with the exception of isolated groups, like some sectors of the Paris proletariat in the years of the great revolution). Legal philosophy, however, was never a pastime for the many; what has to be taken into account here are tendencies among the few. In so far as the intellectual *élites* are concerned, the revival just referred to is obvious. One of the most important consequences of Immanuel Kant's philosophy, in terms of practical effects, was that it "saved," as it were, revealed religion by marshalling it out, firmly but reverently, from the area of philosophical controversy. Kant left a dark room in the house of metaphysics and he also gave ethics a new and firm place, which rendered a compromise with traditional religion possible. The eagerness – and the relief – with which his philosophy was studied by doubting young men who wanted to retain their faith, doubly valuable in the turmoils, dangers and horrors of the French revolution and the Napoleonic wars, is both obvious and moving. It was not until the middle of the century, with evolutionism, Darwinism, and a growing body of scientific observations, that Christianity was again out for trouble for theoretical reasons. Seriously threatened was the Old Testament's description of creation and of human history. Until then,

Christians had accepted that description, with its chronology, as authentic. By 1860 fundamentalism in that sense was no longer a tenable position for Occidental intellectuals; at the same time, comparative studies of religions, systematic text criticism, and archeological evidence hammered more and more vigorously upon the time-honoured Christian image not only of the world of the Old Testament but also of Christ and his teaching. The profound *malaise* of the period is witnessed by many, not only "professional" philosophers, but also French theologians (Ernest Renan) and English poets (Matthew Arnold and lord Tennyson). No gay paganism replaces the stern Christianity of the 19th century, however: the *élites* doubt, but they remain profoundly marked by Christian ethics to the end of the century and beyond.

Although it is true that the 19th century was much more than the 18th, a period marked by Christianity, an important qualification must be made. In the 18th century, nations did not, upon the whole, go to war for the sake of religion, but they took their faith extremely seriously *in terms of action*. They still burnt witches, they still punished dissenters severely. In the 19th century, people did not take their religion as seriously as that. The change of attitudes which explains the difference is, of course, increased tolerance. A question which has to be left unsettled, however, is whether the correct way of describing the development is to say that the 19th century attitude was one of piety enriched by tolerance, or one of faith diminished by tolerance. Whatever formula is used, the fact is that the number of situations where religious considerations were decisive in political, social and ethical issues of importance was steadily decreasing.

Again, we must warn against rash generalizing conclusions. We are referring, unless the contrary is said, to ideas and attitudes in that very narrow, and in most cases only indirectly influential, sector of Occidental societies which took an active interest in legal philosophy and similar branches of learning, with implications for legal philosophy. Even in these *milieux,* important groups, in particular all those connected with or dependent upon the Catholic Church and the firmly established Protestant churches remained essentially faithful to earlier thinking although fundamentalism and belief in verbal inspiration hardly held its own in university theology towards the end of the period. Confronted with the threats due to science as well as to social and modern political development, the Catholic Church went through a period of reaction. Thus the Vatican Council (1869–1870) adopted the dogma of papal infallibility, which created a schism between minorities of liberal Catholics and the vast majority of the Church that remained faithful to Rome.

***

In the realm of "general" philosophy, the 19th century is the German century *par excellence;* it is also the century of the great system-builders. One explanation of the latter characteristic is, of course, that the less explanatory value was granted religion, the more transcendental explanations had to be furnished – and were expected from – secular philosophers.

A great number of 19th century philosophers, both among those essentially engaged in metaphysical speculation and among those principally interested in ethics, social and political questions, exercised such a deep-going influence upon legal thinking in a wide sense that they must be given special treatment in sections of their own. To these belong Immanuel Kant and Jeremy Bentham; although the larger part of their lives was spent before 1800, they both, in highly different ways, dominate 19th century thinking. In the case of Bentham, much of his original thinking in the field of law was revealed to the world as late as the 20th century. Fichte and Hegel also call for sections of their own, while Auguste Comte, Herbert Spencer and John Stuart Mill will be dealt with more summarily in this introductory section. Although all the three exercised a deep-going influence on Occidental *societies* at large, including the general direction of legislative work in many areas, their importance for the development of *law as such* does not seem to be as thorough-going and extensive as that of the writers just mentioned.

A far-reaching general intellectual phenomenon which makes its appearance at the very beginning of the 19th century and which permeates much original thinking in various fields of knowledge and research, ultimately (and rapidly) producing results in such disparate areas as politics and esthetics, is *historicism.* This attitude, or complex of ideas, cannot be pinned down to any one specific philosophical school or thinker, although Montesquieu's sociological relativism is certainly one of the sources. Another, more distant, is British philosophical empiricism. To no small extent, a common sense reaction against the excesses and abuses of the French Revolution would seem to be at the bottom of some branches of historicism. Nor is it easy to define historicism.

One element is a general sense of the value of historically given solutions and institutions, as expressing the cumulated empirical wisdom of generations and as opposed to the airy constructions of 18th century rationalism – voiced most magnificently, by way of reaction to the French Revolution, in the speeches and writings of the English conservative politician and writer *Edmund Burke* (1729–1797). This attitude could lead, as the case was with many representatives of the Romantic literary school in Europe, to an uncritical admiration of the past. In particular, a keen interest in, sometimes a cult of, the Middle Ages characterized the early decades of the 19th century, it found expressions both in literature (Sir Walter Scott's novels being the most famous examples) and in art, under the name of neo-gothicism, favoured well until the middle of the century (the Houses of Parliament in London, Viollet-Le Duc's restorations of French castles, like Pierrefonds, Ludwig II's Neuschwanstein and other castles). In more sophisticated thinking, insight into the uniqueness of the past, and of the passing moment of history was a result of historicism. In this form, historicism undoubtedly represents a lasting step forward in intellectual maturity; the naive way in which institutions and solutions from ancient Greece or Rome had been imitated, e.g., by certain politicians and groups in the course of the French Revolution would be impossible after the Napoleonic wars.

Nationalism and historicism were victorious but not very harmonious neighbours and allies in 1815. Both had been mobilized and put to use when the European states gathered all their forces to defeat Napoleon's supremacy, but there were obvious tensions between them. Nationalism, as we have seen in the preceding section, was to prove the stronger of the two in the long run; it had, or could be given, a broad popular appeal, and it was difficult to reconcile with dynastic and feudal patchwork – completely indifferent to nationality – which history had made of the map of Europe and which historicism wanted to preserve as much as possible. Initially, historicism had the upper hand, supported by the military and political power of the great and small powers that had thrown the Corsican into the sea. We shall come back, in due course, to the political and, indirectly, legal consequences of historicism.

The great philosophical schools, and system-builders, usually kept

Towards a New World: the 19th Century

their importance for the development of *law as such* does not seem to be as thorough-going and extensive as that of the writers just mentioned.

position made it most tempting for the advocates of all imaginable intellectual, political, and social movements to use them as a sort of quarries for arguments. Kant, e.g., could be used by the partisans of the so-called Historical School of lawyers in Germany; he could also be exploited by at least moderate liberals later on in the century. Hegel's impressive but obscure teaching was initially held to justify political *status quo* in Germany, particularly in Prussia. Soon enough, however, the "left-Hegelians" put his ideas to their own use; among them we find the young Karl Marx.

If philosophic idealism (to which we shall soon return) and the more vague and general attitude here referred to as historicism were the predominant movements of ideas in the first three or four decades of the 19th century – the decades of Napoleon, the reaction, and the beginnings of liberalism – it would seem possible, although with some simplifications, to use the label "positivism" for the following decades. In these historicism (still producing and inspiring remarkable scientific results in such fields as comparative linguistics, anthropology, and – of course – history) was to some extent discredited by the failures and excesses of political reaction, the great philosophical system-building had spent its forces and come to a stand-still, liberalism was victorious in many countries and the new political and social problems connected with industrialism cast their shadow over the Occidental public scene.

"Positivism" is at best a vague and ambiguous term. In the interest of clarity, it seems helpful to distinguish between the following uses of the word:

(i) In a "general" philosophical and epistemological context, it is used to denote schools of thought which grant scientific relevance to, or accept as scientific proof, only such phenomena as are "given" (*positum*) sense-data, i.e. perceptible by means of the senses. "Positivism" in this sense can be pushed more or less far, in particular with regard to the degree of certainty which is demanded from evidence and the degree of logical necessity that is demanded from conclusions. In some recent writing, in particular of Marxist inspiration, the term has acquired a slightly negative ring (as a name for idelologically poor, short-sighted and unimaginative fact-collecting).

(ii) In a 19th century "general" philosophical and epistemological context, it is sometimes used, more specifically, to denote the ideas of the French philosopher and sociologist *Auguste Comte* (d. 1857), one of the fathers of the science of sociology. Comte's positivism is really a variant – by some modern standards not very demanding – of positivism as defined under (i). Comte was the first to use the term consistently, however, and he used it as a trade mark for his school of thought, so the word is sometimes used, without warning, for that variant.

(iii) In a "general" legal context, the term stands for such schools of legal thinking as care only for "given" sources and materials (*ius positum*), i.e. such as are actually administered by courts and officers of the law, by custom or by virtue of a legislative act, as opposed, in particular, to such merely pretended or postulated bodies of rules as natural law. Also here, there are variants depending upon the degree of strictness in the requirements to be fulfilled by, e.g. an alleged rule to be accepted as "positive law."

(iv) In a 19th century "general" legal context, the term is frequently used to denote prevailing attitudes among Continental, more particularly German, lawyers from 1830–1840 onwards, until about the end of the century (French lawyers can also be referred to, but a more common term here is the "exegetical school").

(v) In a 19th century English legal context, the word is used – though mostly with the additional epithet "analytical" – to denote the legal philosophy of Jeremy Bentham and John Austin, to which we shall duly return.

(vi) In various contexts, the term appears – but then usually with some explaining epithets as to time, place, and topic – to denote various movements which present at least most of the characteristics defined under (i) and (iii) above.

There was, and there is, of course a connection between the various forms of positivism. They tend to make a "family," sometimes quarrelling but mostly united against enemies from the outside.

Comte's positivism expressed the most spectacular break with idealistic philosophy and metaphysical speculation, although the French thinker laid down with great gusto and fertility a number of highly speculative "natural laws" for the development of sciences and societies. Thus Comte pretended that there are three phases in that development: the "theological," the "metaphysical," and the "positive" stages. In the last-mentioned, where science was to reign over humanity, there would be no need for "law" in the traditional sense; its place was to be taken by sociology. This does not mean, however, that Comte broke with moral values as guiding principles for the future society: "rights" he said, are absurd and immoral; the only right recognized by positivism is to do one's duty.

Neither original, nor – in particular – clear and coherent as a thinker, Comte nevertheless exercised a strong influence by laying the foundations of the systematic empirical study of human societies – *sociology*.

***

Two highly influential English writers should be mentioned in the present general context, although it would also be justifiable to deal with them a little further on, where we discuss the political thinking of the 19th century.

Herbert Spencer (1820–1903), whose great *System of Synthetic Philosophy* exercised a deep-going influence on Victorian England, no more than Comte refrained from a discussion, which would today be considered highly speculative, concerning the ultimate foundations of knowledge and faith and of the processes of development and dissolution which govern the universe. Spencer has retained some of the British heritage of empiricism, but he is also typical for the liberal era by virtue of his firm belief in human progress in all fields; in the future, the moral and social instincts of man shall be more and more strengthened and refined; working for oneself and one's own happiness will coincide with work for the common weal. In terms of practical action, this meant that Spencer could be quoted in support of *laissez-faire* liberalism, which practical liberals, confronted with the consequences of the Industrial Revolution, had had to abandon long before Spencer published his principal works.

The other leading spokesman of British 19th century liberalism was *John Stuart Mill* (1806–1873), son of a radical Scottish economist and philosopher and educated privately, in the thin air of a highly intellectual *milieu*. He was strongly influenced by Jeremy Bentham's utilitarianism (v. sec. 4 below). He reached, like his father, a senior post in the East India Company. For a short period, he was a member of Parliament, where he cast his lot with Gladstone. Through his noble serenity, serious idealism, and also practical common sense, he exercised – and still exercises – a considerable influence, ennobling, by his ethical considerations, both the sometimes rather shallow and negative liberal notion of freedom (*On Liberty*, 1859) and liberal political economy (*Principles of Political Economy*, 1848). Mill was, basically, an empiricist; from this point of departure, he developed a complete epistemological system ("the four inductive methods of science"), which would seem to be, in retrospect, his most important lasting contribution to philosophy. Mill was less radical in his utilitarianism than Bentham; he left, as it were, a privileged position to what is "higher" or "spiritual" when weighing different forms of pleasure; he also showed, in some posthumous essays, a far greater understanding for the ethical values – and the theoretical possibility – of religion than had earlier generations of 19th century radicals. Mill's essay "On Liberty," which deals as much with the dangers coming from oppressive public opinion as with those caused by tyrannic public powers, is likely to be the most important literary monument to the ethical and political thought of Victorian Britain. Mill celebrates freedom, in terms not unlike those of the ancient Greeks, as a good in itself, a "necessary part and condition" of "civilization, instruction, education, culture . . . " Political *régimes* and social systems are evaluated according to their compatibility with individual liberty in this exalted sense. In spite of his high appreciation of liberty, Mill recommended State intervention in industry to a far greater extent than had been admitted by early liberals (the "Manchester school). In Mill's version, liberalism is already becoming the "social *liberalism*" of the next century.

***

In this context, it is impossible to give even the barest outline of the progress of natural science. We have to put up with the sweeping general characteristics given in sec. 1 above. Here, we shall try to characterize the impact of that development on the traditional imprecise and non-experimental disciplines, among which legal philosophy, and legal science as a whole, took a time-honoured place.

Basically, the challenge could be met in three ways. One was capitulation, i.e. by recognizing that what had previously been called "science" could no longer claim that name, by abandoning some of the activities concerned, while carrying on with more modest theoretical pretentions the practically useful ones: a doctrine of interpretation of statutes, or a doctrine of precedents could at any rate be defended as indispensible for the function of the legal system, although on the lower level of craft expertise. Another possible reaction was, of course, to adopt as extensively as possible the methods, habits of thought and terminology of the victorious sciences: what brought progress in one field, it could be claimed, ought to prove equally successful in another. Finally, there was always the possibility of closing, fortifying, and living on in the ivory tower or, more offensively, insisting on, and if possible developing further and motivating more in detail, the uniqueness and value of one's own traditional discipline.

Looking back upon legal science and legal philosophy in the perspective which is possible now, a century and a half later, it seems justifiable to state that all the three possible ways out were tried. As has already been said in the present chapter, legal philosophy (and philosophy as a whole, from the mid 19th century) has successively given up more and more of her once far-reaching explanatory ambitions to deal, very largely, with analysing the language of legal scholars and practitioners. For that purpose, analytical methods characteristic of the exact sciences have very largely been borrowed wherever possible. Moreover, where earlier generations of lawyers either pronounced themselves, with great security, on the strength of theoretical speculation, common sense or more or less deep-going and extensive practical experience – e.g. questions concerning the effects of legislation or the motives of this or that mischief that should be dealt with – empirical social sciences, such as sociology and psychology, have largely taken over the field with their methods, largely modelled upon those of the exact and the natural sciences.

Early in the 19th century, before scholars had realized the breadth and depth of the chasm between natural sciences on the one hand and the humanities and social sciences on the other, there was, among lawyers who wanted to perfect their craft and give it a status – and a chance of development – similar to that of the natural sciences, a strong movement to improve and refine the conceptual apparatus of legal science. The school of *Begriffsjurisprudenz* ("conceptual" or rather "conceptualistic" jurisprudence), that flourished for several decades about the middle of the century in Germany, was, at the outset, not merely a response to the new and precarious situation of legal theory in the presence of the successful new branches of research. There were originally other earlier sources of inspiration, but the ambition to achieve a maximum of precision in descriptions and definitions of legal phenomena was undoubtedly inspired by the new competitive situation. At the root of conceptualism, in its early, naive phases, there was certainly also the idea that legal institutions were "natural" rather than man-made in the sense that to meet the one or the other social need, or to forestall this or that conflict, there was *one* solution dictated by reason. The task of legal scholars, in this perspective, was to analyse carefully, and thus to "purify" legal institutions and legal rules, much as the chemist, by a series of operations, isolates, or purifies, gold or alcohol. It was also held that legal decision-making could be transformed into an entirely objective and scientific activity, similar to, e.g., the analysis of flowers which, by successive examination of their parts and properties, are almost mechanically referred to their proper place in the Linnaean system.

The German *Begriffsjurisprudenz* had a considerable appeal. It was developed – under the influence both of natural law thinking and of the conceptual structures of German idealistic philosophy rather than as a response to the challenge of natural science, – by the law professor *Georg Friedrich Puchta* (d 1846) and carried on with great energy by the great *Rudolf von Ihering* (1818–1892) who explicitly referred to the terminology of the natural science to break down, and then to reconstruct rationally, the "raw material" of legal rules. In 1861, Ihering broke with conceptualism, however, and proclaimed a "pragmatic jurisprudence," to which we shall return in due course (sec. 9 below).

The third possible reaction – to defend the positions of traditional humanities and social sciences on the basis of the originality and uniqueness of their object, viz. man, in his historical and social context, and consequently of the methods called for – was not consciously elaborated and formulated until late in the 19th century. There were, of course, many scholars, in many quarters, who realized more or less clearly the fundamental difference in principle between the exploration of nature and the study of human nature, human relationships and human societies, and who were not troubled by the progress of the experimental sciences. Such "humanistic" fields of research as linguistics, history, anthropology, the history of literature and of the arts and ethnology also made great progress throughout the century, frequently under the inspiration of rationalism and historicism. A regular, philosophically founded "humanistic counter-attack," in the course of which it was attempted to lay down the specific conditions and characteristics of human sciences, did not occur until the end of the century, when in particular the German philosopher *Wilhelm Dilthey* (d. 1911) developed an epistemology of the *Geisteswissenschaften* (sciences of the mind), based upon descriptive psychology and openly acknowledged sets of values. Another prominent German writer, *Ernst Cassirer* (d. 1945) contributed, more critically and with less system-building ambitions, to the epistemology of the historical sciences.

At all times, original and powerful writers, who could not be ranged within this or that specific "school," have exercised an influence which is difficult to measure and define but which may nevertheless be interpreted as symptomatic for the period in which they worked – not least for intellectual needs and yearnings which the "official," institutionalized, organization for the production and dissemination of ideas cannot satisfy. In fact, the number, position and importance of such contributors to the public dialogue of a given period or civilization may be used to measure the relative degree of intellectual "health" and "harmony," or the greater or smaller degree of unreleased tensions in the community concerned. In some periods, for which the term "classic" can be used, the intellectual "establishment" is successful in catching and canalizing all reasonably important expressions of ideas. There is at least some room for dissenters "within the system"; dissent does not mean "heresy." This would seem to have been the case in the great century of Greece and in some short periods of Roman history: the reign of Augustus and the era of Trajan and the Antonines (second century A.D.). At least part of the high Middle Ages seems to correspond to the notion of a "classical" period in this sense, and so does the first half of Louis XIV's *grand siècle* in France. It would seem to be of some importance to stress that although the 19th century was characterized, in the Occident, by a tolerance hardly ever known in earlier periods of history, the number and importance of discordant voices in the public conversation are exceptionally high, compared with previous epochs. Many explanations are of course available – tolerance being one, more wide-spread literacy, and a vastly increased "intellectual market" being another – but it nevertheless seems justified to contend that in spite of enormous scientific, technological and economic progress, radically improved sanitary conditions, drastically lengthened average life expectations for all, or almost all, as a whole "enlightened" governments, relative peace, the 19th century is

Towards a New World: the 19th Century

an epoch of disharmony, heresies, and protest. There is no basic consensus on what is either the good life or the good society. Literature, in some leading countries, tends to take an overall critical and hostile attitude to the society at large; this is true in particular in France, where this particular form of disharmony and tension seems to become endemic, but it is also to a great extent true about Germany and southern Europe. The influence of dissenting philosophers is considerable: the Dane *Søren Kierkegaard* (d. 1855) a radical Christian but also a radical critic of contemporary society, ideals and scholarship; the German pessimistic philosophers *Arthur Schopenhauer* (d. 1860) and *Eduard von Hartmann* (d. 1906); *Friedrich Nietzsche* (d. 1900), whose violent criticism of the unmanly, sentimental and hypocritical Occidental society and whose eloquent cult of superman, "the blonde beast," deeply impressed a whole generation of intellectuals. But in addition to these internationally famous and influential critics, the *bourgeois* society of the 19th century had to face smarting criticism and discontent from all quarters: disappointed radicals, ironic intellectuals, embittered reactionaries. Neither the "proud tower" of official Europe, nor the increasing well-being of the populations express the whole truth; both were continuously criticized and questioned, for good reasons or for bad.

***

To the extent that the law is considered an instrument – one of the instruments – in the service of political power, political and legal thinking is, of course, interwined. In the 19th century, the function of law as a tool for far-reaching reforms of the society – and as an object of reform in itself – was acknowledged more openly and more frequently than had previously been the case: this could be expected, with the idea of progress and the belief in progress gaining more and more ground and with the concomitant successive breakdown of earlier notions of the immutability of law as an expression of its legitimacy and indeed sanctity. On the other hand, however, as has already been stated above, the increasing specialization, and more technical character, of all branches of knowledge and scholarship, as well as the emergence of new social sciences, each with a considerable bearing upon political thought, tended to narrow the scope of that part of the discussion of public affairs where the "law" in a more technical sense was held to be engaged and where, consequently, lawyers had a claim to be consulted as the most competent experts. This tendency had – slowly, in the course of the century – the effect of making lawyers retire to those areas where their expertise was generally recognized, leaving to "general philosophers," economists, sociologists, political scientists and, of course, as ever, prophets and visionaries, the task of drawing up the designs for lofty social constructions; to political leaders was left the practical implementation of such ideas as survived beyond the drawing-board. In both cases, the tendency was, for lawyers, to consider it their task to offer an arsenal of value-neutral tools or part of it.

Although the 19th century saw, at its birth, one of the most powerful dictatorial governments that had ever ruled an Occidental nation – Napoleon's consulate, which in 1804 logically became Napoleon's Empire – the mainstream of political thinking in the West was that movement which summarized, in terms of political action programmes, the principal tenets of Locke and of the moderate French Enlightenment philosophers: the movement to be called "liberalism" (the term seems to have been used first in Spain, in the 1810's; it was soon taken up in France, and in other European countries). That movement had been, and remained, victorious – although with various nuances – in the United States, and it had celebrated a short triumph in France, between 1789 and 1792. The Napoleonic *régime* had not – and could hardly have – any political philosophy of its own. Initially, its justification was to meet the deep need for stability, quiet, and security felt by the vast majority of the French population after a decade of turmoil, change, and terror. When the peace-granting dictator rapidly developed into a rapacious war-lord, that tacit legitimation could no longer be maintained. Defeated, Napoleon could claim nothing but the regards due to genius. His nephew Napoleon III's, attempts to develop in writing, half a century later, a Bonapartist political philosophy were no more rational or successful than any other "philosophy" based upon personal autocratic rule.

The real enemies of liberalism in the course of the 19th century were, in the order of their appearance on the Occidental stage: conservatism, excesses in liberal thinking and socialism.

In retrospect, the Enlightenment philosophers frequently seem to have been uncontested masters of the field in the last fifty years of the 18th century, opposed only by reactionary, less and less powerful churches, and a handful of weak and inefficient princes and noblemen. On the eve of the Revolution, a saying goes, the King of France considered himself to be an abuse. The truth is more complicated, although the opposition against the optimistic liberalism of the Enlightenment had few talented writers at its disposal. One highly gifted French journalist should be mentioned: *Antoine (de) Rivarol* (d. 1801), who had the courage to defend traditional institutions until 1792, when he emigrated and continued his brilliant polemics untill his death.

After the Revolution had shown its true face, the conservative forces rallied. The greatest thinker and writer on this side was undoubtedly the already mentioned English politician and journalist *Edmund Burke,* a poor Irishman who had worked his way up through the corrupt late 18th century Whig establishment. Burke was, politically, an eclectic rather than a fanatic. Thus he recommended "liberal" measures, such as economic liberty and the emancipation of Catholics, to raise Ireland from her depressed state. Broad-minded and perspicacious, Burke realized the weakness of 18th century optimism as a programme for political action, and confronted with the excesses of the French Revolution, his political thinking matured. Respect for the experience expressed in historical institutions, and reluctance to change, where changes could mean irremediable destruction of laboriously gathered values were central elements in Burke's political thought which, in the midst of an intensely active political life, he never had time to develop at length, or more systematically.

During, and in the decade immediately following upon, the Napoleonic wars, the conservative forces had the upper hand; liberalism was on the defensive everywhere in Europe. In these years, a number of conservative or reactionary writers appeared. Most of them were believing and practising Catholics. As early as 1796, the French Vicomte *L.G.A. de Bonald* (d. 1840) wrote, at Heidelberg in Germany, where he had emigrated, his *Théorie du pouvoir politique et religieux,* which is a brilliant and learned plea for absolute monarchy. Count *Joseph-Marie de Maistre* (d. 1821) a Savoyard nobleman who spent a long time as his king's envoy in Russia, developed, in the *Soirées de Saint-Pétersbourg* (1821) and in several pamphlets, coherent antiliberal political and religious convictions. According to de Maistre, who has a strong vein of religious mysticism, the historically given political and religious system, including absolute monarchy (and absolute papacy) has divine sanction, since God has allowed it to last for such a long time. To overturn, or even to reform, the historical *régime* of one's country is thus both a crime and a sin. Similar ideas were expressed, although with less talent, and with a great apparatus of scriptural and historical learning, by the Swiss scholar *K.L. von Haller* (d. 1854), whose great work *Die Restauration der Staatswissenschaften* (6 vol., 1816–1834) enjoyed great prestige in reactionary milieux.

Conservatism never became the relatively complete and relatively uniform ideology that liberalism was, at least in its early stages of development. It was in the nature of things that conservative writers did not propose general systems of government, or complete solutions to social, political and economic problems. Basically they were defending the state of affairs which prevailed at their time or had been prevailing before revolutionary upheavals. This meant, among other things, that since liberal criticism and reform proposals mostly concerned, initially, public law and public institutions, the conservative defence concentrated upon these areas. However, some conservative writers also criticized the uncontrolled growth of industry, the *laissez-faire* policy of liberal governments and the misery of the urban working classes. This particular aspect of conservative criticism undoubtedly contributed both to the modest beginnings of a socially inspired protective legislation (against excessive working hours and particularly heavy work for women and children), which was enacted, in England from the 1830's onwards, and shortly afterwards in other countries.

All over Western Europe, but particularly in Germany, political conservatism was closely allied with a general movement of ideas already referred to above: historicism. Under certain conditions, it could also become an ally of nationalism. This usually came to pass towards the end of the century, when nationalism had assumed, in the then united national states, Germany and Italy, but also in France and, although to a far lesser extent, in Britain, a military or even militaristic character. As long as nationalism was a revolutionary slogan, as it had to be, by definition, both in Italy and in Germany until the 1860's, this alliance occurred only, and rarely, in the previously established national states.

Historicism came to play an important part in the history of European legal thinking, and we shall come back more fully to the German "historical school" below (sec. 8). In this general survey, it is enough to say that one of its practical effects was to prevent legislative reform in many areas, and to give to the study and practice of private law a learned and antiquarian character.

In the course of the 19th century, liberalism and conservatism dominated alternately; from the fall of Napoleon untill about 1830, conservatism characterized most European governments. The following three or four decades saw the heyday of liberalism in England, its short first triumph in France (1830–1851) and at least a clear development towards liberal economic policy in Sweden, Norway and the smaller Continental states. In Germany, Austria, Italy and the Iberian peninsula, reaction ruled, upon the whole undisturbed, until 1848. From 1870 onwards, under the pressure of socialist movements, conservatives and liberals came closer to each other, without merging, however. The fact that the difference, in terms of practical political action, between the two main competitors on the European scene decreased was also due to the simple fact that a number of goals set up by early 19th century liberals were in fact reached in the course of the century. Another explanatory fact is that the leading elements of those classes of society that were the most efficient and powerful advocates of liberalism – the upper middle classes, particularly those engaged in trade and industry – had by the end of the period accumulated wealth and attained a social position which created a far-reaching community of interest between them and the noble and gentle landowners, military officers and higher bureaucrats who were traditionally the staunch supporters of conservative ideas. The economic changes which took place at the end of the century and which revealed both the vulnerability of some branches of industry in the face of international competition and surprising communities of interests between certain industrialists and landowners, including the usually conservative peasantry, contributed to complicate the pattern.

We need not dwell here on details in the evolution of 19th century liberal thinking. Spencer and Stuart Mill, already referred to, were the most influential "general" liberal writers. The main targets of liberalism in the field of legislation remained on the one hand constitutional law, on the other hand such early administrative regulations, from medieval guild bye-laws to mercantilistic detailed legislation, as hampered industry and trade. In the field of private law, the liberals fought against such remnants of patriarchal systems as the subjection and dependence of woman and primogeniture (with regard to the right of succession to land).

***

Since times immemorial, there had been doctrines and programmes of action which can be called socialistic, if by that term we mean, essentially, a more or less complete abolition of private property and a more or less complete collective ownership of land or even movables, whether the collective be the state, a local congregation, a body of local government or a voluntarily formed group of people. In times of disaster, in particular, in the late Middle Ages, in the period of Renascence and Reformation and in the English Civil War, there had been preachers and their sometimes very numerous followers who tried to realise socialist ideals and to overturn the prevailing order of society.

There is, consequently, no reason to be astonished at the emergence of socialist creeds from the early days of industrialism, which undoubtedly meant both misery and, above all, a great insecurity to many people (who had, in all likelihood, starved and suffered as much in their miserable cottages in the rural society they had left, but whose suffering became more visible both by being concentrated in slums which were not idyllic even in summer, when the village cottages had at least had the advantage of being close to nature, and also by being compared with the conspicuous accumulation of wealth of those who profited from industrialism). The early 19th century socialists are usually grouped together under the name of "utopians"; they are thereby distinguished from the later, "scientific" socialism represented by Karl Marx and his pupils, to whom we shall return (sec. 10 below). We need not go into the sometimes highly elaborated and highly ingenious proposals of the early socialists; they exercised little or no influence upon legal thinking. Let us only mention the French nobleman *Count C.-H. de Saint-Simon* (d. 1825), who preached a religiously coloured state socialism, based upon every citizen's right to work; the French business man *F.M.C. Fourier* (d. 1837), who proposed a form of communities *(phalanstères)*, each composed of 400 families, as base of the society; and the workman, politician and journalist *P.J. Proudhon* (d. 1865) who was violently opposed to any hierarchical order, wanted to abolish the monetary system and who formulated the well known slogan "Property is theft."

The effect of utopian socialism upon legislation in the Occident in the 19th century remained indirect: by the pressure exercised by the utopists, both by their appeal to the conscience of the privileged classes, and by the fear of a bloody revolution which they inspired, they undoubtedly lent a tacit but powerful support to those – conservative or liberal – politicians, economists and lawyers, who advocated social reform legislation.

4. Enlightenment Thinking Continued: Jeremy Bentham

Legal philosophy in a narrow sense was only a secondary preoccupation in the thinking of *Jeremy Bentham* (1748–1832) who set out on a career in the legal profession but soon devoted all his time, throughout a long life, to research and authorship on a broad range of subjects, all falling, however, in the fields of philosophy and the social sciences in the broadest sense of the word. Bentham has a claim to be recognized as England's, and one of Europe's, most influential writers in these fields after Locke. He is one of the fathers and pioneers of 19th century liberalism. At the same time, however, his intellectual roots in 18th century rationalism are deep and decisive. It is characteristic that he operates, in his analysis of law and society, with *one* single principle, from which his whole system can be deduced: man's research of pleasure is, according to Bentham, the basis of the whole social order. On the other hand, the adoption of this starting point for the work of building and justifying society – as distinct from, e.g., Locke's affirmation of aboriginal "natural" rights – shows the influence of that empiricism the elaboration of which was the greatest contribution of Britain to "general" philosophy and epistemology in the 18th century. In fact, if his insistence upon *utility*, i.e. capacity to create pleasure as opposed to pain, is the first characteristic of Bentham's doctrine of state and law, the radical and systematic rejection of any theory of natural law is the most characteristic element of his jurisprudential thinking. In this sense, Bentham is not only a "positivist" in the specific and narrow sense of a spokesman of the jurisprudential school of "analytical positivism" (N° v in our enumeration in sec. 3 above), but also a forerunner both of positivism as a general epistemological trend (N° i) and as a general element in 19th century legal thinking (N° iii).

It should be noted, when attempting to define and measure Bentham's influence on his contemporaries and immediate successors, that a considerable proportion of his vast production was not published until after his death; one of his most important treatises in the field of jurisprudence, *The Limits of Jurisprudence Defined,* although written in the 1780's and known to his pupils, *i.a.* John Austin (v. sec 8 below), was edited as late as 1945; one of the greatest works, *The Theory of Legislation,* is a translation into English of "Traité de législation civile et pénale" as published by a French-speaking Swiss pupil in 1802; the English version appeared in 1950. Some works have become available to the public only in the collected works of Bentham (1970).

Bentham's "moral philosophy," to use the term most frequent in his days – today we should rather speak of "psychology" – sets out to explain, discuss and criticize human society on the basis of the empirical observation, already made by Hume and others, that human behaviour is essentially, if not totally, dictated by man's wish to avoid negative perceptions and sensations – "pain" – and to find the opposite, "pleasure." These motives, and nothing in the way either of the defense of "natural rights" or of a "social contract," are the bases of human societies: the avoidance of pain and the research of pleasure makes practically necessary, and consequently justifies, a social organization of some kind. For if each individual pursued his interests regardless of others, the result would be a chaotic state of affairs leading to more pain than pleasure for a great number of men. The object of society, then, is to secure – in Bentham's famous formula, minted already in his *"Fragment on Government (1776)* – *"the greatest happiness of the greatest number."*

The maximation of "happiness" also determines the contents of Bentham's ethics, as a guideline for legislation. "Right and wrong," Bentham says, are "fastened to . . . the two sovereign masters" which "nature" has established to govern mankind, *viz.* pain and pleasure. "It is for them alone to point out what we ought to do, as well as to determine what we shall do." No comments are necessary to demonstrate how far this social philosophy is from the postulates of rationalistic natural law, let alone from a religiously founded law and ethics.

Two major consequences could be drawn from Bentham's starting points, and he spent his laborious life drawing and developing them. In the first place, "philosophers," i.e. social scientists, had to face the task of calculating – for Bentham recommended, and tried to exemplify, a "calculation" in this respect – how the maximum of happiness could be secured to the greatest number of people. In elaborating his principles of calculation, Bentham clearly leaves empiricism and adopts hypotheses which imply not only far-reaching standardizations of human behaviour but also pure fiction. Bentham, like many early economists, operates with a rational man without whom, obviously, no calculation would be possible.

In the second place, Bentham's justification of society, and of the constraint it inevitably implies, goes no further than as follows from its capacity to create the maximum of happiness of the greatest possible number. What goes beyond that cannot be justified. This standpoint makes Bentham a strict, in some respects a ferocious, critic of many, if not most, political and legal institutions of Georgian England. In several cases, he offered alternative solutions, based upon his calculations, to replace the worm-eaten, irrational and unjust institutions he found around him. Bentham paid no regard to history and tradition; in his eyes, they represented no values; history he tended to consider – like many Enlightenment writers – as nothing but a chronicle of crime, superstition and folly.

Three elements of Bentham's legal thinking, in a more narrow sense of the word, will be dealt with here: his general ideas of what law is (as distinct from what it ought to be); the principles underlying his proposals for substantive changes of civil, criminal and procedural law; finally his (posthumously published) principles for the administration of law, in particular the construction of statutes.

Throwing overboard all metaphysical, religious or ethical foundations of law, Bentham describes it as nothing but a system of coercion. Its main characteristics are that it has the form of commands (and prohibitions), that these orders are issued by the "sovereign" i.e. the person or group of persons who are in fact obeyed in the society concerned and, finally, that the sovereign's commands are sanctioned: whoever disobeys, incurs "pain" in the form of a legal sanction. The objection that of all the enactments actually in force, only a few express the present sovereign's commands was met by the ingenious reply that each successive sovereign tacitly accepts, and thus makes his own, "by adoption," the commands of his predecessors.

This view of the law was, not unexpectedly, considered by many critics as primitive, brutal, and insufficient. The absence of any ethical justification was felt to be a serious lack, and the question was raised what made law "binding" upon the subjects. Bentham, of course, had no need for any theory about the "binding" character of law; the question, for him, was whether a given legal system or individual legal rule was efficient or not. If efficient, any system, however tyrannic, would make "law" under Bentham's definition. In actual fact, there is undoubtedly an extremely important ethical assumption at the bottom of Bentham's legal philosophy – the principle of the equality of all men, without which the utilitarian calculation would obviously be impossible, and nonsensical – but that assumption does not find any expression in the description of what the law is (as distinct from what it ought to be). In that description, Bentham does not purport to give more than the observable facts, and that he does, including the possibly quite irrational grounds upon which the sovereign claims, and habitually obtains, obedience. The most salient weak point in Bentham's reasoning, from a strictly theoretical point of view, is that its psychological assumptions are really too crude: the definition does not take into account *custom* as a source of law, and yet custom played a far more important part in Bentham's days than today. *Via* the analysis of custom, the philosopher might have arrived, without inserting any moralizing evaluations of his own, at a more realistic view of the place which ethical convictions, including prevailing ideas about such things as historical legitimacy, do in fact play, e.g., for the purpose of distinguishing a legal system from a mere reign of terror and violence.

By analysing closely the interests engaged, and by discussing clearly and coherently the construction and operation of the mechanisms involved, Bentham rendered most valuable services to the reform of substantive law in the 19th century. Although his international fame and influence were considerable, these services were far more obvious in England than on the Continent, where the initial impact of Roman law, and also law reforms marked both by the humanitarian ethos, the rationalism and the systematizing ambitions of rationalistic natural law writers, had successively introduced important amendments. The difference between Continental law and the archaic – and brutal – law of England became particularly obvious in the former half of the 19th century, after France had adopted her five great Codes (1804–1811), the principal German states had passed Codes of their own (Prussia in 1794, Austria in 1811), and many smaller European states had followed the French example.

In the field of legal procedure, Bentham's radicalism was shocked at the formalism, the delay and the possibilities of vexatious manoeuvres which were very much part of the English court system and procedural law of his days. The philosopher tended to consider the whole system as a plot, by which the members of the legal profession could abuse, in their own interest, the respect, ignorance, and fears of the public. Bentham recommended a radical simplification of procedure, the abolition of many formal rules with regard to trial and hearings, wide discretionary powers for the judge to achieve materially satisfactory results, and a general policy of trying to reconcile the parties as much as possible. In private law, Bentham's main point was that the law should impose as few obstacles and as little delay as possible to that exchange of goods and services which make the economic fortune of a society and thus contributes to the maximum happiness. Rules which could not be defended on rational grounds should be repealed. Security and reliability – which represented important interests – should be weighed against opposing interests, *i.a.*, a reasonably equitable distribution of advantages upon all the members of the community. Bentham's rational approach to private law, and his unhampered radicalism in some respects, came to exercise, directly and indirectly, a deep and widespread influence not only upon law reform but, even more, upon the methods of justifying and criticizing laws and proposed law reforms all over the Western world.

In the field of criminal law, also, Bentham's basic principles meant a new approach. Instead of asking whether a given act deserves punishment, and how severe that punishment should be, he put the question whether, in a given case, the evil which punishment incontestably represents can rationally be expected to be smaller than the evil to be expected if the act is left unpunished or whether a wrong already committed can be repaired by that evil. Rational systematization of crimes, and a consistent proportionality between crime and punishment were also among Bentham's proposals for criminal law reform, a subject in which he took a particularly active interest throughout his later life.

Bentham's discussion of how the law should be administered did not become known until our days. It influenced his contemporaries *via* his pupil, John Austin. If laws were properly drafted – which they were not, in Bentham's view – judges ought to interpret them strictly, i.e. with a view to finding out the actual intentions of the legislature (which, in that case, ought to be based upon the usual utilitarian calculation). In this respect, Bentham seems to share the naive views of Enlightenment lawyers: the idea that the vagueness and ambiguity of language could cause difficulties, and call for specific methods of construction, even in the presence of well-drafted statutes did not seem to occur to him (as it did not occur to Montesquieu or to the Italian criminal law reformer, Marquess Cesare Beccaria, d. 1794, whose highly influential *Dei delitti and delle pene* anticipates many of Bentham's reform proposals). However, Bentham realized that the ideal of the well-drafted statutory text was seldom achieved, and that consequently, the judge was often left in uncertainty about the legislature's actual intentions. *"Strict"* interpretation was impossible; the judge had to perform a "liberal" interpretation, i.e. one which was based upon the hypothetical intention of the lawgiver. Such liberal interpretation, which necessarily implied a restrictive, or an extensive, construction, ought to be performed in the same way as legislation, *viz.* by means of a utilitarian calculation *in casu*. If that operation was carried out correctly, it must necessarily result in a decision which coincides with that which the legislature would have passed, if the case had come under its consideration. In his belief in the infallibility of social and legal mathematics, Bentham is an incurable 18th century optimist.

5. Kant

It has been said about the contribution of the great German thinker *Immanuel Kant* (1724–1804) that philosophy could never more be the same as in earlier, naive days, because Kant had lived. It has also been frequently, and justly, said that Kant's works are among the most intellectually exacting reading that exists. Kant's exceptionally powerful, deep and original intellect, supported by an iron discipline, managed to create a consistent body of philosophical doctrine which is still an object of discussion and in some respects has hardly been refuted until this day. In order to introduce Kantian thinking in the field of legal philosophy and jurisprudence, and to provide criteria for assessing its importace, we cannot avoid a brief survey of that part of his philosophy which was truly revolutionary, viz. his theory of human knowledge.

Immanuel Kant spent the whole of his life in or near the East Prussian city of Königsberg (now "Kaliningrad"), where he held a professorship in logic and metaphysics from 1770 to his death. His peaceful but strenuous existence, characterized by proverbial punctuality and regularity of habits, made him the paragon of the modern university intellectual. However, he took a lively interest in the political

Towards a New World: the 19th Century

and social events of his time. From 1749 to 1797, he published a vast body of learned works, among which the most famous is the *Kritik der reinen Vernunft (Critique of Pure Reason,* 1781). Mention should also be made of his *Critique of Practical Reason (Kritik der praktischen Vernunft,* 1788), and of the great work particularly devoted to questions of ethics and legal philosophy: *Metaphysik der Sitten (Metaphysics of Morals,* 1797).

Kant was a voracious reader, and he was well acquainted with the works of Leibniz, Wolff, Locke, Newton, Hume, and Rousseau, all of whom exercised an important influence upon his thinking. Originally a follower of rationalism, he successively moved towards the empiricism of Hume. His critical mind, however, made him independent towards all the ideas of his predecessors.

Before Kant, philosophers – including Descartes – had basically accepted the idea that true scientific knowledge of the world, or at least some essential parts of it, is unquestionably possible. Kant, in his *Critique of Pure Reason,* takes one further step – which may be considered the initial and fundamental movement of the Kantian intellectual revolution – and puts the question whether an objectively valid cognition is at all possible. Thus, the object of "metaphysics" becomes, in Kant's analysis, not the world, but the intellect itself, the process of cognition as such, and the conditions which make valid cognition possible.

Kant accepts the empiricist standpoint, according to which experience on the basis of sense impressions is a primary source of knowledge. However, sense impressions and experience are not identical; to become experience, the impressions are "processed" by the mind, and thus the propositions about the world coming from sense impressions are really the combined result of two things: of the impact made by outward objects on our senses but also of the structure and operation of the mind. Human cognition, therefore, is never an immediate and true representation of the objects of the outside world – to these objects in themselves, referred to collectively by Kant as *das Ding an sich,* "the object as such," we can never reach – but a knowledge conditioned by the structure and operation of the mind.

When setting out to analyse these built-in conditions of human knowledge, Kant starts from a basic acceptance of the principles of logic, mathematics and physics. These are valid by necessity; Kant calls them *a priori* judgements. All other statements, or judgments, are based upon experience, which shows us their *truth,* i.e. their conformity with an observable reality, but not their *necessity*. Thus they are only relative; for these judgments, Kant uses the term *a posteriori* judgments. Another fundamental distinction refers to analytical judgments, which are necessary and logically demonstrable but do not contribute new knowledge, since they only contain statements about attributes which are by definition part of the object concerned (e.g., the statement that all bodies have an extension in space, since "extension" is a necessary attribute of the concept "body"). All other judgments Kant calls "synthetic": they add something new to our knowledge of the world, as do empirical observations. If there were only analytical judgments *a priori* and synthetical judgments *a posteriori*, how is objectively valid cognition at all possible? This question leads Kant, who refuses to give up the possibility of true scientific knowledge, to what is known as his specific and classical formulation of the problem of knowledge: how are synthetic judgments *a priori* possible? For only synthetic judgments contribute new knowledge, but only *a priori* judgments can claim absolute validity. Kant's answer, which is given in the form of a highly complex analysis of the structure and operation of the mind, is that such judgments are indeed possible. For the structure of our mind provides elements of concepts, which are then tied together into judgments and which are *a priori*, since they are necessary – "built-in," as it were – and not objects of sense perceptions, but which are at the same time synthetic, since they add to our knowledge of reality. Thus, in Kant's view, sense impressions and our understanding are two sources of knowledge, independent of each other, yet complementary; true cognition is the result of the combined operation of the senses and of the preconditioning structure of our minds. That structure comprises two "forms of sensibility," as Kant calls them, viz. space and time, and twelve "categories of understanding" (quantity, quality, relation, modality, each with three possible contents, e.g., for modality: possibility-impossibility, existence-non-existence, necessity-contingency).

Kant's analysis of the conditions for true knowledge is revolutionary at least in two fundamental respects of relevance for legal thinking. In the first place, the inaccessibility of *das Ding an sich*, "the object as such," puts an end to the kind of naive statements about the ultimate nature of reality which had played such an important part in natural law thinking. Moreover, by demonstrating that analytical judgments do not contribute new knowledge, he hits at the very foundations of rationalism, which had been essentially based upon the idea that the logical coherence of descriptions of postulated objects also guaranteed the reality of such objects. At the same time, Kant was convinced that his analysis of the conditions of true knowledge had laid dependable foundations for natural science. There is no need for us to go further into his discussion of these problems. Be it enough to say that in this field, Kant accepted, insofar as the study of the universe as a whole and of living beings is concerned, a notion of teleology, or purposefulness, at least as a provisional hypothesis which helps us better to understand these phenomena. This hypothesis, however, which means a break with the mechanistic assumptions of Newtonian science, introduces a new problem, *viz.* how the ultimate purpose of the universe can be determined.

It is against this background that Kant's discussion of "ideas," or "necessary concepts of reason" must be seen. While stressing emphatically that he is speaking of notions which are outside the reach of any possible scientific knowledge, Kant proposes the three concepts "soul," "world," and "God," which man, in the exercice of his intellectual faculties, *should* adopt, as means of interpreting reality. Again, it is important to stress the revolutionary step made from the unquestioning assumptions of earlier thinkers in these respects.

Coming to Kant's moral and legal philosophy, we are confronted with an initial question of the same fundamental character as the problem of synthetical judgments *a priori:* are there laws which determine men's will *a priori,* and how can such laws claim to be universally valid? Is there, as the philosopher puts it, a *Sittengesetz,* a "moral law?" In his attempt to find an answer, Kant proceeds to study human evaluations. These are of two kinds: judgments of usefulness, which are by definition related to means and thus merely relative, and true moral judgments. Such judgments, however, are mostly essentially subjective, and thus not fit to be considered as universal laws. Nor can a true moral law, of the same kind as the universal laws disclosed by natural science, be an enactment imposed by some outward power and enforced by means of sanctions. Kant's conclusion is that the moral law, if it exists at all, must be of an inward character and it must be of a purely formal character, and thus not contain any specific precepts. As a conclusion of this discussion, Kant formulates his "categorical imperative": "Act only on that maxim through which you can at the same time will that it should become a universal law."

Another formulation given by Kant: "Act as if the maxim of your action were to become through your will a universal law of nature."

Kant's moral law, with its clear emphasis on the acting individual's *will* as the supreme criterion of morality, obviously presupposes man's free will. Again, Kant insists on the hypothetical character of free will: it is not a concept that can be proved or disproved by scientific methods; it is an object of belief, and as such deeply rooted in man's conscience and need for liberty. Kant consistently avoids all confusion between the realm of nature, and of theoretical knowledge, on the one hand, and the moral world on the other hand. The former is the world of *Sein* ("being"), the latter is the universe of *Sollen* ("ought"), and man, he says, is "a citizen of two worlds": as a member of the world of "phenomena," he is subject to causal determination, but as a member of the world of reason and liberty, he is his own law-giver. Kant's exalted opinion of the dignity of mankind has found an expression in a famous passage: "So act as to use humanity, both in your own person and in the person of every other, always at the same time as an end, never simply as a means."

Kant is too much of a realist and an empiricist, however, to overlook the need for a legal order. Whereas the moral law concerns man's will, he states, the laws of the state deals with outward actions. In his treatment of legal questions in a narrow sense, Kant is a precursor of the liberal ideals of the 19th century. To insure a maximum of freedom is an essential goal for the society. At the same time, the rule of law is exalted as the sole purpose of states; it is, in Kant's view, allegiance to a system of laws that constitutes a state in the true sense of the world. The task of the legal system is to lay down the conditions under which the wills of all are brought into harmony with each other, under one common law of liberty. That liberty is, according to Kant, the only "natural right" man can claim by virtue of his being a man. There is, however, Kant concedes, a practical need for coercive power. The legitimacy of that power, according to Kant, is founded upon general consent; Kant operates with a social contract, but only as an explanatory hypothesis, not as a historical fact. As for the actual organization of the society, Kant agrees with Montesquieu in proposing a division of powers. Although he thus adopts some of the democratic and constitutional ideas of the Enlightenment, he refuses to grant active citizenship to women, to apprentices and to wage-earning labourers.

It should be added, by way of conclusion, that Kant like Grotius, took a strong interest in the laws of the international community. In one of his late works, *For an Eternal Peace (Zum ewigen Frieden)* he lays down a body of rules for a future international organization of states, by which all wars should be avoided.

6. The Later German Idealists

Although Immanuel Kant can be justly described as the philosopher whose contribution – together with that of David Hume – meant the end of rationalistic natural law thinking, at least as a mainstream in Occidental legal philosophy, Kant still, in many respects, remains in the 18th century Enlightenment tradition. Thus his point of departure is individualism; the state and its laws have the function of securing a maximum of liberty to the citizens. The further development of German philosophy in the 19th century witnesses the emergence and growth of systems of thought which, increasingly, put the emphasis on the collectivity.

Johann Gottlieb Fichte (d. 1814) sets out, on the foundations laid by Kant, as an individualist; it is the task, according to his early writings, of laws and state to make individual liberty possible. However, more than Kant, Fichte stresses the ethical claims of the collectivity: it is by working for the common weal, and by forgetting completely his self and selfish interests that man realizes his ethical freedom. In his later works, Fichte insists more clearly on the moral duty of becoming, unreservedly, a loyal and active member of the collectivity, which is here understood, in terms already characterized by an almost mystical belief in the state as a supraindividual entity, an independent organism living its own life. No space is left over for the free development of citizens outside the sphere of the state. Towards the end of his life, in his *Staatslehre (Theory of the state,* 1813), Fichte describes the national state as a sort of realization of God on earth, a divine organism, which in the course of future development will grow into a union of the whole of mankind, a mystical body which foreshadows and already to some extent implies a higher life, in which man has conquered and abandoned the realm of physical nature and realized his divine vocation. One consequence, among others, is that no law, or indeed body of ethical precepts, can exist outside the state. In spite of its religious and idealistic inspiration, Fichte's thinking leads to positivism, just as his exalted opinion of the state, in spite of the idea of future all-embracing Christian political unity, leads to, or at least can easily be understood as, an almost religiously founded nationalism. Under the impression of the Napoleonic wars, which ultimately gave rise to strong patriotic and sometimes reformist movements in Germany, the nationalistic component in Fichte's teaching became particularly important; the Romantic movement, at the same time, particularly favoured dim but suggestive ideas about the state as a living organism.

Both these trends – which played an important part in the formation of the Historical School (v. sec. 8 below) – are expressed in the works of the influential philosopher and theologian *Friedrich Schleiermacher* (d. 1834). In the writings of the foremost philosophical spokesman of Romanticism as a literary movement – *Friedrich Schelling* (d. 1854) who equally started as a follower of Kant – the "organism theory" is all-permeating. In Schelling's teaching, the state is an "absolute organism" which leaves no room for that individualism and that insistence on civil freedom which remained an essential element throughout Kant's teaching.

7. Hegel

In the person and writings of *Georg Wilhelm Friedrich Hegel* (1770–1831), who taught at the universities of Jena, Heidelberg and, for the last thirteen years of his life, Berlin, and who has sometimes – ironically, but not without reason – been called "the Prussian State philosopher," German idealism finds its final expression, which at the same time forebodes new, radically anti-idealistic movements. If Kant's works are justly considered to make hard reading, those of Hegel are, both by virtue of their contents and as a result of the extremely complicated and obscure language used, even more difficult to penetrate and to assess. Indeed, even well-prepared readers may frequently doubt whether they have at all grasped Hegel's ideas in all their nuances. Among many works of "general" philosophy – mention should be made of *Phänomenologie des Geistes* (*The Phenomenology of the Spirit*, 1807) and *Wissenschaft der Logik* (*The Science of Logic* 1812–1816) – he wrote *Grundlinien der Philosophie des Rechts* (*Philosophy of Right and Law*, 1820). In spite of his obscurity Hegel has exercised an influence on later thinking that is second to none, including Hume and Kant. The best evidence of the range of that influence is offered by the fact that Karl

Marx, although highly ambivalent in his attitude to Hegel, described himself as a disciple of "that mighty thinker" and that writers as different as John Dewey in the United States and Henri Bergson in France were deeply indebted to him. A school friend of Schelling and of the poet Friedrich Hölderlin, Hegel initially studied Protestant theology at Tübingen and acquired a doctorate in divinity. He was well acquainted with Kant's thinking but his philosophy hardly betrays any Kantian influence.

The two most essential and most well-known concepts in Hegel's thinking are the *Geist*, "Spirit," and the "dialectic process."

By "the Spirit," which according to Hegel expresses itself on different levels – the "absolute," or "World Spirit," which works in philosophy, religion, and the arts, the "objective" or "national" spirit, active in family, society and state, and finally, the individual, or "subjective" spirit – the philosopher understands a real and concrete force, unfolding itself in the course of history. Historicism is another key notion in Hegel's thinking; nothing exists outside the historical process, which coincides with the successive manifestations of the spirit. Hegel insisted strongly on the concrete character of the spirit. Indeed, it could occasionally be impersonated by individuals, such as Napoleon. "I saw the Spirit of the World riding on a white horse," Hegel is reported to have said after he had seen Napoleon in Germany in 1806.

In Hegel's philosophy – which may, from this specific point of view, be called radically rationalistic – thinking and being are one and the same thing. Thinking is the process by which the spirit, in one of its manifestations, becomes conscious of itself; at the same time, the development of all existence, the historical process, concides, as already stated, with the successive realizations of the spirit which, however, also stands for reason. Thus history is an uninterrupted march towards greater and greater rationality in all walks of life. In this sense, everything that exists is, in Hegel's words, basically rational.

The historical process has a dialectic character. "Dialectics" is a term used by philosophers in ancient Greece (e.g., by Plato when describing the progress of the human mind by means of propositions and counter-propositions), in medieval Europe (as a term essentially synonymous with "logic") and later by, e.g., Fichte, when studying the growth of human knowledge. In Hegel's philosophy, the dialectic process – going from one position (thesis) to its opposite (antithesis) and then to a synthesis, in which both synthesis and antithesis are united on a higher level – is characteristic not only of history in the concrete sense of that word, but also of the cognitive process of humanity and of the thinking individual. Again, this means that there is no radical difference between the historical process and the act of thinking that process: what takes place in both is the successive realization of the spirit, which makes use of acting and thinking individuals.

Hegel's ideas about law and state are consistent with these notions of the world order and the historical process. These ideas, which have aroused much enthusiasm, and much indignation depending upon the interpretation given to them, imply in the first place a total negation of any such things as an immutable and universal law of nature. Like all other phenomena, rules are eternally changing in the course of the historical process. Law is, and must be, for Hegel, a historic fact. This does not necessarily mean, however, as some interpreters of the philosopher argued, that since whatever exists, is rational, there could be no room for reform, and further change. It is only if that interpretation is adopted that Hegel could justly be called "the Prussian State philosopher" and understood as if he were of the opinion that the political situation in Germany in his days represented the highest possible rationality and also justice. Convincing evidence has been produced to show that Hegel held basically liberal ideas and looked forward to a state permeated with both more reason and more justice. To some extent, the misunderstanding is likely to be due to the fact that Hegel drew a very sharp dividing line between the state, as a body exclusively devoted to the public weal very much in the exalted sense of the Greek *polis,* and the civil society, which was based upon a concerned with group, class and individual interests.

On the other hand, the very high idea which Hegel harboured concerning the mission of the state as a particularly important and increasingly rational and spiritualized manifestation of the spirit would seem to explain how his philosophy could become – as eventually occurred – an important element in later totalitarian systems. For by stressing the historic and ethical mission and tasks of the state, Hegel grants less and less space to individuals and to individual freedom in the normal and sole comprehensible sense of that term. "Freedom," in Hegel's acception, does not mean the capacity, and the right, to act upon one's own conviction; nor does the word refer to a sphere of action left for individual discretion and protected against the intervention of either the state or third parties. In Hegel's view, freedom means liberation from egoism and egoistic desires. "The highest degree of community," he says, "is the highest freedom." This strange usage – which recalls that underlying Rousseau's contention that by being submitted to the universal will *(la volonté générale)*, men, even defeated minorities, are "forced to be free" – could obviously be exploited by demagogical advocates of totalitarian régimes, and experience shows that this has indeed been the case. Similarly, other elements in Hegel's thinking could easily lend themselves to nationalistic and aggressive interpretations. Thus, in Hegel's opinion, it is part of the dialectic process of history that different nations are successively the tools of the World Spirit at the exclusion of all other nations, whose time may be past or may still be to come. Hegel further contends that since there are neither laws nor contracts between states, certain conflicts between them can only be settled by war; in these, the world history, i.e. the Spirit, is the umpire – a view which can easily be interpreted in the simplistic sense that the actual victor is always right, whatever the motives that prompted him to wage war, and whatever means he uses, the defeated is always wrong, however just his cause may seem.

It is not astonishing that Hegel's followers were from the beginning sharply divided into a conservative wing, which found in the Master's words an irrebuttable presumtion for the rationality and justice of any prevailing state of affairs, and a radical wing, which thought it was their duty to promote, by revolutionary action if needs be, the further self-realization of the spirit.

As already mentioned briefly, a further consequence of Hegel's fundamental ideas and concepts was the rejection of the idea of a natural law, and the unquestioning acceptance of the historically given positive law of each state not only as the sole body of rules to be legally and socially relevant, but also as the only precepts capable to be at all found, ascertained and studied, to the exclusion of any competing claims of an ethical order.

However highly one may think of the depth and width of Hegel's thinking, and however fertile and influential he may justly claim to have been for the further development of philosophy, it seems difficult to deny that, were it only indirectly or even due to misinterpretation, his works have proved, in the light of experience, singularly capable of providing arguments for totalitarian doctrines and régimes.

8. Historicism and Positivism

As is frequently the case in the history of ideas, a reaction against certain exaggerations and weaknesses of Enlightenment thinking in the field of legal philosophy had been slowly gathering strength already in the 18th century. The ignorance and neglect of *history* – both as an irreversible and empirically irrefutable process of change, as an explanatory factor in the analysis of social and psychological phenomena, and as a source of experience – had not gone without censure; already the sociological relativism of Montesquieu contains a seed of criticism and of development in new directions; Burke's, de Bonald's, and de Maistre's reactions, in the political and constitutional fields, were formulated before the end of the century.

A seminal work in the field of law was the German professor *Gustav Hugo's Lehrbuch des Naturrechts, als einer Philosophie des positiven Rechts* (*Textbook of Natural Law, Considered as a Philosophy of Positive Law*, 1798), which came to exercise considerable influence not only in the author's own country but also, e.g., on John Austin in England. Hugo's original contributions are to be found on two levels: on the one hand, he reduces the "philosophy of law," to a great extent, to the systematization of legal rules according to a more or less rational pattern developed, in the course of the 18th century, by several natural law teachers; on the other hand, he demonstrates convicingly that the rules proclaimed by 18th century writers to be part of, or derived from, "natural law," all had already found expression in some given legal system, in some *"positive law."* Hugo is one of the first, if not the first, to use that term in its modern sense (taken over by John Austin, and by him spread over the English-speaking world). By insisting upon the historical foundation of legal rules, even those which claimed the status of "natural," Hugo became a forerunner of the school of thought which was to prevail in early 19th century Germany, the historical school.

Another German scholar who prepared the ground for 19th century historicism was *Justus Möser,* a senior official and historian in the ancient city of Osnabrück. In a great history of his home city, *Osnabrückische Geschichte* (*The History of Osnabrück,* 1768; a third vol. was published in 1824) he described, in great detail, colourfully and lovingly, a fragment of German local history which, under the pen of Voltaire or Gibbon, would probably have become an ironical chronicle of superstition, small-town narrowness of mind, and picturesque folly.

A growing interest in, and respect for, local history, folklore, folk tales and folk songs had been manifest throughout Europe from the middle of the 18th century (in Germany, the most well-known advocate of these branches of scholarship was *J.G. von Herder,* 1744–1803, who exercised a decisive influence on Goethe in his youth; in England, Bishop *Percy's,* d. 1811, publication of *Reliques of Ancient English Poetry,* 1765, and *James Macpherson's,* d. 1796, success with one of the greatest literary hoaxes of all times, the *Poems of Ossian,* in 1765, were expressions of the same tendency).

Thus, in various ways, the ground was prepared for an entirely new, and positive, evaluation also of the legal inheritance of Europe. The igniting spark was given by the Napoleonic wars, in the course of which the French Civil Code was introduced, with greater or smaller modifications, and more or less voluntarily, in countries and territories under French domination, e.g. in the Rhineland, where it remained in force until 1900. The confrontation between this rational, systematic, and "modern" code of laws with the patchwork of Roman law, as transformed by the glossators, postglossators, and later scholars, local laws of various origins, and territorial legislation had the effect of convincing many lawyers of the desirability of radical law reform in Germany. In 1814, *A.F.J. Thibaut* (1772–1840), a university professor and a moderate Enlightenment spokesman (to whose contribution to the doctrine of statutory interpretation we shall come back below, in sec. 12) published a plea for such reform, *Über die Notwendigkeit eines allgemeinen bürgerlichen Rechts für Deutschland (On the Necessity of a General Civil Law for Germany).*

Nationalism, we have stated earlier, successively became one of the strongest elements in early 19th century political ideology. In a discussion of the kind initiated by Thibaut, however, nationalism was unable to indicate the solution; it was in itself ambiguous, for there were two branches of nationalism: one which was based upon historicism, reactionary, and antiquarian; another, which wanted to manifest the greatness and future of one's own nation by radical reform, thereby beating the French on their own ground. Thibaut's proposal found support among the partisans of the latter brand of German patriotism.

Conservative nationalism carried the day, however. Against Thibaut, the young scholar *Friedrich Carl von Savigny* (1779–1861), who was to become one of the leading German lawyers, if not the absolute leader, throughout the first half of the century, published his epoch-making polemical booklet *Vom Berufe unserer Zeit für Gesetzgebung und Rechtswissenschaft* (*On the Vocation of Our Time for Legislation and Legal Science,* 1814). This brilliant pamphlet is an energetic plea against premature legislative initiatives, and at the same time, it formulates a programme of work for German legal science; it became the Credo of what is called the Historical School. Savigny's main point was that the law is a result of "internal, silently working forces" in each nation, and that sudden and "arbitrary" legislative interference would never be able to create true law for a people. This view was developed by G.F. Puchta (whom we have already met as one of the founders of "conceptual jurisprudence," v. sec. 3 above), who introduced the notion of *Volksgeist* ("spirit of the people"). In his further contributions to the debate, Savigny also took up the notion of a "national soul" *(Volksseele),* which is the true creator of the law and which has to be consulted before any changes of the legal system are introduced.

According to Savigny, the real task that had to be tackled by German lawyers was not to draft a national code of laws but to explore the historical foundations of the law as it stood. Such was the influence of this scholar, and of his followers, that this became in fact, to a considerable extent, the programme for generations of legal scholars. Only in the year 1900, after the scholarly analysis, systematization, and description of "Pandect Law," *i.e.* the common Roman law of Germany, as handed over through the centuries, had reached a degree of perfection which could hardly be pushed further, the *Bürgerliches Gesetzbuch,* or Civil Code for the whole German Empire, entered into force, after decades of careful preparation. It may, of course, be said that in postponing the national Code for almost a century, Savigny rendered his country doubtful services. On the other hand, there can be little doubt about the maturity, and high intellectual quality, of the final product. It should also be admitted, in justice, that Savigny was not among those leaders of schools who show the way to others only. His own contributions to that historical exploration of Roman-German law which he preached are of the highest value; his monumental *Geschichte des römischen Rechts im Mittelalter* (*History of Roman Law in the Middle Ages,* 7 vol., 1815–1831) and *System des heutigen römischen Rechts* (*System of Present-day Roman Law,* 8 vol., 1840–1849) are not only masterpieces of scholarship; they are also literary works of high value. Savigny's medieval history is still the most readable general work on medieval legal science. Moreover, Savigny was one of the founders of modern Continental private international law, and he made essential contributions to the development of legal reasoning.

The theoretical foundations of the historical school were severely criticized from the beginning, and it seems obvious that in many respects, they do not sustain a critical examination. The notion of *Volksseele*, or *Volksgeist*, i.e. some kind of collective, national or local consciousness operative in the creation first of custom, later on of legal rules, is unclear, to put it mildly. It is difficult even to imagine, with any degree of precision or vividness, precisely *how* anything in the nature of legal precepts is secreted and distilled out of a scattered collective body. Savigny had to introduce, to save his construction, the idea that from an early date, when articulated rules take the place of vague customary precepts, the *lawyers* assume, as it were, the function of expressing the people's legal convictions and law-making consciousness. However flattering for the legal profession, this is not only a complicated, historically unproved construction it also takes us very far from the basic idea of a *Volksrecht*, that "law of the people," which provided, in the controversy with Thibaut, the moral and historical justification for refusing to initiate law reforms. If the law were, historically, *Juristenrecht*, a "lawyers' law," and not the slow-moving people's, the objections against changes approved by the contemporary legal profession seem to be weak indeed.

Historicism permeated German legal science throughout the 19th century. This was one important heritage of Savigny's school; another – really inherited from the natural law writers and from Hugo – was the preoccupation with the systematics of law, a preoccupation which resulted in the carefully elaborated and meticulous arrangement, divisions and subdivisions of the Civil Code of 1900. The most important single element of the inheritance, however, was strict *positivism*, the rejection of any reference, or appeal, to natural law, or any other body of rules outside the positive law recognized and enforced by the state, sole fountain of justice. This became the tacit creed under which the everyday work of lawyers was performed. For natural reasons, there are few explicit pleas for legal positivism; it is not a doctrine that encourages, or calls for, much theorizing. Some facts and characteristics should be noted, however.

In 1892, the German professor *Karl Bergbohm* published *Jurisprudenz und Rechtsphilosophie*, a work which summarizes and develops the anti-natural law thinking of fully developed positivism. This general attack may seem to be launched late in the day, but it should be remembered that, as we have stated above, natural law remained, i.a., the official legal philosophy of the Catholic Church; even outside the faculties of divinity, it found defenders, and as we shall see below, there was a fairly important "return" of a modified natural law thinking in the last decade of the 19th century. Bergbohm, in his treaty, repeats and expounds upon the traditional arguments against the idea of a law of nature: all ethical precepts, he says, are determined by the society which formulates them; all legal rules are the result of a historical development. There is no room for a natural law besides the positive law of the state.

Two elements of fully developed German 19th century positivism would seem to have carried with them the seeds of that reaction against the movement which occurred in the latter half of the century. On the one hand, prominent representatives of the prevailing "Pandect" school tended to transform law and legal science into a closed intellectual game, which could and should be played without regard to those social, economic, political, humanitarian or other interests and values which, after all, legal rules may be supposed to express, further, and regulate. Not even the great *Bernhard Windscheid* (1817–1892), the unrivalled master of Roman German private law, whose *Pandekten*, (*Pandects*, 1862; seven editions publ. in his lifetime) have been compared with Accursius' *Glossa ordinaria* (chap. 4, sec. 6 above) can be acquitted from the accusation of having excluded considerations of purpose and goal of legal rules and institutions from his work. Other famous representatives of classical 19th century positivism went further, and made the exclusion of all extra-legal elements a particular virtue: "It is quite possible," said *P. Laband* (d. 1918), an important writer in the field of public law, "to determine with precision and completeness the essential characteristics of each legal concept without adding one word about the purpose of the institution concerned."

The second element which also, by its exaggerations, tended to discredit positivism was *conceptualism*, a line of thought which we have already defined and which is expressed in the quotation from Laband; in the long run, it became obvious that legal science incurred the risk of losing that contact with reality without which it can claim no function and no justification.

In the next section, we shall deal with some of the movements which partly replaced positivism at the end of the 19th century.

Towards a New World: the 19th Century

While historicism, positivism and conceptualism dominated in German legal thinking, France went through a development which was, for practical purposes, similar to that which characterized Germany but which had entirely different theoretical foundations.

Before we discuss early 19th century legal thinking in France, some basic facts of decisive importance should be recalled. From the French revolution onwards, nationalism was one of the strongest elements in European thinking in almost all fields; although nationalism draws more attention from historians in those countries where it created conflicts with the prevailing political order, there can be little doubt that it was just as important in those nations where there was no need for changing maps and systems; revolutionary and Napoleonic France was no exception; almost intoxicated by revolutionary zeal and international success, the country was little inclined to listen to foreign ideological influences. In France, therefore, Enlightenment rationalism lived on, at least throughout the Imperial era, as the official ideology of the state. When Catholicism was re-established in 1804, and when, after Napoleon's fall, reactionary ideas got the upper hand for a decade and a half (in fierce controversy with numerous remaining rationalistic and more or less openly pro-revolutionary strongholds), this did not mean that Hume's or Kant's criticism of the basic tenets of rationalistic natural law thinking was accepted. These philosophers were not even known outside narrow specialized circles. Moreover, to the extent French lawyers and legal philosophers were not still dominated by 18th century thinking, they were Catholics. Traditional natural law theories remained and remain, as we remember, the official doctrine of the Roman Church.

Thus whereas in Germany and in England, a new situation had been brought about by the downfall of natural law, France was, upon the whole, untouched by these problems. The French situation was marked by another equally important element: the existence of the Napoleonic Codes: the *Code civil* of 1804, and the four Codes of criminal law, commercial law, civil procedure, and criminal procedure. Of these great statutes, French lawyers were justly proud; in many respects, the *cinq grands Codes* were masterpieces both in substance and in legislative technique. In particular, the *Code civil* was universally greeted as a very fine piece both of legislative wisdom and of draftsmanship. It realized the revolutionary ideal of a clear, laconic, and yet elegant language, which made it possible for all citizens who were not completely illiterate to inform themselves about the contents of the law. It came to pass that the *Code civil* was soon vested with an authority – due to its own intellectual merits but also to its association with the power and glory of the great Emperor – which is very similar to that granted by generations of lawyers to Justinian's *Corpus juris*. This almost religious respect for the Code was largely shared (subject to some exceptions, e.g. disapproval of the abolition of primogeniture in the law of successions – an attitude that led to the splitting up of large landed estates and the creation of too small holdings in the peasantry) also by conservative, and even reactionary critics. The *political* unrest of France gave the *private law* system, thanks to its fundamental stability, a kind of sanctity, and of loftiness, exalted as the Code seemed to be above the everyday bickering of parties and the *coups dÉtat* recurring every ten or twenty years. Throughout the century, it was "the true constitution of France," as a later observer has said.

Finally, the Codes had been carefully prepared; the process of preparation could soon be studied in good and complete publications. The intentions of the legislators were thus mostly possible to ascertain without too much trouble and with considerable certainty (cp. sec. 12 below). In this, the *Code civil* had a great advantage as compared with Justinian's Code and most early codifications: it was a modern instrument of work, expressing contemporary evaluations.

There is no reason to be astonished at the enormous prestige of the Code. Positivism, in the sense of unquestioning acceptance of, and exclusive adherence to, enacted statutory law, thus came natural to French 19th century lawyers.

Intellectually, this raises a problem, however. How could the unbroken belief in rationalistic natural law theories be united, get along, without conflict, with strict positivism? There is nothing new about the problem: medieval lawyers, accepting both natural law and Roman law, had lived with it for centuries. However, they had never professed *strict* positivism – natural law, when it could claim clear support of a religious order, was at least theoretically superior – the Justinian code was distant, in some respects obscure, and could be more easily manipulated than the Napoleonic body of laws; finally, medieval natural law could also be manipulated with greater ease than the early 19th century law of nature, defined in its most subtle details, solemnly adopted by constitutional assemblies and expounded upon by generations of writers.

Enlightenment philosophy and political theory showed the French lawyers a way out of this dilemma (which nothing shows they took very seriously; for the *practising* lawyers, the precedence of the Code, i.e. of strict positivism, caused no doubt). The law of nature, that was an essential part of 18th century legal thinking, was the law of reason. And while Hume, Kant, and others before them had found the impossibility to ascertain objectively what "reason" (whose reason?) commands a stumbling-block in all natural law theories, Rousseau, and the writers and politicians of the French revolution, had found a ready and easy answer, with the great advantage of pragmatical usefulness: the "general will" – *la volonté générale* – expressed reason; and the law expressed *la volonté générale;* the Napoleonic dictatorship had respected one of the basic tenets of revolutionary creeds: *laws* were not enacted by the Emperor without being approved by a "legislative body" *(corps législatif)* and could thus claim the legitimation of the *volonté générale*. In this way, positivism and natural law thinking could live together in a marriage in which there could be little doubt about which of the partners was the strongest.

The first generations of lawyers formulating and implementing this compromise are known under the name *"the exegetic school."* The strict and loyal interpretation of the Code, using such information as could be found in the published preliminary materials, was the essential maxim of these lawyers. It was completed by the assumption, or fiction, that the Code covered all arising problems. This assumption found a legislative justification in the famous article 4 of the *Code civil,* where it is laid down that the judge who refuses to pass a decision under the pretext that the law contains no answer to the problem, or that it is obscure, makes himself guilty of a punishable act. The narrow positivism which resulted is best described by a representative of the "exegetic school," *Demolombe* (d. 1887), whose *Cours de code Napoléon* contains the battle cry of the school: "The (statutory) text above all!" And another academic writer, *Bugnet* (d. 1866) exclaimed: "I do not know of any 'civil law' – I teach the Code Napoléon." Natural law, it was thus held, had had its word, once and for all, in the text of the Code.

This rather primitive form of positivism – which remained predominant in France until the end of the century; the greatest of textbooks, *Baudry Lacantinerie's Cours théorique et pratique de droit civil* (29 vol.) the publication of which began in 1895, is still essentially faithful to its principles – would seem to prove the strength of tradition, of pressure from the surrounding society, and of practical considerations. The most influential drafter of the *Code civil, J.E.M. Portalis* (1746–1807), had expressed, in his introduction *(Discours préliminaire)* to the Code, a far more nuanced, and also realistic, idea of the functioning of a great codification. Admitting openly not only that the laws could "not foresee everything" but also that in such cases, recourse must be had to custom, precedents, and finally to the discretion of the judge, he grants the judge a creative function, which was not recognized by prevailing jurisprudential doctrines until very much later. He also recommends, in the absence of other guidelines, a "return to natural law." However, the text proposed by Portalis to legitimize these ideas was not accepted in the final version of the Code. Napoleon, who seems to have held a fairly naive 18th century view of the possibility to provide answers to all questions in a brief statutory text, is said to have exclaimed "My Code is lost" when he was told that a commentary had been published.

When claiming that answers to all questions should be looked for – and could be found – in statutory texts, both French and German positivists operated with, and on the basis of, an assumption without which this contention would hardly have been able to win the general acceptance with which, after all, it met for a long time. That assumption was that the law constitutes a coherent *system*, characterized by logical consistency and completeness. That claim had not been possible with regard to Justinian law; the lack of systematic arrangement of the *Corpus juris* was criticized already by Renascence lawyers (e.g. *Duarenus,* in his *Commentaria* from 1559). These were also the first to attempt to give the mass of rules of Roman law a rational organization (cp. ch. 5 sec. 5 above).

In the course of the 17th and 18th centuries, several proposals were made both by Roman law writers and by the representatives of rationalistic natural law thinking. *Pufendorf* (v. chap. 6, sec. 4) was particularly active in this respect. He used the different kinds of *duties* as ground of systematization. In France, the efforts to put Roman law into systematic order were carried on by *J. Domat* (d. 1696) in his famous work *Loix civiles dans leur ordre naturel* (1689) and by *R.G. Pothier* (1699–1772) in an equally famous treatise, *Pandectae Justinianae in novum ordinem digestae* (1748); this work exercised a deep-going influence on both the substance and the arrangement of the *Code civil.*

That Code is organized according to a fairly simple pattern:

I. Law of persons; matrimonial law; law of tutorship and guardianship
II. Law of proprietary rights
 1. Property
 2. Limited proprietary rights
III. How property is acquired
 1. Intestate succession and wills
 2. Obligations

It was in Germany that the systematizing work was carried further than elsewhere, both by natural law teachers and by Roman law writers. In the first-mentioned group, the contributions of *Christian Thomasius* (v. ch. 6, sec. 4, above) and *Christian Wolff* (v. ibid.) were particularly important. Wolff used subjective rights as the criteria of classification, and this technique was widely adopted by other lawyers. Both the Prussian General Code of 1794 and the Austrian *Allgemeines Bürgerliches Gesetzbuch* strongly reflect the influence of the natural law teachers. The Austrian Code is divided as follows:

I. Law of persons
II. Law of proprietary rights
 1. Possession, property, security, servitudes, intestate succession
 2. Contracts, marriage settlements, torts
III. General provisions
 1. Creation of rights and duties
 2. Modification of rights and duties
 3. Cessation of rights and duties
 4. Limitation
 5. Acquisition by limitation

In Germany, the work was carried further. G. Hugo's "Lehrbuch" has already been mentioned (sec. 8 above). *Heise's Grundriss eines Systems des gemeinen Zivilrechts zum Behufe von Pandecten-Vorlesungen* (*Outline of a system of General Civil Law for the Purpose of Lectures on the Pandects*, 1807) would seem to close the series of proposals made by Romanists as well as natural law teachers. Heise's system was generally adopted in the 19th century. Further developed in the course of the century it was to determine the structure of the German *Bürgerliches Gesetzbuch* of 1900 – a code, it has been said, in which the dividing line between textbook and code of laws has been blotted out. Its most salient characteristic is the technique of drawing out, as it were, whatever is common for two or more rules and to make that common substance the contents of a "general part" in relation to which the individual rules appear to be specialized applications. Thus, secs. 1–240 contain the "general part" comprising rules common to the whole Code; the second book, "law of obligations" (secs. 241–853) has a general part of its own, and the subdivision on the following level, "law of obligations arising from contract" (§§ 305–361, 433–808a), has in turn a general part, etc.

This thorough-systematization of substantive law was obviously not only a prerequisite for the doctrine, or illusion, of the all-embracing legal system, with an answer to all questions; it also fulfilled the wish of lawyers to achieve a maximum of order and to give their work the same intellectually satisfactory character as the natural sciences.

John Austin (1790–1859) who was for a long time the only, and who remained throughout the 19th century the dominating, representative of analytical jurisprudence in *England,* is important because of the influence which he did in fact exercise rather than because of the originality of the ideas be expressed, for most of his principal ideas drew – as we know now, but as the contemporaries ignored – very heavily on Bentham's posthumously published work.

Austin gave his famous lectures – under the heading *The Province of Jurisprudence Determined* – in the University of London in 1832; together with other works, the lectures were again published, after Austin's death, by his widow; the common name of this posthumous publication (1861–63) was *Lectures on Jurisprudence or the Philosophy of Positive Law.*

Austin professes utilitarianism, but unlike Bentham and most advocates of that basic philosophy of state and law, he is a conservative. He devoted his efforts entirely to the law as it actually was; his great concern was the analysis of the concepts of positive law, and it is by this rigorous and elaborated analysis that he rendered his greatest services to jurisprudence. Austin thoroughly wetted and cleansed, as it were, the conceptual apparatus of legal thinking, but without indulging in exaggerated ideas about the scientific value ot that apparatus.

As for Austin's *general* theory of law we can, for all practical purposes, refer to what has been said above (sec. 4) about Bentham: like his teacher, Austin is far from any natural law, and far from any speculations about the morally binding character of law: it is a system of coercion; legal rules are the commands of the sovereign, i.e. the entity habitually obeyed in the state concerned, and they create duties because they are provided with sanctions. In a somewhat strained way, Austin finds a place for the judge-made common law in this system; it is described as a kind of legislation by tacit delegation.

We can also be very brief in discussing Austin's contribution to legal reasoning and the construction of statutes, for again, Austin very largely builds on Bentham's teaching. However, as a student of the common law of his own time, he is more realistic than his teacher; he gives more attention, and grants greater importance, to customary law, including judge-made law. While statute law emanates directly from the sovereign and is formulated in general propositions, customary law is created for the purpose of individual cases, and is nowhere formulated in a general form. Applying statutory rules and applying customary rules are thus two completely different activities.

When construing a rule of statute law, the judge has to start with its meaning in common usage. The first step is to ascertain that meaning. Austin seems ready to accept, for that process, the traditional methods taught in textbooks from the Middle Ages, but he also counts with the possibility that no clear sense at all can be ascertained. In that hypothesis, Austin proposes – very much like Bentham – that the judge goes on, first to ascertain the *ratio legis*, the purpose of the statute, but eventually – if that purpose cannot be ascertained or if it is manifestly based upon error or ignorance of facts – he has to go on to correct, as it were, the legislature and establish a new rule on the basis of such authorities as can be found and to formulate it as clearly as possible. The "interpreter" of customary law obviously finds himself in an entirely different situation. He does not find a ready-made rule, but has to study existing precedents, interpreting their language in relation to the facts of each case and finally formulating himself that general rule upon which his decision is based.

9. Reactions against Positivism

In the introduction to this chapter, we described the 19th century as a period of "ideological homelessness." What has been said here about positivism would seem to substantiate that judgment at least in one respect: along highly different roads, English, French, and German legal philosophers and lawyers arrived at the same junction – *positivism* – but a short pause at that junction was enough to make them restless; positivism was not the Holy Grail; it could even be considered a name for complete emptiness. So the quest was resumed, eagerly, sometimes almost chaotically. From the last third of the 19th century onwards, the wealth of more or less original, more or less wide-spread, and more or less short-lived theories of law is such that a very strict selection has to be made. We can only discuss, in this chapter, those movements which have had some importance for later developments, which were not merely local, and which still possess, intellectually, something of interest.

Setting aside Marx and early Marxism for treatment in the next section, we shall divide the trends prevailing in late 19th century legal thinking into three groups: in the first place, those with a "utilitarian", "realistic", or "pragmatic" tendency; next, those which imply, in one way or another, a return to natural law or some of its basic tenets; thirdly, those schools of thought which try to enrich traditional legal science – or replace it – with sociological studies and results.

Before going on, however, it is only just to remark that it would be a great error to believe that positivism was "dead" in 1860 or 1870. Upon the whole, *some kind of positivism* – more or less rigorous, more or less elaborate, more or less closed or open to change by other means that formal legislation – would seem to have remained, and to be still, the basic "philosophy" of lawyers in modern society. Throughout the 19th century, this attitude was not only justifiable; it was quite natural: the official society, that "establishment" which expressed its intentions and decisions by means of legislation, (as opposed to "society" as a whole, including private centers of power, public mentality, etc) could upon the whole, albeit with considerable variations, be described in the first place as fundamentally "decent" – decent enough to be in a position to claim not only obedience but also some kind of moral approval or at least tolerance, as being better than in any known past, and preferable to chaos – and in the second place as moving (too slowly according to some, too quickly in the view of others, but nevertheless moving) towards greater perfection. It was for the 20th century, after the collapse of the proud tower of Western Europe, to invent societies on the model of St. Augustine's *magna latrocinia,* "large bands of robbers." Before that, positivism could be justly disparaged as dry, poor and insufficient intellectual and ideological fare; it took the pirate kingdoms of the 20th century to make it *morally* untenable.

Positivism had at least one healthy effect. It directed the attention of lawyers towards their only box of tools – legal language and concepts.

– which had been somewhat neglected in the high-flown eloquence of rationalistic natural law thinking. It deepened their insight and their interest in the law as a system and a machinery of a special kind. Much unclear and insufficiently analysed goods from earlier periods were resolutely thrown overboard.

After half a century of positivism, lawyers were in good control of their machinery. They saw it work more smoothly and efficiently than ever. No wonder that they came back, bewildered, to the question what is the motor of this well-functioning apparatus. If God's will could not be invoked, if the mystic *volonté générale*, or *Volksgeist*, were nothing but fictions, if the "sovereign's commands" implied a circular reasoning to the extent the sovereign claimed a *legal* right to command, not merely brutal force, where was the motor?

Social utility of some kind was the explanation and justification proposed by some lawyers to answer the question of what kept the machine working as it did. The most influential German spokesman of this school of thought – or rather of one among many such schools of thought – was *Rudolf von Ihering,* whom we have already met (sec. 3 above) as a distinguished representative of conceptualism. In 1877 Ihering published the first volume of his work *Der Zweck im Recht (The Purpose in the Law),* which implied a radical break with the conceptualistic tenet that law could be studied and understood without any consideration of the ultimate social purposes and functions pursued by the lawgiver. "The purpose", Ihering now proclaims, "is the creator of the whole law; there is not only single legal rule which was not framed with a view to a purpose, i.e. a practical motive." In order truly to understand a legal rule – and true understanding was obviously a minimum requirement for handling the rule in practice – it is inevitable to study its social function. Going on from the single rules to the legal system at large, Ihering submits that the society, which is the origin of all law, was instituted for the furtherance of common purposes, so that each member, when acting is his own interest, also acts in the interest of others.

By his "purpose theory" *(Zwecktheorie)* Ihering purports both to give law as such a justification and to provide rational guidance for the administration and interpretation of legal rules. His so-called "jurisprudence of interests" was developed in particular by *Ph. Heck* (d. 1943), whose contributions were made in the 20th century, however, and thus fall outside the present survey. Although Ihering and his pupils undoubtedly exercised a healthy influence by drawing attention to the social functions of law, they tended to forget that in a modern society, the task of finding the ultimate and superior purpose of a legal rule or a legal institution may be extremely complicated, since the legal solution finally adopted by the state may be a compromise between irreconcilable purposes and between interests of opposing groups. Ihering himself was well aware of the antagonistic element in the creation of law; his work *Der Kampf ums Recht – ("The Struggle about Law",* from 1872) shows his deep insight into the mechanisms by which a rule of law comes into existence. This means, however, that the capacity of the "purpose" to guide lawyers to the correct solution of a conflict is smaller than Ihering claims.

Two other important German writers should be mentioned. *E.R. Bierling* (d. 1919), author of *Kritik der juristischen Grundbegriffe (Critique of Fundamental Legal Concepts,* 1877–1883) and of *Juristische Prinzipienlehre (The Doctrine of Legal Principles,* 5 vol. 1894–1917), elaborated a "psychological theory of law" on the bases of "general" epistemological positivism: the law, in Bierling's view, is nothing but a human response to empirical facts; not only external events or states of affairs, however, but also psychological facts contribute to "create law." Legal rules, according to Bierling, are such norms as are mutually recognized as such by the members of the community, both those entitled to the benefits of a given rule – and able to invoke it in his favour – and those bound by it. *Otto von Gierke* (d. 1921) – best known as one of the greatest historians of German law of the late 19th century and as an undefatigable defender of the Germanic element in a legal tradition where the Roman elements tended to dominate completely – also fought positivism and stressed the element of commonly held values and ethical convictions as an indispensible foundation of a working legal system. Although Gierke's emphasis on the collective and corporate elements in German public law tradition (the notions of "Estate", or *Stand,* and of *Gemeinde* and *Genossenschaft,* "parish" or other local community, "guilde") was to make him influential in certain rather doubtful 20th century schools of thought, he represents, in many respects, a return to the basic tenets both of the historical school and, beyond it, to certain elements of natural law, a term which he in fact uses to denote the legal convictions of the general public.

In France, the reaction against positivism did not come until the last decade of the 19th century. The principal opponent was *François Gény*

(1861–1938); most of his work was published after the turn of the century, but intellectually, Gény belongs to the period now under consideration. He marks the end of the almost secular predominance of the exegetic school. Gény's most important contribution, in the perspective of history, belongs to the field of legal reasoning, but his ideas in that field are intimately connected with his general views of law, its origin, development and function. Gény's bestknown works are *Méthode et sources en droit privé positif* (*"Method and Sources in Positive Private Law,* 1899) and *Science et technique en droit privé positif ("Science and Technique in Positive Private Law,"* 1914–1924).

Gény's work should be seen, in the first place, as a reaction against the French version of legal positivism; he criticizes at great length, and with a wealth of arguments, the idea that the law foresees and covers all imaginable conflicts; he also attacks the tenets of conceptualism, according to which the solution of any conflict submitted to a court could be deduced, objectively, from the law by use of the conceptual apparatus of legal science. The lawyer – both scholar and practitioner, including the judge – must leave his ivory tower, Gény contends, and look for solutions outside; he should try to make "the nature of things" *(la nature des choses)* the basis of his decisions. This concept, Gény admits, is vague, but for that very reason, it is also fertile, for it represents that living law which can fill out the gaps of written law and which also gives legal development its direction for the future. In this "state of nature", the lawyer finds, according to Gény, the *"given* law", a kind of spontaneous creation, born out of the necessities of the concrete social relationships that characterize, and indeed constitute, the life of the community. To this spontaneous birth of legal solutions, positive law, and legal science, give that formal shape which is, in Gény's vocabulary, "technique." The term "science", he reserves for that part of the lawyer's activity which purports to find, in concrete cases, what is "given", what is, according to the "nature of things", the proper solution of the case. When searching for that solution, the judge's work – transcending those "exegetical" labours which gave their name to the school criticized by Gény – has the character of a *libre recherche scientifique* ("free scientific research"). When adopting this terminology, Gény undoubtedly wants to express the intellectual ambitions of his work: his judge is performing a sociological research, he is "scientific." Looking more closely at Gény's description of that research, however, we find that his judge is not merely out for a set of empirical facts: he also searches for *a social evaluation of these facts,* indeed for a *norm.* It is that norm which is hidden under the purportedly "objective", and "scientific" term "nature of things": the "natural" here means that which is socially acceptable and accepted – in short: *what is right.* In this sense, Gény represents a return to natural law. Not, of course – as has been amply demonstrated by his critics – a natural law in the sense of an immutable, everywhere identical body of precepts. Far from that, Gény would seem to anticipate that strong movement of ideas which emerged in Europe, particularly in Germany, after the second Great War and which tried to formulate a "relative" or "historically given" natural law: a body of basic rules which are "natural" in the sense of obvious, and necessary, expressions of the ethical convictions of a given community at a given stage of its development. For all the intelligence and impartiality of Gény's effort to give the quest for the "natural solution" a scientific, i.e., an objective, character in the sense of the empirical social sciences, that effort is doomed to fail. Sooner or later, the "research" preached by Gény passes the inevitable frontier and becomes a value-based decision.

Gény reserves his "free scientific research" for those situations where statutory law gives no answer. Shortly after the end of the 19th century, a school of thought with far more radical ideas about the liberty of the judge raised rapid – and short-lived – interest in Germany. It was called the "Free Law School." Sociology, and its specialized subdivisions sociology of law and criminology, had made considerable progress in the latter half of the century. The German *Max Weber* (1864–1920) and the Frenchman *Léon Duguit* (1859–1928), the greatest thinkers of the new science, did not publish their most influential works before the turn of the century, but sociological thinking had produced many results of obvious interest to lawyers.

One result of the progress of sociology was that some spokesmen of this new branch of empirical research denied the "scientific" character of traditional legal science and claimed that term for their own exclusive use. The true science of the law, wrote the German sociologist *Eugen Ehrlich* (d. 1922), is legal sociology; traditional jurisprudence is merely a technique, "the art of adapting the law to the special needs of legal science." The French sociologist *Emile Durckheim* (d. 1917), more generous, granted the law a special position as the "most stable element" of social organization; wherever that organization had extended its sway over a new field of human life and relationship, the law followed.

The most extreme expressions of belief in the possibility of replacing completely law and traditional legal science by sociology emanate from the above-mentioned "Free Law School." Already in 1885, the German professor O. *Bülow* (d. 1907) had submitted that it is, in fact, the judge who creates law; the legislator merely prepares it. In 1903 Eugen Ehrlich delivered a lecture under the heading *Freie Rechtsfindung und freie Rechtswissenschaft (Free Finding of the Law and Free Legal Science)*, in which he developed Bülow's theses in a more radical way; all attempts by the lawgiver to exclude or limit the influence of the human personalities entrusted with the implementation of legal rules were utterly vain. Ehrlich went on to exalt the "free search for the law" at the expense of "mechanical application" of statutory provisions. The most efficient prophet of the "Free Law Movement" was, however, H. Kantorowicz (d. 1940), who published in 1906, under the pseudonym Gnaeus Flavius, his manifest *Der Kampf um die Rechtswissenschaft (The Struggle about Legal Science)*, a dramatic and radical pamphlet, which caused much discussion for some time. Kantorowicz, in fact, never claimed that the judge ought to be free to decide in flat contradiction with clear statutory provisions. That, however, was about the limit. Enactments, the "free law" advocates held, neither could nor ought to provide more than a vast field, within which the solution was to be found, with great liberty for the judge to find the proper solution according to the "living law," i.e. legal and ethical convictions prevailing in the community (and shared by the judge).

Although, as already stated, the "Free Law Movement" was a fashion of short duration, it did reflect serious problems and serious preoccupations towards the end of the 19th century. Lawyers had become more and more aware of the insufficiency of codified law and its inability to cover all situations, especially in a quickly changing society; such a society was Continental Europe under the influence of the rapidly advancing industrial revolution (cp. sec. 1 and 2 above). These preoccupations, which were of course closely connected with the most serious problem of the period, "the social question" – i.e. how and upon what conditions the growing working class population could be peacefully integrated, or reintegrated, in the framework of *bourgeois* society – had been brought home to lawyers with such strength that we find their echo in two codes: in the German Code of 1900, where the famous "general clause" of art. 242 instructs the judge to interpret contractual obligations according to "good custom" *(gute Sitten)*, and art. 1 of the Swiss Code of 1901, where it is laid down that whenever the law remains silent, the judge shall first consult custom, then, in the absence of custom, formulate that rule which he would have laid down had he been legislator. These enactments express growing insight both in the limited possibilities of codification and in the problems of interpretation, to which we shall return shortly (sec. 12).

10. Marx and Early Marxism

To the author of a work, however modest, on the history of political and legal ideas, the mere decision to have a heading which contains the name "Marx" or the term "Marxism" way well seem like opening a large window, facing the Atlantic, in a house on a beach, while a tempest comes in from the sea: the situation is not easy to master. So much turbulent air presses on to enter the room. Let us remind the reader, therefore, that this is neither a textbook of economic history, of social or political theory in general, or of the philosophy of history; nor is it a polemical tract. Our main concern is the *historical development* of *legal* thinking, and while discussion of that topic in a textbook of this kind cannot – for reasons set out in the preface – be carried out without a good deal of general historical and other data being summarily presented, the window looking out upon the sea cannot be thrown wide open to all the winds that tend to blow furiously as soon as the name of Marx has been pronounced. The truth is that however profoundly Marxism – or at least political movements claiming that name, with or without added qualifying epithets – has come to modify legal realities in the societies where that school of thought prevails, the thinking and doctrines of Karl Marx and of his followers are, among all the great schools and movements of its kind, the one which has given least attention, and granted least importance, to *the law* in any or all of its many possible roles and functions. In fact, as a school of thought – which is something entirely different from a social and political system – Marxism would seem to be the only major trend to reject the law, at least in the long range time perspective, as an instrument of political, social and economic organization.

The lack of interest which Marxism shows with regard to the law as an object of deeper reflection does not automatically lead to historians of legal philosophy showing a corresponding lack of interest in Marxism. It indicates, however, that this school of thought cannot claim, in this context, the large space which should be natural in a history of economic or political thinking.

Karl Marx(1818–1883), the son of a lawyer, a Jew who had converted to Protestantism, took up legal studies at the university of Bonn and later at Berlin. In the course of his academic career, which ended with a doctorate in philosophy, he heard lectures by Savigny, wrote a monograph on legal theory and also made some translation work in the legal field. Philosophy, however, was the main object of his intellectual interest; he belonged to the pupils of Hegel and his thought was deeply marked forever by the problems and methods of the Berlin philosopher. Marx' activity as a radical journalist in the Rhineland, then under Prussian rule, ended with his being exiled to France and Belgium. He collaborates with another young German radical, *Friedrich Engels* (d. 1895) and gets into touch with socialist and communist groups. In 1848, Marx and Engels draft, for a communist organization of German workers in London, the "Communist Manifest" of 24 February, 1848. From 1849 Marx lives in London, in poverty if not in actual want, intensely engaged in writing historical and critical works. Of the most influential among them all, *The Capital,* the first volume was published in 1867; books II and III were published by Engels after Marx' death.

In his very vast production, Marx himself did not present any coherent or elaborated legal theory. He has, particularly in his earliest writings, given many critical points of view relating to legal or nearlying problems, but mostly *en passant,* as it were, while dealing more fully with economic or other questions. His attitude in matters connected with legal theory seems to have changed rather frequently; thus, while he supported and proposed, especially as a young journalist, legislative measures implying social reform, even in questions of a narrow scope, we find in his later work strong expressions of what amounts to a complete rejection of the law and of a legal system, as a form for organizing a society. Thus, when critics refer to "Marxist philosophy of law," they speak about the ideas of Friedrich Engels, of the leader of the Russian Bolschevik revolution, *Vladimir Iljitj Lenin* (d. 1924) or, most frequently, of the vast body of later writing where those elements of legal thinking which can be found in the works of the founders are interpreted, analysed and elaborated by modern Marxist scholars. Some branches of this Marxist or Marxism-inspired writing – which falls outside the present survey – are strongly marked by the fact that Marxism, in one or the other of the many variants actually extant, has been made the officially approved state theory (often expounded and defended with the severity characteristic of an exclusive state religion) of a number of states. This very special situation naturally gives these branches of Marxist literature a function and a character which are different from those of scholarly writing in the Occident. Thus one of the functions of Marx exegeses in the Communist countries would seem to be to justify the "practice" of the writer's own State or communist party by providing scriptural evidence for the necessity of that practice or at least its compatibility with true Marxism.

In spite of the meagreness of Marx' own legal thinking and of the innumerable variations in later Marxist writing, there are features which are common to all Marxist movements and which distinguish these from other schools of thought in legal theory, even from such as represent highly "radical" opinions (whatever that battered term may stand for in modern debate). These common features would seem to be on the one hand a basic conception of human societies and their development, on the other hand an equally basic epistemological and methodological outlook.

As for the Marxist conception of society and history, Marx (and his pupils) not only embrace a coherent radically "materialistic" view of the world – "idealism" is a highly pejorative term in Marxist language: it stands for "unscientific" thinking and was used not only against philosophical enemies but also against earlier, utopian socialist movements and writers. In "materialism" as such, there is nothing original. Auguste Comte's "positivism" is hardly less radical in its negation of "spiritual" explanations of the world and of history. What makes Marx' originality in this field is the consistency with which he analysed, from his materialistic point of departure, the structure and development of human societies, from the earliest times to his own days.

Physical objects, "material" things, according to Marx, are the only tangible realities. Such ideas and concepts as "justice" or "righteousness" exist only in the brains of man. The contents of these psychic phenomena are – to simplify radically – determined by the prevailing principles of distribution and use of material things in the society concerned. In fact, "ideas" are so heavily determined by these realities that no real governing effect can be ascribed to them. The most important element in the prevailing social system is the production of material objects in the society; this production is a result of the cooperation of the "productive forces" – raw materials, capital and manpower – under certain "conditions of production," i.e. principles for the mutual relations of the productive forces. These principles are in turn determined by the actually existing distribution of material goods upon the individuals and – more important in the Marxist perspective – upon the *classes* into which society is divided.

In this analytical pattern, the law, like all other expressions of culture, belongs to the "superstructure" which has grown upon the foundations laid by and consisting in the process of production. Like all other elements of the superstructure the law reflects – to simplify fairly radically again – prevailing conditions of production in an essentially passive and dependent way. Thus the law cannot claim any decisive or active influence upon these conditions. Marx characterizes the legal system of each historically given society – whatever idealistic colours or terms may be used to depict or describe it – as a system of coercion intended to promote and safeguard the interests of the ruling class and, consequently, to keep the underprivileged class or classes at bay.

In this perspective, history is essentially the story of classes struggling for control of the material goods available. From Hegel, Marx had taken over – albeit, of course, with the important modifications made necessary by his basic materialism – the idea of history as a "dialectic" process, i.e. a chain of events moving from one stage of development in its opposite; between these two poles – "thesis" and "antithesis" in the Hegelian pattern – there emerges a "synthesis" which constitutes, in its turn, the point of departure, the first pole, or "thesis," of the next movement. History, in this view, is the successive change of the conditions of production due to modifications in the process of production, which result in certain states of affairs, e.g. the feudal rules on land tenure, becoming "inadequate;" this creates tensions which result in a crisis and in the transition to the next phase of development.

Marx, who was in his best moments a very concise writer, describes his position in a famous and frequently quoted passage (from the preface of his Critique of Political Economy, transl. by Stone): "In the social production which men carry on they enter into definite relations that are indispensable and independent of their will; these relations of production correspond to a definite stage of development of their material powers of production. The sum total of these relations of production constitute the economic structure of society – the real foundation, on which rise legal and political superstructures and to which correspond definite forms of social consciousness. The mode of production in material life determines the general character of the social, political, and spiritual processes of life. It is not the consciousness of men that determines their existence, but, on the contrary, their social existence determines their consciousness. At a certain stage of their development, the material forces of production in one society came in conflict with the existing relations of production, or – what is but a legal expression for the same thing – with the property relations within which they had been at work before. From forms of development of the forces of production these relations turn into their fetters. Then comes the period of social revolution. With the change of the economic foundation the entire immense superstructure is more or less rapidly transformed. In considering such transformations the distinction should always be made between the material transformation of the economic conditions of production, which can be determined with the precision of natural science, and the legal, political, religious, esthetic or philosophic – in short ideological, forms in which men become conscious of this conflict and fight it out."

Marx knew a Europe of incipient or early industrialism; in England, however, where he spent his last thirty years and wrote his most mature work, industrialism was undoubtedly "ripe" and had produced its fruits in most respects relevant to political and economic theory. The "conditions of production" thus known to Marx were characterized by the fact that "capital" (goods, plant, machines) was owned by a relatively small group, the *bourgeoisie,* while the productive factor "manpower" was represented by growing masses of paupers, who were attracted to the industial centres from overpopulated rural areas; these masses frequently or mostly lived in deepest material, cultural and even moral misery. Marx devoted deep-going studies to this state of affairs. Much has been learnt and can still be learnt from his masterly analysis of the human condition in the world of large industrial plants, with a rigid distribution of tasks – with the result that the individual worker never finishes a product and is thus deprived of the pride and satisfaction of ever handling, let alone marketing, the fruit of his labour – and in large cities with no other links between their inhabitants than common insecurity, squalor and anonymity. A key concept in Marx' analysis is "alienation" – the *state* of "being alien," or "foreign," as well as the *process* leading to that state.

While it should be emphasized – here as so often when trying to present Marx' views – that different reading versions are possible at least in many details, the generally accepted interpretation is that the social, legal and economic conditions of his times would inevitably, as a determined phase in the dialectic process of history, lead to crisis and catastrophe. This process could hardly take any other form, against the given background, than a revolution carried out by the oppressed class, the proletariat. It is perfectly consistent with Marx' theoretical points of departure that this revolution should be followed by the "dictatorship of the proletariat": the new ruling class should, like all its predecessors in history, take the political and legal machinery into its service in order to promote its own interests and oppress its enemies. Needless to say that in a long-range perspective this idea – which implies that an oppressed majority would become oppressive while remaining a majority – gives rise to many difficult questions: how and how long would the identity of the group "proletariat" be maintained after it had reached dictatorship? how and by whom would its rule be managed in concrete terms?

It is more difficult to obtain a precise idea of the next phase of development, and it is even more difficult to make that phase fit into the pattern of the dialectic process of history. For – according to most qualified Marx scholars – that development would lead to a final stage: the classless society, where a new man, no longer reduced to a piece of goods on a market, and thus no longer alienated, would come into existence. Marx' statements about this final stage – where the dialectic swing of the pendulum has consequently come to a rest – are neither extensive nor clear. It seems fairly obvious, however, that his ideas have at least some utopian elements.

The most widely accepted interpretation of Marx is that in this final phase of history the legal system, and the whole state apparatus, would – the term is Friedrich Engels' – "wither away." Since that apparatus is essentially a mechanism of coercion, there would be no need for it in the classless society. Similarly, the units of productive work – in particular industrial establishments – would undergo radical changes; management, i.e. leadership related to men, would be replaced by "the administration of things and the direction of the process of production" (again, we are using Engels' terms). It has been contended that Marx (or Engels) can hardly have meant that even such "neutral" rules as, e.g., traffic regulations, and the organization needed to implement them, should become superfluous in the classless society and consequently "wither away." No clear answer to that question can be found in Marx' or Engels' own works. It does not seem unfair to say that the classless society very much remains an incomplete sketch of a political programme. The way in which the theories, ideas and prophecies of the fathers of Marxism were explained and ultimately put into practice by Lenin and others falls outside a history limited to the West and coming to an end about 1900.

The second – and far more esoteric – main feature which is common to the original teaching of Marx and to all those later movements which may justly claim to be Marxist is the so-called *dialectic method* which the master had inherited from Hegel but developed into a highly complex and sophisticated body of epistemological principles.

Drastic simplification is inevitable when trying to present the method in this context. As it seems to be understood by most of those who claim to command it fully and some who claim to be practising it, it is based upon a theory of knowledge, according to which the actual work of scholars, their theoretical analysis of the phenomena they are studying, implies a kind of reciprocal acting, a "dialectic relationship," between the student and the sector of reality he studies: while he receives impulses from the object of his study, he also acts upon that object. An important concept in the Marxist world of ideas is "practice" – i.e. acting (transforming principles, ideas, etc. into action). Marx and his followers seem to reject the idea of a decisive and reasonably clear-cut dividing line between the theoretical study of reality (observation without interfering) and the active handling of it. Science, it is held, implies "practice" and ought to do so. This means, i.a., that the idea of "objectivity" as a possible or at least desirable ideal for scholarly work is rejected.

It would seem superfluous to underline the profound difference between the Marxist epistemology and that elaborated in the course of the last century – first in the exact and natural sciences and later also in the fields of humanities and social science – and now generally prevailing outside Marxist circles. This is not to say that Marxism has not contributed to a deeper understanding of the problems of objectivity. It has served as a warning against certain forms of too anxiously rigorous positivism which has sometimes tended, particularly in some sciences, to reduce "scientific" to a synonym of "trivial," or "obvious." It has also made scholars more conscious about the many subtle and treacherous ways in which prejudice and implied value judgments can thwart even the most honest attempts at objectivity, – e.g. by influencing the initial formulation of problems or the choice of objects of study. Nevertheless, Marxist epistemology and method inspire serious misgivings. The fact that complete objectivity is not possible to achieve – that in the humanities and social sciences, no absolutely clean and razor-sharp line can be drawn between the observer and the object observed – is no more a reason to give up the quest for objectivity than the impossibility to achieve complete safety on the road would provide an argument for abandoning all attempts to make them safer. Upon the whole, it would seem that Marxist epistemology and method admit, to a greater extent than traditional, more or less elaborately positivistic standards and methods, an arbitrary choice both of questions, basic assuptions and methods of verification; for all these elements of scholarly work, it seems possible to arrive at desired results by manipulation, or by adoption of Marxist axioms. The most obvious example is the basic assumption of the dialectic process of history – a theory which is, of course, not only unproved but also, in its general form, impossible to prove. Marxist reasoning (as distinct from the reasoning of Karl Marx) frequently gives a strong impression of being carried out in a closed room, cut off by initially adopted principles from that surrounding reality which it is, after all, the task of science to study and to understand as freely and as completely as possible.

11. The Turn of the Century

In the preface of the present work, we have given our reasons for making an end at the last turn of a century: carrying "history" too far, and covering under that heading what is really "contemporary" may imply a particularly treacherous kind of intellectual dishonesty, *viz.* to describe ideas and theories that still stir up academic or political dust, with the historian's pretention to objectivity, fairness, distance and overview. The proper date for "the end of history" may be discussed. Within certain limits, one date may be as good as another. We have chosen 1900, i.a., because a number of important events in the peaceful chronicle we are relating happened shortly after that year. It could, of course, have been 1914. Any year *after* the first Great War would however be too late, in my view. The year 1900 has obvious almost æsthetic advantages. What happened afterwards is, in the still rather slow-moving world of legal thinking, "contemporary," should be studied as such, and consequently falls outside the present book.

Making a halt on the threshold of the century, we shall devote a few remarks to what seemed to be, then, the situation of legal thinking and what seemed to be the possibilities and prospects for that branch of learning and research. Knowing, as we now do, what happened next, it would seem to be of some interest to follow, be it only in the barest outline, those lines of development which proved to have a future, and to ask why these survived, while other tendencies, schools, and attempts were doomed to fail.

Looking back, in 1984, four trends in legal thinking would seem to have made, in the course of the century, a sufficiently strong case to claim our attention. Of these four, only two enjoyed, at the turn of the century, a position which justified the guess that they were to continue and to produce important results in years to come.

The first among these two was what we may call the *sociological*, or social science-oriented research. The continuation of this branch of legal theory must have seemed imperative, not only to "progressive" legal scholars. It must have been clear, given the general intellectual climate of the time, in particular the immense prestige of *empirical* sciences in all fields, that if legal thinking was to retain its "scientific" character both in the academic community and outside, it simply had to make its empirical foundations broader and deeper.

The second trend that could be looked upon with considerable confidence already at the turn of the century was the continued rather narrow and down-to-earth analysis of interpretation of statutes, the proper use of precedents, the most rational arguments – in short *legal reasoning*. No outsider would care very much for that branch of legal thinking; it would continue to be laughed at or admired as *arcana* of the lawyers' craft. As long as there was a law, it would remain. It could hardly be foreseen, however, that this field of study would loom as large as it has done in the latter half of the 20th century (various hermeneutical and "rhetorical" movements in Continental Europe).

The important part played in the 20th century by the two remaining trends, out of the "winning" four, was difficult or impossible to foresee.

This is true, in the first place, about the strong current of *natural law thinking* which appeared in the wake of the second World War and not only lasted, in academic circles (with the emphasis on Germany) for a couple of decades, but also – and that is more important – inspired the creation of national constitutions and international conventions granting an elaborate and in some cases remarkably effective protection of human rights. This non-revolutionary movement produced, in a short time, results which come close to those of the breakthrough of Enlightenment thinking in the United States and in France in the last quarter of the 18th century. In the year 1900, most competent observers in the West (outside the limited world of confessional Catholic institutions) were firmly entrenched in positivism of some kind. They would no doubt have considered this return of natural law thinking as an entirely unexpected and almost shocking echo from a past which they thought already both distant and safely buried. Even though the natural law revival seems to have come to an end – for how long? – in the world of learning, its results outside that world not only remain but are energetically defended and expounded upon. "Human rights" have become almost an independent branch of legal science. As long as that is the case – and there seem to be good reasons to believe it will last for a long time – natural law ideas retain, as it were, the position of a discharged but not disabled soldier whose services may still be wanted in a major crisis.

The fourth leading trend in 20th century legal thinking appears, in retrospective, as unexpected as the natural law revival. It is *the formal and logical analysis of law as a structure*. Within this broad description, there are today many movements to enumerate: the "pure law theory" of the Austrian *Hans Kelsen,* the analyses of legal language by the Uppsala school *(Axel Hägerström)* and the Scandinavian realists, similar enquiries by English and Continental philosophers and lawyers under the influence of philosophical movements (the Cambridge and Vienna schools in the first decades of the 20th century, deontic logic, system theory and other lines of investigation, some related to the computer revolution). Upon the whole, this branch of research would seem to be today, together with the empirical, social science-oriented, the most vigorous branch on the old tree of legal thinking.

Looking back, there seems to be at least some logic in the development we have outlined. Few words are needed to explain why the claim for extended, and deepened, empirical knowledge about the law as a social phenomenon has remained, and remains, strong. Questions and methods may be subject to much discussion, and their usefulness may be doubted, but it is the present writer's conviction that a legal science or, for that matter, legal philosophy which does not develop in continuous cooperation with, and with contributions of its own to, empirical social science will die from isolation and starvation. The search for more, and better, empirical knowledge has been for a long time and will certainly be, the most important highway of any branch of learning towards the future.

There are hardly any reasons to discuss the continued growth of scholarly interest in legal reasoning. Good workmen have to take care of, and improve, their tools. On the other hand, this is an occupation which – beyond a certain limit – faces the risk of sterility; there is some evidence for this in the many generations of textbooks on interpretation, from the late Middle Ages onwards.

The return of natural law is, of course, largely explained by events in contemporary history. On the other hand, there is no obvious reason why the despair and bitterness caused by the war and the preceding events should be channelled precisely in this direction. It seems to indicate a latent presence of natural law thinking. Let us remember of an observation already made, *à propos* earlier crises in the history of legal philosophy: the idea of some sort of "natural law" be it only a vague standard of common decency, that man can find for himself and apply, is psychologically irresistible.

The emergence and growth of formal analysis of the law as a structure calls for more afterthought. In some respects, this development is "natural" in so much as it corresponds to, and presupposes, a phase of rapid evolution in mathematics and logic from the latter half of the 19th century onwards. There would seem to be, on the other hand, a strong element of "intellectual self-defence" in the movement – and thus both an illustration of the homelessness, and a continuation of the somewhat disoriented quest for something to replace natural law, which we discussed in sec. 1 of the present chapter. In an epistemological situation where only two forms of knowledge were recognized as "truly scientific" – empirical knowledge of the world outside and that knowledge about the laws of intellectual operations which is embodied in mathematics and logic – and where the connection with ethics and with a system of values which was traditional in legal philosophy threatened to strike the whole discipline off from the list of recognized "sciences," one salvage operation was to become some kind of "applied sociology"; the other was to cut all relations *both* with the social sciences *and* with traditional value-based neighbours. The first and most radical attempt to "save" legal thinking as a truly scientific discipline was made by Kelsen and implied, precisely, this operation. Kelsen's theory of law is "pure," as its author called it, in the sense that its object are legal norms and their internal relations – nothing else. It is a "grammar of norms"; the relations of these to other fields of knowledge are entirely left out. Later scholars of the same or of similar inspiration have not always respected Kelsen's drastic delimitation of the field of study, but on the whole, the Austrian lawyer has been of fundamental importance for many different schools of thought. The future, and possibilities of meaningful development, of these lines of research may well be the principal question concerning the general direction of legal thinking in the next century.

12. *Legal Reasoning in the 19th Century*

While most textbooks and articles dealing with the theoretical problems related to legal thinking still express, throughout the 19th century, the experience and ideas which had been successively accumulated from the glossators onwards, some innovations can be observed, particularly in Germany, in the wake of the Historical School. The leader of that school, Savigny (v. sec. 8 above), made one of the most influential contributions to the discussion of statutory interpretation; we shall come back to his theories. The impact of Bentham's and Austin's analytical positivism upon interpretation as well as the tenets of the French exegetical school in this area have already been dealt with. We shall therefore concentrate our attention, in this section, to the German development, to the consequences upon interpretation of the new methods of preparing legislation which became predominant with the emergence of parliaments, and finally to some lines of development which did not come into fruition until the following century.

The "general" science of hermeneutics made a considerable step forward with the Romantic movement. With its deep interest both in history and in the irrational elements in all human activities, it broke with the naive rationalism and firm belief in the one-dimensional clarity and completeness of human languages which had been characteristic of the Enlightenment and which had caused even such experienced, pragmatic and eminently intelligent thinkers as Montesquieu to believe in the possibility of short exhaustive statutory texts and in the judge-automaton who processed given facts into a decision without any value judgment or any hesitation. The leading philosopher in the field of hermeneutics was the theologian *F.D.E. Schleiermacher* (d. 1834). In the course of the century, a growing number of scholars with various backgrounds began to lay the foundations of modern hermeneutics without, however, breaking radically with the traditions accumulated in the fields of theology, law, and philology.

A number of works of some importance were published before Savigny, in the first part of his great *System des heutigen Römischen Rechts* (1840), laid the foundations of all later jurisprudential discussion of the subject on the Continent. In this growing *corpus* of writings, where new tendencies are gradually expressed, mention should be made of a work by Savigny's most important opponent in matters of legislative policy, the Heidelberg professor A.F.J. Thibaut. This distinguished and influential jurist, who represented the persisting trend of Elightenment rationalism and who was influenced by the legislative ideas of the French revolution and the Napoleonic codifications, was critical, indeed contemptuous, of the prevailing theories of interpretation, which lacked, in his view, both true systematic consistency and sufficient completeness. However, in terms of practical results, Thibaut is not far remote from the level, and the ideas, represented by, among others, Glück (v. chap. 6, sec. 9, above). He adopts the main division into grammatical and logical interpretation, and goes on to subdivide the latter into two groups: interpretation based upon the legislator's intentions, and interpretation which follows the (objective) *ratio legis*. What is common to both is that they constitute attempts to find, albeit in different ways, the "spirit of the statute" ("Geist des Gesetzes"). Unlike his predecessors, Thibaut makes energetic efforts to study the relationship between logical and purely linguistic interpretation, and he points out that it is when logical and linguistic interpretation clash – in other words, when considerations of a substantive character lead away from a *verbatim* reading – that there is reason to speak of "restrictive," or "extensive" interpretation. In cases where the process of "logical" interpretation leads to clear results after the "grammatical" interpretation has failed, the term "declaratory" interpretation is used. Thibaut rejects the idea of a specifically "political" method of construction. Moreover, he sharply condemns most of the medieval apparatus of terms and concepts which still appeared in most traditional expositions of legal hermeneutics. Against historical methods, which would lead the practising lawyer into useless antiquarian investigations and easily give free play to arbitrary decisions, Thibaut launches vigorous attacks characterized by the irony so efficiently deployed by the sceptics of the Enlightenment.

The most salient features of Thibaut's doctrine are a distrust both of free methods and of extensive catalogues of concepts, terms and specific intellectual processes. Thibaut makes use only of the two notions of "interpretation according to the legislator's intentions" and "interpretation according to the *ratio legis,* i.e. a method based upon consideration of the actual consequences of one or the other solution *in casu.* The conclusions of the analysis are presented in an order of priority where the wording of the statute comes first, the *ratio legis* next, and the legislative intentions last.

In Savigny's work, it is difficult to single out specific concrete questions where this writer's treatment of the theory of interpretation constitutes a decisive break with earlier traditions. In the same way as Hugo Grotius occupied, in his day, an almost undisputed position as the father of the rationalist school of natural law, even though many of his ideas can be found in earlier writers, it seems correct to say, with regard to Savigny, that his discussion of the problems of interpretation assumed its particular importance and gained its particular influence less through original and creative individual features than by virtue of the fact that a universally admired and influential leader in the world of legal science recapitulates, with great learning, good sense and formal brilliance, those ideas and methods which had proved, in the long process of earlier discussion, to be viable and fertile. If any element in Savigny's analysis is to be singled out for particular mention, the most obvious feature in his clear insight into a fact which many earlier, naive or unimaginative, expounders of Justinian law had overlooked, viz. the historical relativity and the inevitable incompleteness of any set of legislative solutions and, concomitantly, the recognition of the contin uous creative work which is performed by courts and practitioners within the framework of the texts. "Interpretation" appears in Savigny's version, as an element in the continuous growth of the living law, not as a mechanical solution of nice questions within a system claiming to be complete once and for all and in some way withdrawn from the historical process. These ideas were by no means new, but with Savigny they have the character of fundamental, axiomatic starting points, not only of safety valves reluctantly admitted to avoid unacceptable results. Generally speaking, Savigny stresses repeatedly that interpretation is really an *art*, albeit subject to strict norms. In individual questions, Savigny mostly adopts traditional solutions.

One of the pillars upon which all earlier hermeneutic writing was based, viz. the idea of an ascertainable, consistent, and all-pervading "legislator's will" – a notion originally going back to the Emperor Justinian – underwent important changes in the course of the 19th century. From the French Revolution onwards, and especially after 1848, some kind of representative assembly with an increasing influence upon the process of legislation became a standard element in European constitutions. This meant, obviously, that statutes could no longer be considered the expressions of a single individual's will or even as volitions of a small group of advisers or political leaders. More often than not, the texts expressed political compromises and were thus, in principle, not "willed" by anyone, even if the ascertaining of individual volitions in the numerous membership of modern Parliaments had been practically feasible. The modern technique of legislation also meant, however, that special formalized texts – commonly referred to as "legislative material" or *travaux préparatoires,* and mostly composed of commission reports, government bills, possibly with comments on the interpretation of the proposed statute, and opinions of parliamentary committees – became available to lawyers as a matter of course. These documents frequently contained not only accounts of the legislative process and of general policy considerations but also fairly detailed comments on the true meaning or indeed the recommended construction of individual provisions.

Thus, at the same time as naive references to the "lawgiver's will" became more and more difficult to justify, well-defined, technically sophisticated and strictly formalized "supplementing bases" for an interpretation founded upon legislative intentions came into existence. When legislation became the business of a parliamentary body – as had been the case in Britain and Sweden since the Middle Ages – Governments, which still largely kept the initiative in matters of legislation, had to convey to a new group of persons the justification and the meaning of proposed enactments. At the same time, since the parliamentary body itself was formally or actually regarded at the *legislature* – or at least as one of the bodies covered by that term – *dicta* originating from parliamentary work assumed particular importance as sources of information about "legislative intentions."

Brief mention should be made of what may be called an intermediate stage – although the technique thus referred to still finds favour in certain cases – namely the so-called "referendum to the public" whereby proposed statutes were published and the general public was invited to give its opinion on the text. Particularly common in the period 1770–1830, under the influence of Rousseau and other 18th-century philosophers active in the domain of political science, this method has survived, in a modified form, in those countries where persons and organizations to whom a proposed statute is of particular concern are invited to give their opinion before the bill is finally submitted to the legislature.

The measure of importance given to the various and often quite numerous opinions expressed in the course of the regular process of legislation by parliamentary assemblies depended, it would seem, chiefly upon two circumstances: prevailing constitutional theories about the identity and composition of the legislature and prevailing theories about the reasons *why* legislative intentions should be of importance for the construction of statutes. In countries where Montesquieu's doctrine of the division of powers was more or less strictly adhered to – as was the case in France from the time of the First Empire, in theory if not in fact – it was only logical that particular stress should be laid upon parliamentary opinions. This is obviously even more true where Rousseau's theory of the *souveraineté du peuple* was adopted. Where the situation was more complex, as in Sweden (at least after the Constitution of 1809) and in most German states, particularly Prussia after the constitutions granted in the first half of the 19th century, parliament had no such claim to exclusive attention. Government bills and papers also could be held to express, to some extent, the "legislator's" intentions.

The appearance of reports from commissions of enquiry and parliamentary reports is a *sine qua non* for the controversy between those two schools in modern discussion which are, not very happily, designated as "subjective" and "objective." The former of these is characterized by the decisive importance attributed to the "preparatory works," whereas the latter insists on the actual social function of the piece of legislation, to the extent this can be ascertained by studying the statute "at work;" in this latter perspective, the *travaux préparatoires* are considered rather as historical evidence without immediate interest for the solution of those individual problems which emerge in the course of time, perhaps decades or even centuries after the "legislator" acted and in such circumstances that it is obvious that the framers of the text had never given them a thought.

The modern discussion concerning "subjective" and "objective" interpretation started – for all practical purposes we can confine ourselves to the German discussion, for nowhere else were these questions debated so early or with such richness of argument – within the historical framework of early constitutionalism, roughly about 1830–40. It is enough to state that most of the principal arguments used in later discussion were known by about 1840 (a full and interesting discussion, by R. von Mohl, is found in the *Archiv des Kriminalrechts* as early as 1842, pp. 246 ff.).

With the importance attributed, in Continental legal thinking, to the preparatory material as an aid in the construction of statutes, a further difference between legal reasoning in the common law of England and the technique of argumentation prevailing in Continental law came into existence. English courts – which had, of course, lived with parliamentary legislation for centuries and with printed reports of parliamentary proceedings for a very long time before French and German lawyers had any reason to pay attention to the phenomenon, possibilities, and problems of preparatory materials – refused to accept *travaux préparatoires* as aids in the interpretation of statutes. This, in turn – but this complex problem cannot be discussed here – may have contributed to those differences in legislative technique between Continental Europe and the common law countries, in particular Britain, which became more and more visible in the course of the 19th century, as the two systems were improved and elaborated each on its basic assumptions.

Some short concluding remarks should be given on the development of hermeneutics towards the turn of the century and onwards.

The theories of interpretation in the field of legal thinking was, of course, gradually influenced by the analysis of the notions of "understanding" and "interpretation" which was initiated in particular by German late 19th century "New Kantians," like *W. Dilthey* (d. 1911) and continued in the 20th century by, e.g., *E. Cassirer,* and the Italian *E. Betti,* later by the "Frankfurt School" with *F. Gadamer.* A second source of influence were the theories of modern semantics and psychology concerning the conditions of linguistic communication and linguistic understanding. The implicit basic assumption of all earlier hermeneutical theories was, in the field of law, not only the idea of a rational legislator but also unlimited faith in the power of expression of natural languages or at least in the possibility of arriving, after various obscurities had been removed, at an absolute and unambiguous meaning, applicable without difficulty to individual cases. In other words, an undoubted starting point was that by a sufficiently energetic and competent process of interpretation one could always find *one* answer, *the* correct answer, to a given problem. Modern hermeneutics represents, on this score, a far less optimistic attitude. "Interpretation" was more and more considered as one among several processes in the administration of legal rules, and lawyers became prepared to accept situations where "interpretation" simply gives no answer and where there is no alternative to going on, within the loose framework furnished by that preliminary intellectual process and by accepted standards of reasoning, to solve the problem, ultimately on the basis of an individual value judgment. This "semantic resignation" also had the consequence that even those legal writers who advocated a "subjective" method of interpretation became aware, to a greater extent than earlier, of the fact that the use of *travaux préparatoires* is less an investigation of a real, historical, "legislative will" than a conscious choice of a set of given, formalized "supplementing bases" for purposes of statutory construction and that these bases could provide certain general guidelines and individual examples, but hardly indications of a "will" in any reasonable psychological sense.

The last characteristic element of the modern development – a development which may be said, in short, to imply a "disintellectualization" of interpretation in relation to the hermeneutic views held by scholastics, humanists and rationalists – was the increasing consciousness of the function of laws and statutory texts as purpose-directed social means of governing and controlling, among and in addition to other such means. The conception of such texts as *canones,* venerable in themselves, would seem to have been replaced by the attitude that they are essentially *tools,* in the service of specific interests and needs. There is certainly nothing entirely new in this idea; it would be foolish to underestimate the practical wisdom and knowledge of ancient and medieval lawyers on this point (as, in all likelihood, with regard to the insufficiency of language as a means of communication). What is new is rather the fact that the idea has been openly recognized, expressed, and used for the elaboration of more sophisticated theories purporting to analyse and describe tha realities of the law and its administration. We have already quoted the *dictum* of R. von Ihering, "Der Zweck ist der Schöpfer des ganzen Rechts." This utilitarian outlook gradually coloured the predominating idea of statutory texts, their authors and their use.

Concluding Remarks

More than once, in the preceding pages, the work of modern legal philosophers has been described as a losing battle; in a long-range perspective, taking into account the earliest times, it seems to be the defence of an ever-dwindling province. In fact, all-embracing doctrines presented with perfect certitude have been continuously exchanged against more and more pusillanimous provisional hypotheses on smaller and smaller problems and with lower and lower explanatory power. This is said neither to deprecate the efforts of modern thinkers nor to defend the vast ambitions of their predecessors; it is a statement of facts; such have been, and such are, the conditions under which this particular branch of social and human science must accept to work. The latest developments, which tend to deprive legal thinking of what may well be its largest province, which is claimed by the empirical social sciences, and at the same time to transform an increasing part of its metropolitan area into an exact science, a logic inspired by mathematics, seems to threaten the very identity of a pursuit carried on since the days of the Jonian philosophers and, in all likelihood, but unknown to us, much earlier.

There is hardly ever much point in deploring the direction taken by a branch of science; even if one does not believe in inexorable and inevitable dialectic in the march of history, in science or elsewhere, there are usually imperative reasons for the main orientation of a given discipline at a given moment; errors and exaggerations of the past frequently explain and justify prevailing tendencies. However, having come to the end of this survey, the writer begs the reader's indulgence for one concluding wish: there is, and there will always be, a need for a legal thinking which is neither exclusively "social," nor exclusively "logical" but which remains – with all the frailty and all the risks this implies – a *human science*. Some of the deepest and, as experience shows, most indispensable sources of Occidental legal thinking spring forth from ground which belongs to the *litterae humaniores* rather than to any other branch of scholarship; there is a risk for these sources to run dry if the efforts of legal philosophers are exclusively directed towards problems and methods which are foreign to the humanities. In the last decades, a reaction, which is encouraging from this point of view, has been gathering strength. There is no reason to give up hope for the future.

Alphabetical Index

A Treatise of Human Nature   181
A Vindication of the Government of New England Churches   186
ab omnibus approbetur   150
Abélard, Pierre   108
Academia   30
Accursius   117
actio popularis   26
Acts of the Apostles   77
Aegean islands   15
Africa   136, 172
Alaric   52
Alaska   185, 230
Albert the Great   109
Alcuin   94
Alexander of Hales   108
Alexander the Great   17, 19, 35, 38, 73, 224
Alexandria   79
alienation   287
Allgemeines Bürgerliches Gesetzbuch, s Austrian Code of Private Law   174
Allgemeines Landrecht s Prussian Civil Code   174
Alpine countries   102
Althusius, Johannes   152
Ambrose, St   88, 89
America   172
American Declaration of Independence   173
American Revolution   152, 173
Amicus Plato, sed amicior veritas   36
Amyot   148
An Enquiry concerning Human Understanding   181
An Enquiry concerning the Principles of Morals   181
An Essay concerning Human Understanding   192
analogy   67
Anglican   183
Anthony, Mark   62
Antigone   27
Antiochia   79
Antisthenes   41
antithesis   285
Antonines   242
Arabs   95, 106
Aragon   105
Aramaeic   87
arbor actionum ("Tree of actionts")   121
Archiv des Kriminalrechts   298
aristocracy   14, 35, 39
Aristotelian   22
Aristotelian logic   107, 122
Aristotelian philosophy   99
Aristotelianism   109
Aristotle   19, 24, 25, 35 ff, 71, 124, 195, 218
Aristotle's Topics   36
Aristotle's Ethics   109
arithmetics   107
Arnold, Matthew   233
art of printing   98
Asia   172
Asia Minor   15, 17, 82
Assyrians   73
astronomy   107
Athens   16, 17, 24, 29
auctoritas   169, 218
Augustine, St   52, 73, 88, 89, 103,

142, 276
Augustus 55
Aurelius, Marcus 43, 62
Ausführliche Erläuterung der Pandecten nach Hellfeld 208
Austin, John 237, 250, 253, 264, 274, 293
Australia 230
Austria 102, 105, 137, 171, 227, 228, 247
Austria-Hungary 225
Austrian Code of Private Law 174
authority 119, 169
authority (auctoritas) 107
Auxerre, William of 118

Babylonian Captivity 73
Babylonian Captivity of the papacy 99
Babylonians 73
Bacon, Francis 147, 183
Bacon, Roger 113, 124, 177
Bade 227
Baldus degli Ubaldi 125, 148, 207
Balkans 227
Barbarossa, Frederick 119
Barbeyrac, Jean 191
Bartolomeu Dias 136
Bartolus of Sassoferrato 125, 148, 161, 207
Bassianus, Johannes 121
Baudry Lacantinerie 271
Bavaria 105, 227
Bayle 180
Beccaria, Cesare de 180, 208, 254
Begriffsjurisprudenz 240, 241
Belgium 228, 230
Bengal 172
Bentham, Jeremy 181, 234, 237, 238, 249, 293
Bergbohm, Karl 267
Bergson, Henri 261
Berytos 48
Betti, E 298
BGB, s Civil Code of Germany 53
Bierling, E R 278

bishops 79
Bismarck 225
Black Death 106
Blackstone's Commentaries 41
Bodin, Jean 151
Boethius 94
Bohemia 102, 105, 137, 171
Bologna 117
Bonald, LGA de 245, 264
Bonaparte, Napoleon 174, 224
Boniface VIII 104
bonum commune 112
Bordeaux 196
Borgia, Cesare 149
Bourbons 226
bourgeois 137
bourgeois society 243
bourgeoisie 286
Bracton 128, 182
Brandenburg 105
Brazil 136
Britain 296
British Empire 230
Bruno 177
Bugnet 271
Bulgarus 117
Burgundians 80, 95
Burke, Edmund 235, 245, 264
Burlamaqui 191
Burma 230
Bülow, O 281
Bürgerliches Gesetzbuch, or Civil Code for the German Empire 175, 266

Cabinet 200
Cabral 136
California 185
Caligula 51
Calvin, Jean 139, 147
Calvinism 139, 144
Cambridge 117
Cambridge school 291
Canada 230
canon law 100, 103
canonists 100, 130
Canossa 104

Alphabetical Index

Cape Horn   136
Cape of Good Hope   136
capitularia (of the early Frank Kings)   129
Caribbean islands   136
Carolingians   94
Cartesian philosophy   187, 206
Cartesius   177
Cassiodorus   94
Cassirer, Ernst   242, 298
Castille   105
categorical imperative   257
Catholic Church   233, 268
Catholic Church (in the Middle Ages)   101 f
Cavaliers   185
Cavendish   158
Cavour, Count Camillo   228
Caesar, Julius   50
censorship   176
Charlemagne   94
Charles I (of England)   158, 184
Charles II (of England)   158, 184
Charles the Bald (Emperor)   94
Charles V (Emperor)   137
checks and balances   200
China   136
Chinese   172
Chinese Empire   228
Christianity   53, 71, 232
Chrysippus   43
Church   85, 183
Cicero's "On the Laws (De legibus)"   62
Cicero's De inventione   107
Cicero, Marcus Tullius   43, 46, 60, 61, 68, 71, 161
City of God   92
city-state   18, 20
Civil Code   65, 174, 176, 226
Civil Code of Germany   53 f s Bügerliches gesetzbuch
Civil code, 1804   220, 231, 296
civil procedure   269
civil rights   204
civitas terrena (the worldly State)   91

Claims against the Tyrants   152
classes   195, 285
classical learning   89
classical learning (in the Early Church)   89
Clive   172
Code civil, s French Civil Code
Code for Sweden and Finland, 1734   175
Code Napoléon   271
Code of Civil Procedure   174
Code of Commercial Law   174
Code of Penal Procedure   174
Codes of criminal law   269
cogito, ergo sum   178
Coimbra   125
Coke, Edward   184
collegia   56
colonialism   221
Colonna, Egidius   148
Columbus   136
Commentaria   161, 272
Commentaries   41
Commentarii de iure civili   163
commentators   125
commercial law   269
commission reports   296
common law   183
Communism   205
commutative justice   40
Comte, Auguste   234, 236, 237
conceptualistic jurisprudence   240
Concordia discordantium Canonum (Harmony of discordant canons)   129
conditions of production   285
Condorcet   180
conference in Berlin in 1884   228
Confessiones   89
Congo   228, 230
Conring, Hermann   162
conservatism   244, 246
Constance   99
Constantine the Great   79
Constantinople   52, 79
Constitutio Antoniniana   66
Constitution of the United

Alphabetical Index

States 197
constructio (putting together) 163
Continental Europe 281
contracts should be kept 156
Controversiae illustres 115
Copernicus 98, 177
corps législatif 271
corpus Christianum 98
Corpus juris civilis 37, 47, 58, 60, 66, 100, 117, 163
corpus mysticum 85, 91, 103
council 99
Council of Basle 99
Council of Chalcedon 79
Counter-Reformation 140
Cours de code Napoléon 271
Cours théorique et pratique de droit civil 271
Covenant 73, 152
Crates 41
Crimean war 224
criminal procedure 269
Critique of Practical Reason (Kritik der praktischen Vernuft 255
Cromwell 158, 184
Crown 200
Crusades 106
curriculum of studies 106
cyclical process of history 167
Cyclops 26
Cynics 25, 41, 71
Cyrus 73

d'Alembert 180
Danish and Norwegian National Codes of 1683 and 1687 175
Dante Alighieri 148
Danube valley 228
dark centuries 93, 100
Darwinism 232
das Ding an sich 255, 256
De Civitate Dei (On the City of God) 90, 91, 103
De iure naturae et gentium (On the Law of Nature and of Nations) 188
De jure belli ac pacis libri tres (Three Books on the Law of War and Peace) 154
De l'esprit des Lois (The Spirit of Laws) 197
de Maistre 264
De officio hominis et civis iuxta legem naturalem (On the Duties of a Man and Citizen under the Law of Nature) 188
De Principe (On the Prince) 149
De regimine principum (On the Rule of Princes) 109, 148
De republica Anglorum, On the State of England 183
De Trinitate (On Trinity) 89
De vera religione (On True Religion) 89
Declaration of the Rights of Men and Citizens 174
Declarations of Rights (1776 and 1789) 220
decreta 58
decretal letters 129
decretals 129
Decretists 100
Decretum 129
Defensor pacis (The Defender of Peace) 149
definitions 124
Dei delitti e delle pene 180
democracy 14, 35, 39
Democritos 27
Demolombe 271
Demosthenes 22
Denmark 102, 105, 138, 228
Der Kampf ums Recht 278
Der Zweck im Recht (The Purpose in the Law) 277
Der Zweck ist der Schöpfer des ganzen Rechts 300
Descartes 158, 170, 255
Deuteronomium 74
Dewey, John 261
dialectic 163
dialectic process 261
dialectics 107, 261
dictatorship of the proletariat 287

Alphabetical Index

Dictionnaire historique et critique 180
Diderot, Denis 180
Die Restauration der Staatswissenschaften 246
Diet of Roncaglia 119
Digest 58
Dijon, Academy of 25, 41, 201, 203
Dike 26
Dilthey, Wilhelm 241, 298
diocesis 79
Diocletian 52
Diogenes 41
Discours préliminaire of the French Civil Code 272
disputations 107
distribution of power, in Aristotle's work 38
distributive justice 40
Divine Reason 62
divisio 123
divisio (organizing into groups) 163
division of powers 34, 258
doctrinal 209
Doctrine of Legal Principles 278
doctrine of predestination 90
dogmatic 119
Domat, Jean 134, 176, 272
dominate 49, 52
Dominican 99, 109
dominus et deus 52
Domitian 51
Doneau, Hugues, s Donellus
Donellus, Hugo 162 f, 189
Dorian states 16
Dorians 15
Du contrat social (On the Social Contract 1762) 202
Duarenus 161, 272
Duguit, Léon 280
Durckheim, Emile 280

Earl of Shaftesbury 191
East Africa 230
Eastern Empire 18
Eastern religions 77
economics 186
edict 55, 58
edictum perpetuum 56
Education 232
Edward I 150
Egypt 230
Ehrlich, Eugen 280, 281
elegant jurisprudence 146, 151, 162
emancipation of Catholics 225, 245
Emperor 101
Emperor (in the Middle Ages) 101 f
Empire 172
empiricism 35, 113, 114
empiricist theory of knowledge 192
Enchiridion 43
Encyclopédie 180
Engels, Friedrich 287
England 102, 128, 138, 170, 222
Enlightenment 180, 208, 219, 264, 269
English Civil War 248
English Parliament 200
entelechy 110
Epictetus 43, 62
Epicurean school 25, 42
Epicureans 71
Epicurus 41
episcopos 79
epistola decretalis 129
equality 215
equity 41, 55
eschatological 85
esprit général 198
Estates General 152, 173, 174
Estonia 171
Etymologiae 94
etymology 87
euangelion 75
executive power 200
Exodus 74
experience 114
extensive 163
extensive construction 67

Alphabetical Index

family, in Aristotle's work 37
Fathers of the Church 85, 88, 141
Federal Constitution (of the United States) 172
Federation 227
feudal society 98
Fichte, Johann Gottlieb 234, 259, 261
Filmer, Sir Robert 185
Finland 102, 106, 138, 228
First Great War 290
Flavius 281
Fontenelle 180
For an Eternal Peace (Zum ewigen Frieden) 259
forms of government 34, 39
Forster, V V 207
Fortescue, John 183
Fourier, F M C 248
Fragment on Government 250
France 65, 102, 105, 138, 222, 230
France, in the 19th century 65
Franciscans 99, 115
Franco-German war (1870-71) 214
Frankfurt School 298
Franklin, Benjamin 173
Franks 80, 95
fraternity 215
Frederick the Great 175
Free Finding of the Law and Free Legal Science 281
Free Law School 280, 281
Freie Rechtsfindung und freie Rechtswissenschaft 281
French Cinq Grands Codes 220
French Civil Code 174, 265
French Enlightenment 244
French exegetical school 293
French Revolution 214, 219, 234, 296
Fundamenta juris naturae et gentium, Foundations of the Law of Nature and of Nations, 1709 190
fundamentalism 233

Gadamer, F 298

Gaius 61
Galilei 177
Geist "Spirit" 261
Geist des Gesetzes 294
Geisteswissenschaften (sciences of the mind) 242
Gemeinde 278
general spirit 198, 199
general will 204
Geneva 139, 145, 201
Genossenschaft 278
Gentiles 74, 83
Gény, Franois 278, 279, 280
geographic discoveries 98
geometry 107
Georgian England 200
German 227
German Bürgerliches Gesetzbuch of 1900 273
German Code of Private Law 175
German Empire 224
Germanic law 128
Germanic tribes 18
Germany 102, 171, 222, 230, 247
Geschichte des römischen Rechts im Mittelalter (History of Roman Law in the Middle Ages 266
Gibbon 264
Gierke, Otto von 278
Gladstone 238
Glanvill 128, 182
Glorious Revolution of 1688 140, 184, 191, 193
Glossa ordinaria 122, 268
glossae 117
glossators 117
Glück, Fredrich Christian 208, 294
God, or Nature (Deus sive natura) 178
Goethe 223
golden ages 167
good custom 281
Gospels 76
Gothic architecture 186
government bills 296
grace 72, 90, 91
grammar 107

308

Alphabetical Index

grammatical   210
grammatical interpretation   163, 210
grand siècle   171
Gratianus   129
Great Plague   106
Great Schism   99, 105, 130
Greco-Roman culture   98
Greece   82, 261
Greek fathers   86, 215
Greek science   48
Greek science, in Roman law training   48
Gregory the Great   94
Gregory VII   104
Grotius, Hugo   116, 153, 273, 295
Grundlinien der Philosophie des Rechts (Philosophy of Right and Law   260
Grundriss eines Systems des gemeinen Zivilrechts zum Behufe von Pandecten-Vorlesungen   273
Gustav Hugo   264

Habsburg   102, 137, 171, 227, 228
Haller, K L von   246
Hanover   227
Harrington, James   184
Hartmann, Edward von   243
Hebrew   87
Heck, Ph   277
hedonist   42
Hegel, Georg Wilhelm Friedrich   234, 260
Heise   273
Hellenes   15
Hellenistic   20, 24, 41
Hellenistic science   69
Henry IV   104
Heraclitos   27
Herbert Spencer   234, 238
Herder, J G von   265
Hermagoras from Temnos   68
hermeneutics   293
Hesiod   26
hierarchy of virtues   33

Hincmar   94
Hippo   89
historical process   261
Historical school   236, 260, 266, 293
historicism   234, 235, 246
Hobbes, Thomas   42, 153, 178, 184, 188, 193
Hotman, François   152, 163
Holy Alliance   224
Holy Roman Empire of German nationality   96, 137, 227
Homeric poems   25, 26
homo mensura maxim   27
homo novus   61
honorarium   48
Hooker, Richard   183
Hotomanus, François   163
House of Commons   200
House of Lords   200
House of Saxony   101
Hugo   117
Hugo, Gustav   264
human laws   156
human rights   219
humanitarianism   182
Hume, David   181, 210, 214, 255, 260, 269
Hungary   102, 106, 171, 228
Huns   18, 95
Hus, Jan   139
Hägerström, Axel   291
Hölderlin, Friedrich   261

Iberian peninsula   102, 228, 247
idea of progress   167
ideological homelessness   214
Ihering, Rudolf von   67, 241, 277, 278, 300
Iliad   15
imbecillitas   188
imperative law   115
Imperial Constitutions   58
Imperial legislation, in the Roman Empire   58
In hoc signo vinces   79
India   172

Alphabetical Index

Indian Ocean   136
indicative law   115
individual, in Aristotle's work   37
individual rights   182
Indo-China   225, 230
Industrial Revolution   20, 230
inscriptions   22
Institutes   61
Institutes of the Laws of England   184
Institutiones   58, 161
interpolations   59
Interpres sive de interpretatione libri duo (The Interpreter, or Two Books on Interpretation)   207
interpretatio   67, 69
interpretation   24, 163, 209, 298
Investiture Contest   104
Ionians   15
Irenaeus   77
Irnerius   117
Isidore of Seville   94
Isocrates   22
isonomy   16
Italian style   146
Italy   102, 105, 171, 228, 230, 247
ius positum   237

Jacobus   117
Jahve   74
James I (of England)   183
James II (of England)   191, 193
Jansenism   147
Jerusalem   73
Jews   77
John Duns Scotus   113
Jonian philosophers   301
Judaism   73
judicial power   200
Jupiter   74
Jurisconsultus sive de optimo genere juris interpretandi   163
Jurisprudenz und Rechtsphilosophie   267
Juristenrecht   267
Juristische Prinzipienlehre   278

jus civile   55, 66
jus commune   127
jus gentium   56, 66, 94
jus gentium naturale   115
jus gentium secundarium   116
jus honorarium (or praetorium)   55
Jus naturae methodo scientifica pertractatum (The Law of Nature Treated with Scientific Method)   190
jus naturale   94
jus positivum   113
jus respondendi   57
justice (according to Plato)   33
justice, according to Aristotle   40
Justinian   57, 58, 80, 95, 218
Justinian code   270
justitia commutativa   40
justitia distributiva   40
justum bellum   157
justum pretium   40

Kant, Immanuel   181, 214, 232, 234, 236, 254, 260, 269
Kantorowicz   281
Kelsen, Hans   291
Kierkegaard, Søren   243
Kritik der juristischen Grundbegriffe   278
Kritik der reinen Vernuft (Critique of Pure Reason, 1781)   255
Königsberg   254

la volonté générale   263, 271
Laband, P   268
Lacedæmon   15
laissez-faire   246
Langobards   80, 95
Last Judgment   168
latifundia   51
Latin America   228
Latin Fathers   86
Latins   86
Law of Citations   57
law of nature   14, 74
law of the people   267

Alphabetical Index

Law of the Twelve Tables 49, 54, 60
Law-State 195
lawyers' law 267
lectures 107
Lectures on Jurisprudence or the Philosophy of Positive Law 274
left-Hegelians 236
legal 209
legal decision-making (v political) 65
legal hermeneutics 208
legal philosophy 131
legal reasoning 130
legal reasoning (in medieval law) 130 f
legal support 219
leges barbarorum 59
legislation by the assembled people, at Rome 54
legislative material 296
legislative technique 298
legitimate self-defence 157
Lehbuch des Naturrechts, als einer Philosophie des positiven Rechts 264
Lehrbuch 273
Leibniz, Gottfried Wilhelm 179, 255
Leon (Kingdom of) 105
Lerinum, Vincent of 142
Les loix civiles dans leur ordre naturel(The Civil Laws in their Natural Order) 176
Les six livres de la République (Six Books on the State) 151
Levellers 184
Leviathan 158
lex aeterna 62, 91, 110, 111
lex divina 111
lex humana 111
lex naturalis 108, 110
lex regia de imperio 95
lex temporalis 91
Liber Extra 130
liberal arts 107
Limits of Jurisprudence De-fined 249
Livonia 171
Livy 54
local law 127
Locke, John 134, 147, 169, 170, 182, 184, 186, 193, 199, 204, 244, 249, 255
logical 163, 210, 301
logos 44
Loix Civiles dans leur ordre naturel 272
lord Tennyson 233
Louis the Pious 94
Louis XIV 171, 196, 199, 222, 242
Louis-Napoléon 226
Louis-Philippe 226
Louisiana 185
Ludwig IIs Neuschwanstein 235
Lugdunum 77
Luther, Martin 139, 147
Lutheranism 144
Lyceum 25, 35, 41
Lyons 77
Lysias 22

Macau 136
Macedonia 17, 37
Machiavelli, Niccolo 149
Macpherson, James 265
Magellan 136
Magna charta 184
magnum latrocinium 73
de Maistre, Joseph-Marie 245
majeutic 30
mandata 58
Marathon 17
Mare liberum (On the Freedom of the High Seas) 154
Marsilius of Padua 149
Martin Luther 139
Martinus 117
Marx, Karl 236, 248, 276, 282
Marxism 276, 282
Mason, George 186
Massachusetts 185
Maurus, Rabanus 94
Maxentius 79

Alphabetical Index

Mayflower 185
Mecklenburg 227
Melanchton, Filip 146
mendicant orders 99
Messiah 75
Metaphysik der Sitten (Metaphysics of Morals, 1797) 255
Method and Sources in Positive Private Law 279
Méthode et sources en droit privé positif 279
Metternich 224
Mexico 230
Middle Ages 98, 248
modern 132
Modestinus 57
Mohammed 80
Mohl, R von 298
Monarchomachs 152
monarchy 14, 34, 49
monarchy, in ancient Rome 49
monetary economy 15
Monica, St 89
Montaigne, Michel de 42, 147, 176
Montesquieu, Charles de 169, 170, 182, 186, 195, 196, 208, 234, 254, 258, 264, 294, 297
moral law 257
mos gallicus 162
mos italicus 146
Moses 74
Mount Sinai 74
music 107
Möser, Justus 264

Naples 109
Napoleon 222, 224, 244
Napoleon III 226, 244
Narva 172
National Assembly 174
nationalism 235, 246
natural inclinations 111
natural law 28, 39, 42, 86, 108, 114, 120, 144, 182, 198, 271
natural man 193, 198
natural rights 159
naturalistic 28

naturalistic natural law 14, 158
nature 72, 83, 84, 202
Nature, in Christian theology 72
Neothomism 134
Nero 51, 77
Netherlands 102, 138, 170, 228
New Kantians 298
New Testament 76, 82
New Zealand 230
Newton 255
Newton, Sir Isaac 177
Newtonian mechanistic thinking 187
Nicomachean Ethics 39
Nietzsche, Friedrich 243
nobilitas 50, 61
noblesse d'épée (nobility of the sword) 196
noblesse de robe (nobility of the robe) 196
nominalism 113
Normans 105
North Africa 225
North American 220
North and Central Africa 230
North, Sir Thomas 148
Norway 102, 105, 138, 228, 247
notitia rerum humanarum atque divinarum 169
Nova methodus discendae docendaeque jurisprudentiae, A New Method for Learning and Teaching Law 179
Novellae 58

object as such 255
objective 298
objective theory of values 32
Occam, William of 113, 124
ochlocracy 35, 39
Octavianus, s Augustus 50
Odyssey 15, 26
Of the Laws of Ecclesiastical Polity 183
old age pension schemes 232
Old Testament 74, 152
oligarchy 35, 39

Alphabetical Index

On Crime and Punishment 180
On Duties (De officiis) 62
On Liberty 238
On the City of God 91
On the Laws (De legibus) 62
On the Orator (De oratore) 62
On the State (De republica) 62
Opinions of Paul 61
Orange, William of 191, 193
orbs 222
organism theory 260
Oriental religions 71
Origenes 87
Osnabrück 264
Osnabrück Geschichte (The History of Osnabrück) 264
Ostrogoths 80, 95
Otto the Great (German Emperor) 96
Otto von Bismarck-Schönhausen 227
Ottoman Empire 228
Oxford 117, 125

pacta sunt servanda 155, 157
Pakistan 172
Palestine 73
Panaitius 43
Pandect Law 266
Pandectae Justinianae in novum ordinem digestae 272
Pandectists 209
Pandects 58, 161, 268
Pandekten 268
pantheism 178
papacy 79, 92, 129, 138
Papinian 57
papyrus documents 22
Parallell Lives of Plutarch 148
Paris 117
parish 85
Parliament 105
Parliament (of England) 105, 150
Parliamentary reform 225
partitio (splitting up into elements) 163
Pascal, Blaise 147, 158, 176, 177

Patriarcha (The Patriarch) 185
Patriarchs 74
Patricians 49
Patristics 86
Paul, St 57, 81, 87, 111
Paul's letter to the Romans 83
Paul's letters 77
peace 92
Pelagianism 144
Pelagius 90
Peloponnesian war 17, 30
Peloponnese 15, 16
Penal Code 174
Percy, Bishop 265
Peripathetic 22
Peripathetic school 25, 35
Persia 17
Persian Letters (1721) 196
Peterloo 225
phalanstéres 248
Phariseans 76, 82
Philip ("le Bel"), King of France 104 f
Phillip of Macedonia 17
Philo from Alexandria 75
philological interpretation 210
philosophical construction 210
Phänomenologie des Geistes (The Phenomenology of the Spirit) 260
Pierrefonds 235
Pilate 76
Pilgrim Fathers 185
Piraeus 17
Pius IX 228
Plassey 172
Plato 19, 25, 29, 33 ff, 71, 107, 195, 261
Plato's "Laws" 34
Plato's "Republic" 31 f
Plato's "Statesman" 33
Plato's Timaios 108
Platonism 30 ff
Plebeians 49
Plutarch 148
Poems of Ossian 265
Poitiers, battle of (732 AD) 80

Alphabetical Index

Poland   102, 105, 137, 171, 225
polis   15, 18, 31, 33, 64
political and legal decision-making   65
political decision-making (v legal)   65
political interpretation   210
political science   169, 182
polytheism   77
Pomerania   171
Pompey   73
Pope   79, 101
Portalis, J E M   272
Portugal   102, 105, 228, 230
Poseidonius from Rhodes   43
positive law   39, 111, 264
positive law (jus positivum)   108
positivism   236, 276
postglossators   125
Pothier, R G   272
praetor   55
praetor peregrinus   55, 66
Prague   125
principate   49, 51
Principles for a New Science   179
Principles of Political Economy   238
private international law   267
private property   87, 203, 248
procedure   23
productive forces   285
progress of arts and sciences   201
proper price   40
property   193
Prophets   74
proselytes   83
Protagoras   27
Proudhon, P.J   248
prudentia   48
Prussia   105, 171, 224, 227
Prussian Civil Code of 1794   174, 220
Pseudo-Isidorian Decretals   129
public health services   232
Puchta, Georg Friedrich   241, 266
Pufendorf, Samuel   178, 186, 187, 207, 272

Puritans   183
purpose theory   277
Pythagoras   27

Quesnay, François   186
quadrivium   107
quod omnes tangit   150

ratio   169, 218
ratio legis   211, 294
ratio scripta   120
rational   199
rationalism   109, 114, 172, 178
rationalist   29, 32
rationalistic   28
rationalistic natural law   14, 153
reason   119, 169
reason (ratio)   107
reception, of Roman law in Western Europe   59
Rechtsstaat   195, 219, 220, 228
référé législatif   208
Reflections on the Rise and Fall of the Roman Empire (Considérations sur les causes de la grandeur des Romains et de leur décadence)   196
Reformation   98, 248
Relectio de Indis   116
Reliques of Ancient English Poetry   265
René Descartes   146, 177
Renan, Ernest   233
Renascence   60, 99, 121, 133, 141, 146, 148, 155, 162, 178, 248
Republic   36, 49
Republic, in ancient Rome   49
Restoration (English)   185
restrictive   163
restrictive construction   67
revelation   72
rhetorics   107
Rhine principalities   105
Rimini, Gregor of   115
Rivarol, Antoine (de)   245
Roman army   77
Roman Empire   20, 94, 119

Alphabetical Index

Roman law 24, 46, 47, 53, 99, 168
Roman law (ancient) 46 ff
Roman law, in modern times 53
Roman law, in the Middle Ages 47 ff
Roman lawyers 218
Roman lawyers, training 48
Rome, Goddess 77
Romulus Augustulus 52
Rousseau, Jean-Jacques 169, 170, 173, 182, 191, 219, 255, 263, 297
Royal Navy (British) 226
Rudolf von Ihering 241, 277
rule of law 219
Rules of Ulpian 61
Russia 137, 151, 170, 171, 230

Sabine, GH 20
Saint-Simon C-H de 248
Salamis 17
salvation 72, 83
Sardinia 224, 228
Savigny, Friedrich Carl von 265, 293 ff
Saxonian dynasty 104
Saxony 105, 227
Saxony-Weimar 227
Scandinavian realists 291
Scandinavians 80
scepticism 42
Sceptics 25, 71
Schelling, Friedrich 260
Schleiermacher, FDE 294
Schleiermacher, Friedrich 260
Scholasticism 146
Scholastics 107, 166, 195, 218
school of philosophy 22
Schopenhauer, Arthur 243
Science et technique en droit privé positif (Science and Technique in Positive Private Law, 1914-1924) 279
Scienza nuova prima 179
Scotland 138
Scott, Sir Walter 235
scriptum 69, 163
Second Reich 228

secularized natural law 155
Sein ("being") 258
Selden, John 184
Senate 49
senatus-consulta 55
Seneca 43, 62
sententia 69, 163
sententia legis 209
Sententiae 94
Seven Years' War 171
Sinn des Gesetzes 209
Sittengesetz 257
slave 15
slavery 45, 87
Slavs 80
Slesvig 224
Smith, Adam 186
Smith, Thomas 183
social animal 86
social contract 28, 33, 152, 185, 193, 215, 258
socialism 34, 205
socialitas 188, 193
sociial insurance 232
Socrates 28, 29
Soirées de Saint-Pétersbourg 245
Sollen ("ought") 258
Solomon 73
Solon 26, 54
Solon's 24
sophia 25
Sophists 25, 26, 28
Sophocles 27
South and East Africa 230
souveraineté du peuple 297
sovereignty 151
Sozialstaat 220
Spain 105, 136, 171, 228, 230, 244
Spanish armada 138
Sparta 15, 16
Spencer 247
Spencer, Herbert 234, 238
spheres of interest 230
Spinoza, Baruch 178
spirit of the statute 294
Staatslehre 259
Stagira 35

Alphabetical Index

Stand (Estate) 278
State Church 160
status legales 69
Stoa or Stoic school 25
Stoa poikile 43
Stoic doctrine 44 f
Stoic philosophy 47
Stoicism 43
Stoics 71
Stroux, Joh 68
Stryk, Samuel 162
Stuart 138
Stuart dynasty 193
Stuart Mill, John 234, 238, 247
Sturm and Drang 186
style of reasoning 68
style of reasoning, of Roman lawyers 68
Suarez, Francisco 116
subjective 298
subjective right 114
Summa Theologica 109
superstructure 285
Sweden 102, 106, 128, 137, 138, 170, 171, 228, 247, 296, 297
Swedish Rural Code of 1350 175
syllogism 124
synthesis 285
System des heutigen Römischen Rechts 294
System des heutigen römischen Rects (System of Present-day Roman Law) 266
System of Synthetic Philosophy 238

Tacitus 77
Tagaste 89
teaching methods 130
teaching methods (medieval law) 130 f
technological gap 221
Ten Commandments 74
Textbook of Natural Law, Considered as a Philosophy of Positive Law, 1798) 264
Tharsus in Cilicia (Asia Minor) 82

The Province of Jurisprudence Determined 274
Themis 26
Theoderic the Great 80
Theodosius 79
Theodosius II 58
theological 14, 28
Theophrastos 22
Théorie du pouvoir politique et religieux 245
Theory of Legislation 250
theory of status 68
Theory of the state 259
Thermopylae 17
thesis 285
Thibaut, AFJ 265, 294, 295
Tierney, B 150
thing 96
thing (assembly among the Germanic peoples) 96
Third Estate 152, 199
Thirty Year's War 137, 140
Thomas of Aquino, St 109, 124, 155, 183
Thomasius, Christian 187, 189, 273
Thomism 115, 141
Timaios 107
topics 123
Tories 225
Trajan 242
travaux préparatoires 298
Tribonianus 58, 161
Tudor 138, 183
Turin 228
Turks 171
Two Treatises of Government 192
Tübingen 261
tyranny 35
tyrant 16, 30
Tyrrell, James 184

Ulpian 57
United States 221, 222, 228, 230, 244
universities 106
Uppsala 125

316

Alphabetical Index

Uppsala school 291
usus modernus ("modern usage") 162
utopism 34

Vandals 80, 91, 95
Vasco da Gama 136
Vasquez, Fernando 115
Vatican Council (1869-1870) 233
Vattel 191
verbum 69
Vico, Giambattista 179
Victor Emanuel, King of Sardinia 228
Victorian England 226, 238
Wieacker, Franz 145
Vienna 171, 228
Vienna school 291
Villey, M 114
Vindiciae contra tyrannos 152
Viollet-Le Duc 235
Visigoths 52, 80, 91, 95
Vitoria, Francisco de 116
Vocation of Our Time for Legislation and Legal Science 266
Volksgeist 267, 277
Volksrecht 267
Volksseele 267
volonté générale 204, 219, 271, 277
Voltaire 167, 180, 264
voluntarism 113

voluntaristic 14
Vom Berufe unserer Zeit für Gesetzgebung und Rechtswissenschaft 266
war of all against all (bellum omnium erga omnes) 159
Waterloo 222, 225
Weber, Max 280
Weigel 188
Weimar 223
Western Empire 18
whig (ie liberal) interpretation of history 166
Whigs 225
Windscheid, Bernhard 268
Wise, John 186, 189
Wissenschaft der Logik (The Science of Logic) 260
Wolff, Christian 187, 190, 255, 273
working class population 281
world law, in Stoic philosophy 44
world soul, in Stoic philosophy 44, 62
World Spirit 263
Wurtemberg 227
Wycliffe 139

Zeno 25, 43
Zeus 74
Zwecktheorie 277
Zwingli, Ulrich 139, 147